Effa Okupa

International Bibliography of African Customary Law

Monographs

from the

International African Institute

London

International African Institute

LIT

Effa Okupa

International Bibliography of African Customary Law

Ius non scriptum

International African Institute

LIT

Cover illustration: Queen Mother's head, Benin, by kind permission of the British Museum.

Die Deutsche Bibliothek – CIP-Einheitsaufnahme

Okupa, Effa
International Bibliography of African Customary Law : Ius non scriptum / Effa Okupa. – Hamburg : LIT, 1998
(Monographs from the International African Institute (London) ; 4.)
ISBN 3-8258-4009-3

NE: GT

Grindelberg 15a 20144 Hamburg Tel. 040–44 64 46 Fax 040–44 14 22

Distributed in North America by:

Transaction Publishers
New Brunswick (U.S.A.) and London (U.K.)

Transaction Publishers
Rutgers University
35 Berrue Circle
Piscataway, NJ 08854

Tel.: (732) 445 – 2280
Fax: (732) 445 – 3138
for orders (U.S. only):
toll free 888-999-6778

PREFACE

The study, analysis and reporting of African customary laws, which in an earlier period were largely limited to the work, first of missionaries and travellers, and then of district officers and ethnographers, as well as of a few African writers such as Dr J.B. Danquah in Ghana, decisively moved into the mainstream of legal scholarship after World War II with the appearance of learned journals such as the Journal of African Law devoted to the field, the creation of posts and centres, and the development of initiatives often government inspired or conducted for the systematic investigation and reform of the customary laws in the countries of Africa.

This expansion was a global phenomenon and concern. Although much of the activity was located in the African countries themselves foreign countries, notably Britain, France, the United States, Belgium, Germany, but also many others around the world took part in this movement too.

The institutions and processes of African customary laws. and the challenges posed by it, became a required part of the worldwide agenda of comparative and jurisprudential studies. (The work of Max Gluckman, an anthropologist with a special interest in African indigenous laws exemplified this trend and supported it.) Is African indigenous law "really law": and do we have to modify our definition of "law" to accommodate it? Or, contrariwise is one justified in rejecting the claims of African customary and unlegislated norms to be part of the law family? Such were the fundamental questions among others, which the newfound concern with customary laws, and especially those of Africa, had to confront.

The growth worldwide of scholarly and practical interest in African customary laws, and the phenomenal expansion in published books, articles, papers, reports and government documents relating to them, have led to major problems for the student of African indigenous laws. The participation of disciplines other than the legal and the anthropological - such as history, geography, economics, sociology, politics - in the study of and writing about African laws, and the consequent multiplication of relevant sources, create special difficulties for the researcher. Where should he or she look for material? Has the researcher neglected some valuable reference of which he or she was unaware?

With this in mind one turns eagerly to bibliographies of the subject. The outstanding work done by Professor Jacques Vanderlinden of the University Libre de Bruxelles in accumulating and publishing bibliographical materials must be mentioned here. But this effort, like other less ambitious ones has its limits. Only one who has tried to compile a bibliography (as the present writer assisted in doing for the Restatement of African Law Project) is aware of the enormity and demands of the task. Searching the world's literature for references; deciding whether an item should be listed, and if so under what heading; verifying the publication details including title, author, place and date of publication and so on - these are arduous, unrewarding and often unappreciated burdens.

Dr Okupa, whose present work is intended to take this process further, mentions, justifiably, the frequent errors and deficiencies she has found in earlier citations, which have then to be checked and corrected. But the present work goes much farther than this in its gleaning of references in distant fields of publication. Truly is it described as an "international bibliography". The author had to decide, when faced with the wealth of material which her researches had thrown up, what limits to impose. She correctly and realistically decided that the work should be confined to materials relating to the “anglophone” part of Africa. One cannot quarrel with her decision.

The ambit of the Bibliography is for me amply demonstrated by the fact that, even concerning areas of law or peoples with whose institutions I am especially familiar, I have found many relevant references in her work of which I was unaware.

The work is arranged in chapters organised around fields or topics. This permits the author to add invaluable critical commentary and explanation to the bare references. Her position on major issues, such as on the future of African customary laws in the legal systems of African states is made clear, and is presented helpfully and convincingly. Her work investigating customary laws in the field incidentally validates these opinions.

Of the utility of the present work there can be no doubt. Future generations of scholars and researchers in the field of African indigenous laws will bless the name of Dr Okupa, who has, by the publication of the present volume, enormously reduced the burden on them.

Antony Allott
Emeritus Professor of African Law
University of London

Even if the compiler and author of *International Bibliography of African Customary Law: Jus non Scriptum*, Effa Okupa, submitted an affidavit to state that the following preface is its author's invention, I would swear that what I have to say about the origin of this bibliography might be invented, but is true in a spiritual sense. As the Italians put it: *Si non é vero, é bene trovato*.

The idea of compiling this bibliography, its design, the composition of the chapter, the introductory notes by the compiler, must, I am sure, have been conceptualised, step by step, when Effa travelled the long and dusty ways from Windhoek to Opuwo and beyond up to where the Kunene river meanders; the river that, according to modern international law, forms the border between Namibia and Angola. For Effa's Ovahimba, this border is not important. The Kunene river is the lifeline of Okaoko and the Kunene does not divide the land of the Ovahimba: it is the source which nourishes its environment.

Each time when Effa returned from the Himba, we sooner or later discussed another aspect of African Customary Law. It was the time when the preparation of the Faculty of Law of the University of Narnibia had begun. What role would customary law play in the curriculum? How would we structure its teaching? Was customary law worth being considered as a necessary element in a modern law curriculum? If yes (and we both supported it), what would be the material to rely on?

The Himba are present throughout this bibliography and I believe it is good that after Effa's exposure to, and involvement with, the Himba this bibliography was the result. But of course, this book is not just about the Ovahimba.

This book is an indispensable tool for all who are in one way or the other concerned with customary law as lecturers, researchers, law appliers and law reformers. Why do I think it indispensable? This question can only be answered when one looks at other sources available to the customary and African law scholar. Jacques Vanderlinden's bibliographies of African law are known to all who work in the field.[1] Norbert Rouland summarised in his introduction to *Anthropologie Jurisdique* the most common source books, textbooks and bibliographies.[2] The author of this preface can also refer to a bibliographical publication on Namibian Customary law.[3] We may find here and there annotated bibliographies. But, they did nor dare to do what this bibliography has done: to write the bibliographical data into an African context. After generations of missionaries, anthropologists and lawyers, whose first interest was to force African customary law into the Procrustean bed of either the bible, civilisation or a western paradigm of Rule of Law, African Customary Law begins to breathe again: to breathe the air of Africa. The flexibility of customary law stands a chance against Rule of Law campaigners who have never tried to understand the origins of customary law, but also never left the positivistic education behind which taught them a very narrow concept of Rule of Law.

This bibliography does not glorify the great African past, it does not deny the many inroads made during and by colonialism, nor does it repeat the mistakes that were made by many scholars in Southern Africa (and elsewhere) for whom the Roman-law-based modern law provided a structure that African customary law had to follow. Instead it opens avenues for customary law to live the life of any other law: the life which encompasses change and development.

The vision of this bibliography is of the dignity of Africa and its mission is to rediscover the principles of African Customary law. Gordon Woodman and A.O. Obilade conclude their introduction to *African Law and Legal Theory* by stating that there is no imminent prospect of the emergence of an African legal theory.[4] However, they put this statement into a sub-section of a chapter entitled 'The Need for an African Legal Theory'. Okupa's bibliography is not a direct response to this need but is certainly an indirect one. Her bibliographical data appear in a provocative order under provocative headings and include aspects not usually found in scholarly work. In this sense, she has directly responded to the need for African legal theory. She has responded by crossing borders and by putting her own accent on the material.

Manfred 0 Hinz
Professor of Law
University of Namibia
Windhoek, December 1997.

1 Covering the time from 1947 to 1989 and published in four volumes by Presses Universitaires de Bruxelles.

2. N Rouland, *Antropologie juridique*, Paris 1988 (Presses Universitaires de France).

3. W. W. Hillebrecht, *Bibliography of Works Relevant to the Study of Customary Law and Traditional Administration of Justice in Namibia*, Windhoek, 1991 (Cass).

4. Gordon R. Woodmann and A.0. Obilade, 'Introduction' in *African Law and Legal Theory*, Aldershot, Singapore, Sydney, (Dartmouth): XXV.

Contents

Statutes

Treaties

Acknowledgements

There is a yawning gap in the literature of African customary law, and in the writing of this bibliography I encountered many virtuous persons. I am enormously grateful to the Librarians at the Institute of Advanced Legal Studies; the Librarians at University College London Institute of Archaeology; the British Library of Political and Economic Science, and the Librarians at the School of Oriental and African Studies, especially Mr David Hall of the International African Bibliography.

In spite of the Librarians, the collection would not have been ready for publication without the support of Dr. Werner Menski and Prof. Murray Last. I am tremendously grateful.

I owe the *ovaHimba* enormous debt of gratitude. I have gained from their humility, and the importance that they attach to the systematic, consistent development of their indigenous law.

My greatest obligation is to my family, Ade and Kwesi for their reasonableness and patience during the compilation of the bibliography and the writing of the headnotes.

Finally, I am particularly grateful to the numerous authors whose works are quoted in the bibliography, without their writing, there would have been no bibliography.

This *ius non scriptum* is the outcome of everybody's support, but the mistakes are mine alone and my word processor that has a will of its own.

Glossary

In Otjiherero plurals are formed by using a number of prefixes, such as *oma-*, *ova-*, *ovi-*, *otu-* and *ozo.* I have entered the plural form separately for words that appear frequently.

!	indicates a palatal click before the word, for example *!Noreseb*
eanda	the matriclan, the matrilineage, plural *omaanda*
Mukuru	The Supreme Deity who created the earth
ohakera	the child's cattle endowment, plural *ozohakera*
okurumatisa	oral will
omuHimba	a *Himba* man, woman or child; a person, plural *ovaHimba*
ondjova wife	a man's first wife under indigenous law
onganda	a village, *Himba* semi-permanent family living-quarters, plural *ozonganda*
oruzo	patriclan, patrilineage, plural *otuzo*
ousemba	right or rights
oveta	justice, law, personal integrity
ovitunya	marriage settlement, bridewealth, brideprice
ovivareke	contractual betrothal gifts
ozonganda	villages, semi-permanent living quarters (plural)

Introduction

Has customary law a future?

There are many factors responsible for the longevity and resilience of African indigenous laws, even in the face of the authoritative modernity of state law and military decrees. Why has customary law not fallen into abeyance? One of the aims of this book is to answer the question and for African customary law to be taken seriously.

Today, African customary law is still the law that regulates the lives of most people in rural Africa, especially children, who because of their minority, do not have a choice of law. An understanding of customary law is crucial for the protection and survival of the poor and powerless. This fact, on its own, should be taken seriously by IMF, foreign investment and trade, Law Reform Committees and Law Commissions all over the non-western world. In essence, this collection of bibliographies also aims to show that customary law should remain a valuable framework of reference for teachers, researchers, adjudicators and Africanists in the construction of modern law.

But some members of the African elite see their people's indigenous laws as a liability that they must transcend in order to be modern. Modernism for the sake of modernity does not mean jettisoning what was before, and is meaningful to the majority; there should be continuity in change.

The imposed colonial laws of Roman-Dutch law, Civil law and Common law are part of the problems of African states South of the Sahara, because the laws have been utilised by the post-independence political elite in Africa, to reinforce their position as the adoptive ruling class, who have been christened the '*Wa Benzi*, the *Ova Benzi*', meaning people of the Mercedes Benz. The law of non-imposition of law only goes to show that for the majority of the citizens of the new states, the laws cloned from the colonial countries have been irrelevant to what the people do and the factors that determine their life style. The consequence of this non-imposition of law is that only the bureaucratic elite make the choice of relying on the imposed law and customary law when it suits them.

This book focuses only on African customary law to encourage further research into the indigenous laws of the people of Africa. It is necessary for me to explain the use of the term 'indigenous law'. In some of the references in the sixteen chapters, we shall see that various terms have been used by scholars to designate the system of laws, norms or customs found in Africa. Sometimes, it is referred to as 'native law', 'native laws and customs', 'native customary law', 'primitive law', 'folk law', 'informal law', 'living law', 'positive morality', 'non-state law', 'non-government law', 'autogenous regulation', 'native justice', 'indigenous law', 'customary law', 'people's law', 'vernacular law'. There is an on-going debate among international Africanists as to the conceptual question of nomenclature, and the nature of African law. The terminology argument either illuminates or conceals the scholar's preference of the meaning of 'law' as it applies to the African phenomena.

My preference is for the use of 'indigenous law' when it is applied to a particular community, 'tribe' or ethnic group, for example, the Akan indigenous law, Dinka indigenous law, the *Himba*, the Nuer, the Talensi, the Yeke, because the ethical basis of the principles of their law is indigenous to that particular community. African indigenous laws are a related family of laws composed of principles of moral philosophy and prescriptions of behaviours recognised by the dominant patrilineal or matrilineal groups within each specific society. State law is manifestly only one form of law in African states, accordingly, the indigenous laws of the various 'tribes' or communities within the state could be termed the 'customary law' in contradistinction to the state law.

Indigenous law in its second millennium

Ankermann, (1905:55) argued that, "as far as we know, Africa has never invented anything, but has only received from others". But Africa and its people have been around for thousands of years. Why are they treated with so much disdain? Not many writers who underrate Africa for its lack of invention can survive the hostile environment.

Even a simple human intellectual activity such as the formulation of law is purported to have been received by Africans. This is one of those assumptions about Africa that has perpetuated the myth that Africa has no laws. Today, archaeologists, ethno-archaeologists and oral historians are beginning to piece the evidence together that there were multi-ethnic city states, as well as stateless societies in pre-colonial Africa since the beginning of the first millennium.[1] There were public infrastructures of roads, city walls and market spaces, as well as exchange standards in gold dust, gold ingots, brass ingots, cowrie shells and barter.

There was justice; anarchy did not reign. According to the records of Arab geographers and historians, African kings were renowned for their sense of justice.[2] The communities formulated their own laws setting out some basic legal principles to meet their needs. Hence the contents of this book are divided into sixteen substantial chapters to enable the researchers to examine the various applicable aspects of the indigenous law.

It is a person's relationship to his or her community and the character of the person that make up the indigenous law and count as virtues and justice. Indigenous law is the acceptable norms that most people in the community comply with.

---

[1] For details see:
D. W. Phillipson, (1993) *African archaeology*. Cambridge: Cambridge University Press.
Graham Connah, (1987) *African civilisations*. Cambridge: Cambridge University Press.
T. Shaw, P. Sinclair, B. Andah and A. Okpoko (1993) *The archaeology of Africa: Food, metals and towns*. London: Routledge.
Vansina, J. (1990) *Paths in the rainforest: Toward a history of a political tradition in Equatorial Africa*. London: James Currey.

[2] See generally:
J. M. Cuoq, (1975) *Recueil des sources arabes concernant l'Afrique occidentale du V11e au XV1e siècle: Bilad al-Sudan*. Paris: Centre National de la Reserche Scientifique.
J. F. P. Hopkins, and N. Levtzion, (tran, & eds.) (1981) *Corpus of early Arabic sources for West African history*. Cambridge: Cambridge University Press. (Fontes historiae Africanae, series Arabica 1V)
Fisher, H. (1982) 'Early Arabic sources and the Almoravid conquest of Ghana'. Journal of African History. Vol. 23. No. 4, pp. 549-560
As-Sa'di (1964) Ta'rikh es-Sudan. Translated by O. Houdas, (ed.) (1913-1914) Paris: Adrien-Maisonneuve.

Customary law need not be written to become law, hence the title of this volume is, *ius non scriptum*. Common law is the collective tribal indigenous laws of English, Irish and Welsh men and women. The Scottish tribe is in the second millennium of Roman law. One could as well ask, what laws existed in Europe before the Roman conquest?

The disintegration of pre-colonial African empires, states and their legal institutions could have been brought about by a combination of many lethal situations: disintegration of families during the slave trade, the spread of Islamic conquest, Christian missionaries against heathenism[3] and the white men's aggression. In the nineteenth century, Africans were traumatised. One needs only to follow the collapse of the Soviet Empire in our life time to understand how the breakup of the African kingdoms impacted on the people.

The structure of the bibliography

As a result of the historical accident of colonialism, most African states now have several models of law: their many indigenous laws; the legal extensions imposed by the colonial powers: Common law, Civil law, Roman-Dutch law, and by Islamic conquest of some communities by Sharia law, and finally Hindu law. Some African political elite also flirted with Socialist law. The collection in this bibliography would have been too unwielding and might have become an amalgam of all these European laws of Africa, in English, French, German and Portuguese. It would have been too complex for most indigenous laws relegated to the index reference. It would not have served the needs of diligent customary law researchers who require published field work in indigenous laws, in archaeology, in anthropology, in oral history and in languages. I have an awesome admiration for Vanderlinden (1992) who compiled *Bibliographies internationales de la doctrine juridique africaine*. See chapter 16.

However, without intending to follow the artificial colonial boundaries, my intention at first was to collect indigenous law references on a linguistic basis. For example, the Akan, Bemba, Dogon, Dyola, Edo, Gikuyu, Ibo, Igala, Mbaka, Mende, Mossi, Mwa, Shona, Talensi, Temne, Xhosa, Yoruba, Zande, and the Khoisan languages of !Kung, Nama and Khomani. There has always been small-scale movement of people and some of these people have inter-married for centuries. For example, bridewealth, *lobola, aseda, ovitunya* is a common contractual element of the formalities of marriage found under most indigenous laws. Generally, matrilineal societies have small bridewealth and patrilineal societies have large bridewealth. See chapter 11.

It became obvious, however that a linguistics-based reference system would cut across too many boundaries. Take a situation like Central Africa comprising Angola, Burundi, Cameroon, the Central African Republic, Congo, Equatorial Guinea, Gabon, Rwanda, and Zaïre. Their land was carved up between Belgium, Britain, France, Germany, and Portugal. Accordingly, I settled for only the collection of essays and papers from common law jurisdiction in English speaking African countries. Even that has its inherent problems. After the 1914-1918 War, under the Treaty of Versailles, Germany was stripped of all her African territories. See chapter 1. Cameroon, a former German territory, was carved out between France and Britain and now has common law and French civil law.

---

[3] There were numerous Catholic and Protestant missions to Africa from the colonial powers as well as from other European states: Basel Mission, Finnish Mission Society, Norwegian Mission Society, Swedish Mission Society, American Presbyterians, Free Methodists and Seventh Day Adventist.

Botswana, Lesotho, Namibia, South Africa, Swaziland and Zimbabwe have common law and Roman-Dutch law. The former British territories with common law jurisdiction are: Gambia, Ghana, Nigeria and Sierra Leone in West Africa, and Kenya, Malawi, Sudan, and Uganda; Tanganyika was formerly German East Africa.

The bibliography is not exhaustive. Some countries have more published papers than others, however as a result of the long isolation of South African customary law scholarship, the works of some South African legal writers have been omitted. References for Islamic and Hindu law have also been left out.

As there are many questions that torment researchers of customary law, some inter-disciplinary materials in oral history, archaeology, ethnography and philosophy have been included. A clue to the answers may be found in the inter-disciplinary materials.

The compiling of the references was in itself an odyssey that deserves a separate volume. It was my good fortune to start the chasing of obscure references in the first-class Libraries of the School of Oriental and African Studies where every esoteric journal or periodical on Africa could be located, the Library of the Institute of Advanced Legal Studies, UCL Institute of Archaeology, and the Library of the Courtauld Institute. Being a diligent footnote reader and index guide, I followed many trails in search of the correct citations, and I found many inaccuracies. I was almost driven mad by some of the citations of references in non-legal academic journals. Incredible as it is, even some writers managed to cite their own papers wrongly in different journals. Sometimes dates, volumes, page numbers and end page number are inaccurate, and the problem was compounded by reference searches in French, German, Italian, Portuguese or Spanish journals for research materials on Africa law. Many interesting references have been missed, and sometimes customary law does not even rate an index reference.

Some deficiencies in references have been remedied and, unwittingly, I may have let a few slip through the net, in spite of the excellent libraries, but I have tried to maintain a certain amount of accuracy. Inevitably, there will be a few errors. However, I have adopted a very simple technique of referencing to help researchers with problems with foreign exchange who send abroad for photo copies to know exactly how many pages there are in the articles. First, the surname of the author is cited, followed by his or her initials, date, title of the paper, name of periodical or journal, volume: Vol. and number, No. and pp. for pages. The reference for a book has the same format as that of a periodical, but the place of publication and the publishers of the book are also cited. If an author has three or four publications in the same year, it is denoted by a b c etc.: thus (1992a) (1992b) (1992c).

The chapters

The aim of chapter 1 is to reconstruct the quiet legal struggle of indigenous laws, against the imposition of German civil law and English common law. German colonial territories were discussed because German East Africa, Tanganyika, later renamed Tanzania, and German South West Africa, renamed Namibia, and half of Cameroon now, have common law jurisdiction. An analysis of the attempted codification of indigenous law is explained.

The natives were governed by 'indirect rule' as long as they were submissive, paid their head or hut tax, and let themselves be flogged or imprisoned for criminal offences. A brief discussion on the further attempts to modernise indigenous laws by recording them is also narrated. This was followed by a rush of law and economic self-determinism, law and development, law and human rights, law and whatever else. All in the name of modernising indigenous laws, but indigenous laws triumphed over them.

It was not possible in chapter 2 to meet all the requirements of customary law researchers. Important references in Dutch, German, Japanese, Russian and Swedish have been left out, because the researchers who can read those languages know the research libraries to find the appropriate references.

Chapter 3 is an outline on some African chiefs and councillors and their position today. These were the men of power who told the rest of the people what to do, and some were priests and healers who knew about the fertility of land and women. These chiefs were the men who were coerced into concluding Protection Treaties with the colonial powers. The all-powerful District Officer, Resident Officer, District Commissioner or the Native Commissioner, as he was known in African territories with white settlers, is also introduced in this chapter, as well as in chapters 1 and 9.

Chapter 4 is a brief child ethnography. It has not been easy balancing the child law of an androgynous community with that of a patrilineal community. However, the consequences of growing up in matrilineal, patrilineal or duolineal transmission systems are established in some detail. Many children develop under different legal institutions, and the various roles the institutions play in the children's education are examined. The role of the paternal uncles as the children's ombudsmen in matrilineal societies is also examined.

Chapter 5 explains simple contract that people entered into. Many Africans have traded internally in gold, ivories, slaves, textiles, kola, yam, pottery, cattle, goats; sheep, palm oil and palm wine for a very long time. Some have conducted long-distance trading with literate Arab communities.

Chapter 6 examines the administration of criminal law under colonial rule, as well as under indigenous law. See also chapter 9. Criminal law is another problematic area of the indigenous law, because some small-scale societies, like the *ovaHimba* do not kill criminals, whereas other groups use the system of the poison ordeals to administer 'justice'. Under indigenous law, after the open, fair criminal trial, the poison ordeal was manipulated and administered by the court to rid the community of murderers. Most people know the guilty party. The court, having gathered information as well as hearing the parties, must perform a public duty by letting the poison ordeal give a reasonable verdict and the punishment, death by the poison ordeal. But the poison can not discriminate deliberately between the innocent and the guilty party. Therefore, with the herbalists' sound knowledge of the local pharmacology of lethal poisons, the dosage is manipulated to let the guilty party die and the innocent party survive.

Chapter 7 defines cultural property and the modern statutory law prohibiting their export and international laws governing their return. The topics covered by the selected books, essays and monographs in periodicals on cultural property vary from general aesthetic descriptions to fakes and authenticity, restitution of illicitly removed cultural property, recovery of stolen cultural objects and the European art market for African antiquities.

The chapter also attempts an explanation of how the objects found their way to the European and American art markets. What could be done to compensate Africans for the loss of their cultural property?

Chapter 8 examines what causes disapprobation of indigenous law and the general ignorance about indigenous law. The missionaries who were mostly liable for the dissemination of irrational information about indigenous law wanted polygynists annihilated and their idols burnt. The chapter also discusses some traditional practices disapproved of by the state. From the empirical evidence, it is apparent that most people take the indigenous law very seriously.

In chapter, 9 we shall see how the people have devised ways of settling their disputes. We examine pre-colonial courts and the official native courts with hand-picked chiefs or headmen with their native assessors. The complaints procedure is discussed as well as a case study. There was no evidence of *lex talionis* under matrilineal indigenous law. In short what was most evident is the role of mediation and compensatory justice.

Chapter 10 is a 'demystification' of indigenous law because it is buttressed by philosophy and theology. The principles of indigenous law have been uninfluenced by Judaeo-Christian ethics, and law and morals have not yet separated. Some indigenous law thinkers have attempted to answer some questions and a study of the references in this chapter will explain the resilience of indigenous law.

In chapter 11 the formation of marriage is a very serious business not to be entrusted to only the couple. Child betrothal is examined as well as the ubiquitous bridewealth. As usual, one has to weigh the formalities of patrilineal and matrilineal forms of marriages and the consequence on divorce on the parties.

Chapter 12 is a brief history of African legal anthropology from Sarbah (1897) to the grand imperial anthropologists and to the opening of Law Schools in Africa. Sack (1992) has written a very exhilarating introduction to law and anthropology.

Land and family property, chapter 13, is the only area of customary law where there have been radical changes and the indigenous law is being swept aside to some extent as a few people appropriate more indigenous land for themselves.

Chapter 14 is an examination of a girl's prescriptive right to a husband. The girl-child has a right to a husband, the boy-child has a duty to marry. Sororate and levirate polygyny are examined

Chapter 15 comprises an examination of succession and inheritance rules under polygyny, monogamy, patrilineal, matrilineal and duolineal systems and who gets what.

Chapter 16 is a compilation of a bibliography of bibliographies that a researcher could explore for more materials. The conclusion that one comes to is that African states need to find more money to pay for journals and periodicals and research reports on customary law.

Headnotes

The treatment of the headnotes is necessarily brief, for the point of the exercise is to encourage the researcher to use the bibliographic tool. I did not use indigenous words from many ethnic groups as it might have made the text too difficult to read. However, the indigenous words used in the text are in italics. As well as the glossary, with their approximate English meaning to clarify the concept under discussion, contextual explanation of the *Otjiherero* terms used is also provided.

The language spoken by the *ovaHimba* with whom I did my field work is *Otjiherero* and the orthography has been influenced by Afrikaans and English. The rights of the child, for example can be *ousemba womuatje* or *ousemba omuatje*. The latter as it is spoken is the model that I have used in the headnotes. This also applies to the plural *ousemba wovanatje*, children's rights,or *ousemba ovanatje*. In some words like the sacred fire, *okuruuo*, I retained the triple vowel rather than writing *okuruwo*. Thus the plural in the headnotes is *omaruuo*, not *omaruwo*. The prefix *omu* for singular becomes *ova* for plural, *omuHimba* is an individual *Himba* person; *ovaHimba* are the *Himba* people.

The glossary is appended immediately after this introduction to encourage the diligent reader to study the simple terms as well as prevent leafing forwards and backwards in search of meaning. I have kept the use of indigenous words to the barest minimum.

Can indigenous law survive? Like other ancient traditions in the world, indigenous law is changing in terms of its own priority. Indigenous law is not rooted in the past, because today, indigenous law is reflecting changes in the society. It is even meeting the needs of graduates. Today, Africans have been humiliated by technological inferiority, but their contribution to humanity in the protection of their children should not be underrated.

Reference

Ankermann, B. (1905) 'Kulturkreise und Kulturschichten in Afrika'. Zeitschrift für Ethnologie. Vol. 37, pp. 54-84.

Chapter 1 — Attempted reform of indigenous laws

The purpose of this chapter is to explain the attempts by the colonial powers to codify the system of 'native laws and customs' found in Africa, but they did not have a *tabula rasa* within which to inscribe the colonial law.

Since colonialism, drastic measures have been applied to African indigenous laws to clone or to transform them into western law with an African backdrop. After the attempted codification, there followed a period of the recording, the restatement, and the unification of African customary law. Today, it has become development and harmonisation of customary law for social engineering. The indigenous laws are still with us, albeit a modified version of their former selves for the survival of the majority subject to them. What is responsible for the resilience and longevity of indigenous law?

Throughout this book, we shall see that the majority of the rural people have had only very limited direct involvement with the changing political and statutory legal power structures in their new states.

1.1 Thumbnail legal history

It is essential to give a thumbnail reconstruction of the legal history of the colonisation of Africa South of the Sahara to simplify this chapter. In pre-colonial Africa, the missionaries, adventurers and traders had found systems of family law, family property, succession, inheritance, criminal law and compensatory justice, but it was not the positivist law that they knew. Nevertheless, the early Europeans had co-existed peacefully with the natives.

The slave trade having been abolished, it became respectable to acquire cheap and profitable colonies with docile labour. German scholars had argued that Britain became enormously rich and successful because of her overseas territories, and that Germany should emulate Britain and provide land that was rich in mineral resources for its immigrants. However, von Strandmann (1993) has recently refuted the economic argument, pointing out that the colonial trade at the height of German colonialism was only one per cent of Germany's total trade. In view of this insignificant amount, Germany did not need colonies to increase its trade. What Germany acquired from her colonies towards the closing years of the 19th century was international prestige rather than economic profit. For, it was Germany that after all skilfully convened the Signatory Powers of the Berlin Africa Conference of 1884/85, where Africa was dismembered and the fate of the natives was sealed.[4] The Conference also balanced the might of Germany and the United Kingdom.

Iliffe (1995) recently explained that there was no single motive for the partition of Africa. During the 1870s Africa accounted for little more than five per cent of Britain's trade, most of it with Egypt and South Africa. "Africa was partitioned not only because European statesmen or soldiers willed it, but because they for the first time possessed the technological capacity to do it".

---

[4] For details on the Signatory Powers of the Berlin Africa Act, see Edward Hertslet (1896:317).

However, Britain and Germany imputed Treaty making status to the local kings and councillors in their territories, and impliedly recognised their authority to sign or make their mark, as their consent to be bound by the Protection treaty. See chapter 3. Not only were the native customs recognised by the colonial treaties, but Article 111 paragraph 2 of the Berlin Africa Conference had also expressly guaranteed to the natives, freedom of conscience and religious toleration. The colonial powers were bound to respect the existing customs and usages prevailing in the territory. Be that as it may, the freedom of conscience and religious toleration did not extend to some spheres of indigenous laws and cultural property. See chapter 7. The existence of indigenous laws was one of the reasons for the attempted codification of the various indigenous laws within the new colonial territories.

1.2 Attempted codification

The period of colonialism was also the height of codification in Germany; the German Code of Criminal and Civil Procedure had been promulgated in 1877, and the German Civil Code in 1896, accordingly, the Reichstag also decided to codify native customs in the German colonies of Cameroon, German East Africa, German South West Africa and Togo. The argument was that if a code of indigenous customs was available, the colonial legal administrators would then be consistent in their application of native law. German jurisprudence would apply to the Germans, and native law, as the compilers deemed it to be, would apply to the natives in the form of a code. However, in any litigation between a German and an African, German law would prevail.

Germany was determined to codify the native laws and customs of their territories (German South West Africa, German East Africa, Cameroon and Togo), because "no new law can be created unless the old law is known". Accordingly, the Reichstag requested the Reich Chancellor's representatives to collect material concerning native laws and produce an authentic compilation of the laws of the natives (Lyall 1980). Dr. Albert Hermann Post (1887) asserted that the indigenous laws of the natives could be ascertained by means of questionnaires sent out to Africa. From the analysis of the materials obtained from the territories, the jurists in Germany would be able to extract, formulate and codify the various principles of native customs.

Some jurists did not advocate the codification of native customs and traditions by questionnaires, because it would put indigenous customs into a primitive ethnographic straight jacket, preventing any further development of the rational thought of the natives. If the natives were satisfied with their family, succession, divorce and inheritance customs why superimpose another law or codify their law? Meinhof (1908) explained that the unqualified application of European forms of 'code' to the natives must inevitably lead to all sorts of inconveniences.

But Germany was determined to codify the native laws and customs of the protectorates. Whether or not the questionnaires were prepared in Berlin, Bremen, or Cameroon was irrelevant. Meinhof argued that the codification of native laws by means of questionnaires prepared in Europe, by those without knowledge of the practical realities, would be inadequate. It can now be stated more firmly that questionnaires prepared by those without an understanding of the ethical and political content of indigenous law would be inappropriate. A further criticism of the questionnaires was that they reflected the misconceptions already held about the African's 'primitive mentality'. This was after the publication of Ankermann, (1905) and Lucien Lévy-Brühl's infamous book, *Les fonctions mentales dans les sociétés inférieures* (1910).

As an example, we can take question number 9 from the German questionnaire to illustrate some misconceptions.

QUESTION: Is there fictitious marriage, perhaps a marriage with a plant, a tool or a picture, with an animal or a spirit?

This question and many more indicated the thinking of the German legal ethnologists of the time. The questionnaires served imperialist propaganda by disseminating irrational material about natives who invented nothing, but only receive. One could almost conclude that the interpretation of the questionnaires was the origin of the invention of disapprobation of African indigenous laws. See chapter 8.

The answers to the questionnaires were returned to Germany, analysed, compiled and published in pamphlets, but there was no speedy and authentic restatement of native law. At the end of the First World War, under the Treaty of Versailles, Germany had to renounce all her rights and titles over the African colonies, and the codification project was abandoned.

Meanwhile, Britain with its jurisdiction of common law was not interested in the codification of indigenous laws, it was not necessary for its political programme. An indigenous law which was not posited could not be law, and Britain simply imposed its own brand of Austinian legal principles on the natives of its territories and protectorates. See chapters 3 & 8. A few kings who had opposed colonial administration were deposed to reduce their power, and some hand-picked loyal natives who had declared openly for Britain were appointed as advisers to the District Officer (DO) or District Commissioner, (DC) Resident Commissioner (RC) or Native Commissioner (NC) as they were called in territories with white settlers.[5] The DOs and NCs were appointed from colonial headquarters and a policy of indirect rule emerged. Indirect rule had been devised and used in the Sokoto Caliphate of Nigeria and the idea was transferred to other colonies and protectorates.

The District Officer or Native Commissioner presided over the native court, and in his absence, the Assistant DO, DC, RC or NC was the President of the Court. He prescribed the manner and form of procedure to be observed in the native court, the times and places in which courts should be held. He would decide the principle of native law applicable to the case, provided however that such principles were not repugnant to natural justice or morality; inconsistent with the statute law, which was also applicable in England and Wales. Furthermore, the NC or the DO decided the applicability of morality and repugnancy to the peculiar circumstances of a case. Local customs could be thrown out as repugnant to morality. However, the DO, DC, RC, or NC did not apply principles of native law to 'educated detribalised' natives. The District Officer or Native Commissioner was a very powerful man.

---

[5] For further details see:
Authoritative general history of Africa
R. Oliver and J. D. Fage (eds.) (1975-86) The Cambridge history of Africa. 8 vols. Cambridge: Cambridge University Press
J. Ki-Zerbo et al. (1981-1993) UNESCO general history of Africa. 8 vols. London
J. Vansina (1978) African history. London
J. F. A. Ajayi and M. Crowder (eds.) (1985) Historical atlas of Africa. Cambridge: Cambridge University Press
John Iliffe (1995) Africans: The history of a continent. Cambridge: Cambridge University Press.

1.3 Development, reform and social change

After independence from the colonial powers, attempts were made by some of the newly created Law Reform Commissions to record or to integrate principles of indigenous law into statutory law, but the colonial criminal statutes were retained by the new elite. The first serious attempt by many Law Reform Commissions was a restructuring of the courts to ensure state supervision of justice at the local level of traditional courts. This would bring the native courts into the mainstream of the courts system and deprive them of criminal jurisdiction. Many people disagreed and argued that it would destroy their traditional compensatory justice system, which has survived even the colonial administration. Their argument was that a community with tradition of compensating the victim and his or her *eanda* has very little crime, delinquent children or criminal litigation. See chapter 6. There were different ways of doing customary law.

The School of Oriental and African Studies (SOAS), University of London also initiated a project of restatement of African customary law. The SOAS project made its point that customary law had rules that could be written down. This enabled many lawyers, reformers, draftspersons, academics and parliamentarians not conversant with the miscellaneous indigenous laws to understand the rules and principles. Essentially, this meant a restatement for the *Wa Benzi*, as the ordinary people themselves already know the law. Furthermore, it meant a law-divide of two models of law, the written customary law model, and a continuation of the imposed colonial system.

Accordingly, the argument of the nationalists was that the new states should unify the indigenous laws and the inherited common law, since it is mostly lawyers' law, and has no practical relevance to the majority of the citizens. Not only should the states claim political independence, they should also proclaim legal independence by accepting the values generated by their own society.

Law and development died quietly and its position was taken over by international human rights law. Many African states are parties to the law making Conventions and have ratified several treaties with the hope of transforming their societies. The nationalists argued that the customary international law values embedded in international law are not shared by the majority of their citizens in the rural areas. The objectors contend that it is a new imposition of international human rights law by the former colonial powers to destabilise the new states and renew their power over the natives. If someone in a village invoked an international norm in the traditional courts what has it solved?

Thus this chapter includes some materials on codification, the recording of customary law, social changes, development and law reform. This chapter may also be used in tandem with the material in chapter 8.

1.4 Bibliography

African Studies Branch of the Colonial Office, (1949) 'Methods of recording native customary law'. Journal of African Administration. Vol. 1, No. 3, pp. 130-136.

Afrika-Instituut, (1956). *The future of customary law in Africa.* Report of the Proceedings of a Symposium in Amsterdam. Leiden.

Conference on the Integration of Customary and Modern Legal Systems in Africa, 1964. Ibadan. Nigeria. *Integration of customary and modern legal systems in Africa.* New York: Holmes & Meier.

Future of Customary Law in Africa. International Symposium on the Future of Customary Law in Africa. Amsterdam 1955. Leiden Universitaire.

The harmonisation of African law (1972) Instituto Italo-Africano. Milano: Giuffrè Editore.

'*Integration of customary and modern legal systems in Africa*' (1971) A conference held at Ibadan on 24-29 August 1964. New York: Africana Publishing Corporation.

'Integration of customary and modern legal systems in Africa'. (1964) Journal of African Law. Vol. 8, No. 2, pp. 55-58.

'Integration of laws in Cameroons'. (1964) Journal of African Law. Vol. 8, No. 2, pp. 153-154.

Laws of Lerotholi: Basutoland 1946.

The move towards codification. (1958) Journal of African Law Vol. 2, No. 2, pp. 73-81.

Natal Code of Native Law. (1891) Reproduced in full in African Studies. Vol. 2, pp. 1-26.

Natal Code of Native Law: Proclamation No. 168, 1932. Witwatersrand University Press.

Natal Code, Law No. 19 of 1891.

Report and proceedings of the Government Commission on native law and customs, 1883. Shannon: Irish University Press, reprint 1970.

Agbede, I. O. (1972) 'Conflict between customary and non-customary systems of law'. Verfassung und Recht in Übersee. Vol. 5, pp. 415-422.

Agbede, O. (1975) 'Towards unification of municipal laws in Africa: Nigerian experience'. Verfassung und Recht in Übersee. Vol. 8, pp. 423-433.

Agondjo-Okawe, P. L. 'Les domaines d'application des droits traditionnels'. Encyclopédie juridique de l'Afrique. Vol. 1, pp. 405-421.

Aguda, A. (1973) 'Legal development in Botswana from 1885-1966'. Botswana Notes and Records. Vol. 5, pp. 52-63.

Ajayi, F. A. (1960) 'The interaction of English law with customary law in Western Nigeria'. Journal of African Law. Vol. 4, No. 1, pp. 40-50.

Ajayi, F. A. (1960) 'The interaction of English law with customary law in Western Nigeria'. Pt. 2. Journal of African Law. Vol. 4, No. 2, pp. 98-114.

Akpaloo, G. A. (1994) 'The impact of legislations on the customary practices of the Ga-Dangme people of South Eastern Ghana'. Law & Anthropology. Vol. 7, pp. 203-238.

Akweenda, S. (1989) *International law and the protection of Namibia's territorial integrity: Boundaries and territorial claims.* London: PhD. Thesis LSE, University of London.

Ali, O. H. (1971) 'The conversion of customary law to written law'. The Sudan Law Journal and Reports, pp. 147-161.

Alliot, M. (1967) 'Problèmes de l'unification des droits Africains'. Journal of African Law. Vol. 11, No. 2, pp. 86-98.

Allott, A. N. (1957) 'Gold Coast law reform'. West Africa. pp. 105 & 127.

Allott, A. N. (1959) 'The unity of African law'. Journal of African Administration. Vol. 11, pp. 72-83.

Allott, A. N. (1961) 'The changing law in a changing Africa'. Sociologus. Vol. 11, pp. 115-131.

Allott, A. N. (1963) 'Codification and unification of law in Africa'. Africa Quarterly Vol. 3. No. 1, pp. 187-200.

Allott, A. N. (1965) 'Towards the unification of laws in Africa'. International and Comparative Law Quarterly. Vol. 14, pp. 366-389.

Allott, A. N. (1966) 'The codification of the law of civil wrongs in common law African countries'. Sociologus. Vol. 16, pp. 101-122.

Allott, A. N. (1968) 'The unification of laws in Africa'. American Journal of Comparative Law. Vol. 16, pp. 51-87.

Allott, A. N. (1977) 'The people as law-makers: Custom, practice and public opinion as source of law in Africa and England'. Journal of African Law. Vol. 21. No. 1, pp. 1-23

Allott, A. N. (1984) 'Development for what? False gods and holy writ'. Human Rights and Development. Third World Legal Studies. pp. 1-9.

Allott, A. N. (ed.) (1960) '*The future of law in Africa*'. Record of Proceedings of the London Conference 28 December 1959 to 8 January 1960. London: Butterworths.

Allott, A. N. (ed.) (1962) *Judicial and legal systems in Africa*. London: Butterworths.

Allott, A. N. and Woodman, G. R. (1985) *People's law and state law: The Bellagio Papers*. Dordrecht: Foris Publications.

Allott, A. N., Anozie, I. O. and Read, J. S. (1963a) 'Codification and unification of laws in Africa'. Colloquium on African law, London, June 1963. Journal of African Law. Vol. 7, No. 2, pp. 72-83.

Anderson, J. N. D. (1957) 'The conflict of laws in Northern Nigeria'. Journal of African Law. Vol. 1, No. 1, pp. 87-98.

Anderson, J. N. D. (1960) 'Colonial law in tropical Africa: The conflict between English, Islamic and customary law'. Indiana Law Journal. Vol. 35. pp. 433-442.

Anderson, J. N. D. (1963) *Changing law in developing countries*. London: Allen & Unwin.

Ankermann, B. (1905) 'Kulturkreise und Kulturschichten in Africa'. Zeitschrift für Ethnologie. Vol. 37, pp. 54-84.

Arty, A. (ed.) (1990) *Post-modern law, enlightenment, revolution, and the death of man.* Edinburgh: Edinburgh University Press.

Asmis, W. (1913) 'Law and policy relating to the natives of the Gold Coast and Nigeria'. Journal of the African Society. Vol. 12, pp. 17-51 & pp. 136-164.

Baade, H. W. (1963) *African law: New law for new nations.* Dobbs Ferry: Oceana.

Baxi, U. (1979) 'Law and 'development'. Verfassung und Recht in Übersee. Vol. 12, pp. 97-114.

Benda-Beckmann, F. von (1981) 'Some comments on the problems of comparing the relationship between traditional and state systems of administration of justice in Africa and Indonesia'. Journal of Legal Pluralism. Vol. 19, pp. 165-175.

Bennett, T. W. and Vermeulen, T. (1980) 'Codification of customary law'. Journal of African Law. Vol. 24, No. 2, pp. 206-219.

Bentham, J. (1822) 'Codification proposal addressed to all nations professing liberal opinions'. Bowring J. (ed.) *Bentham Works.* Vol. 1V. Edinburgh: William Tait.

Bentsi-Enchill, K. (1969) 'The colonial heritage of legal pluralism'. Zambia Law Journal. Vol. 1, No. 2, pp. 1-30.

Bentsi-Enchill, K. (1971) 'Choice of law in Ghana since 1960'. University of Ghana Law Journal. Vol. 8, pp. 59-75.

Berghe, P. L. van den (1973) 'Pluralism'. In Honigmann, J. J. (ed.) *Handbook of social and cultural anthropology.* Chicago: Rand McNally.

Blanc-Jouvan, X. (1964) 'Development of a new code in Madagascar'. Africa Today. Vol. 11, pp. 7-9.

Blanc-Jouvan, X. (1977) 'La résistance du droit africain à la modernisation'. Revue Sénégalaise de droit'. Vol. 21, pp. 21-44.

Burman, S. B. and Harrell-Bond, B. E. (eds.) (1979) *The imposition of law.* New York, London: Academic Press.

Chiba, M. (1986) *Asian indigenous law: In interaction with received law.* London: KPI Ltd.

Conac, G. (ed.) (1980) *Dynamiques et finalités des droits africains.* Paris: Economica.

Contini, P. (1969) *The Somali republic: An experiment in legal integration.* London: Cass.

Cooper, R. M. (1971) 'Uganda's Law Development Centre'. Review of the International Commission of Jurists. Vol. 7, pp. 33-37.

Cotran, E. (1963) 'The unification of laws in East Africa'. Journal of Modern African Studies. Vol. 1, No. 2, pp. 209-220.

Cotran, E. (1965) 'Integration of courts and application of customary law in Tanganyika'. East African Law Journal. No. 1, pp. 102-123.

Cotran, E. (1966) 'The place and future of customary law in East Africa'. East Africa Law Today. No. 5, pp. 72-92.

Cotran, E. (1968) 'Integration of courts and application of customary law in Kenya'. East African Law Journal. No. 4, pp. 14-20.

Danquah, J. B. (1928) *Gold Coast: Akan laws and customs and the Akim Abuakwa constitution.* London: G. Routledge and sons.

Davies, O. (1967) *West Africa before the Europeans.* London: Methuen.

Davis, P. D. (1956) 'Transition from primitive to modern law in the African Gold Coast'. Intramural Law Review. Vol. 11, pp. 118-130.

Deng, F. M. (1969) 'The future of customary law in the Sudan'. Malaya Law Review. Vol. 11, pp. 268-286.

Deng, F. M. (1971) *Tradition and modernization: A challenge for law among the Dinka of the Sudan.* New Haven: Yale University Press.

Drechsler, H. (1980) *'Let us die fighting'. The struggle of the Herero and Nama against German imperialism 1884-1915.* London: Zed Press.

Ekow-Daniels, W. C. (1962) 'Unifying African law'. West Africa. No. 2350 p. 650

Ekow-Daniels, W. C. (1964) 'The interaction of English law with customary law in West Africa'. International and Comparative Law Quarterly. No. 13, pp. 574-616.

Elias, T. O. (1954) 'Customary law the limits of its validity in colonial law'. African Studies. Vol. 13, Nos. 3-4, pp. 97-107.

Elias, T. O. (1958) *Impact of English law on Nigerian customary law.* Lagos: Government Printer.

Elias, T. O. (1962) *Ghana and Sierra Leone: The development of their laws and constitution.* London: Stevens and Sons.

Elias, T. O. (1970) 'Law in a developing society'. Nigeria Law Journal. Vol. 4. pp. 1-19.

Engo, P. B. (1964) 'Some aspects of legal reform in Cameroon'. Abbia. Vol. 6, pp. 159-171.

Fallers, L. A. (1956) 'Changing customary law in Busoga district of Uganda'. Journal of African Administration. Vol. 8. pp. 139-144.

Fallers, L. (1962) 'Customary law in the new African states'. Law and Contemporary Problems. Vol. 27, No. 4, pp. 605-616.

Fitzpatrick, P. (1990) 'The desperate vacuum: Imperialism and law in the experience of enlightenment'. In Arty, A. (ed.) *Post-modern law, enlightenment, revolution and the death of man.* Edinburgh: Edinburgh University Press, pp. 90-107.

Gaay Fortman, B. de and Mihyo, P. (1993) 'A false start: Law and development in the context of a colonial legacy'. Verfassung und Recht in Übersee. Vol. 26, pp. 136-161.

Gadacz, R. R. (1987) 'Folk law and legal pluralism'. Legal Studies Forum. Vol. 11, pp. 125-144.

Ghai, Y. (1987) 'Law, development and African scholarship'. Modern Law Review. Vol. 50, pp. 750-776.

Ghai, Y. (1991) 'The role of law in the transition of societies. The African experience. Journal of African Law. Vol. 35, Nos. 1 & 2, pp. 8-20.

Gilissen, J. (ed.) (1960) *The recording of customary law in British Africa and the restatement of African Law Project.* La redaction des coutumes dans le passé et dans le presént. Bruxelles.

Gluckman, M. (1956) *Custom and conflict in Africa.* Oxford: Basil Blackwell.

Gordon, R. J. (1991) 'Customary law in Namibia: What should be done'? Vanderbilt Journal on Transnational Law. Vol. 24, No. 4, pp. 633-651.

Green, L. C. (1968) *The common law and native systems of law.* In Wilson, R. R. (ed.) International and comparative law of the Commonwealth. Durham: Duke University Press.

Griffiths, J. (1986) 'What is legal pluralism'? Journal of Legal Pluralism. No. 24, pp. 1-55.

Hag Ali, O. (1970) 'Conversion of customary law to written law'. Sudan Law Journal. pp. 147-161.

Hannigan, A. St. J. J. (1956) 'The impact of English law upon the existing Gold Coast custom and the possible development of the resulting system'. Journal of African Administration. No. 8, pp. 126-132.

Hannigan, A. St. J. J. (1961) 'The imposition of Western law forms upon primitive societies. Comparative Studies in Society and History. Vol. 4, pp. 1-9.

Harvey, W. B. (1962) 'The evolution of Ghana law since independence'. Law and Contemporary Problems. Vol. 27, No. 4, pp. 581-604.

Hazard, J. N. (1971) 'Revolutionary socialism and African law reform'. Association of the Bar of New York Record. Vol. 26, pp. 358-368.

Hertslet, E. (1896) *The map of Africa by treaty. Abyssinia to Great Britain.* London: Harrison & Sons

Hilaire, J. (1964) 'Nos ancêtres les Gaulois'. Annales africaines. pp. 7-77.

Holleman, J. F. (1973) 'Trouble-cases and trouble-less cases in the study of customary law and legal reform'. Law and Society Review. Vol. 7, pp. 585-610.

Hooker, M. B. (1975) *Legal pluralism: An introduction to colonial and neo-colonial laws.* Oxford: Oxford University Press.

Iliffe, J. (1971) *The integration of customary and modern legal systems in Africa.* New York: Africana.

Iliffe, J. (1995) *Africans: The history of a continent.* Cambridge: Cambridge University Press.

James, R. W. (1967)'Judicial development in customary law'. Journal of the Denning Law Society. Vol. 2, pp. 41-58.

Kahn-Freund, O. (1969) 'Law reform in Kenya'. East African Law Journal. Vol. 5. pp. 54-87.

Karibi-Whyte, A. G. (1966) 'The reception of English law in Sierra Leon. A historical treatment'. Sierra Leone Studies. pp. 109-118.

Kerr, A. J. (1958) 'The reception and codification of systems of law in Southern Africa'. Journal of African Law. Vol. 2, No. 2, pp. 82-100.

Kerr, A. J. (1997) 'The Bill of rights in the new constitution and customary law'. The South African Law Journal. Vol. 114, pp. 346-355.

Kiapi, A. (1991) 'African concept of law and law reform in Uganda'. Journal of African Religion and Philosophy. Vol. 2, No. 1, pp. 59-62.

Koyama, D. S. (1980) *Customary law in a changing society.* Cape Town: Juta.

Krzeczunowicz, G. (1963) 'A new legislative approach to customary law: The repeals provisions of the Ethiopian Civil Code of 1960'. Journal of Ethiopian Studies. Vol. 1, pp. 57-67.

Krzeczunowicz, G. (1965) 'Code and custom in Ethiopia'. Journal of Ethiopian Law. Vol. 2, pp. 425-439.

Kucklick, J. (1978) 'The sins of the fathers: British anthropology and African colonial administration'. Research in Sociology of Knowledge, Science and Art. No. 1, 93-119.

Kuper, H. and Kuper, L. (eds.) (1965) *African law: Adaptation and development.* Berkeley: University of California Press.

Kuper, L. and Smith, M. G. (eds.) (1971) *Pluralism in Africa.* Berkeley: University of California Press.

Lang, J. H. A. (1961) 'The inheritance of common law'. Universitas. Vol. 4, No. 6, pp. 175-177.

Le Roy, E. (1978) 'La vie du droit en Afrique'. Recueil Penant. Vol. 761. pp. 315-323.

Le Roy, E. (1979) 'African traditional law and modernity'. Revenue Monchanin. Vol. 12, No. 4, pp. 35-43.

Levasseur, A. A. (1971) 'The modernization of law in Africa with particular reference to family law in the Ivory Coast'. In Foster, P. and Zolberg, A. (eds.) *Ghana and the Ivory Coast: Perspectives on modernization.* pp. 151-166. Chicago: University of Chicago Press.

Lévy-Brühl, L. (1910) *Les fonctions mentales dans les sociétiés inferieurs.* Paris: Alcan.

Lewin, J. (1938) 'The recognition of native law and custom in British Africa'. Journal of Comparative Legislation. No. 20, pp. 16-23.

Lewis-Barned, J. F. de S. (1963) 'Integration of judicial systems: The recent reform of the local courts appeal system in Tanganyika'. Journal of African Law. Vol. 7, No. 2, pp. 84-93.

Low, D. A. (1973) *Lion rampant: Essays in the study of British imperialism*. London: Frank Cass.

Lugard, F. J. L. (1922) *The dual mandate in British Tropical Africa*. London: Frank Cass & Co.

Lyall, A. B. (1980) *The social origin of property and contract: A study of East Africa before 1918*. London: PhD. Thesis. LSE, University of London.

Mann, K. and Roberts, R. (eds.) (1991) *Law in colonial Africa*. London: Heinemann.

Meinhof, K. (1908) 'The codification of native law in German colonies'. Journal of the African Society Vol. 7. pp. 159-164.

Mensah-Brown, A. K. (1976) *Introduction to law in contemporary Africa*. New York: Coneh Magazine Ltd.

Mommsen, W. J. and Moor de, J. A. (eds.) (1992) *European expansion and law: The encounter of European and indigenous law in 19th and 20th century Africa and Asia*. Oxford: Berg.

Moore, S. F. (1970) 'Politics, procedures and norms in changing Chagga law'. Africa. Vol. 40, pp. 321-343.

Moore, S. F. (1973) 'Law and social change: The semi-autonomous social field as an appropriate subject of study'. Law and Society Review. Vol. 7, No. 4, pp. 719-746.

Moore, S. F. (1986) 'Legal systems of the world: An introductory guide to classification, typological interpretations and bibliographical resources'. In Lipson, L and Wheeler, S. (eds.) *Law and the social sciences*. pp. 11-62. New York: Russel Sage Foundation.

Morris, H. F. (1968) 'Marriage law in Uganda: Sixty years of attempted reform'. In Anderson, J. N. D. (ed.) *Family law in Asia and Africa*. London: Allen & Unwin.

Morse, B. W. and Woodman, G. R. (eds.) (1987) *Indigenous law and the state*. Dordrecht: Foris Publications.

Morse, B. W. and Woodman, G. R. (eds.) (1988) *Indigenous law and the state*. Dordrecht: Foris Publication.

Mqete, R. B. (1989) 'Traditionalism in modern African legal systems with specific reference to the legal position in Southern Africa'. Law & Anthropology. Vol. 4, pp. 17-26.

Mustafa, Z. (1973) 'Opting out of the common law: Recent developments in the legal system of the Sudan'. Journal of African Law. Vol. 17, No. 2, pp. 133-147.

Naib, R. M. (1982) 'Modernization without westernization'. Journal of Law and Society. Vol. 1, No. 1, pp. 59-66.

Nhlapo, R. T. (1984) 'The position of customary law in South Africa. Law and Anthropology'. Vol. 4, pp. 47-57.

Nicholson, M. E. R. (1973) Change without conflict: a case study of legal change in Tanzania. Law and Society Review. Vol. 7, pp. 747-766.

Nkrumah, K. (1962) 'Law in Africa'. Address at the Opening of the Ghana Law School, 4 January 1962. Journal of African Law. Vol. 6, No. 2, pp. 103-112.

Ntumy, M. A. (1982) 'The conceptual relationship between law and development and its implications for development in Africa'. Nigerian Journal of Development. No. 2, pp. 11-

Nwabara, S. N. (1979) 'The received' Nigerian law and the challenge of legal independence'. Journal of Asian and African Studies. No. 14, pp. 99-108.

Obol-Ochola, J. Y. (1970) 'The application of customary law in Uganda: Judicial ambivalence, indifference and sabotage'. Eastern Africa Law Review. No, 3, pp. 175-179.

Obol-Ochola, J. Y. (1971) Customary law and national development in Uganda. Vierteljahresberichte. No. 43, pp. 1-29.

Ojwang, J. B. (1985) 'European law in Africa: Wherefore?' In Jorgensen, S., Pöyhönen, J. and Varga, C. (eds.) *Tradition and progress in modern legal cultures,* pp. 141-147. Stuttgart: Steiner Verlag Wiesbaden,

Ojwang, J. B. (1989) 'The meaning, content and significance of tribal law in an emergent nation: The Kenya case'. Law and Anthropology. Vol. 4, pp. 125-140.

Ojwang, J. (1986) 'Legal transplantation: Rethinking the role and significance of Western law in Africa'. In Sack, P and Minchin, E. (eds.) *Legal pluralism. Proceedings of the Canberra Workshop V11.* Canberra Law Department, Research School of Social Sciences, Australia National University, pp. 99-123.

Okoth-Ogendo, H. W. O. (1970) 'Law reform and African law in East Africa'. East African Journal. Vol. 7, pp. 19-25.

Ollennu, N. A. (1961) 'The influence of English law on West Africa. Journal of African Law. Vol. 5, No. 1, pp. 21-35.

Ollennu, N. A. (1970) 'Law reform in Ghana in the 1970s'. University of Ghana Law Journal No. 7, pp. 1-30.

Ollennu, N. A. (1971) 'The changing law and law reform in Ghana. Journal of African Law. Vol. 15, No. 2, pp. 132-179.

Orban, F. A. (1971) 'African law revision'. East African Law Journal. Vol. 7, pp. 56-68.

Orde-Browne, G. St. J. (1933) 'British justice and the African'. Journal of Royal African Society. Vol. 32, pp. 148-159.

Park, A. E. W. (1963) *The sources of Nigerian law.* London: Sweet & Maxwell.

Paul, J. C. N. (1979) 'Introduction: *Traditional* v *Modern legal systems*'. Verfassung und Recht in Übersee. Vol. 12, pp. 95-96.

Phillips, A. (1955) The future of customary law in Africa. Journal of African Administration. Vol. 7, pp. 151-159.

Pogucki, R. J. H. (1956) 'A note on the codification of customary land law on the Gold Coast'. Journal of African Administration. Vol. 8, No. 4, pp. 192-196.

Pogucki, R. J. H. (1962) 'Notes on codification of land law and registration of titles to land'. Ghana Bulletin of Agricultural Economics. Vol. 2, pp. 21-25.

Poirier, J. (1963) *Le probleme de la redactions des droits coutumiers d'Afrique noire. Etudes de droit contemporain.* Paris: Cujas.

Post, A. H. (1887) *Afrikanische Jurisprudenz: ethnologisch-juristische Beiträge zur Kenntnis der einheimischen Rechte Afrikas.* Oldenburg: Schulze.

Prillaman, J. L. (1966) 'Integration of tribal courts into the national judiciary of Liberia: The rule of the local courts adviser. Liberia Law Journal. pp. 43-67.

Proehl, P. O. and Richardson, H. J. (1970) 'Crossroads for law in Africa'. UCLA Law Review. Vol. 18, pp. 219-251.

Randa, H. (1987) *Problems of interaction between the imposed English system of law and the Luo customary law in Kenya.* Juris Dok, Lund: University of Lund.

Rattray, R. S. (1929) *Ashanti law and constitution.* London: Oxford University Press.

Redmayne, A. and Rogers, C. (1983) 'Research on customary law in German East Africa'. Journal of African Law Vol. 27, No. 1, pp. 22-41.

Reyntjens, F. and Wolf-Phillips, L. (1984) 'Revolution in the legal systems of third world states'. In Marasinghe, M. L. and Conklin, W. E. (eds.) *Essays on third world perspectives in jurisprudence.* Singapore: Malayan Law Journal Pte. Ltd.

Roberts, S. (1971a) 'The recording of customary law: Some problems of method'. Botswana Notes and Records. Vol. 3, pp. 12-21.

Roberts, S. (1971b) 'The recording of customary law, with appendix'. Botswana Notes and Records. Vol. 3, pp. 12-21.

Roberts, S. (1983) 'Imposition, choice and change: Some conflicting perceptions on the relationship between state law and indigenous institutions in contemporary Africa'. Jahrbuch für Afrikanisches Recht. Vol. 2, pp. 99-106.

Roberts-Wray, K. (1957) 'The need for study of native law'. Journal of African Law Vol. 1, No. 2, pp.82-86.

Roberts-Wray, K. (1960) 'The adaptation of imported law in Africa'. Journal of African Law. Vol. 4, No. 2, pp. 66-78.

Rwezaura, B. A. (1983) *Traditionalism and law reform in Africa*. Saarbrucken: Europa Institut der Universität de Saarland.

Rwezaura, B. A. (1987) 'State law and customary law: reflections on their relationship in contemporary Tanzania'. Vorträge, Reden und Berichte aus dem Europa-Institut. Saarbrucken No. 83, pp. 1-21.

Said, E. (1993) *Culture and imperialism*. London: Chatto & Windus.

Salacuse, J. W. (1968) 'Developments in African law'. Africa Report. Vol. 13, pp. 39-45.

Salter, D. R. and Ojwang, J. B. (1985) 'Law Reform in Africa: A comparative study of Tanzanian and Kenyan experiments'. Verfassung und Recht in Übersee. Vol. 18, pp. 123-138.

Sawyerr, G. F. A. (1967) 'Internal conflict of laws in East Africa'. In Sawyerr, G. F. A. (ed.) *East African law and social change*. Nairobi: East African Publishing House, pp. 110-171.

Sedler, R. A. (1968) 'Law reform in the emerging nations of sub-Saharan Africa: Social change and the development of the modern legal system'. St. Louis University Law Journal. Vol. 13, pp. 195-257.

Seidman, R. B. (1965) 'The inarticulate premise'. Journal of Modern African Studies. No. 3, pp. 567-587.

Seidman, R. B. (1978) *State, law and development*. London: Croom Helm.

Seidman, R. B. (1982) 'On restructuring the colonial state: How a Bill became a law in Zimbabwe. Africa. Vol. 52, No. 3, pp. 56-76.

Seidman, R. B. (1992) 'The fatal race: Law-making and the implementation of development goals'. Third World Legal Studies. pp. 79-98.

Sevareid, P. (1983) 'The future of customary law'. Africana Journal. Vol. 14, No. 1, pp. 34-47.

Simons, H. J. (1938) 'The study of native law in South Africa'. Bantu Studies. Vol. 12, pp. 237-242.

Singer, N. J. (1972) 'Ethiopian civil code and the recognition of customary law'. Houston Law Review. Vol. 9, pp. 460-494.

Smith, D. C. (1989) *Did colonialism capture the peasantry: A case study of the Kagera* district. Uppsala: Scandinavian Institute of African Studies.

Snyder, F. G. (1980) 'Law and development in light of dependency theory'. Law and Society Review. Vol. 14, No. 3, pp. 723-804.

Snyder, F. G. (1986) *Capitalism and legal change: An African transformation*. London: Academic Press.

Sousa Santos, B. de (1984) 'From customary law to popular justice'. Journal of African Law. Vol. 28, Nos. 1-2, pp. 90-98.

Stafford, W. G. (1935) *Native law as practised in Natal.* Johannesburg: Witwatersrand University Press.

Stafford, W. G. and Franklin, E. (1950) *Principles of native law and the natal Code.* Pietermaritzburg: Shuter & Shooter.

Stoljar, S. J. (ed.) (1977) *Problems of codification.* Canberra: Dept. of Law, Research School of Social Sciences, Australian National University.

Strandman, H. P. von (1993) 'Germany and its relationship with Namibia in colonial times'. Windhoek: The Namibian-German Foundation for Cultural Co-operation. (Unpublished Paper).

Tanner, R. E. S. (1966) 'The codification of customary law in Tanzania'. East African Law Review. Vol. 2, pp. 105-116.

Tejada, F. E. de. (1979) 'The future of Bantu law'. In Hutley, F. C., Kamenka, E. and Tay, A. E. (eds.) *Law and the future of society.* Weisbaden: Franz Steiner, pp. 303-315.

Theodoropoulos, C. (1982) 'Legal dualism in Namibia: The present as history. Eastern '. Africa Law Review. Vol. 15, pp. 20-65.

Twining, W. (1963) 'The restatement of African customary law: A comment'. The Journal of Modern African Studies. Vol. 1, pp. 221-228.

Twining, W. (1964) *The place of customary law in the national legal systems of East Africa.* University of Chicago Law School.

Umozurike, U. O. (1970) 'International Law and colonialism in Africa'. Eastern Africa Law Review. Vol. 3, No. 1, pp. 47-82.

Unsworth, E. G. (1944) 'Conflict of law in Africa'. Human Problems. pp. 49-55.

Van Niekerk, B. J. (1970) 'Customary law in Botswana: Substitution or adaptation'? Comparative and International Law Journal of South Africa. Vol. 3, pp. 242-247.

Vanderlinden, J. (1959) 'The recording of customary law in France during the 15th & 16th centuries and the recording of African customary laws'. Journal of African Law Vol. 3, No. 3, pp. 165-175.

Vanderlinden, J. (1966) 'Civil law and common law influences on the developing law of Ethiopia'. Buffalo Law Review. Vol. 16, pp. 250-266.

Vanderlinden, J. (1983) *Les systèmes juridiques africains.* Paris: PUJ 'Que sais-je' series. No. 210.

Varga, C. (1976) *Modernization of law and its codificational trends in the Afro-Asiatic legal development.* Budapest: Institute for World Economy of Hungarian Academy of Science. (Studies on developing countries).

Verhelst, T. (1968) *Safeguarding African customary law: Judicial and legislative processes for its adaptation and integration.* (Occasional Paper No. 7). Los Angeles: African Studies Centre, University of California.

Wanjala, S. C. (1989) 'The relevance and position of customary law in Kenya's legal system'. Law and Anthropology. No. 4, pp. 141-151.

Whitefield, G. M. B. (1929) *South African native law.* Cape Town: Juta & Co.

Wilson, R. R. (ed.) (1968) *International and comparative law of the Commonwealth.* Durham: Duke University Press.

Witbooi, H. (1900) *The Hendrik Witbooi papers.* Translated by A. Heywood and E. Maasdorp, annotated by B. Lau. Windhoek: Archeia.

Woodman, G. R. (1968) 'Common customs of Ghana: Common law or customary law?' University of Ghana Law Journal. Vol. 5, pp. 1-5.

Woodman, G. R. (1969) 'Some realism about customary law: The West African experience'. Wisconsin Law Review. pp. 128-152.

Woodman, G. R. (1989) 'The peculiar policy of recognition of indigenous laws in British colonial Africa: A preliminary discussion'. Verfassung und Recht in Übersee. No. 22, pp. 273-284.

Woodman, G. (1974) 'British legislation as a source of Ghanaian law: From colonialism to technical aid.'. Verfassung und Recht in Übersee. Vol. 7, pp. 19-32.

Woodman, G. (1993) 'Customary laws: the internal contemporary challenge to African states'. Norwich Seminar: Unpublished paper.

Wright, A. C. A. (1943) 'The interaction of various systems of law and customs in British Somaliland and their relation with social life'. Journal of East Africa Natural History Society. Vol. 17, pp. 62-102.

Wright, C. T. H. (1901) 'German methods of development in Africa'. Journal of the African Society. Vol. 1, pp. 23-38.

Yusuf, A. B. (1982) *The Nigerian legal system: Pluralism and conflict of laws in the Northern States.* New Delhi: National.

Zaka, S. J. L. (1969) 'Revision and unification of African legal systems: The Uganda experience'. In Carter, G. M. and Paden, A. (1969) *Expanding horizons in African Studies.* Evanston: Northwestern University Press. pp. 157-168.

Chapter 2 — Case books and legal research

There are very few case books on customary law, but there are many important decisions on indigenous family and succession law that still act as precedent for customary law cases. Any trawl through the various early Law Reports, Digests and Reviews would yield rich harvest, because judgments on indigenous law cases were widely reported, as they were deemed to be unrepugnant to equity and good sense.

Usually good Law Libraries have a long list of law periodicals, accordingly only the names of the Law Reports are cited without the full bibliographic details.

A Law Report sets out the judgment of the bench and the *ratio decidendi* of the case. The case is identified by the names of the parties, the date of the hearing, the name of the court and the names of the presiding judge or judges. A further help for the researcher using Law Reports is that other cases judicially considered in the determination of that particular case, as well as cases referred to in the judgment, are also cited.

Most of the capital cities in Africa have National Archives and Documentation Centres. Some pre-independence legal papers are also held in customary courts, the old Chief's courts, now renamed 'community courts', 'people's courts' or 'lower courts'. A few traditional judges in the Chiefs' Courts, or Headmen's Courts had court clerks who kept records of the proceedings. See chapter 3. There are records of decisions reached in Native Tribunals, the Council of Headmen, as well as papers of Regional and National Council of Chiefs and Headmen. A few states have Houses of Chiefs. And there are Official Gazettes of Administration and Files of the Resident Commissioner, District Officer or Native Commissioner.

Furthermore, a few established law firms in some states now have fifty year old client files, of non-contentious material that could be used for compilation of principles of customary law, precedents and case books. There are many unpublished law papers available for consultation in the various offices of African Law Journals that have suspended publication, as well as in the Faculty of Law Reference libraries in some African universities.

2.1 Fieldwork

To understand the nature of African peoples' concept of the living indigenous law extensive fieldwork is essential. Participant observation in indigenous legal research is an attempt to participate in, and to understand the nature of everyday reality of the group, thus identifying the principles of behaviour that function as law. A real participant observer does not live in the Governor's residence, then drives out daily to interview important 'natives'. The only way of knowing the people's daily reality is to live with them for as long as possible. From daily contact with the group one will then acquire the everyday language of communication. There are many people in the rural heartland who have virtually no contact with the outside world, and a few make occasional forays to regional capitals.

The research method used for this book was to conduct in-depth interviews singly, visiting the sages, old people who did not move around, as well as searching for widows, widowers, and girls in sororate or levirate polygyny. Sometimes in the evenings the discussions involved between five to seven people. The questionnaires I had prepared were found to be useless, as nobody could read or write. The questionnaires were used by me and with the help of an interpreter for major philosophical discussions, and when the court was sitting.

Anyone could come to me at any time to talk, or to correct any statement they had made. Young children, too, liked being asked questions. It is not ethical to ask children certain questions, even if parents and guardians had given their consent, one asked only simple harmless questions. Here is a sample of my under-seven questionnaire:

What is your surname? Does it demonstrate affiliation to an *eanda* or *oruzo*? Are there names for girls, boys, born in the morning, afternoon, evening or night, or days of the week? Will you change your name on going to school? Do you have anything more to tell me about names? Where do babies come from? Are you a naughty child? Does O'mama smack you when you are naughty? Does Baba smack your big brother when he is naughty? Do you know what actions are good? Can you distinguish good actions from bad actions? What do you do in the *onganda*? Do you have any livestock? How did you acquire them? Do you own any cattle jointly with O'mama, baba, brothers and sisters?

Several children thus, became very informative sources for my research on social life. No man, woman or child was personally identified, anonymity was considered very important because of the bickering among co-wives. I did not want everybody to know who supplied what information.

When one talks to interviewees, how does one know that the answer to a question is actually relevant, or even correct? As a participant observer, with two experimental groups and two control groups, one weighs the evidence provided by one group against the control group. A right answer cannot be deduced if it is inconsistent with the legal institutions. For example, it is an established principle of *Himba* duolineal transmission law that a woman is the mother of only the children whom she physically brought into the world. Thus, talking about matrilineal adoption of children is an unruly horse that no self-respecting maternal uncle will ride.

The information gathered was cross-checked again. The control groups and the experimental groups were reversed in order to verify each other's data and supplement the original version. After analysing and assessing the information, the findings were discussed with several sages, singly or in twos for comment. The information is further cross-checked with oral historians, archaeologists, linguists and with archival sources.

2.2 Use of indigenous concepts

English jurisprudence has its own elaborate vocabulary but sometimes the appropriate indigenous equivalent can not be formulated. This is a major reason for using the indigenous words. I found that the English equivalent is often not as subtle as the *Himba* concept, for any translation is only an equivalent English meaning of the indigenous concept. Take a simple word like *eanda*. Every *Himba* child who is over seven years old or so, knows his or her name and his or her *eanda* and *onganda*. Now, *eanda* can be translated as meaning 'matriclan', 'matrilineal', 'matriarchy', but this is not what the *Himba* mean, or what their over-sevens mean by *eanda*. *Eanda* means the blood bond, clinging unto the umbilical cord, the direct maternal link.

The use of indigenous words is not meant to make understanding the ethnography difficult for the interested reader; it is only that one is trying to get the *Himba* concepts across smoothly. I always asked whether a *Himba* would understand the English approximation of the ethnography that I have reported.

2.3 Bibliography

Abuja Law Reports
Africa Court of Appeal Reports
African Law Digest
African Law Reports
African Law Reports: Malawi series
African Law Reports: Sierra Leone series
All Nigeria Law Reports
Annual Survey of African Law

Botswana Law Reports
Buganda Customary Law Reports
Butterworth South African Law Review

Decisions and Appeal cases in the court of the Resident Commissioner of Basutoland, the Special court of Bechuanaland Protectorate.
Digest of Decisions of the Court of Appeal for East Africa
Digest of East African Civil Law Reports
Digest of the Supreme Court
Digest of West African and Kenya Law Report

East Africa Digest
East Africa Law Reports
East African Protectorate Law Reports
Eastern Africa Law Reports
Eastern Africa Law Review

Federal High Court of Nigeria Law Reports
Federation of Nigeria Law Reports
Federation of Rhodesia and Nyasaland Law Reports

Gambia Law Reports
Ghana Law Reports
Ghana Law Reports Digest
Ghana Law Reports: Current Cases
Ghana Law Reports: Unreported High Court Judgments
Gold Coast Law Reports

High Courts of Nigeria Law Reports

Judgments of the Supreme Court of Nigeria

Kampala Law Reports
Kenya High Court Digest
Kenya Law Reports

Kings Law Reports
Kwara Law Review

Lagos High Court Reports
Law Librarian: Bulletin of the British and Irish Association of Law Librarians
Law Reports of Anambra State of Nigeria
Law Reports of Courts of Nigeria
Law Reports of Kenya
Law Reports of Tanzania
Law Reports of High Court of Zanzibar
Law Reports of the Court of Appeal for Eastern Africa
Law Reports of Northern Rhodesia
Lesotho Law Reports
Liberia Law Reports

Malawi Law Reports

Native Appeal Court Reports
Nigerian Bulletin of Contemporary Law
Nigeria Court of Appeal Reports
Nigerian Criminal Reports
Nigerian Commercial Law Reports
Nigerian Current Law Reports
Nigeria Lagos High Court Report
Nigerian Law Reports
Nigerian Reports of Appeal Cases
Nigeria Weekly Law Reports
Northern Region of Nigeria Law Reports
National Archives and Documentation Centres

Plateau Law Reports
Prentice Hall Weekly Legal Service
Privy Council Judicial Committee: All England Law Report

Quarterly Law Reports of Nigeria

Reserved Judgments of the Supreme Court of Nigeria
Rhodesian Law Reports

Selected judgments of the Divisional Courts of the Gold Coast Colony 1921-1925, 1931-1937. Accra, London
Sierra Leone Law Recorder
Sierra Leone Law Reports
South African Law Reports
South African Law Reports: Cape Provincial Division
South African Law Reports: Orange Free State
South African Criminal Law Reports
Southern Rhodesian Law Reports
Supreme Court Monthly Law Reports (Nigeria)
Supreme Court of Nigeria Judgments

Supreme Court of Nigeria Law Reports
Supreme Court Reporter (Nigeria)

Tanzania Law Reports
The High Commission Territories Law Reports 1926-1966. Maseru, Lesotho.

Uganda Protectorate Law Reports

West African Court of Appeal Reports Selected Judgments 1930-1955 includes cases from Gambia, Gold Coast, Nigeria and Sierra Leone.
West African Law Reports
West African Supreme Courts Weekly Law Report
Western Nigeria Law Reports

Zambia Law Reports
Zambia High Court: Selected Judgments
Zimbabwe Law Reports
Zimbabwe Law Review

Ali, O. H. (1971) 'The conversion of customary law to written law'. The Sudan Law Journal and Reports, pp. 147-161.

Allott, A. N. (1953) 'Method of legal research into customary law'. Journal of African Administration. Vol. 5, No. 4, pp. 172-177.

Aubert, V. (1963) 'Researches in the sociology of law'. The American Behavioural Scientist. Vol. 7, No. 4, pp. 16-20.

Bainbridge, J. S. (1972) *The study and teaching of law in Africa.* Hackensack, N.J.: Fred B. Rothman & Co.

Barnard, A. and Good, A. (1984) *Research practices in the study of kinship.* London: Academic Press.

Bennett, T. W. (1980) 'Conflict of laws in South Africa: Cases involving customary law'. Tydskrif vir Hedendaagse Romeins-Hollandse Reg. No, 43, pp. 27-38.

Chanock, M. (1989) 'Writing South African legal history: A prospectus'. Journal of African History. Vol. 30, pp. 265-288.

Chiduo, V. (1986) 'Problems of libraries in the Third World: The experience of the university of Dar es Salaam'. Botswana Library Association Journal. Vol. 8, No. 1, pp. 14-18.

Cotran, E. (1987) *Casebook on Kenya Customary Law.* Abingdon: Professional Books and Nairobi University Press.

Crowder, M. (1986) 'The book crisis: Africa's other famine'. African Research & Documentation. No. 41, pp. 1-6.

Curtin, P. D. (1970) 'Field techniques for collecting and processing oral data'. Journal of African History. Vol. 9, No. 3, pp. 367-385.

Danquah, J. B. (1928) *Cases in Akan law, decisions delivered by Sir Ofori Atta, Paramount chief of Akim Abuakwa, with introduction, synopses and notes.* London: George Routledge & Sons.

Dias, C. J. (et al.) (1981) *Lawyers in the third world: Comparative and developmental perspectives.* Uppsala: Scandinavian Institute of African Studies.

Doorly, A. M. (1950) *A digest with subject headings arranged alphabetically of the reports of cases decided in the West African Court of Appeal in the years 1930-1941 and in the Judicial Committee of the Privy Council in final appeals in the years 1929-1930.* Accra: Government Printer.

Duncan, P. (1960) *Sotho laws and customs. A handbook based on decided cases in Basutoland together with the laws of Lerotholi.* Cape Town: Oxford University Press.

Earnshaw, A. (1910) *Gold Coast Judgments. Reports of 18 cases decided.* Judgments delivered at Cape Coast Castle, Gold Coast Colony, 1909-1910. London:

Elias, T. O. (1958) 'The problem of reducing customary laws to writing'. In*British Legal Papers presented to the Fifth International Congress of Comparative Law.* Bruxelles 4-9 August 1958. London: Stevens & Sons, pp. 57-69.

Epstein, A. L. (1954) *Juridical techniques and the judicial process: A study in customary law.* The Rhodes-Livingstone Papers, No. 23. Manchester: Manchester University Press.

Epstein, A. L. (1967) 'The case method in the field of law'. In Epstein, A. L. (ed.) *The craft of social anthropology.* London: Tavistock Publications, pp. 205-231.

Ghai, Y. (1987) 'Law, development and African scholarship'. Modern Law Review. Vol. 50, No. 4, pp. 750-776.

Gluckman, M. (1973) 'Limitations of the case-method in the study of tribal law'. Law and Society Review. Vol. 7, pp. 611-641.

Goldblatt, I. (1937) 'A social study of law'. South African Journal of Science. Vol. 34, pp. 455-462.

Griffith, W. B. (1935) *A digest of and index to the reports of cases decided in the Supreme Court of the Gold Coast Colony, 1844-1931.* Accra: Government Printer.

Gulliver, P. (1969) 'Introduction to case studies of law in non-western societies. In Nader, L. (ed.) *Law in culture and society.* Chicago: Aldine.

Hall, R. de Z. (1938) 'The study of native court records as a method of ethnological inquiry'. Africa. Vol. 11, pp. 412-427.

Hollander, B. (1961) *Colonial justice: The unique achievement of the Privy Council's Committee of Judges.* London: Bowes & Bowes.

Holleman, J. F. (1974) *Issues in African law.* The Hague: Mouton.

Hund, J. G. (1974) 'The roles of theory and method in investigating primitive law'. The Comparative and International Law Journal of Southern Africa. No. 7, pp. 208-214.

Lewin, J. (1938) 'The recording of customary law and custom'. Journal of the Royal African Society. Vol. 37, pp. 483-493.

Limb, P. (1996) 'An A-Z of African Studies on the Internet'. African Research and Documentation. No. 70, pp. 58-68.

McNeil, I. R. (1967) 'Research in East African law'. East African Law Journal. Vol. 3, pp. 47-78.

Milner, A. (1968) 'The African Law Reports'. Law Library Journal. Vol. 61, pp. 11-42.

Milner, A. (ed.) (1971) *Modern African contract cases*. Oxford: The African Law Reports.

Mutungi, O. K. (1973) 'The communication of law under conditions of development: The Kenya case'. East African Law Journal. Vol. 9, No. 1, pp. 11-42.

Olaitan, M. O. (1982) *Cases on Nigerian land law. Index 1971-1975*. Lagos: Libriservice Publications.

Olaitan, M. O. (ed.) (1978) *Cases on Nigerian land law. Index 1880-1970*. Lagos: Lagos University Library.

Phillipson, D. (1988) 'Are Africanist publications available in Africa?' African Archaeological Review. Vol. 6, Editorial, pp. 1-2.

Poulter, S. (1975) 'An essay on African customary law research techniques: Some experiences from Lesotho'. Journal of Southern African Studies. No. 1, pp. 181-193.

Prinsloo, M. W. (1993) 'Field research in indigenous law'. Zeitschrift für Vergleichende Rechts wissenschaft. Vol. 92, pp. 221-236.

Redmayne, A. and Rogers, C. (1983) 'Research on customary law in German East Africa. Questionnaire concerning the laws of the natives in the German colonies'. Journal of African Law. Vol. 27, No. 1, pp. 22-41.

Redwar, H. W. H. (1909) *Cases reported in Redwar's comments on some of the Ordinances of the Gold Coast colony, 1889-1989*. London.

Renner, P. A. (1915) Gold Coast Reports (1861-1914) relating to the Gold Coast and the colony of Nigeria. London: Sweet & Maxwell.

Rhoads, J. B. (1983) *The role of archives and records management in national information systems*. Paris: UNESCO.

Roberts, S. (1971) 'The recording of customary law: Some problems of method'. Botswana Notes and Records. Vol. 3, pp. 12-21.

Samuels, H. (1986) 'Who controls the past'? American Archivist. Vol. 49, pp. 109-124.

Sarbah, J. M. (1897) *Fanti customary laws: A brief introduction to the principles of the native laws and customs of the Fanti and Akan sections of the Gold Coast, with a selection of cases thereon decided in the law courts* London: Clowes & Sons Ltd.

Sarbah, J. M. (1904) *Fanti Law Reports: Reports of decided cases on Fanti customary laws 1845-1903.* London: William Clowes & Sons Ltd.

Sarbah, J. M. (1906) *Fanti national constitution and Fanti Law Reports.* London: William Clowes & Sons Ltd.

Schapera, I. (1949) *Some problems of anthropological research in Kenya colony.* London: Oxford University Press, for the International African Institute.

Sedler, R. (1970) 'Law reporting in Anglophonic Africa: Some observations'. American Journal of Comparative Law. Vol. 18, pp. 831-840.

Singer, N. J. (1973) 'The use of writing as a factor in the integration of African legal systems: The case of the Cambata' (Ethiopia). Law in Rural Africa. Vol. 22, pp. 57-68.

Sinitsina, I. (1987) 'African legal tradition: J. M Sarbah, J. B. Danquah, N. A. Ollennu'. Journal of African Law. Vol. 31. pp. 44-57.

Snyder, F. G. (1973) 'The use of oral data in legal anthropology: A Senegalese example'. Journal of African Law. Vol. 17, No. 2, pp. 196-215.

Tetteh, K. (1971) 'Law reporting in Anglophone Africa'. International Comparative Law Quarterly. Vol. 20, pp. 87-98.

Thomas, P. A. (1971) 'Legal education in Africa: with special reference to Zambia'. Northern Ireland Legal Quarterly, Vol. 22, pp. 3-37.

Twining, W. L. (1962) 'Legal studies at the University of Khartoum'. Journal of African Law. Vol. 6, No. 2, pp. 145-150.

Twining, W. L. (1964) *The place of the customary law in the National Legal systems of East Africa.* Chicago: University of Chicago.

Twining, W. (1966) 'Legal education within East Africa'. East Africa Law Today. pp. 116-117.

Twining, W. (1973) 'Law and anthropology: A case study in inter-disciplinary collaboration'. Law and Society Review Vol. 7, No. 4, pp. 561-583.

Twining, W. and Quick, E. V. (1994) *Legal records in the Commonwealth.* Aldershot: Dartmouth.

Wilson, R. R. (ed.) (1968) *International and comparative law of the Commonwealth.* Durham: Duke University Press.

Chapter 3 — Chieftaincy

The chapter on chieftaincy could have been incorporated into the chapters on attempted reform of indigenous law, customary law, criminal law and dispute settlement, but as there are many references, I decided that Chieftaincy should stand on its own. The Chiefs and the councillors deserve a special chapter, because customary lawyers have neglected the process by which colonial administrators intervened in the indigenous legal system.

Although the legal history of Africa is dominated and determined by the colonial experience, legal researchers should not forget the role of Kings and traditional rulers in pre-colonial administration; because in the memorable one liner: "Those who ignore history are doomed to repeat it".

In the various African kingdoms, these Kings have different titles such as, the Asantehene, Alake, Emir, Ga Manche, Kabaka, Oba, Ooni, Omuhona, Sultan, Talon-Na, and many more. Before Columbus reached America, Joao Afonso d'Aveiro had been received in 1486 in the court of the Oba of Benin. Other Kings and chiefs had long distance trade with literate societies North of the Sahara who recorded the transactions in Arabic. The communities who lived along the East African coastline traded with Arabs resulting in the Swahili language, a mixture of Bantu, Arabic and Sahelian loan words. (Wright 1993) British, Dutch, French, Germans, Italians, Portuguese and Spaniards traded with Africans before the trade in human beings.

Some kingdoms consisted of a courageous and powerful person, the King, the Queen mother, a paramount chief, councillors, territorial chiefs, district or divisional chiefs, clan chiefs and village heads. Furthermore, there were the Kingmakers, as well as many palace officers such as the controller of the treasury, the master of the horses, commander in-chief of the army, the army of tribute collectors, the keepers of cultural property, the interpreters, keepers of food barns, the chief diviner, that is the in-house chaplain, the master of rituals and his retinue, the chief physician who advises on health care, the King's drummers and musicians, the poets, story tellers, the sculptors, dancers, actors, officers who made the court regalia, the domestics who carried out the domestic chores, the fathers-in-law, brothers-in-law of the harem polygyny, palace attendants, farmers, smiths, door keepers, a fleet of carriers, keepers of the shrines and altars, pages, army of cooks, drink brewers, herders, bailees, and those whose only function was to wash and dress a deceased king for the final journey to his ancestors. And there was the rest of the rural population.

However, under colonial administration, there could not possibly be a Queen in England and some native Kings in the colonies. Accordingly, in some of the territories where colonial authorities were very powerful, surreptitiously, some kings were called Paramount Chiefs or Chiefs to put them in their place with their underlings. Or perhaps, the colonisers were ignorant of the traditions of the people and the role of the Kings in African societies. A study in Afro-colonial linguistics should prove very educative.

3.1 Treaties

In Africa, a power to annex and settle in the hinterland accrued to the colonial power that was the first to raise its flag on an African coastal strip. The implication of the 'Hinterland doctrine', according to Akweenda (1989), was that the colonial powers should not encroach on each other's sphere of influence. Belgium, Britain, France, Germany, Holland, Italy, Portugal and Spain assumed sovereignty over lands in Africa. They did not assume sovereignty by force, but by Protection Treaties which they negotiated with the Kings and the councillors. Germany and others were following the practice of the British Government who entered into treaties with Chiefs in New Zealand. Some African Kings signed, and others made their marks on the document as their consent to be bound, and the colonisers claimed sovereignty over the land and the 'natives'.

It was accepted by the colonisers that Kings, Paramount chiefs and councillors who received foreign dignitaries had full powers to govern and represent their 'tribes' in the negotiations and acceptance of treaties. The colonial powers did not negotiate the text of the treaty, and the content of the obligations imposed on the natives. The Treaty was written in English or German, and the Chiefs had no copies of the text that had been interpreted for them by the missionaries. In the Report on the Natives of SWA and their Treatment by Germany (1918:32) it was reported that Leutwein wryly commented:

It is not necessary to believe, however, that the chiefs sat like German law students over their *corpus iuris* perusing the contents of the agreements with a view to getting a full knowledge of their contents.

Was it a Treaty, a Gentlemen's Agreement or a Contract that the Kings had concluded? Whatever it was, it created obligations, yet conferred no rights on the natives as the colonial powers had no reciprocal duties.

As a consequence of the 'breach' of the treaties, the colonial powers unleashed their superior technological fire power on the natives. Britain embarked on punitive expeditions against some of the colonies (see chapter 7) and Germany launched a vigorous war of annihilation against the rebellious tribesmen who had only bows and arrows, assegais and kieries. The colonisers had inexhaustible supplies of ammunition for the repeating rifles and 'guns that made so much noise'. The civilised nations in Christendom looked on at this massacre of innocent natives in their homeland, and approved it, until Germany unleashed its full military might on them in the 1914-1918 War.

3.2 Chiefs by gazette

After the death of the leaders and many of their people, some of the Kings who survived were deposed, 'dethroned', 'destooled', 'deskinned', exiled or abdicated, in some territories in Africa. The new Imperial power created new chiefs by gazette or warrant. Against principles of indigenous law some gazetted chiefs were promoted to Paramount chiefs. Some of the deposed pre-colonial chiefs held hereditary titles and those who did not have hereditary titles had been nominated by the Queen mother and their election or rejection had been ratified by the Kingmakers.

Most gazetted chiefs did not enjoy the loyalty of their people. In the chain of 'indirect rule' these gazetted chiefs who were paid a monthly stipend and allowances to induce them to stay on or reward them for their loyalty, appointed district sub chiefs who nominated village headmen. Some unpopular chiefs by gazette allotted land to kinsmen.

The gazetted chiefs were directly responsible to the Native Commissioner, or District Commissioner or District Officer, as they were known in some new colonies.

Furthermore, the gazetted chiefs had bigger post-colonial boundaries to administer and these included many acephalous societies that had not been under any hereditary ruler. They were also in charge of reporting unnatural deaths, the prevention of crimes, introducing new Government legislation to their people and of collecting head or hut tax. Any gazetted chief, sub chief or headman who disobeyed the DC, DO could be deposed, suspended from employment, fined or his stipend was reduced.

As was explained in chapter 9, under pre-colonial indigenous administration, the King's court was the final court of appeal in litigation concerning chieftaincy, land, and loan of equipment. See chapter 5. However, not many cases got that far, but the ones that did were adjudicated quickly and wisely and there were no lashes. Law and order, divorce, inheritance, crime, and the preservation of the countryside were dealt with at the village or *onganda* level.

The new colonial administration reorganised the Chiefs' courts in some of their territories into A. B. C. D. Grade courts, and the proceedings of each court were to be recorded. The Grade A Court had civil, criminal and matrimonial jurisdiction, but no Christian marriage dispute was heard by the Chief. The Grade B Court could administer 12 strokes or a fine of £50, the Grade C could also give 12 strokes or a fine of £10 and the Grade D Court was for theft of farm produce or livestock and administered 12 lashes or a fine of £5 and imprisonment for three months. The whip and prison were the remedies for most offences. There was no evidence to support flogging under indigenous law. The DO or the NC sanctioned the floggings of natives, because it legitimated his own preference. The interpretation of the indigenous law for the Native Commissioner or District Officer was left in the hands of elderly men who toed the line and many started adapting indigenous law for their benefit in the power game between them and the NC, DC and DO. If the gazetted chiefs disapproved of women's activity, the District Commissioner declared that activity a breach of indigenous law and restated it.

The DO, NC determined the costs between the parties. Thus, the gazetted chiefs lost their indigenous power of imposing compensatory justice, because the administration determined the level of fines for each court. The District Officer, or District Commissioner or Native Commissioner was the final native court of appeal, but litigants could appeal to the Supreme Court. There were a few famous appeals in the West Africa Supreme Court, but Olivier (1961:227) and Gordon (1991:89) noted that a survey of the Southern Africa Supreme Court records from 1920-1985 did not produce even one appeal. The answer is or ought to be, a very short one. The administration of the Native Commissioner was undemocratic and oppressive. Very few natives dared to appeal against the judgement of the Native Commissioner, District Commissioner or District Officer. Not appealing to a higher court was following their instinct of survival, an important safeguard for peaceful co-existence. From the experience gained from the deposed chiefs, the natives knew that resistance to the legal administration of the DO or the NC was doomed from the beginning and some people manipulated colonial adjudication for their own advantages.

The colonisers may have brought peace between the various tribes, but they did not bring peace within the tribe. It was left to the indigenous laws to preserve the people's own legal autonomy and to regulate matters among them. In essence, that has remained the pattern until today. As constitutional lawyers would know, most Constitutions of African states acknowledge the presence and activity of indigenous laws.

3.3 Fountain of culture

Apart from adjudication, the pre-colonial indigenous rulers were crucial in the preservation of cultural heritage. See chapter 7. The continuity of tradition in arts, music, poetry and religion was very important, as some Kings had almost divine status. They were the custodians of some of the important objects for divination, because they had duties to the ancestors of their tribes which gave the Kings their mystical divinity.

These were pre-literate societies and researchers will have to rely on archaeological findings for the non-judicial roles of the Kings. The life-size anthropomorphic archaeological discoveries of Nok, in Jos Plateau, Fagg (1979), Shaw (1981) are radiocarbon dated between fifth-third centuries BC. However, the most exciting 9th century AD archaeological objects were unearthed at Igbo Ukwu, the grave site of a very important man, probably a priest sitting on a stool surrounded by religious and cultural artefacts. But the most significant archaeological finds were at Ife, Willett (1967) Garlake (1974) Eyo (1974). These were life size bronzes and terracottas kept in shrines or on altars inside the palace.

Bronzes and ivories of the Kings of Benin that had been displayed in the palace since the Portuguese first visited Benin were plundered by members of the British punitive expedition. Gold cast or gold plated objects, ceremonial objects, staff of state were also pillaged in the Gold Coast. See chapter 8. Further ritual objects were removed and burnt by missionaries when the people refused to abandon their 'paganism' for another form of 'paganism'.

3.4 New states v traditional states

Post-independence states inherited the colonial legacy of chieftaincy which predated colonialism. During indirect rule, most chiefs had governed their people in Edo, Luganda, Oshivambo, Twi or Yoruba and their children were educated by either the patriclan or the matriclan. See chapter 4. But post-independence leaders were mainly those able to read English, French, German or Portuguese who were the new indigenous literate elite. The new Presidents and Prime Ministers realised that the traditional rulers represented the mass of the rural people, but they, the new elite have only the authority inherited from the colonial powers.

Some African leaders reinstalled the surviving heirs of the hereditary rulers who had been deposed, and the deposed reverted to their status before being gazetted or warranted. In some states, those who were loyal to the new political leaders survived. There were many long-running chieftaincy litigations, because some tribes had different periods of interregnum. An interregnum stretches from a hypothetical one year period of gestation and parturition of the new King, to five or in some cases ten years. Accordingly, in some areas, hereditary heirs and heir presumptive mounted several succession litigations. Who should succeed? The first son of the first wife, or the competent, educated son of the second, third or subsequent wives, or the chief's sister's first son or educated nephews or uncles? Or sons of the princes? The role of the Queen mother and Kingmakers had fallen into disrepute during the colonial rule, but was activated post-independence.

The reactionary kingdoms and chiefdoms who were in the pre-independence opposition parties were blamed for lack of development. How could the chiefs attract government funding to their districts if their people voted for the opposition?

Sekou Touré harassed some of his chiefs into an early grave. Julius Nyerere abolished chieftaincy. Kwame Nkrumah destooled and deskinned rulers who did not toe the political line, and the Kabaka was forced into exile by Milton Obote. Tubman, of 'a thousand umbrellas' unleashed a war on his up-country elite, and the numerous coups d'etat of men with guns in some post-independent states exterminated their 'VIPs of waste'. Other chiefs obligingly died and a few abdicated.

The Chief's Court was reorganised into the lower rung of the statutory court and were called Magistrates or Community courts without the Chiefs. Houses of Chiefs analogous to the British House of Lords were created in some state capitals.

Traditional rulers and indigenous laws are blamed for Africa's under-development, for lack of human rights, and children's rights, for the non emancipation of women, and for the law's inability to develop the state. Instead of blaming African states for what they did not achieve, we should try at least to acknowledge what the traditional states achieved.

3.5 Bibliography

'Chieftaincy and the state in Africa'. (1987) Journal of Legal Pluralism and Unofficial Law. Special Issue. Nos. 25 & 26. pp. 1-339.

Abrahams, R. G. (1965) 'Neighbourhood organisations: A major sub-system among the Northern Nyamwezi'. Africa. No. 35, pp. 168-186.

Abrahams, R. G. (1967) *The political organisation of Unyamwezi*. Cambridge: Cambridge University Press.

Abrahams, R. G. (1981) *The Nyamwezi today: A Tanzanian people in the 1970s*. Cambridge: Cambridge University Press.

Abrahams, R. G. (1989) 'Law and order and the state in the Nyamwezi and Sukuma area of Tanzania'. Africa. No. 59, pp. 356-370.

Adelaja, K. (1976) 'Traditional power control among the Mossi and Yoruba: A comparative study'. Présence Africaine. No. 97, pp. 43-57.

Adu, A. L. (1948) *The role of chiefs in Akan social structure: An essay*. Accra: Government Press.

Afigbo, A. E. (1972) *The warrant chiefs: Indirect rule in South-Eastern Nigeria 1891-1929*. London: Longman.

Ahurwendeire, H. R. (1984) 'The story of the drum kingdom in South-West Uganda'. Uganda Journal. Vol. 4 pp. 69-90.

Aidoo, A. A. (1977) 'Asante Queen mothers in government and politics in the nineteenth century'. Journal of the Historical Society of Nigeria. Vol. 9, pp. 1-13.

Akpan, N. U. (1955) 'Have traditional authorities a place in modern local government systems? Journal of African Administration. No. 7, pp. 109-116.

Akweenda, S. (1989) *International law and the protection of Namibia's territorial integrity: Boundaries and territorial claims*. London: PhD. Thesis LSE. University of London.

Alexandre, P. (1970) 'Chiefs, commandants and clerks'. In Crowder, M. and Ikime, O. (eds.) *West African chiefs*. Ile-Ife: University of Ife Press.

Annor, K. P. (1985) 'Cultural and social identities in Africa: Chieftaincy and political change in Ghana'. Verfassung und Recht in Übersee. Vol. 18, pp. 153-156.

Anoff, W. C. (1981) 'The role of the chiefs in the Gold Coast society'. West African Review. No. 25. pp. 163-165.

Ansere, J. K. (1977) 'Local Government and chieftaincy'. Ghana Journal of Sociology No. 11, pp. 71-78.

Apter, A. H. (1983) 'In praise of high office: The politics of panegyric among three Southern-Bantu tribes'. Anthropos. Vol. 78, pp. 149-168.

Arbousset, F. R. (1957) 'Chefferies Africaines'. Encyclopedie Mensuelle d'Outre-Mer. October. pp. 278-280.

Arhin, K. (1966) 'Diffuse authority among the coastal Fanti'. Ghana Notes and Queries. No. 9, pp. 66-70.

Arhin, K. (1973) 'Chieftaincy'. Ghana Today. No. 2, pp. 1-5.

Arhin, K. (1983) 'Rank and class among the Asante and Fante in the 19th century'. Africa. No. 53, No. 1, pp. 2-22.

Arhin, K. (1985) *Traditional rule in Ghana: Past and present.* Accra: Sedco Publishing.

Armstrong, R. G. (1952) *State formation in negro Africa.* PhD Thesis. University of Chicago.

Arnott, D. W. (1958) 'Councils and courts among the Tiv: Traditional concepts and alien institutions in a non-Moslem tribe of Northern Nigeria'. Journal of African Law. Vol. 2, No. 1, pp. 19 25.

Ayeni, V. (1985) 'Traditional rulers as Ombudsmen: In search of a role for natural rulers in contemporary Nigeria'. In Aborisade, O. (ed.) *Local government and the traditional rulers in Nigeria.* Ile-Ife: University of Ife Press.

Aylttey, G. N. N. (1981) *Indigenous African institutions.* New York: Transnational Publishers Inc.

Baesjou, R. (1979) *An Asante embassy on the Gold Coast: The mission of Akyempon Yaw to Elmina 1869-1872.* African Social Research Documents. No. 11. Leiden: Africa Studies Centre.

Banton, M. (1954) 'Tribal headmen in Free town'. Journal of African Administration. Vol. 6, No. 3, pp. 140-144.

Bassing, A. (1973) 'Grave monuments of the Dakakari'. African Arts. Vol. 6, No. 4, pp. 36-39.

Beattie, J. (1964) 'Bunyoro: An African feudality?' Journal of African History. No. 5, pp. 24-35.

Benda-Beckmann, F. von (1981) 'Some comments on problems of comparing the relationship between traditional and state systems of administration of justice in Africa and Indonesia'. Journal of Legal Pluralism. No. 19, pp. 165-173.

Bovill, E. W. (1958) *The golden trade of the Moors.* Oxford: Oxford University Press.

Buell, R. L. (1928) 'Chieftains enthroned British rule in Nigeria as a significant colonial experiment'. Asia. pp. 56-62.

Bukurura, S. H. (1994a) *Sungusungu: Vigilantes in West Central Tanzania.* Cambridge: PhD Thesis. Churchill College, University of Cambridge.

Bukurura, S. H. (1994b) 'The maintenance of order in rural Tanzania'. Journal of Legal Pluralism and Unofficial Law. No. 34. pp. 1-29.

Burman, S. B. (1981) *Chiefdoms, politics and alien law: Basutoland under Cape rule 1871-1884.* London: MacMillan.

Busia, K. A. (1951) *The position of the chief in the modern political system of Ashanti: A study of the influence of contemporary social changes on Ashanti political institutions.* London: Oxford University Press.

Buxton, J. (1963) *Chiefs and strangers.* Oxford: Clarendon Press.

Cannadine, D. and Price, S. (eds.) (1987) *Rituals of royalty: Power and ceremonial in traditional societies.* Cambridge: Cambridge University Press.

Cohen, D. L. (1972) 'The concept of charisma and the analysis of leadership'. Political Studies. Vol. 20, pp. 299-305.

Colson, E. (1953) 'Social control and vengeance in Plateau Tonga Society'. Africa. Vol. 23, No. 3, pp. 199-212.

Comaroff, J. (1974) 'Chiefship in a South African homeland'. Journal of Southern African Studies. Vol. 1, No. 1, pp. 36-51.

Comaroff, J. (1978) 'Rules and rulers: Political processes in a Tswana chiefdom'. Man. Vol. 13, pp. 1-20.

Connah, G. (1987) *African civilizations: Pre colonial cities and states in tropical Africa, an archaeological perspective.* Cambridge: Cambridge University Press. Cambridge: Cambridge University Press.

Cory, H. (1951) Ntemi: *The traditional rites in connection with the burial, election, enthronement and magical powers of a Sukuma chief. in Tanganyika.* London: Macmillan.

Crowder, M. (1964) 'Indirect rule: French and British style'. Africa. No. 34, pp. 167-205.

Crowder, M. and Ikime, O (eds.) (1970) *West African chiefs: Their changing status under colonial rule and independence.* Ile-Ife: University of Ife Press.

Daannaa, H. S. (1992) The impact of state law on custom and leadership in a post-colonial state: A legal historical case study of centralised Wa and acephalous Chakali in Northern Ghana. London: Ph. D. Thesis LSE, University of London.

Daannaa, H. S. (1994) 'The acephalous society and the indirect rule system in Africa. British colonial administrative policy in retrospect'. Journal of Legal Pluralism No. 34 pp. 61-85.

Daniels, W. C. (1972) 'Jurisdiction of the High Court of Ghana in chieftaincy matters'. Review of Ghana Law Journal. No. 4, pp. 81-92.

Doornbos, M. R. (1973) 'Some structural aspects of regional government in Uganda and Ghana'. Journal of Administration Overseas, No. 12, pp. 88-100.

Doornbos, M. R. (1978) *Not all the king's men: Inequality as a political instrument in Ankole, Uganda.* The Hague: Mouton.

Dorward, D. C. (1969) 'The development of British colonial administration among the Tiv, 1900-1949'. African Affairs. No. 68, pp. 316-333.

Drucker-Brown, S. (1978) 'The structure of the Mamprussi kingdom and the cult of naam'. In Claessen, H. J. M. and Skalnik, P. (eds.) *The study of the early state'.* The Hague: Mouton.

Drucker-Brown, S. (1988) 'L'intronisation du roi Mamprusi'. Journal des Africanistes. Vol. 58, No. 1, pp. 485-501.

Earle, T. (1991) 'The evolution of chiefdoms'. In Earle T. (ed.) *Chiefdoms: Power, economy and ideology.* Cambridge: Cambridge University Press.

Escedy, C. S. (1972) 'Some questions on the political evolution of the traditional state in Africa, South of the Sahara'. Néprajzi Ertesitö. No. 54, pp. 189-215.

Evans-Pritchard, E. E. (1950) *The Nuer: A description of the modes of livelihood and political institutions of a Nilotic people.* Oxford: Clarendon Press.

Eyo, E. (1974) 'Odo Ogbe Street and Lafogido: Contrasting archaeological sties at Ile Ife Western Nigeria'. W. A. J. A. Vol. 4, pp. 99-109.

Fagg, B. (1979) *Nok Terracottas.* London: Ethnographica Ltd.

Fallers, L. A. (ed.) (1964) *The king's men: Leadership and status in Buganda on the eve of independence.* Chicago: University of Chicago Press.

Fallers, L. (1955) 'The predicament of the modern African chief: An instance from Uganda'. American Anthropologist. No. 56, pp. 290-305.

Fallers, L. (1956) *Bantu bureaucracy: A century of political evolution among the Basoga of Uganda.* Chicago: University of Chicago Press.

Ferguson, P. and Wilks, I. (1970) 'Chiefs, constitutions and the British in Northern Ghana'. In Crowder, M. and Ikime, O. (eds.) *West African chiefs: Their changing status under colonial rule and independence.* New York: Africana Publishing and University of Ife Press.

Forde, D. and Kaberry, P. (eds.) (1967) *West African kingdoms in the nineteenth century.* Cambridge: Cambridge University Press.

Fortes, M. and Evans-Pritchards, E. (1940) *African political systems.* London: Oxford University Press.

Fraser, D. and Cole, H. (eds.) (1972) *African art and leadership.* Madison: University of Wisconsin Press.

Garbett, G. K. (1966) 'The Rhodesian chiefs dilemma: Government officer or tribal leader'. Race. Vol. 8, pp. 113-128.

Garlake, P. S. (1974) 'Excavations at Obalara's land, Ife: An interim report'. West African Journal of Archaeology. Vol. 4, pp. 111-148.

Gartrell, B. (1983) 'British administrators, colonial chiefs and the comfort of tradition: An example from Uganda'. African Studies Review. No. 26, pp. 1-23.

Geschiere, P. (1982) *Village communities and the state-changing relations among the Maka of Southern Cameroon since the colonial conquest.* London: Kegan Paul International.

Ghai, Y. P. and McAuslan, J. P. W. B. (1970) *Public law and political change in Kenya: A study of the legal framework of government from colonial times to the present.* Nairobi: Oxford University Press.

Gillett, S. (1973) 'The survival of chieftaincy in Botswana'. African Affairs. No. 72. pp. 179-185.

Gluckman, M. (1949) 'The village headman in British Central Africa'. Africa. Vol. 19, pp. 89-94.

Gluckman, M. (1961) 'The role of the Barotse king in the judicial process'. Stanford Law Review. No. 114. pp. 110-119.

Gluckman, M. (1963) *Order and rebellion in tribal Africa.* London: Cohen and West.

Goldschmidt, J. E. (1981) *National and indigenous constitutional law in Ghana: Their development and their relation to each other.* Leiden: PhD Thesis. University of Leiden.

Goody, J. R. (1971) *Technology, tradition and the state in West Africa.* London: Oxford University Press.

Goody, J. R. and Braimah, J. A. (1987) *Salaga: The struggle for power.* London: Longmans.

Goody, J. (1966) *Succession to high office.* Cambridge: Cambridge University Press.

Gordon, R. J. (1991) 'Vernacular law and the future of human rights in Namibia'. Acta Juridica pp. 86-103.

Graf, W. D. (1983) 'Nigerian elite consolidation and African elite theories'. Verfassung und Recht in Übersee. Vol. 16, pp. 119-138.

Greuel, P. J. (1971) 'The leopard-skin chief: An examination of political power among the Nuer'. American Anthropologist. Vol. 73, pp. 1115-1120.

Gulliver, P. H. (1963) *Social control in an African society.* London: Routledge & Kegan Paul.

Haight, B. (1972) 'A note on the leopard-skin chief'. American Anthropologist. Vol. 74, pp. 1313-1318.

Hailey, W. M. (1950a) *Native administration in the British African territories.* London: His Majesty Stationery Office.

Hailey, W. M. (1950b) *Native administration in the British African territories. Pt. 1. East Africa: Uganda, Kenya, Tanganyika.* London: HMSO.

Hailey, W. M. (1951a) *Native administration in the British African territories. Pt. 3. West Africa: Nigeria, Gold Coast, Sierra Leone, Gambia.* London: HMSO.

Hailey, W. M. (1951b) *Native administration in the British African territories.. Pt. 4. A general survey of the system of native administration.* London: HMSO.

Hailey, W. M. (1953) *Native administration in the British African territories. Pt. 5. High Commission Territories: Basutoland, Bechuanaland Protectorate and Swaziland.* London: HMSO.

Hall, M. (1987) *The changing past: Farmers, kings and traders in Southern Africa 200-1860.* Cape Town: David Philip.

Hammett, I. (1975) *Chieftainship and legitimacy: An anthropological study of executive law in lesotho.* London: Routledge and Kegan Paul.

Hannigan, A. St. J. J. (1955) 'Local government in the Gold Coast'. Journal of African Administration. No. 7, pp. 116-123.

Henige, D. (1975) 'Akan stool succession under colonial rule: continuity or change'. Journal of African Studies. No. 16, pp. 285-293.

Holleman, J. F. (1969) *Chief, council and commissioner: Some problems of government in Rhodesia.* Assen, The Netherlands: Royal van Gorkum Ltd for Afrika-Studie Centrum.

Howan, R. (1956) 'African leadership in transition: An outline' Journal of African Administration No. 8, pp. 117-126.

Ijagbemi, E. A. (1973) 'A note on Temne kingship in the early nineteenth century'. Tarikh. Vol. 4, pp. 24-30.

Jingoes, St. J. (1975) *A chief is a chief by the people.* Oxford: Oxford University Press.

Konings, P. (1986) *The state and rural class formation in Ghana: A comparative analysis.* London: KPI.

Kumado, C. E. K. (1974) *Customary constitutional rules and procedures for enstoolment and destoolment of a chief among the anlo-Ewe.* Accra: PhD Thesis. University of Ghana.

Kumado, C. E. K. (1989) 'Chiefs as judges in traditional constitutional litigation in Ghana'. Law & Anthropology. Vol. 4, pp. 225-257.

Kumado, C. E. K. (1990-1992) 'Chieftaincy and the law in modern Ghana'. University of Ghana Law Journal. Vol. 18, pp. 194-216.

Kuper, H. (1947) *An African aristocracy: Rank among the Swazi.* London: Oxford University Press.

Kyei, A. K. (1977) 'Chieftaincy under the law'. Ghana Journal of Sociology. No. 11, pp.36-47.

Ladouceur, P. (1972) 'The Yendi chieftaincy dispute and Ghanaian politics'. Canadian Journal of African Studies. Vol. 6, pp. 97-117.

Ladouceur, P. (1979) *Chieftaincy and politicians in Northern Ghana*. London: Longmans.

Law, R. (1976) 'Horse, firearms and political power in pre-colonial West Africa'. Past and Present. Vol. 72, pp. 112-132.

Law, R. (1977) *The Oyo empire c1600-c1836*. Oxford: Oxford University Press.

Law, R. (1982) 'Making sense of a traditional narrative: Political disintegration of the kingdom of Oyo'. Cahiers d'Etudes Africaine Vol. 22, Nos. 3 & 4, pp. 387-403.

Lawal, L. (1978) 'Legitimacy and political authority in the traditional political system of the Yoruba of the Oyo state in Nigeria'. Journal of the Historical Society of Sierra Leone. Vol. 2, pp. 31-43.

Le Roy, E. (1979) 'Les chefferies traditionnelles et le problème de leur intégration en Afrique noire'. In Conac, G. (ed.) *Les institutions administratives des états francophones d'Afrique noire*. Paris: Economica.

Levtzion, N. (1968) Muslims and chiefs in West Africa. Oxford: Clarendon Press.

Levtzion, N. (1973) *Ancient Ghana and Mali*. London: Methuen.

Lloyd, P. C. (1959) 'The traditional political system of the Yoruba'. Southwestern Journal of Anthropology. Vol. 10, No. 4, pp. 366-384.

Lombard, J. (1967) *'Autorités traditionnelles et pouvoirs Européens en Afrique noire*. Paris: Armand Collins.

Lugard, F. D. (1970) *The dual mandate in British tropical Africa*. London: Frank Cass.

MacLean, J. (ed.) (1906) *A compendium of Kafir laws and customs, including genealogical tables of Kafir chiefs and various tribal census returns*. Grahamstown: J. Slater.

Mair, L. P. (1958) 'African chiefs today'. Africa. Vol. 28, pp. 197-205.

Mair, L. P. (1966) *Primitive government*. Harmondsworth: Penguin.

Mair, L. P. (1977) *African kingdoms*. London: Oxford University Press.

McCaskie, T. C. (1972) 'Innovational eclecticism: The Asante empire and Europe in the nineteenth century'. Comparative Studies in Society and History. Vol. 14, pp. 30-45.

McIntosh, S. K. and McIntosh, R. J. (1984) 'The early city in West Africa: Towards an understanding'. African Archaeological Review. Vol. 2, pp. 73-98.

Mensah-Brown A. K. (1969) 'Chiefs and the law in Ghana'. Journal of African Law. Vol. 13, pp. 57-63.

Mensah-Brown, A. K. , (1967) 'An African chiefdom in modern Ghana'. Présence Africaine Vol. 62, pp. 94-120.

Middleton, J. (1970) 'The roles of chiefs and headmen among the Lugbara of Uganda'. In Middleton, J. (ed.) *Black Africa: Its people and their cultures today*. London: Collier-Macmillan.

Middleton, J. and Tait, D. (eds.) (1958) *Tribes without rulers: Studies in African segmentary systems*. London: Routledge and Keegan Paul.

Miller, N. N. (1968) 'The political survival of traditional leadership'. Journal of Modern African Studies. Vol. 6. pp. 183-201.

Moore, S. F. (1970) 'Politics, procedures and norms in changing Chagga law'. Afrika. Vol. 40, pp. 321-343.

Morris, M and Read, J. (1972) *Indirect rule and the search for justice, essays in East African legal history*. London: Oxford University Press.

Mukasa, H. (1946) 'The rule of the kings of Buganda'. Uganda Journal. Vol. 10. pp. 136-143.

Munger, E. S. (1971) *Chief Gatsha Buthelezi of the Zulus: South Africa's dynamic new political personality*. Hanover: American Universities Field Staff.

Nadel, S. F. (1942) *A black Byzantium: The kingdom of Nupe in Nigeria*. London: Oxford University Press for the International Institute of African Languages and Cultures.

Nana Atta, K. B. (1977) 'Litigation in chieftaincy'. Ghana Journal of Sociology. No. 11, pp. 58-77.

Nana, A. B. (1977) 'Modernization of the institution of chieftaincy'. Ghana Journal of Sociology. No. 11, pp. 12-37.

Nevadomsky, J and Inneh, D. E. (1983) 'Kingship succession rituals in Benin'. African Arts. No. 17, pp.47-48.

Newbury, D. (1992) *Kings and clans: Ijwi Island and the Lake Kivú rift, 1780-1840*. Madison: University of Wisconsin.

Nieuwaal, E. A. B. van (1991) The Togolese chiefs: Caught between the Scylla and Charibdis? Afrika Focus. Vol. 7, pp. 121-152.

Nkiwi, P. N. (1976) *Traditional Government and social change: A study of the political institutions among the Kom of the Cameroon Grassfields*. Fribourg: The University Press.

Nzimiro, I. (1972) *Studies in Ibo political systems: Chieftaincy and politics in four Niger States*. London: Frank Cass.

Obeng, E. E. (1988) *Ancient Ashanti chieftaincy*. Tema: Ghana Publishing Co.

Ochieng, W. R. (1972) 'Colonial African chiefs: Were they primarily self-seeking scoundrels'. In Ogot, B. A. (ed.) *Politics and nationalism in colonial Kenya*. Nariobi: East African Publishing House.

Offiong, D. A. (1984) 'The status of Ibibio chiefs'. Anthropological Quarterly. Vol. 57, no. 4, pp. 100-113.

Ofori-Boateng, J. (1974) 'Chieftaincy matters and proceedings'. The Review of Ghana Law. Vol. 6, No. 2, pp. 93-105.

Ogot, B. (1964) 'From chief to president: A study in traditional and modern African leadership'. In Fröhlich, W. (ed.) *Afrika im Wandel seiner* Gessellschaftsfornen. Leiden: Brill, pp. 84-97.

Okeke, I. R. (1994) *The chieftaincy institution and government recognised traditional rules in Anambra State*. Enugu: Media Forum Nigeria.

Olivier, M. J. (1961) *Inboorlingbeleid en administrasie in Mandaatgebied van Suidwes-Africa*. Stellenbosch: D. Phil. Thesis. University of Stellenbosch, South Africa.

Ollennu, N. A. (1976) 'Chieftaincy under the law'. In Ekow-Daniels, W. C. and Woodman, G. (eds.) *Essays in Ghanaian Law 1896-1976*. Legon: The Faculty of Law. University of Ghana, pp. 38-56.

Omoding-Okwalinga, J. (1984) 'Chiefs in Uganda'. Uganda Journal. No. 41. pp. 23-31.

Ottenberg, S. (1971) *Leadership and authority in an African society: The Afrikpo village group*. Seattle: Washington University Press.

Oyemakinde, W. (1978) 'The chief law and the regulation of traditional cheiftaincy in Yorubaland'. Journal of the Historical Society in Nigeria. No. 9, pp. 63-74.

Packard, R. M. (1981) *Chieftainship and cosmology: A historical study of political competition*. Bloomington: Indiana University Press.

Patton, S. F. (1984) 'The Asante umbrella'. African Arts. No. 17. pp. 64-72.

Perham, M. (1934) 'A restatement of indirect rule'. Africa. No. 6, pp. 321-334.

Perham, M. (1937) *Native administration in Nigeria*. London: Oxford University Press.

Phillipson, D. W. (1993) *African archaeology*. Cambridge: Cambridge University Press.

Proctor, J. M. (1968) 'The house of chiefs and the political development of Botswana'. Journal of Modern African Studies. No. 6, pp. 59-79.

Quarcoo, A. K. (1977) 'Chieftaincy as a socio-political institution of Ghana'. Ghana Journal of Sociology. No. 11, 44-57.

Quinlan, T. (1988) 'The perpetuation of myths: A case study on 'tribe' and 'chief'' in South Africa'. Journal of Legal Pluralism. No. 27, pp. 79-115.

Ranger, T. (1982) 'Tradition and travesty: Chiefs and the administration in Makoni district, Zimbabwe 1960-1980'. Africa. No. 52, pp. 20-41.

Ratnam, K. K. (1964) 'Charisma and political leadership'. Political Studies. No. 12, pp. 341-354.

Rattray, R. S. (1929) *Ashanti law and constitution*. Oxford: Clarendon Press.

Ray, B. (1990) *Myth, ritual and kingship in Buganda.* Oxford: Oxford University

Richards, A. I. (ed.) (1959) *East African chiefs: A study of political development in some Uganda and Tanganyika tribes.* London: Faber & Faber.

Roberts, B. (1974) *The Zulu kings.* New York: Charles Scribner & Sons.

Robertson, A. F. (ed.) (1982) *Uganda's first republic: Chiefs, administrators and politicians, 1967-1971.* Cambridge: African Studies Centre.

Rubin, L. (1967) 'Chieftaincy and the adaptation of customary law in Ghana'. In Butler, J. and Castagno, A. (eds.) *Boston papers on Africa: Transition in African politics.* New York: Praeger.

Sansom, B. (1974) 'Traditional rulers and their realms'. In Hammond-Tooke, W. D. (ed.) *The Bantu speaking peoples of Southern Africa.* London: Routledge & Kegan Paul.

Sarbah, J. M. (1906) *Fanti national constitution: A short treatise on the constitution and Government of the Fanti, Asanti and other Akan tribes of West Africa.* London: William Clowes & Sons Ltd.

Schapera, I. (1956) *Government and politics in tribal societies.* Josiah Mason Lectures delivered at the University of Birmingham. London: Watts.

Schapera, I. (1963) 'Kinship and politics in Tswana history'. Journal of the Royal Anthropological Institute. Vol. 93, pp. 159-173.

Schapera, I. (1966) 'Tswana chiefs as innovators'. Kroniek van Afrika. No. 6, pp. 157-168.

Schapera, I. (1969) 'Uniformity and variation in chief-made law: A Tswana case study'. In Nader (ed.) *Law in culture and society*, Chicago: Aldine Publishing, pp. 230-244.

Schapera, I. (1970) *Tribal innovators: Tswana chiefs and social change 1795-1940.* London: The Athlone Press.

Service, E. (1975) *Origins of the state and civilization.* New York: W. W. Norton.

Shaw, T. (1970) *Igbo Ukwu: An account of archaeological discoveries in East Nigeria.* London: Faber & Faber.

Shaw, T. (1981) 'The Nok sculptures of Nigeria'. Scientific America. Vol. 244, pp. 154-166.

Smith, E. W. (1926) *The golden stool.* London: Holborn Publishing House.

Solanke, L. (1929) 'The constitution of the 'Oba' House-the Royal House in Yoruba polity'. WASU. pp. 7-12.

Sutton, I. (1984) 'Law, chieftaincy and conflict in colonial Ghana: The Ada case'. African Affairs. Vol. 83, No. 330, pp. 41-62.

Tagarts, F. S. B. (1934) 'The African chief under European rule'. Africa. No. 4, pp. 63-76.

Tangri, R. (1980) 'Paramount chiefs and central government in Sierra Leone'. African Studies. No. 39, pp. 183-195.

Temple, C. L. (1968) *Native races and their rulers*. London: Frank Cass.

Tignor, R. L. (1971) 'Colonial chiefs in chiefless societies'. Journal of Modern African Studies. Vol. 9, pp. 339-359.

Tobi, N. (1969) 'The Austinian legal positivism and the Nigerian legal system: A critical examination'. The Lawyer. Vol. 3, No. 2, pp. 49-59.

Tosh, J. (1978) *Clan leaders and colonial chiefs in Lango: The political history of an East African stateless society c. 1800-1939*. Oxford: Clarendon Press.

Tosh, J. A. (1973) 'Colonial chiefs in a stateless society. A case study from Northern Uganda'. Journal of African History. Vol. 14, pp. 473-490.

Umozurike, U. O. (1979) 'Treaties concluded by Europeans with African kings and chiefs before the 20th century. International Law and Colonialism in Africa. pp. 39-50.

Vansina, J. (1962a) 'A comparison of African kingdoms'. Africa. No. 32, pp. 324-334.

Vansina, J. (1962b) *L'evolution du royaume de Rwanda des origines à 1900*. Bruxelles: ARSOM.

Vansina, J. (1990) *Paths in the rainforest: Toward a history of a political tradition in equatorial Africa*. London: James Currey.

Webster, J. B. (1984) 'Through the palace gates, chiefs and chronology, developing reliable dating structures'. History in Africa. No. 11, pp. 337-349.

Wilks, I. (1975) *Asante in the nineteenth century*. Cambridge: Cambridge University Press.

Willett, F. (1967) *Ife in the history of West African sculptures*. London: Thames & Hudson.

Williams, D. (1966) 'The changing role of chiefs in Africa'. Optima. No. 16. pp. 215-220.

Woodburn, J. (1982) 'Egalitarian societies'. Man. Vol. 17, pp. 431-451.

Wright, H. T. (1993) 'Trade and politics on the Eastern littoral of Africa, A.D. 800-1300'. In Shaw, T., Sinclair, P., Andah, B., and Okpoko, A. (eds.) *The archaeology of Africa: Food, metals and towns*. London: Routledge, pp. 659-672.

Wunsch, J. A. (1976) 'Traditional authorities, innovation and development policy'. Journal of Developing Areas. Vol. 11, pp. 357-372.

Yelpaala, K. (1983) 'Circular arguments and self-fulfilling definitions: Statelessness and the Dagaaba'. History in Africa. No. 10. pp. 349-385.

Zahan, D. (1967) 'The Mossi kingdom'. In Forde, D. and Kaberry, P, M. (eds.) *West African kingdoms in the nineteenth century*. London: Oxford University Press.

Chapter 4 — Concept of the child

The headnotes to this chapter will be too brief for a detailed child ethnography under indigenous law, plus the legal complexities of the duolineal transmission system of the *eanda* and *oruzo* and patriliny in the rearing of children. However, the emphasis will be on matriliny as most people write on patriliny. The function of matriliny is to protect wives and their children and their property.

Children are the wealth of the people subject to indigenous law. Children hold a privilege position, for they confer status on their progenitors. Most husbands of the patrilineage or matrilineage like many children, because children are an extraordinary gift from the ancestors. Men want homes that are full of children who exemplify their virility, whereas most women are more concerned with staying alive rather than dying in child birth.

Under indigenous law, if the question, "Who is a child?" is put to the elders, invariably, the answer is any boy or girl, man or woman, who had undergone all the customary rites, but had not undertaken the responsibility of marriage for procreation. Thus, every unmarried man or woman remains a child of the matrilineage or patrilineage.

However, under most indigenous laws, there are different stages of childhood.

1. Infancy, from 0 to 7 years, as the child is dependent on its family.

2. Childhood in matrilineal societies is from about 8 to 12 years when the child is a dependent of the maternal uncles in the *eanda*

3. Youth is from about 13 to 25 years, when the person is technically still a child unless he or she has married and has a child or children.

In matrilineal societies the family consists of a husband, his brothers and sisters, and the sisters' children, his parents and maternal aunts, grandparents and his *eanda* and *oruzo*. A man's wife or wives and their children are not related to the husband's family, because his wife or wives are not bound to him by ties of blood, even if they have a dozen children. He has no *oruzo* authority to do what he likes with his wife, or wives and their children. They are still attached to their matrilineage by their umbilical cords, the blood tie. A matrilineal husband is not the patriarchal head of the family, he is just another member of his *eanda* family. A husband is only the progenitor of the next generation. The family is not a private matter for fathers, because the interests of women and children are governed by *eanda* justice.

4.1 The child in utero

Among the *Himba*, and in most other ethnic groups, the processes of menstruation, conception and the reproduction of another being are tantamount to religious experiences that affect everybody in a small-scale community. According to *Himba*ian morality, a pregnant woman must refrain from sexual intercourse during the last three months of pregnancy, because of fear of infecting the foetus or of causing a miscarriage. This prohibition of sexual intercourse for the last term before the child is born is upheld very strictly in polygynous marriages. The pregnant woman simply comes off the polygynous rota.

In indigenous jurisprudence, the child *en ventre sa mere* is acknowledged to be a child in being, therefore he or she has a claim right on the *eanda* to be born alive. Every precaution is therefore taken to protect the life of this child *en ventre sa mere*, who has the transmissible *eanda* right of being in *utero*. I was assured that there was no abortion. The enforced celibacy rule about abstaining from sexual intercourse during the last term helps to ensure that. Adultery and abortion did not generate any argument in matrilineal societies, because the answers are very clear. Children are born into the *eanda*, descent is matrilineal and, in particular, children are valued per se by the *eanda*.

Some Herero women explained that they had heard about therapeutic abortions in the hospitals to save the lives of very sick pregnant women. They thought this was justified to save the women.

In some patrilineal societies, a father could 'adopt' his daughter's child born outside marriage, especially if the progenitor was someone nominated by him, in order to keep his family line alive. In other patrilineal societies, the pregnant unmarried girl must identify the man, and he was obliged to marry her and was granted a divorce only when the child attained the age of seven or eight.

4.2 Death is dancing with us

Child birth is an endurance test, and a life and death struggle for the rural woman, and for the survival of the child. Even if child birth is universal, this is still worth reiterating, because to bring a new human being into the world could also mean the death of mother and child. This reflects the cardinal virtues of courage and adherence to matriliny in many societies. As they say, death is just sitting over there, across the *onganda*, dancing with the woman in labour.

In matrilineal societies, more often than not, every child is born within the bosom of its mother's matrilineage. If the practice that a pregnant woman should be returned to her *onganda* was not adhered to, and the woman should die giving birth in her husband's *onganda*, everyone knows that the deceased woman's *eanda* would claim extortionate compensation for negligence in the conduct of the confinement. It was agreed that in the long run, in order to reduce conflict within the community, it made economic sense for the society if a pregnant woman returned to her *eanda*. The matriclan has a legal obligation to keep her alive, because it was one of the finer points of advancing the legal bridewealth to help towards her maintenance. One of the greatest disasters for a community was for a pregnant woman to die. Her death would not only be unnatural, it would be catastrophic for her, and the potential members of the population, the single child, twins or triplets whom she is carrying.

In pre-colonial times, the place of birth used to be very important, but today some children are born in state hospitals and maternity wards in the big towns. All these children are born 'outside' the *eanda*, but they do not become the ethnic group of the town where they were born, by virtue of being born 'outside'. They retain their mother or father's ethnic identify, as *ius sanguinis* takes priority over the place of birth. Just as in Britain, a person can be British, yet remain quintessentially English, Irish, Scot or Welsh.

The infant's birth in the maternal *onganda* incorporates the new baby into its mother's *eanda*, because descent is matrilineal. Being born in the *onganda* is a bonding between the baby and its *eanda*. The birth in the *onganda* of the child who will one day inherit their estate, further affirms the obligations of the maternal males for the woman's children.

Having taken all the necessary precautions, the child still has a right to be born whole and perfect. A disabled child exists as a perpetual reproach to its mother and her family, because invariably it is always assumed to be the mother who brings about the disability. In most cases a woman with a disabled child is kicked out of the matrimonial *onganda*, back to her family, for she should not contaminate the man's home. The husband could demand the return of the bridewealth, because he had not got what he bargained for: a whole and perfect child. Potential husbands do not like paying bridewealth into a home with a disabled person because they fear it is endemic.

The birth of twins gave the patrilineal Yoruba and matrilineal *Himba* a special cause to celebrate the admission of more new members to the community. Twins represent tremendous blessings as they bring riches and good fortune. The parents of twins are entitled to receive gifts and are permitted to entreat for gifts for the twins from the community. This can be seen as an invitation to other *ozonganda* to partake in the good fortune. The *Himba* also credit twins with psychic powers to ward off the threat of lightning.

In some other communities which abhor twins, and multiple births, customary neonaticide is practised, and both twins, or a single twin was ritually killed. Noenaticide may also have to do with nutrition, as in the case of most mammals. If a rat has too many in her litter and cannot feed all of them, she will kill off some of the pups to make the others survive. The unfortunate human twin for neonaticide was usually the underweight infant, or the child who howled for too long, or the one that came out with its feet first, so endangering the life of its mother, or the child born with its cutting teeth. The child is not abandoned, but is buried with its placenta so that it could find another mother for its rebirth

Abiku, *ogbanje* and other variations on the name, is a child of special phenomenon who deserves an explanation. *Abiku* is an unfortunate child destined to make several cycles of birth, death, rebirth and death to the same traumatised mother until the deceased child is cremated to terminate the perpetual cycle of reappearance and disappearance.[6] Only cremation guaranteed his or her non-return, for if an arm or a leg was amputated the child would still reappear. A woman had given birth eighth times and only the eight child survived as the seventh had been cremated.

4.3 Naming ceremony

There is also feasting for the mother who survived the birth agony, as well as preparation for the ceremony of name-giving. Meanwhile, the surviving infant wears special jewellery and amulets to ward off evil and guard him or her against premature death. Between ten to fourteen days, when the umbilical cord has healed, the infant's naming ceremony takes place during his or her presentation to the *eanda* and introduction to the patrilineage.

The right to a name is one of the basic rights of the child under indigenous law. Of all the gifts the child will receive, the most distinctive and lasting is the name. The name is the child's private property. The name would show that the bearer is an omu*Himba*, a Mossi, a Mende, an Akan. The infant's name is a vehicle of meaning that is supposed to embody the child's personality, emotions, the child's potential physical and moral stature. Some names connote the social significance of the birth, day of the week, morning, high noon or night, family mores, religious and philosophical understanding

---

6 An archaeologist explained to me the unusual practice of African cremation in antiquity. The place of burial had a stone bowl, pestle and mortar as grave goods, but a child's bowl had no pestle and mortar.

of the family. A name could also represent the parents' idea of freedom, because the parents, too, have come of age. If the child is their first, it will conclude the parent's status as children of their parents.

The child is carried to the *okuruuo* by a maternal aunt. The infant is thoroughly inspected for any physical defects by the *eanda* men who are never present during labour, and if a defect is found, they prepare for the wrath of the *oruzo*. In the presence of both patrilineal and matrilineal relatives, the infant is transferred to its father's arms for further examination, then passed round to those who have a right to name the infant. The child is given about six names from both sides of the family, reflecting the politics and poetry of the times. The subtleties in the meaning of the names also describe the humour or creativity of the name givers. Under indigenous law a name is not a trivial thing like naming a black, beautiful girl as Rose. Only the children who go to School make a unilateral change of name for a biblical name such as Ezekiel, Joshua, Jeremiah, Solomon, Moses, Zadoc, Peter as in many parts of Africa. These names are only for the school teachers, but not for the *eanda* and *oruzo*

The child is breast fed for a long time, probably eighteen months to two to three years, perhaps as contraception, the mothers explained. As pastoralists, the *ovaHimba* women are aware that mother's milk is better for the infant than cows' and goats' milk, although both may be in plentiful supply. The possible reason for the preference of mother's milk as it was explained to me, was because in the first and second year in the life of the human child, growth is very rapid and the child must be kept healthy. Secondly, infant mortality is highest in the first and second year. Accordingly, the *ovaHimba* mothers are aware of the positive immunity that is passed to the child in the mother's milk. If the mother does not have sufficient milk, the spider web of the *eanda* sisterhood comes to her rescue.

4.4 *Ohakera*

Among some pastoralists, every infant son or daughter born alive in a particular family will receive identical property of *ohakera* (plural: *ozohakera*). Here we find cattle equality, because children are equal. As they say, the child's sex at birth has nothing to do with the child. He or she did not choose it. It was decided by the ancestors, and nobody chooses their ancestors. *Ohakera* is the child cattle endowment, and it is set aside from the rest of the cattle that the child acquires later by purchase or by inheritance. *Ohakera* consists of a cow or two, a heifer and a ewe lamb. The precise composition of the endowment depends on the husbandry status of the givers. *Ohakera* is the par excellence social indicator of good parents' obligations to make provisions for the children. It is not bribery with cattle, because the children are not old enough to appreciate the intrinsic value of cattle. It is insurance, an economic investment for the teenage years. Matrilineal children do not inherit the paternal cattle wealth, but are instead given their own in infancy.

Should a child die before the age of seven or eight years, the *ohakera* reverts to the donors, or the donors' *omaanda*. Should a pregnant woman's husband predecease her, the progeny *en ventre sa mere* gets nothing, because under some indigenous law, the child *in utero* must be born alive before he or she acquires a property right to the special gift of *ohakera*. In this uncomplicated way, succession to a deceased child's cattle property is regulated.

A child earns his or her *ohakera* by virtue of being born alive, it is his or her just desert. It ensures cattle equality in the sense that everyone has *ohakera*, and the acquisition of *ohakera* assigns to children and adult children their obligations and rights in the community. The owner of the *ohakera* herd also owns the young animals, so with a natural talent for looking after animals, anyone can become quite rich in cattle. Accordingly, no one needs to complain of social injustice. The very rich cattle owners do not feel threatened that the not so rich cattle owners will steal their cattle, because there is no injustice in the original principle of acquisition.

The *ohakera* endowment is an up-front maintenance payment, the child has no further claims or entitlement to his or her father's cattle. *Ohakera* justice is a moral and legal entitlement, and this is one of the reasons of matriliny sex equality. The duality of the *eanda* and *oruzo* justice means that children's rights are quaranteed by the obligations of members of their dual descent, and social co-operation between the generations in the interest of children. They argue that social co-operation in rearing children within such a unit benefits everyone.

4.5 'Adoption'

From being a toddler to about the age of seven, a child has to learn and accept the ethics and culture of the community. The *ovaHimba* for example are a working family: father, mother, children, uncles, aunts, wives, nieces, nephews, able grandparents and great aunts, all have to work. Indigenous law does not regard work in the family as child labour, or exploitation of the children. Every member of the *onganda* is obliged to make contributions according to his or her age. Among pastoralists, boys and girls tend the kid goats, ewe lamb and heifers, they must know the natural mother of the numerous young animals, even if the young ewe will go to its own mother.

When children of the matriclan are between seven and eight years old, they are prepared for distant 'adoption' by their matrilineal relatives. Under indigenous law this extended sojourn with the matriclan is not adoption, or fostering, or guardianship. It is more like raising one's heirs. It is the parents and the child's patriclan who decide when a child is ready for the separation to the *eanda*.

The sojourn with the matrilineage is discussed in great detail with the children and they have a say in the proceedings. The child would be maintained and supported by the matriclan who assume parental responsibilities for the child. The transfer of the child from the patriclan to the matriclan is a very important indigenous law institution for socialisation of children. The children do not lose contact with their biological parents but some of the older men informed me that when they left the patriclan for the matriclan, they did not return until they were well into adulthood. Nowadays, however, some children return home more often because of the availability of transport.

Under the indigenous law of matriliny, since men cannot become pregnant and reproduce, they have a responsibility to rear the children of their female blood relatives with altruism, because they know that in return, their own children will be reared by their maternal blood relatives. It is a reversal of sex roles where the men are responsible for the rearing of children and the transmission of traditions to the next generation. Hence fatherly irresponsibility is not condoned, because it means that another man has to pick up the cattle burden of rearing the child, thus bridewealth is used to deny irresponsible men access to *eanda* women, as procreation is a potentially dangerous activity for women and burdensome for their *eanda*.

The reproductive control of men by men is based on indigenous law principles of justice for children. Children cannot make claims on the *eanda* if their mothers did not bring any bridewealth or *ohakera* cattle into the *eanda* capital. Thus the children may have claims on the *eanda*, but they cannot make the claim if there are no cattle assets to share. Justice is for living children as well as for those yet to be born. Small-scale societies maintain equilibria in their various legal institutions, because of the conventions which are inseparable from the indigenous law that lead to social justice for all.

The men 'adopt' their sisters' children, their nephews, nieces and cousins of the *eanda* blood. An uncle was defined as "a man who loves children". Bringing up children is the most important job fit for a man. The argument was that it was best for children to be educated by their maternal male relatives. It makes the children independent very early in life, and created bonds between children, parents, and the *eanda*. The children were also linked to their maternal and paternal grandparents and the wider community.

Under indigenous law, in case of the dissolution of the marriage of the child's parents or death of the parents, the child continued with his or her education in the *eanda* uninterrupted and would have known mainly his or her maternal family. Childless monogamous couples, although considered 'immature' are not excluded from taking on *eanda* nephews and nieces. It is every maternal uncle's legal obligation to raise his nephews and nieces.

4.6 Otjiwondo: age-group, age set

The births of children in the *ozonganda* are not registered, so adults and children grow up not knowing their chronological age; but the births of children in hospitals are registered. However, for the purpose of free existence, dates of births are irrelevant. After a few months, a participant observer usually gives up asking "How old is that child? What of that girl?" It is not necessary to know the chronological age precisely. The various pieces of jewellery worn by boys and girls define their ages and were just as serviceable for them. In some ethnic groups, boys and girls and young adults adorn themselves with many kinds of jewellery, necklaces, belts and anklets. There are various pieces of jewellery for the under fives, under ten, for puberty, for the married, the bereaved and the old. Every item of jewellery is significant.

The *Himba* reckons births, deaths and marriages by the seasons, for example, they say, "three or four rainy seasons ago", or "four winters ago when mother died". The most common form of reckoning is by the *otjiwondo* (plural *oviwondo*), an age-grade association of boys who were circumcised in the same season. The girls who have had their first menstruation in the same season also form their own age set. This means technically that there are more girls age groups than boys' age groups, since the latter were formed at irregular intervals. *Himba* boys must be circumcised, but there is no clitoridectomy for girls. The act of circumcision, that is the removal of the foreskin from the penis, is not accompanied by any religious ritual, it has no religious significance and it is simply a rite de passage to a half adulthood of life cycle. The circumcision marks the change of status from childhood to puberty.

At the first sign of the menstrual flow, its arrival becomes news. It is advertised in the *onganda*, because it is everybody's business. A child has suddenly become a woman who will fill the *onganda* with children and more cattle. Menstrual bleeding means fertility and reproduction. If she is betrothed, her prospective husband will bring gifts. If she has not been spoken for, a menstruating girl will attract all the unengaged men hovering in the various *ozonganda*.

When an *otjiwondo* was declared, the boys nearing or just past puberty, that is about 12-14 years old, returned home to their patriclan, to undergo *sukareka*, circumcision. It was performed mostly in the winter months to avoid infection. Some veterans explained that in their time there were a dozen or more boys in their *oruzo* for *sukareka*. The circumcision operation was performed on all the boys in one ceremony. The boys are encouraged not to howl like girls, but to behave as men who will soon get married.

Boys who were circumcised together bonded as great friends for life, and formed a unique brotherhood of the *otjiwondo*. The circumcision *otjiwondo* was given a distinguished name approved by the sages. The name should commemorate an outstanding event within five years. If the proclamation circumcision *otjiwondo* was named after an animal, it became sacred to that age-set, and the brotherhood should neither kill nor eat their icon. An *otjiwondo* could also be named after a big event, rather than an animal. Gibson (1977:67) described the chronology of *otjiwondo* as epochs, an institution. The *otjiwondo* fulfilled a quasi-annual chronology based upon important episodes and occasional conditions of the region in which they live. In Gibson's study of the age groups and epochs, it was found that some of the epoch names could be identified historically. The epoch name *'jonyosi yomutjira'* signified the appearance of Haley's comet in 1910. This simply indicated that the *ovaHimba* had some knowledge of astronomy.

Apart from being an efficient indigenous news broadcasting system, the *otjiwondo* was also a mutual aid association for the brotherhood of men, and the sisterhood of women. The women's *otjiwondo* helped each other at childbirth, lying in, and looking after their sick members. Many members of the *otjiwondo* appeared at all functions affecting the members or their *omaanda*, on occasions such as births, deaths, marriages, feasts of menstruation, sickness, court hearings and cattle crisis. The large numbers who attend the functions gave the members much needed moral support and reinforce the interdependence of the community.

4.7 Ombudsmanship that shines like the sun

We have seen that under indigenous law the *eanda* and *oruzo* assign responsibility for the care of the very young children, first to their procreators, then to their maternal uncles. Thus the *eanda* and *oruzo* ensure the best interest of the children by allocating consensus for the welfare of the children between the *eanda* males and *oruzo* males. In matriliny the *eanda* and *oruzo* are about balance, the equilibrium between men and women, who must reproduce and rear the next generation of children for the common good of the community. Flekkøy (1993) explained that it was the Norwegians who gave the world the first official position of an Ombudsman for Children in 1981.[7]

In matrilineal societies the ombudsmanship of the paternal uncles, great uncles and grandfathers is constituted to avoid the complete withdrawal of the children from their father's patrilineage. The

---

[7] Flekkøy M. G. (1993) *Children's rights. Reflections on and consequences of the use of developmental psychology in working for the interests of children.* Gent: University of Gent.

The concept of an 'ombudsman' or 'ombudsmen' is ancient. From Roman Law one could deduce that the tribunes of the plebes held the position of contemporary ombudsmen. Thomas (1976:16) noted that the first two (tribuni) were created in 494BC but by 449 BC their number had risen to 10. Their original function was probably to protect plebeians from arrest and punishment by patrician magistrates. Zaman (1995:4) explained that the Control Yan of the Chinese Han Dynasty (206-BC-220 AD) and the Censors of the seventeenth century American Colonies had the same function. There is also the classical Islamic institutions of the Mohtasib and Nazurala Mazalim, and the Turkish institution of the Quad-ulQudat concerned with scrutinising the action of administrators. How did only the Swedes have an ombudsman? Zaman (1995:4) suggests the inspiration for the Swedish ombudsman came from King Charles X11's short exile in Turkey in 1709, on his return he appointed the Comptroller-General as the first official with duties to scrutinise the action of royal servants.

motive is virtuous, so that the children themselves could cultivate the friendship of adult men of outstanding virtues. This is an exceptional friendship, the friendship of fathers and sons, of uncles, nephews and nieces. It is only natural, according to the *Himba*, that the paternal uncles should be the safeguarders of the children in distant matrilineage.

The *Himba* explained that their remote ancestors laid down the separate responsibilities with the ombudsmanship web that bind both families with mutual threads of rights and duties. The *oruzo* begets children, formulates moral principles, and implements the legal rules, but the *eanda* has blood line, cattle capital and the physical custody of the child. The women admitted that ombudsmanship is just and fair, because the *eanda* and *oruzo* are not in conflict. It is not an issue of male versus female. Brothers and fathers have found out that children living only with their mothers tend to be poor. Accordingly, *Himba* women's healthy survival as a group depends on their men, in fact their brothers and uncles, rearing the next generation of *ovaHimba* children.

As already explained, children in matrilineal societies do not inherit their father's wealth; therefore, the ombudsmen are concerned only with the character building of the children. There is no potential for conflict between children and the ombudsmen. The children are not their parents' insurance against old age, or their parents' pension benefits scheme. Neither are the ombudsmen desperate men who hang unto their children as pension fodder. Matrilineal fathers' dreams, or expectations are thrust not on their own children but on their sisters' children, their nephews and nieces. The major motive for the ombudsmen's concern with their blood children is ethical consideration, doing what is morally required of men to comply with the justice system of their community. Indigenous justice requires that the ombudsmen see to it that the children develop in a 'good direction'.

The ombudsmen and the *eanda* cannot own children in common or jointly. Although title to land is held jointly, and adultery may not be a ground for divorce, but when it comes to children, we see a different pattern. Children cannot be jointly owned. They cannot be owned by the begetters and they cannot be owned by the rearers, Therefore, the ombudsmen as the *otuzo* watchdogs within the *eanda* protects, as it were their genes and the well-being of the next generation.

Having sent the children to their maternal uncles, the ombudsmen participate in all the determinations that affect the children, because such resolutions cannot be left solely to the maternal uncles. The most substantial consultations are when marriages are being arranged for the youngsters or in the arrangements of child betrothal. This consultation is significant because of its implications for reproducing the next generation. Children cannot choose their parents, but at least the ombudsmen in their urge for self-preservation can help the children yet unborn by seeking to ensure that would-be parents make good marriages. The ombudsmen will not permit maternal males to sacrifice the children for bridewealth cattle.

The ombudsmen also have a final say in the divorce proceedings of a couple and in disputes about succession to cattle property if the *eanda* appeals to the *oruzo* court. Sometimes, on the grounds of complaints from the children about their *omaanda*, the ombudsmen make suggestions to the *eanda*. The ombudsmen are concerned with the living child as well as the funeral arrangements for a dead child, but only the *eanda* who had brought the child into the world is empowered to bury the dead.

Children brought up under the ethical standards of the *eanda* and *oruzo* know that they have to live within the community, accept the *eanda* redress, or the *oruzo* ombudsmen compensatory justice, and the matter ends there.

To conclude this essay on child ethnography, we must remember that more children are being born in polygynous marriages, and more are surviving, and indigenous jurisprudence still governs their lives.

Indigenous child law is crucial to an understanding of the survival and protection of African children within the bigger units of the matriclan or patriclan. In essence, the people's own legal philosophy about child rearing should remain a valuable framework of reference in constructing an effective modern child law.

4.8 Bibliography

Achebe, C. C. (1980) 'Literary insights into the *ogbanje* phenomenon'. Journal of African Studies. Vol. 7, No. 1, pp. 31-38.

Akoto, E, and Hill, A. G. (1988) 'Morbidité, malnutrition et mortalité des enfants'. In Tabutin, D. (ed.) *Population et sociétés en Afrique au Sud du Sahara*. Paris: L'Harmattan, pp. 309-334.

An-Na'im, A. (1994) 'Cultural transformation and normative consensus on the best interests of the child'. In Alston, P. (ed.) *The best interest of the child*. Oxford: Clarendon Press, pp. 62-116.

Arens, W. (1979) *The man-eating myth, anthropology and anthropophagy*. Oxford: Oxford University Press.

Aries, P. (1962) *Centuries of childhood*. London: Cape.

Armstrong, A. (1990) 'Maintenance statutes in six countries in Southern Africa'. Journal of African Law. Vol. 34, No. 2, pp. 132-144.

Barker, D. (1975) *Unmarried fathers*. London: Hutchinson.

Barry, H. and Paxson, L. M. (1971) 'Infancy and early childhood: Cross-cultural codes'. Ethnology. Vol. 2, No. 10, pp. 466-508.

Barsh, L. R. (1989) 'The draft Convention on the Rights of the Child: A case of eruocentrism in standard setting'. Nordic Journal of International Law. Vol. 58, pp. 24-53.

Baxter, P. and Almagor, U. (eds.) (1978) *Age, generation and time: Some features of East African age organization*. New York: St. Martin's Press.

Bean, P. (ed.) (1984) *Adoption: Essays in social policy, law and sociology*. London: Tavistock.

Beckstrom, J. H. (1972) 'Adoption in Ethiopia ten years after the civil code'. Journal of African Law. Vol. 16, No. 2, pp. 145-168.

Boswell, J. (1988) *The kindness of strangers: The abandonment of children in Western Europe from late antiquity to the Renaissance*. New York: Pantheon Books.

Bouthoul, G. (1970) *L'Infanticide différé*. Paris: Hachette.

Brown, S. (1991) *Late Carthaginian child sacrifice in their Mediterranean context*. Sheffield: Sheffield Academic Press, University of Sheffield.

Burman, E. (1994) 'Innocents abroad: Western fantasies of the childhood in the iconography of emergencies'. Disasters: Journal of Disaster Studies and Management. Vol. 18, No. 3, pp. 238-251.

Burman, E. (1996) 'Local, global or globalized? Child development and international child rights legislation'. Childhood: A Global Journal of Child Research. Vol. 3, No. 1, pp. 45-66.

Caldwell, J. C. (1976) *The socio-economic explanation of high fertility: Papers on the Yoruba Society of Nigeria.* Canberra: Dept. of Demography, Australian National University.

Caldwell, J. C. and Caldwell, P. (1981) 'The function of child spacing in traditional societies and the direction of change and in the reduction of postnatal abstinence'. In Page, H. J. and Lesthaeghe, R. (eds.) *Child spacing in tropical Africa.* London: Academic Press, pp. 73-92. 181-200.

Cameron, A. and Kuhrt, A. (1983) *Images of women in antiquity.* Detroit: Wayne State University Press.

Chipande, G. H. R. (1987) 'Adoption among female headed households: The case of Malawi'. Development and Change. Vol. 18, No. 2, pp. 315-327.

Clark, J. P. (1963) 'Abiku' In Moore, G and Beier, U. (eds.) *Modern poetry from Africa.* London: Penguin Books.

Cooter, R. (ed.) (1992) *In the name of the child.* London: Routledge.

Cotran, E. (1971) 'Comments and case notes: Custody of children under customary law'. East African Law Journal. Vol. 4, pp. 153-154.

Dall, K. N. (1991) *The African girl child: Challenges and prospects in the 1990s.* New York: UNICEF.

Daly, M. and Wilson, M. (1981) 'Abuse and neglect of children in evolutionary perspective'. In Alexander, R. and Tinkle, D. W. (eds.) *Natural selection and social behaviour.* New York: Chiron Press.

Dannert, E. (1880a) 'Customs of the ovaHerero at the birth of a child'. Folk-Lore Journal. Vol. 2, Pt. 4, July 1880, pp. 62-68.

Dannert, E. (1880b) 'Customs and ceremonies of the ovaHerero at the birth of twins'. Folk-Lore Journal. Vol. 2, Pt. 4, pp. 104-114.

Dingwall, R., Eekelaar, J. and Murray, T. (1983) *The protection of children: State intervention and family life.* Oxford: Basil Blackwell.

Ebeku, K. S. A. (1994) 'The legal status of Nigerian children born by a widow: *Chinweze* v *Masi* revisited'. Journal of African Law. Vol. 38, No. 1, pp. 46-60.

Edwards, W. (1929) 'From birth to death'. NADA. No. 7, pp. 16-25.

Eekelaar, J. (1991) 'Are parents morally obliged to care for their children?' Oxford Journal of Legal Studies Vol. 11, No. 3, pp. 340-353.

Eibl-Eibesfeldt, I. (1979) 'Children's behaviour: !ko-San, Yanomani, Himba and Eipo cultures'. Cultures. pp. 24-36.

Ekow-Daniels, W. C. (1977) 'The effect of marriage on the status of children in Ghana'. In Roberts, S. (ed.) *Law and the family in Africa.* The Hague: Mouton. pp. 159-168.

Els, J. (1984) *The life cycle of the Himba of Kaokoland.* Stellenbosch: PhD. Thesis, University of Stellenbosch, South Africa.

Fortes, M. (1959) 'Descent, filiation and affinity'. Man. No. 59, pp. 193-197.

Fortes, M. (1974) 'The first-born'. Journal of Child Psychology and Psychiatry. Vol. 15, pp. 81-104.

Fox, L. F. (ed.) (1967) *East African childhood.* Nairobi: Oxford University Press.

Gelfand, M. (1971) *Diet and tradition in an African culture.* Edinburgh & London: E. & S. Livingstone.

Goody, J. (1959) 'The mother's brother and the sister's son in West Africa'. Journal of the Royal Anthropological Institute Vol. 89, pp. 59-88.

Granzberg, G. (1973) 'Twin infanticide: A cross-cultural test of a materialist explanation'. Ethos. Vol. 1, No. 4, pp. 405-412.

Gray, F. H. (1981) 'Birth intervals, postpartum sexual abstinence and child health. In Page, H. J. and Lesthaeghe, (eds.) *Child spacing in tropical Africa.* London: Academic Press, pp. 93-110.

Griffiths, A. (1984) 'Support for women with dependent children in Botswana'. Journal of Legal Pluralism. Vol. 23, pp. 1-15.

Hardman, C. (1973) 'Can there be an anthropology of children'? Journal of the Anthropological Society of Oxford. Vol. 6, No. 2, pp. 85-99.

Harunah, H. B. (1993) 'Pawnship in pre-colonial Etsako society and culture'. African Notes: Journal of the Institute of African Studies. University of Ibadan. Vol. 17, Nos. 1& 2, pp. 1-12.

Hodges, J. and Hussain, A. (1979) 'La police des familles'. Ideology and Consciousness. No. 5, pp. 87-123.

Holman, R. (1973) *Trading in children: A study of private fostering.* London: Routledge.

Howman, E. G. (1929) 'Notes on the consequences of childless marriages among natives. NADA. No. 7, p. 8

Juma, W. (1960) 'The Sukuma societies for young men and women'. Tanzania Notes and Records. Vol. 54, pp. 27-29.

Kabeberi, J. (1990) *The child:Custody, care and maintenance.* Nairobi: Oxford University Press.

Kasunmu, A. B. (1964) The principle of acknowledgement or recognition of paternity under customary law in Nigeria. International and Comparative Law Quarterly. Vol. 13, pp. 1093-1104.

Kerr, A. J. (1965) 'Does a minor need two natural guardians in two systems of law to assist him at the same time. South African Law Journal. Vol. 82, pp. 487-494.

Kerr, A. J. (1973) 'Guardianship of children of Bantu customary unions: The inter-personal conflict of laws problem'. South African Law Journal. Vol. 90, pp. 4-11.

Kidd, D. (1906) *Savage childhood: A study of Kafir children.* New York: Negro Universities Press.

Kirk, L. (1975)' Estimating the ages of children in non literate populations: A field method'. Journal of Cross-cultural Psychology. Vol. 6, No. 2, pp. 238-249.

Koner, M. and Worthman, C. (1980) 'Nursing frequency, gonadal function and birth spacing among !Kung hunter gatherers'. Science. No. 207, pp. 788-791.

Kreager, P. (1980) *Traditional adoption practices in Africa, Asia, Europe and Latin America.* Research for Action, No. 6, London: International Planned Parenthood Federation.

Lafon, B. E. (1976) *Adoption: A comparative approach in English, French and customary laws.'* Licence en droit. Yaounde: University of Yaounde.

Lambo, T. A. (1975) *The child and the mother-child relationship in major cultures of Africa.* Carnets de l'Enfance. Vol. 10. UNICEF.

Mallows, M. (1991) 'Transracial adoption: The most open adoption'. In Mullender, A. (ed.) *Open adoption: The philosophy and the practice.* London: British Agencies for Adoption and Fostering.

McCall, D. F. (1974) 'Who owns the child? Descent systems and the social position of women in Gur myth and society'. Journal of African Studies. Vol. 1, No. 3, pp. 252-284.

Mensa-Bonsu, H. J. A. N. and Dowuona-Hammond, C. (eds.) (1994) *The rights of the child in Ghana: Perspectives.* Accra: Woeli Publishing Services.

Mobolade, T. (1973) 'The concept of *abiku*'. African Arts. Vol. 11, No. 1. pp. 62-64.

Molokomme, A. (1991) *Children of the fence: The maintenance of extra-marital children under law and practice in Botswana.* Leiden: Africa Studies Centre, Research Report.

Molokomme, A. (1994) 'Caught between indigenous law and state law: The strategies of mothers in maintenance cases in a Banwaketse village'. Law and Anthropology. Vol. 7, pp. 287-310.

Mosca, P. G. (1975) *Child sacrifice in Canaenite and Isrealite religion.* PhD. Thesis. Harvard University.

Mueller, E. (1976) 'The economic value of children in peasant agriculture'. In Rider, G. (ed.) *Population and development: The search for selective interventions.* Baltimore: John Hopkins University Press.

Muranga, M. (1989) 'Theophoric names: The Christian element with special reference to South Western Uganda'. The African Mind. Vol. 1, No. 1, pp. 91-99.

Muriithi, N. (1995) 'What is my name'? African Studies Review & Newsletter. Vol. 17, No. 1, pp. 21-23.

Nadi, B. (1958) 'Adoption among the Oromo of Sawa'. University College Addis Ababa Ethnological Society Bulletin. Vol. 8, pp. 83-92.

O'Collins, M. (1984) 'The influence of western adoption laws on customary adoption in the Third World'. In Bean, P. (ed.) *Adoption essays in social policy, law and sociology*. London: Tavistock Press, pp. 288-304.

O'Neill, O. (1988) 'Children's rights and children's lives'. Ethics. No. 98, pp. 445-463.

O'Neill, O. and Ruddick, W. (eds.) (1979) *Having children: Philosophical and legal reflection on parenthood.* New York: Oxford University Press.

Ohuche, R. O. and Otaala, B. (eds.) (1981) *The African child and his environment.* Oxford: Pergamon Press for the United Nations Environment Programme.

Ojofeitimi, E. O. and Elegbe, I. (1984) 'Mother's beliefs as to causation and prevention of birth defects in Ile-Ife, Nigeria'. Journal of the Royal Society of Health. Vol. 104, No. 3, pp. 116-118.

Ominde, S. H. (1952) *The Luo girl from infancy to marriage.* Nairobi: East African Literature Bureau.

Otlhogile, B. (1990) 'Infanticide in Bechaunaland: A footnote to Schapera'. Journal of African Law. Vol. 34, No. 2, pp. 159-162.

Ottenberg, S. (1989) *Boyhood rituals in an African society.* Seattle: University of Washington Press.

Page, H. J. and Lesthaeghe, R. (1981) *Child-spacing.* London: Academic Press.

Pauwels, J. M. (1969) 'Legitimation of children in customary law in Kinshasa'. In Gluckman, M. (ed.) *Ideas and procedures in African customary law*, Oxford: Oxford University Press. For the International African Institute, pp. 223-235.

Quartey-Papafio, A. B. (1913) 'The use of names among the Gas or Accra people of the Gold Coast'. Journal of the African Society. Vol. 13, pp. 167-182.

Raum, O. F. (1940) *Chaga childhood.* London: Oxford University Press for the International African Institute.

Read, J. S. (1993) 'Protecting Uganda's children: A new model child law for an African state'. Journal of Child Law. Vol. 5, No. 4, pp. 170-177.

Read, M. (1959) *Children of their fathers: Growing up among the Ngoni of Nyasaland.* London: Methuen & Co.

Renteln, A. D. (1994) Is the cultural defense detrimental to the health of children? Law and Anthropology. Vol. 7, pp. 27-106.

Riesman, P. (1992) *First find your child a good mother: The construction of self in two African communities.* New Brunswick, N. J.: Rutgers University Press.

Ross, W. D. (tr.)(1984) *Aristotle: The Nicomachean ethics.* Oxford: Oxford University Press.

Rwezaura, B. A. (1986-87) 'Tanzania: More protection for children'. Journal of Family Law. Vol. 25, pp. 261-267.

Rwezaura, B. A. and Wanitzer, U. (1988) 'The law and practice relating to the adoption of children in Tanzania'. Journal of African Law. Vol. 32, No. 2, pp. 124-163.

Shelton, A. (1969) 'Igbo child-raising, eldership and dependence: Further notes for gerontologists and others. The Gerontologist. Vol. 8, No. 4, pp. 236-241.

Simmance, A. J. F. (1959) 'The adoption of children among the Kikuyu of Kiambu district'. Journal of African Law. Vol. 3, pp. 33-38.

Soyinka, W. (1963) 'Abiku' in Moore, G. and Beier, U. (eds.) *Modern poetry from Africa.* London: Penguin Books.

Thompson, B. (1991) 'Child abuse in Sierra Leone: Normative disparities'. International Journal of Law and the Family. Vol. 5, No. 1, pp. 13-23.

Thompson, B. (1992) 'Africa's Charter on children's rights: A normative break with cultural traditionalism'. International and Comparative Law Quarterly. Vol. 41, pp. 432-444.

Tomasevski, K. (ed.) (1986) *The right to food: Guide through applicable international law.* Dordrecht: Martinus Nijhoff.

Tredinnick, A. W. and Fairburn, A. C. (1980) 'The baby removed from its parents: Prophylaxis with justice'. New Law Journal. 19 June, pp. 498-500.

Uzodike, E. N. (1990) 'Custody of children in Nigeria: Statutory, judicial and customary aspects'. International and Comparative Law Quarterly. Vol. 39, pp. 419-433.

Wolf, J. J. de (1983) 'Circumcision and initiation in Western Kenya and Eastern Uganda'. Anthropos. Vol. 78, pp. 369-410.

Woodman, G. R. (1975) 'Two many illegitimate children?' University of Ghana Law Journal. Vol. 12, No. 1, pp. 51-59.

Zulu, A. H. (1947) 'Parent-child relations'. Race Relations. Vol. 14, No. 4, pp. 146-149.

Chapter 5 — Contract

For a very long time, many people in Africa under indigenous law have made oral contracts using either gold dust, gold ingots, brass rods or cowrie shells as a medium of exchange. There was a well-developed exchange sector between the interiors of Africa, and with the communities that had long distance trans-Saharan trade routes, and the East African coastline. There were intra-regional and inter-regional trade network that became the slave routes.

The mass of the agricultural and pastoral population benefited from selling to the petty traders who traded with the powerful middle men between the Arabs and the Europeans. They bought ivory, gold, ebony, rhino horn, slaves, copper and exotic animals. Some of these middle men became rich and powerful because they controlled the trade. See chapter 3.

Barter, where X swaps goods that are superfluous to his or her requirements, in exchange for Y's superfluous goods, has been excluded because money payment has become the dominant exchange standard. In this very brief headnote, I shall examine an under researched area of the law: how people in the rural areas contracted for services, sale of goods, and loan of equipments under customary law. The ubiquitous bridewealth will also be examined as it is the contract par excellence in indigenous law. Bailment, sale, loans and the remedies provided for their breach will be discussed.

Who has capacity to contract under indigenous law? Adult men and women have capacity to enter contractual agreements. However, in matrilineal societies, a husband cannot sell his wife's property with or without her permission. Neither can any adult member sell off family property, nor *eanda* property, without the consent of the family. See chapter 13. Although minor children own the property given or bequeathed to them, they cannot alienate the property without the authority of their parents, maternal or paternal uncles. See chapter 4.

Men and women have to pay for the services of herbalists, for prescriptions for themselves and for cures for their children's various ailments. If within the *eanda* or *oruzo* there was nobody capable of performing circumcision, facial and bodily scarification, bonesetting, teeth extraction, the expertise of the specialist has to be negotiated and paid for whether or not this produced good results. Furthermore, some people have to contract for labour to help with digging, building, planting or harvesting when able-bodied adult men were unavailable, as well as negotiate for loans of implements. The contracting parties set out their own terms.

5.1 Sale

For there to be a sale under indigenous law, the specific objects for sale should be available for the buyer to see, for example, 10 baskets of corn, 10 bundles of yam, 10 bags of sorghum, 10 ivory tusks. The objects have to be in existence. Next season's kola nuts, or the contents of the next day's fishing baskets cannot be sold. The seller sells only what exists and what the vendor can see and what can be bargained for, the vendor also guarantees latent defects.

The buyer can pay the price immediately or put down a deposit towards the price of the goods. However, the deposit would be forfeited if the buyer failed to pay the balance after the terms of recovery have been breached. Or the purchaser can negotiate deferred payment, but without incurring liability for interest.

If the full price or part-payment has been made, the vendor is liable for damage to the object while awaiting delivery or collection by the purchaser. However, the most important constituent of indigenous law of sale is that the seller has title, owns the object of sale. The buyer having paid the price in good faith, must be guaranteed against the curse and the taboo of the real owner.

5.2 Sale of palm wine, kwacha and home-made brews

Wine is essential to many people's lives, and wine is used to celebrate births, betrothals, circumcisions, marriages and deaths. In some places, wine is sold in calabashes or in other vessels. The seller tells the buyer the price of the calabash of wine according to the size of the container. In some places, the containers are not sold with the wine, so the seller collects the calabashes when they are empty.

Usually, no buyer enters into a contract to buy wine without first tasting the liquid for quality. The buyer, too, before using the wine pours some on the ground as libation to the ancestors. The buyer can negotiate a reduction in price before tasting, because after tasting the wine, the buyer must make a final offer to the seller. Having tasted the wine, the buyer has not got much bargaining power left. A buyer cannot go around all the palm wine and kwacha sellers tasting their wares.

If the offer is accepted, the price is paid, and the containers of wine are collected by the buyer or delivered by the seller who arranges to collect the empty containers at a specified day. If the vendor agrees to deliver, the wine must be delivered at the pre-arranged time, or the vendor will bear the loss for deterioration in the quality of the wine. If an empty vessel is broken before the day fixed for collection, then the buyer is liable for replacement, if it as after the collection date, the seller bears the loss.

Usually, palm wine is sold in the original containers in which the wine was collected, because the seller cannot guarantee the quality of the wine after it is transferred from one vessel into another that might not be airtight, and should be thoroughly rinsed out before putting the fresh wine into the buyer's containers. In this instance, the buyer is liable for deterioration, but the seller may lose the palm wine drinking fraternity if rapid deterioration sets in before the wine is consumed.

Some home-made brews are sold by the ladle from the vat and large pots used for storing millet within which it was brewed. After tasting, offer and acceptance, the buyer decides on the number of ladlefuls to be transferred into the buyer's container. The buyer is liable for contamination.

5.3 Loan

During times of famine or scarcity, loans for consumption are made to neighbours and friends in front of witnesses. Loans of foodstuff such as yams, maize, oil, meat, kola and many more are made; in return, the exact quantity and quality of the foodstuffs are returned, not in species because it has been consumed. There is no interest charge for loans for consumption, but there is an action for the non-return of the foodstuff. See chapter 9.

Furthermore, there is loan for the use of a person's farming implements, fishing or hunting equipments, (hoes, axes, arrow heads, spear heads, fish hooks) and even pottery and jewellery. It is not hire, as there is no payment for the use of the equipment, but the precise objects are returned after use. The borrower is liable for damage, destruction or loss of the equipment. As no interest is chargeable, the borrower sometimes hands over some object to the creditor as security for the loan. When the debt is discharged, the specific object is returned.

The lender of objects for use or for consumption has an action against the borrower in the first instance court. The borrowers and agnates are liable for unjust enrichment. See chapter 9. Usually, the borrowers avoid the strong arm of indigenous law village opprobrium. It is an infringement of the taboo if objects are not restored to the lender, the consequences of the taboo are more terrifying than starving to death next time round.

5.4 Bailment

In pastoral communities where people own vast herds of cattle, large flocks of sheep and goats, some of the animals are bailed to poor agnates or *eanda*. The distribution of the animals to different areas of the tribal homeland prevents the decimation of all the bailor's animals by cattle disease.

The bailor's oral contract with the bailee guarantees that the bailee and his family have an interest in the progeny of the cattle capital. The bailee has a duty of care to take the cattle out for grazing. The bailee milks the cows and uses the milk for food and makes yoghurt.

Bailment among pastoralists is like the loan for use of farming, hunting, fishing or building implements, only that with loan of equipments, the bailor does not share in any increment generated by the loan of the tools. Whereas, in bailment, bailor and bailee share the young animals produced by the cattle capital.

The contract of bailment is revocable, if the bailee starved the cattle, ate some of the capital investment or bailed them out to another bailee. Furthermore, when the contract expires and the animals are returned, the bailee has to prove that any missing capital investment were killed either by wild beasts or by lightning. The bailee would produce the hide as evidence to substantiate the number of missing animals. Bailors are usually very powerful men, accordingly, the remedies of the bailors in case of conversion, are restitution by the bailee and his *eanda,* or the bailor's bodyguards will visit the fractious bailee and his family, who will be reduced to slavery.

5.5 Ubiquitous bridewealth

The relationship between a husband and wife is fraught with indigenous law contracts. The formation of marriage and divorce have been discussed in chapter 11.

The giving of bridewealth is the indigenous licence to procreate another human being and it is not bestowed freely. The bridewealth is a distinct contractual agreement that has nothing to do with either the gifts to the bride, her mother, her sister, favourite aunt or the expenses incurred in feasting. Among some people, indigenous law does not stipulate the fixed amount of bridewealth that ought to be offered to the bride's family. It is open to the parties to negotiate their own bridewealth. In a typically expansive Eastern State of Nigeria legislation, Limitation of Dowry Law, 1956, section 3(a) provides:

> Where no incidental expenses of a marriage are paid by the husband or intended husband or on his behalf dowry shall not exceed in amount or value the sum of thirty pounds.

This was an attempt to institutionalise a fixed dowry. The fixed dowry in Eastern Nigeria was unenforceable, and the patrilineal fathers circumvented the law and negotiated privately as they had always done in pre-statutory society.

However, according to the general principles of indigenous contract law, there must be an agreement for a fixed number of oxen, heifers and/or sheep, gold, ivory, cloth or whatsoever the parties had agreed upon. The object for bridewealth and the quantity are fixed by negotiations. The oral contract of bridewealth is a hard bargain. Some examples of their legal reasoning may be useful for clarifying the contractual obligations of the parties. If, for example, the in-laws could not or would not pay the balance of the bridewealth, at what point in time would they go to the *oruzo* court for arbitration? If their daughter's/niece's husband predeceased her, could the young widow elect to marry or not to marry her brother-in-law? If their niece, daughter died, could her corpse be returned to the *onganda*? Of course only part of the bridewealth would be refunded if she died in childbirth. Would the in-laws want to marry the deceased wife's sister? See chapter 14. The answers to these questions and many more were incorporated into the oral agreements that they had the foresight to negotiate.

When the bridewealth had been fixed, it could be negotiated to be paid by instalment, but most people do not like to be indebted to their in-laws. Only the very poor negotiate for payment by instalments. On the other hand, only desperate would-be-laws, too, accepted virilocal marriage for their girl on an instalment basis, for their girl might have ended up being a third or fourth wife.

Furthermore, the bridewealth should not have a condition attached to it, such as whether or not the girl would have babies. If there was such a condition, then there would be no transfer of the bride to the groom's family. But if a family accepted the virilocal transfer of their daughter with a condition of pregnancy attached, then the groom's family would be obliged to pay double after the birth of the first child. If the groom's family could not or would not pay the balance of the bridewealth, then they would go before the *oruzo* court for arbitration. See chapter 9.

Since most marriages are virilocal, the economics of maintenance of the woman have to be sorted out. In spite of the bridewealth, the groom who is taking his bride away from her family and home has a contractual obligation to provide for her. Had it not been for the marriage and subsequent child bearing, she would have been supported by the *eanda*. By contracting a virilocal marriage and living with him, she has acquired a right to be maintained and supported by him for the duration of the marriage. The groom would maintain her and her offspring until the dissolution of the marriage, when liability for maintenance terminates and she would rely on the marriage bridewealth.

Meanwhile, if her husband should die, the proferment of bridewealth to the woman's family does not give her de facto possession of her deceased husband's corpse. It is an implied term of the bridewealth contract that a wife has no property in her deceased husband, because the possessory right in her husband's body reverts to his patrilineage after death.

5.6 Bibliography

Achike, O. (1975) Some aspects of African customary law of contract. In Elias, T. O., Nwabara, S. N. and Akpamgbo, C. O. (eds.) *African Indigenous Laws*. Enugu: Government Printer, pp. 313-333.

Agboyibor, Y. (1982) 'Généralités sur le droit de la responsibilité 'civile'. Encycopedie juridique de l'Afrique. Vol. 9, pp. 279-282.

Allott, A. N. (1975) 'Credit and the law in Africa: A special study of some legal aspects of economic development'. Journal of African Law. Vol. 19, Nos. 1 & 2 pp. 73-82.

Ardener, S. (1964) 'The comparative study of rotating credit associations'. Journal of the Royal Anthropological Institute. Vol. 94, pp. 201-229.

Arhin, K. (1990) 'Trade, accumulation and the state in Asante in the nineteenth century'. Africa. Vol. 60, No. No. 4, pp. 524-537.

Babafemi, F. O. B. (1974) Trade narks and the illiterate: A critique of the judicial attitude. Journal of African Law. Vol. 18, No. 2, pp. 180-182.

Bohannan, P. (1955) 'Some principles of exchange and investment among the Tiv'. American Anthropologist. No. 57, pp. 60-70.

Bohannan, P. and Bohannan, L. (1968) *Tiv economy*. London: Longmans, Green & Co.

Bohannan, P. and Dalton, G. (eds.) (1962) *Markets in Africa*. Evanston: Northwestern University Press.

Bovill, E. (1968) *The golden trade of the Moors*. Oxford: Oxford University Press.

Carroll, D. W. (1967) 'Customary commercial law in Northern Nigeria'. Law in Society. No. 3, pp. 73-100.

Colson, E. (1974) *Tradition and contract*. Chicago: Aldine Publishers.

Daaku, K. (1971) 'Trade and trading patterns of the Akan in the 17th & 18th centuries'. In Meillassoux, C. (ed.) *The development of indigenous trade and markets in West Africa*. Oxford: Oxford University Press, pp. 68-81.

Danquah, J. B. (1928) *Akan laws and customs*. London: Routledge, pp. 219-220.

Danquah, J. B. (1951) *Obligations in Akan society*. London: Bureau of Current Affairs.

Elias, T. O. (1956) *The nature of African law*. Manchester: Manchester University Press, pp. 166-182.

Farnsworth, E. A. (1969) 'The development of the civil law of obligations in new states: Senegal, Madagascar and Ethiopia'. In Dainow, J. (ed.) *Essays on the civil law of obligations*. Baton Rouge: Louisiana State University Press, pp. 51-72.

Garrard, T. F. (1982) 'Myth and metrology: The early trans-Saharan gold trade'. Journal of African History. Vol. 23, pp. 443-461.

Ghai, Y. P. (1969) 'Customary contracts and transactions in Kenya'. In Gluckman, M. (ed.) *Ideas and procedures in African customary law*. Oxford: Oxford University Press for the International African Institute, pp. 333-346.

Gluckman, M. (1965a) 'The importance of obligation in contract'. In Gluckman, M. *The ideas in Barotse jurisprudence*. New Haven: Yale University Press, pp. 170-203.

Gluckman, M. (1965b) Obligation and debt. In Gluckman, M. *The ideas in Barotse jurisprudence*. New Haven: Yale University Press, pp. 242-272.

Gray, R. and Birmingham, D. (1970) *Precolonial African trade: Essays on trade in Central and Eastern Africa before 1900.* London: Oxford University Press.

Hill, P. (1963) *Migrant cocoa farmers of Southern Ghana*. Cambridge: Cambridge University Press.

Hoebel, E. A. (1964) Status and contract in primitive society. In Northorn, F. S. C. and Livingston, H. H. (eds.) *Cross-cultural understanding: Epistemology in Anthropology*. New York: Harper & Row.

James, E. T. (1953) 'Bahima cattle transactions'. Uganda Journal. pp. 74-75.

Kapferer, B. (ed.) (1976) *Transaction and meaning: Directions in the anthropology of exchange and symbolic behaviour*. Philadelphia: Institute for the Study of Human issues.

Le Roy, E. (1973a) *Anthropologie historique et juridique des contrats en Afrique noire, en Grèce et à Rome.* Document Pédagogique No. 4, Paris-Brazzaville: LAJP

Le Roy, E. (1973b) 'Le systeme contractuel du droit traditionnel Wolof''. Law in Rural Africa. Vol. 22, pp. 45-56.

Lewis, I. M. (1959) 'Clanship and contract in Northern Somaliland'. Africa. No. 29, pp. 274-293.

Lyall, A. B. (1980) *The social origin of property and contract: A study of East Africa before 1918.* London: PhD Thesis. London School of Economics. University of London.

Lyall, A. (1986) 'Traditional contracts in German East Africa: The transition from pre-capitalist forms'. Journal of African Law. Vol. 30, No. 2, pp. 91-129.

Mahoney, N. (1977) 'Contract and neighbourly exchange among the Birwa of Botswana'. Journal of African Law. Vol. 21, No. 1, pp. 40-65.

Mauss, M. (1966) *The gift: Forms and functions of exchange in archaic societies*. London: Cohen & West.

Mauss, M. (1970) *The gift, forms and function of exchange in archaic societies*. London: Routledge & Kegan Paul.

McCarthy, P. (1968) 'De facto and customary partnerships in Ethiopian law'. Journal of Ethiopian Law. No. 5, pp. 105-122.

Meillassoux, C. (ed.) (1971) *The development of indigenous trade and markets in West Africa.* Oxford: Oxford University Press.

Moore, S. F. (1972) 'Legal liability and evolutionary interpretation: Some aspects of strict liability, self-help and collective responsibility'. In Gluckman, M. (ed.) *The allocation of responsibility*. Manchester: Manchester University Press.

Moore, S. F. (1991) 'From giving and lending to selling: Property transactions reflecting historical changes on Kilimanjaro'. In Mann, K. and Roberts, R. (eds.) *Law in colonial Africa.* Portsmouth: Heinemann, pp. 108-127.

Olawoye, C. O. (1978) 'The question of accountability in the customary law of pledge'. Journal of African Law. Vol. 22, No. 2, pp. 125-132.

Roberts, S. (1969) 'The Malete law of contract: A reply'. Botswana Notes and Records. No. 2, pp. 62-63.

Schapera, I. (1965) 'Contract in Tswana case law'. Journal of African Law. Vol. 9, No. 3, pp. 142-153.

Schapera, I. (1969) 'Contract in Tswana law'. In Gluckman, M. (ed.) *Ideas and procedures in African customary law.* Oxford: Oxford University Press for the International African Institute, pp. 318-332.

Sheriff, A. (1987) *Slaves, spices and ivory in Zanzibar: Integration of an East African commercial empire into the world economy 1770-1873.* London: James Currey.

Turton, N., Griffin, J. B. and Lewen, R. W. (1936) 'Native agreements and Buganda native laws'. Laws of the Uganda Protectorate. Vol. 6, pp. 1365-1523.

Uchendu, V. C. (1964) 'Livestock tenancy among Igbo of Southern Nigeria'. African Studies. Vol. 23, No. 2, pp. 89-94.

Uchendu, V. C. (1967) 'Some principles of haggling in peasant markets'. Economic Development and Cultural Change. Vol. 16, No. 1, pp. 37-50.

Walker, J. M. (1968) 'Bamalete contract law'. Botswana Notes and Records. No. 1, pp. 65-76.

Woodman, G. R. (1967) 'Development in pledges of land in Ghanaian customary law'. Journal of African Law. Vol. 11, No. 1, pp. 8-26.

Chapter 6 — Criminal law, witchcraft, ordeals

Materials on tort and crime have been brought together in this chapter because they were indistinguishable under the various indigenous laws. A taxonomy of some indigenous offences, ordeals and witchcraft will be examined as witches were invariably easy targets in most societies. An exposition of how the traditional courts conduct trials of men and women who flaunt the indigenous moral law will be given in chapter 9.

The principles of indigenous law for the redress of fatal injuries, non-fatal injuries, and damage caused by animals and things were compensation and just 'deserts' because liability was strict. Under matriliny, the *eanda* was strictly liable, and the agnates were also strictly liable under some patrilineage system for those unable to pay compensatory fine.

It is a myth that pre-colonial African societies were anarchical and brutal; a society where tribesmen were nearly always at the ready to throw poisoned spear heads at each other. Violence and cruelty in human societies have nothing to do with men's ethnic origin, as illustrated by twentieth century wars, when millions of people were slaughtered in Europe, and hundreds of thousands died in the Africa Campaigns against Germany. Killing with either guns that killed ten people at once, or with arrow heads that killed one at a time, is still tantamount to killing fellow human beings. As such, African societies did not have a monopoly of violence, some indigenous communities were as beastly and cruel as the societies of the colonial powers. The myth of violence and brutality were perpetuated to justify the application of colonial penal laws, public hangings and incarceration. Most human beings white or black want to stay alive, to be healthy, and to get on with the chores of survival. Members of every community require peace and security among themselves to go about their social obligations without interference from those who do not comply, this is an important reason for preferring the compensatory justice of indigenous law.

6.1 Administration of criminal law

This chapter cannot be understood without a brief historical reference to the colonial administration of criminal law. The colonial powers appropriated the administration of customary criminal law to augment their power, and to submit the natives to the colonisers' form of justice without compensation. Criminal prosecution also changed the power relationship between the natives and the administrators.

As was reported in chapter 1, some Kings, Chiefs and Councillors who had opposed colonialisation were deposed, tried and exiled to other colonies by the new administration. Hand-picked loyal natives were appointed to work with the District Officer, or District Commissioner, or the Native Commissioner, as they were called in some territories. In colonial administration, 'indirect rule' was the most effective way devised to police thousands of natives, and eliminate the last vestiges of power of the former indigenous aristocracy and uphold the superiority of the few white people.

The power to prosecute and administer the criminal law enabled the administrators to sanction flogging the natives into reluctant obedience, or of inflicting death sentence by public hangings. The criminal law and the prerogative of judicial execution of natives were very important in the social control scheme of the administrators. It put the fear of the white rulers into the natives as the administrators had the power of life and floggings over them. As Anthony Kirk-Greene (1980:42) wisely noted, "the European DC wore the bullet-proof waistcoat of his white skin: it might not stop the bullet, but it nearly always stopped the other party from firing".

Meanwhile, all offences against the person, offences against government property and theft should be reported to the DC, DO, NC's representatives who would prosecute the offenders. In short, all criminal proceedings would be heard in the new criminal courts created by the administration. Prisons were built; juveniles, men and women were incarcerated and at the end of their sentences, they became a new class of detribalised native criminals.

6.2 Principles of tortious liability

Indigenous societies had tort liability, and the unwritten ethical rules of right conduct that restrained some members within the village group and the wider community from oppressive actions, and from wanton killing of one another. People tended to carve out certain areas for themselves because they knew each other and they inter-married. Most people do not believe that human beings are naturally beastly. Why should human beings be beastly to other human beings like themselves who did not harbour any hostile intention of bewitching their family.

The majority of people subject to indigenous laws have little or no experience of the modern penal laws of their country or the Biblical Ten Commandments, as the foundations for why they should do the right act. They followed their unwritten indigenous rules of social behaviour about how they should live in a society, and theirs is basically a just society. For example, let us take the Offences against the Person Act, 1861 applicable in colonial territories. Most natives refrained from murdering each other not because of the statute, fear of public hangings or prison, but because murder is seen as immoral. It is the wrong act to do. It is not tolerated behaviour. It is wrong to kill human beings wantonly or perversely. Furthermore, they do not recognise the lawful killing by the Government of anyone, nobody has a right to the life and death of another human being. It is considered immoral to deprive a person of his or her most valuable possession: life. By killing a human being, the killer has not only killed a potential procreator of other human beings, but has also actually killed life itself. Accordingly, a murderer does not deserve to die, two immoralities cannot make a virtue, and one will only be adding insult to the murderous injury by taking the killer's life. Hence witches were not allowed to go on a killing of their own, only after a fair trial that the group has the judicial capacity to activate the poison ordeal.

The indigenous principle not to deprive a person of his or her life except by the community, is not grounded on the authority of the statute or divine authority. Their indigenous laws that do not postulate that divine commandment or statutory power are their ethical laws. According to some sages, indigenous moral laws have existed for a very long time, they do not know how their ancestors agreed to regulate their societies by such laws. But it is certain that, as rational living beings, most adult men and women must have agreed that murder would not be tolerated, for the simple reason that such an act is against another human being. Since they were "all equal share-holders in their community" they accepted that as justice. There was real justice in their community that pivots on their ethical values. See chapter 11.

6.3 Hidden indigenous law

The indigenous criminal legal system did not disappear in spite of the determined efforts of the administrators to squash indigenous criminal law trials. The people considered it an injustice if the offender or his patrilineage did not make proper compensation to the victim and the victim's family.

A taxonomy of indigenous offences or tortious liability would include murder, manslaughter, malice, slander, insulting behaviour, as well as theft of property damage caused by animals and things and strict liability for act of minors.

Homicides occur, but most do not get to the statutory trial court, because they are tried in the local traditional courts. Most people will not jettison the indigenous courts in favour of the statutory courts for such an act will produce instability and lack of cohesion in the majority of indigenous law institutions. Furthermore, the parties still have to live in the same community. The purpose of the ultimate punishment of indigenous law is compensatory justice to improve the quality of life of the deceased's family and the deceased's community. Compensation is a more effective deterrent than incarceration.

Under the indigenous offences against the person, is the crime of the accidental killing in defence of oneself, or of a member of one's family, or under provocation. The offence of manslaughter is followed by the lesser offences of the tort action for assault and maiming of a person. The adultery of a young wife of child bearing age is also put under this heading, because her husband could demand compensation from the other party for the offence against his virility.

Under the category of offences against property and animal trespass indigenous law has included the fraudulent conversion of bailment cattle and the wrong-doing against children's property, that is theft of their matrilineal inheritance. Sometimes a child labours for many years for a maternal uncle who dies leaving the child nothing to inherit.

The refusal to refund the bridewealth on divorce, where there are no children, also comes under property. It was pointed out that the preservation of the environment and wild life should come under the heading of property, because the wanton destruction of community trees is an offence against community property. Moreover, some trees cannot be used for building or for firewood because they give off noxious fumes, accordingly the trees should be preserved and not slashed and burnt for farming. Grazing land, too, has its rules, as it is sometimes easily over-grazed, because grazing levels have to be maintained.

The offences that affect reputation are bad luck, witchcraft and slander. The words 'witchcraft and slander' tend to have identical meaning in some places. If you slandered a person you were implying that the person is a witch. Infertility and childlessness are instances of being bewitched, and the offence of bewitching is tried in the Chief's court if the bewitcher does not admit liability. See chapter 9.

'Bewitching' it was argued was the real cause of misfortune, because witches operated on their own. In some matrilineal pastoral communities, if a person wanted to know the real cause of his or her misfortune, he or she would bring in elders skilled in interpreting the configurations of the entrails of specially slaughtered animals. If the intestines proved that a person was bewitched, then *okuhuhura* was performed to heal the sick or the bewitched person. In other societies, a person accused of witchcraft or sorcery, because the *actus reus* is difficult to prove, is tried by the poison ordeal to prove the innocence or guilt of the alleged witch.

Cloning the former administrators, some literate conservatives wish to retain the flogging of wilful children and juvenile offenders. But, most non-literate, non-violent people subject to the indigenous law of compensatory justice find flogging abhorrent. Flogging is put in the same category as torturing and reducing a child to the status of a beast. Flogging, it was explained, disregarded the obligations of the matrilineage and patrilineage to support the young offender. Furthermore, flogging violates the 'rights' of a victim who wants compensation or monetary value, and who derives no pleasure in the torture and reduction of a thief to the status of a beast.

6.4 Compensatory justice

The purpose of compensatory justice in indigenous law is to maintain equilibria in the institutions of the patrilineage and matrilineage, age groups, (important route to power) religions, among sons, daughters, nephews and nieces, and in the community generally, which is clearly a major motive for wanting compensatory justice. Compensation satisfies the victim, or the victim's *eanda,* it punishes the offender, as well as his or her agnates. Furthermore, compensatory justice deters the young from criminality. Agnates who are made vicariously liable work very hard to accumulate wealth, and they resent members who dissipate the patrimony or the *eanda* inheritance on compensation. A few people should not be allowed to make life more difficult for others.

Some people in rural Africa have more confidence in their own equity of compensatory justice than in the punishment of incarceration. Why should free men be taken away from their responsibility and locked up for months and years? Prison, the *Himba* assured me, turns bad men into predators. Imprisonment of men is seen as morally indefensible. Heads of families, the *eanda* and *oruzo* should take responsibilities for looking after their young and maintain indigenous institution of justice.

Indigenous law has a repertoire of how to punish offenders, not by pain, suffering, incarceration or public hangings, but compensatory justice. According to the indigenous law, if two, three, or ten people should steal one cow, they paid a compensatory fine of six head of cattle per offender. The offenders are severely punished as a deterrent because they did not respect the other's property. The criminals who have jointly committed a crime cannot gain any advantage for themselves by their numbers. They cannot profit from their crime, individually or in a group.

The meaning of indigenous justice is in the interpretation according to the community, and that is the very basis of indigenous moral law. See chapter 10. However, if some people choose to behave like non-humans and harm others, then the offenders should be given their 'deserved deserts' or 'just deserts'. Their just deserts are: the repair of the damage, restitution of the property, cattle compensation or the monetary value, plus costs for the sitting of the court. Punitive damages were reserved for the fatal injury of women of child bearing age, because of the loss of their procreating capacity, and loss of expectation of life. Compensation for the unmarried man was loss of earning capacity. The restitution is first to the victim of the theft, or of the injury, and secondly, to the deceased victim's family or *eanda.* One of the reasons given by matriliny for their 'just deserts' theory is that it acts as deterrence to the other members of the community. Compensatory justice means that there is no revenge or self-help by the injured party's agnates. One always expects that the equilibrium will be restored.

6.5 Trial by ordeal

Trial by poison ordeal is usually reserved by the Mano and Efik of West Africa for a murderer and for a person who causes misfortune or death by witchcraft. Only survival from the poison ordeal could vindicate the person who causes death by witchcraft.

It must be recalled, however, that since time immemorial some African boys have been circumcised and the desensitised head of the penis covered with medicinal leaves. African herbalists treated dysentery, malaria, aches and pains, and have made facial and bodily scarifications that did not develop into keloids. Some people extracted two or four lower incisors and filed the upper incisors. The gap-toothed lower jaw and the inverted upper incisors are the distinctive recognition marks and the identification of skeletal remains of some ethnic groups. Furthermore, there were cases of inoculation against small pox and snakebites. Incisions with metal knives were made in different parts of the body, and a paste made by grinding the heads of several poisonous snakes mixed with medicinal plants, was regularly applied to the cuts for a couple of weeks.

Thus, there are many herbalists in African societies who have sound knowledge of the pharmacopoeia and potency of medicinal plants, poisonous plants and lethal bark extracts. See Iwu 1993. The poison ordeal was used in some societies as a means of invoking the aid of the supernatural in ridding the community of its dangerous members. This illustrated the use and abuse of power. The powerful argue that murderers and witches should not operate outside of the group judicial extermination system. Only the community, after a fair criminal trial, had the right of judicial execution of criminals by the poison ordeal. The Efik used the Calabar beans, and the Mano the sasswood.

The poison is lethal. It will kill the innocent as well as the guilty, because it cannot distinguish between the parties. However, to prove his or her innocence or guilt, the alleged murderer or witch was required to drink the poison. Before being condemned to the poison ordeal, the court must have heard the evidence, and must have given the person a fair, public trial. The guilty cannot escape the consciousness of guilt and in conformity with indigenous justice, the guilty must die. Accordingly, the dosage of the poison ordeal is manipulated to that effect. Some societies have no oathing before the ordeal. When the guilty held the container with trembling hands and drank very slowly (looking around and telling everybody that he or she is still alive), the poison was readily absorbed into the bloodstream. According to the opinion of the judges, the innocent person was given a non-lethal version of the drink. The plant extract causes emesis and is vomited and the innocent survives.

6.6 Bibliography

Customary criminal law in Kenya (1963) Journal of African Law. Vol. 7, pp. 1-3.

'Dead legalism in place of live justice: Plea for punishments suited to African conditions'. East Africa and Rhodesia. 20 April 1950. Vol. 26, pp. 1026-1027.

Kenya (1963) *Report on the Customary Criminal Offences in Nairobi*. Nairobi: Government Printer.

'Record of the conference on penal problems in East Africa', (1966) The University College, Dar es Salaam. January 1966. East African Law Journal Vol. 2, No. 1, pp. 1-71.

Abel, R. L. (1969) 'Customary law of wrongs in Kenya: An essay in research method'. American Journal of Comparative Law. Vol. 17, pp. 573-626.

Abel, R. L. (1970) 'Case method research in the customary laws of wrongs in Kenya'. East African Law Journal. Vol. 6, pp. 20-60.

Adesanya, S. A. (1969) 'The exclusion of the application of the Nigerian codified form of common law of evidence from the customary courts and the machinery for filling the gaps'. Northern Ireland Legal Quarterly. Vol. 20, pp. 349-369.

Aguda, T. A. (1963) 'Mens rea in Nigerian law'. London: PhD. Thesis. University of London.

Aidoo, A. (1957/8) 'Some aspects of proof and application of customary law in Ghana'. Obiter. Vol. 1, pp. 26-31.

Ajibola, B. (ed.) (1990) *Compensation and remedies for victims of crime*. Lagos: Federal Ministry of Justice.

Akanki, O. (1970) 'Proof of customary law in Nigerian courts'. Nigerian Law Journal. Vol. 4, pp. 20-36.

Allott, A. N. (1964) 'Evidence in African customary law'. In Gilissen, J. (ed.) *La preuve*. Recueils de la Societé Jean Bodin. Vol. 18, Brussels: Libraire Encylopédique, pp. 59-80.

Allott, A. N. (1966) 'The codification of the law of civil wrongs in common law African countries'. Sociologus. Vol. 16, pp. 101-121.

Aremu, L. O. (1980)'Criminal responsibility for homicide in Nigeria and supernatural beliefs'. International and Comparative Law Quarterly. No. 29, pp. 112-131.

Ashton, H. (1952) *The Basuto*. Oxford University Press, pp. 255-275.

Asuni, T. (1969) 'Homicide in Western Nigeria'. British Journal of Psychiatry, pp. 1105-1113.

Bacon, M. K., Child, I. L. and Barry, H. (1963) 'A cross-cultural study of correlates of crime'. Journal of Abnormal and Social Psychology. Vol. 66, No. 4, pp. 291-300.

Barlow, T. B. (1939) 'Vicarious liability in South African native law'. South African Law Journal. Vol. 56. pp. 233-235.

Bascom, W. (1980) *Sixteen cowries: Yoruba divination from Africa to the New World.* Bloomington: Indiana University Press.

Beidelman, T. O. (1963) 'Witchcraft in Ukaguru'. In Middleton, J. and Winter, E. H. (eds.) *Witchcraft and sorcery in East Africa*. London: Routledge and Kegan Paul.

Bennett, T. W. and Scholtz, W. M. (1979) 'Witchcraft': A problem of fault and causation'. Comparative and International Law Journal of Southern Africa. Vol. 12, pp. 288-301.

Bentzon, A. W. (1966) 'The structure of the judicial system and its function in a developing society'. Acta Sociologica. Vol. 10, pp. 121-145.

Bienen, L. (1974) 'Criminal homicide in Western Nigeria 1966-1972'. Journal of African Law. Vol. 18, No. 1, pp. 34-56.

Black, D. (1987) 'Compensation and the social structure of misfortune'. Law and Society Review. Vol. 21, pp. 563-584.

Boehringer, G. H. (1971) Aspects of penal policy in Africa with special reference to Tanzania'. Journal of of African Law. Vol. 15, No. 2, pp. 182-211.

Bohannan, P. (1957) *Justice and judgement among the Tiv*. Oxford: Oxford University Press, pp. 34-51.

Bohannan, P. (ed.) (1960) *African homicide and suicide*. Princeton, NJ: Princeton University Press.

Braithwaite, J. (1989) *Crime, shame and reintegration*. Cambridge: Cambridge University Press.

Brewer, I. G. (1974) 'Sources of the criminal law of Botswana'. Journal of African Law. Vol. 18, No. 1, pp. 24-36.

Brietzke, P. H. (1972) 'Witchcraft and law in Malawi'. East African Law Journal. No. 8, pp. 1-24.

Brietzke, P. (1974) 'Murder and manslaughter in Malawi's traditional courts'. Journal of African Law. Vol. 18, No. 1, pp. 34-56.

Brillon, Y. (1980) *Ethnocriminologie de l'Afrique noire*. Paris: Vrin.

Bringer, P. (1981) 'The abiding influence of English and French criminal law in one African country: Some remarks regarding the machinery of criminal justice in Cameroon'. Journal of African Law. Vol. 25, No. 1, pp. 1-13.

Brown, D. (1965) *Criminal procedure in Uganda and Kenya*. London: Sweet & Maxwell.

Brown, D. (1966) 'The award of compensation in criminal cases in East Africa'. Journal of African Law. Vol. 10, No. pp. 33-39.

Brown, D. (1966) 'The award of compensation in criminal cases in East Africa'. Journal of African Law. Vol. 10, pp. 33-39.

Brown, D. (1970) *Criminal procedure in Uganda and Kenya*. London: Sweet and Maxwell.

Bukurura, S. H. (1994a) *Sungusungu: Vigilantes in West Central Tanzania*. Cambridge: PhD Thesis. Churchill College, University of Cambridge.

Bukurura, S. H. (1994b) 'The maintenance of order in rural Tanzania: The case of Sungusungu'. Journal of Legal Pluralism and Unofficial Law. No. 34. pp. 1-29.

Burbridge, A. (1940) 'A witch doctor's power'. NADA. pp. 8-18.

Burns, F. M. (1910) 'Trial by ordeal among the Bantu Kavirondo'. Anthropos. Vol. 5, p. 808.

Burns, F. M. (1910) Trial by ordeal among the Bantu-Kavirondo. Anthropos. Vol. 5, pp. 808.

Bushe, H. G. (1935) 'Criminal justice in East Africa'. Journal of the Africa Society. pp. 117-128.

Bussani, M. (1996) 'Tort law and development: Insights into the case if Ethiopia and Eritrea' Journal of African Law. Vol. 40, No. 1, pp. 43-52.

Bwongwong'a, M. (1994) *Procedures in criminal law in Kenya.* Nairobi: East African Educational Publishers.

Chamblis, W. J. and Seidman, R. B. (1982) *Law, order and power.* Reading, MA: Addison-Wesley Publishers.

Christelow, A. (1987) 'Property and theft in Kano at the dawn of the groundnut boom, 1912-1914'. International Journal of African Historical Studies. Vol. 20, pp. 225-243.

Chukkol, K. S. (1981) *Supernatural beliefs and the criminal law in Nigeria: A critical appraisal.* Zaria: Ahmadu Bello University.

Chukkol, K. S. (1983) 'Supernatural beliefs and criminal law in Nigeria'. Journal of the Indian Law Institute. No. 25, pp. 444-474.

Clifford, W. (1964) 'The African view of crime'. British Journal of Criminology. pp. 477-486.

Clifford, W. (1966) 'Crime and culture: An African study'. Canadian Journal of Corrections. No. 8, pp. 157-166.

Clifford, W. (1974) *An introduction to African criminology.* Nairobi: Oxford University Press.

Coldham, S. (1995) 'Legal responses to state corruption in Commonwealth Africa.' Journal of African Law. Vol. 39, No. 2, pp. 115-126.

Collingwood, J. J. R. (1967) *Criminal law of East and Central Africa.* London: Sweet & Maxwell.

Contini, P. (1971) 'The evolution of blood-money for homicide in Somalia'. Journal of African Law. Vol. 15, No. 1, pp. 77-84.

Cotran, E. (1963) *Report on Customary Criminal Offences in Kenya.* Nairobi: Government Printer.

Cotran, E. (1967) The position of customary criminal law in African countries, In Sawyerr, G. F. A. (ed.) *East African Law and Social Change.* pp. 14-25.Nairobi: East African Publishing House.

Crawford, J. R. (1967) *Witchcraft and sorcery in Rhodesia.* London: Oxford University Press.

Crick, M. (1993) Witchcraft and sorcery in Africa. In Hughes, J. (ed.) *Faces of culture: Explorations in anthropology.* St. Lucia: University of Queensland.

Culwick, G. M. (1934) 'Religious and economic sanctions in a Bantu tribe'. First International Congress of Anthropological and Ethnological Sciences. London.

Cutshall, C. R. (1982) 'Culprits, culpability and crime: Stocktheft among the Ila of Zambia'. African Studies Review. Vol. 25, No. 1I, pp. 4-26.

Dambazau, A. B. (1994) Law and criminality in Nigeria. Ibadan: University Press, Plc.

Date-Bah, S. K. (1970) 'A restatement of the application of the customary law of slander'. Review of Ghana Law. Vol. 2, pp. 150-152.

Deng, F. M. (1965) 'The family and the law of Torts in African customary law'. Sudan Law Journal and Reports. pp. 535-

Devine, W. A. (1932) 'The habitual criminal'. NADA. No. 10, pp. 21-23.

Diamond, S. (1971) 'The rule of law versus the order of custom'. Social Research Vol. 38, pp. 42-72.

Doherty, O. (1990) *Criminal procedure in Nigeria: Law and practice*. London: Blackstone.

Dorsinfang-Smet, A. (1963) 'Réflexions sur les modes de preuve dans l'action judiciaire des societiés dites primitives'. In Gilissen, J. (ed.) *Recueils de la Societe J. Bodin pour l'histoire comparative des institutions. La preuve,* Vol. 18, pp. 15-35.

Douglas, M. (ed.) (1970) *Witchcraft confessions and accusations*. London: Tavistock.

Durand, P. P. (1970) 'Customary oathing and the legal process in Kenya'. Journal of African Law. Vol. 14, pp. 17-33.

Ebo, C. (1979) 'Indigenous law and justice: Some major concepts and practices.' Vierteljahresberichte. Vol. 76, pp. 139-148.

El Dareer, A. (1982) *Women, why do you weep? Circumcision and its consequences*. London: Zed Press.

Elias, T. O. (1954) 'Insult as an offence in African customary law'. African Affairs. Vol. 53, pp. 66-69.

Elias, T. O. (1962) 'Some considerations on the administration of criminal justice in Nigeria'. International Review of Criminal Policy. pp. 3-10.

Elias, T. O. (1971) 'Traditional and modern criminal policies'. Non-Institutional Treatment of Offenders. Paris. pp. 325-334.

Elias, T. O. (ed.) (1970) The prison system in Nigeria'. Lagos: Government Printer.

Epstein, A. L. (1954) *Juridical techniques and the judicial process: A study in African customary law*. Manchester: Manchester University Press for the Rhodes-Livingstone Institute Paper. No. 23, pp. 20-21.

Epstein, A. L. (1969) 'Injury and liability in African customary law in Zambia'. In Gluckman, M. (ed.) *Ideas and procedures in African customary law*. London: Oxford University Press for the International African Institute. pp. 292-303.

Epstein, A. L. (1972) 'Sanctions'. International Encyclopedia of Social Sciences. Vols. 13-14, pp. 1-5.

Evans-Pritchard, E. E. (1931) 'Sorcery and native opinion'. Africa. No. 4, pp. 22-54.

Evans-Pritchard, E. E. (1935) 'Witchcraft'. Africa. Vol. 8, pp. 417-422.

Evans-Pritchard, E. E. (1937) *Witchcraft, oracles and magic among the Azande of the Anglo-Egyptian Sudan.* Oxford: Clarendon Press.

Farwell, B. (1986) *The Great War in Africa 1914-1918.* New York: W. W. Norton.

Finch, C. S. (1990) *The African background to medical science.* London: Karnak House.

Fisiy, C. and Geschiere, P. (1990) 'Judges and witches, or, how is the state to deal with witchcraft? Examples from South-East Cameroon'. Cahiers d'Etudes Africaines. Vol. 118, pp. 135-156.

Foucault, M. (1977) *Discipline and punish: The birth of the prison.* London: Allen Lane.

Frimpong, K. and McCall Smith, A. (1992) *The criminal law of Botswana.* Cape Town: Juta & Co.

Furnas, D. W., Ashraf, S., Hombergh, P. van den, Froeling, F. and Nunda, I. M. (eds.) (1985) 'Traditional craniotomies of the Kisii tribe of Kenya'. Ann. Plastic Surgery. Vol. 15, No. 6, p 538.

Gluckman, M. (1963a) *Order and rebellion in tribal Africa.* London: Routledge and Kegan Paul, pp. 178-206.

Gluckman, M. (1963b) 'The reasonable man in Barotse law'. In Gluckman, M. (ed.) *Order and rebellion in tribal Africa.* London: Cohen & West, pp. 178-207.

Gluckman, M. (1965) *Politics, law and ritual in tribal society.* Chicago: Aldine Press.

Gray, J. (1958) 'Opinions of assessors in criminal trials in East Africa as to native custom'. Journal of African Law. Vol. 2, No. 1, pp. 5-18.

Greer, G. (1984) *Sex and destiny: The politics of human fertility.* London: Secker and Warburg.

Guidy, W. J. (1987) 'Excision? Mutilation sexuelle? Mythe ou réalité?' Présence Africaine. No. 142, pp. 53-58.

Gutmann, B. (1926) Das recht der Dschagga. Krueger Felix (ed.) Siebentes stück. Abbandlungen der sachischen staatlichen Forscbungsinstitute Forschunginstitut für Pscychologie Nr. 7.

Hamilton, R. (1935) 'Criminal justice in East Africa'. Journal of African Society. pp. 7-26.

Hannigan, A. St. J. (1958) 'Native custom: Its similarity to English conventional custom and its mode of proof'. Journal of African Law. Vol. 2, No. 2, pp. 101-115.

Hatchard, J. and Ndulo, M. (1994) *Readings in criminal law and criminology in Zambia.* London, James Currey.

Heald, S. (1986) 'Witches and thieves: Deviant motivations in Gisu society'. Man, NS. Vol. 21, No. 1, pp. 65-78.

Hedges, R. Y. (1962) *Introduction to the criminal law of Nigeria.* London: Sweet & Maxwell.

Henry, A. F. and Short, J. F. (1954) *Suicide and homicide*. New York: The Free Press of Glencoe.

Holleman, J. F. (1955) 'Indigenous administration of justice'. NADA pp. 41-47.

Honderich, T. (1969) *Punishment: The supposed justification*. London: Hutchinson.

Hone, H. R. (1939) 'The native of Uganda and the criminal law'. Journal of Comparative Legislation and International Law. pp. 179-197.

Hopkins, E. (1973) 'The politics of crime: Aggression and control in a colonial context'. American Anthropologist Vol. 75, Nos. 3 & 4, pp. 731-742.

Hoske, F. (1982) *The Hosken Report: Genital and sexual mutilation of females*. Lexington, Mass: Women's International Network News.

Howell, P. P. (1952) 'Some observations on the distributions of bloodwealth among the Nuer'. Man. No. 52. pp. 19-21.

Howell, P. P. (1954) *A manual of Nuer law: Being an account of customary law, its evolution and development in the courts established by the Sudan Government*. London: Oxford University Press.

Howman, R. (1948) Witchcraft and the law. NADA. No. 25, pp. 7-18.

Huber, H. (1959) 'Ritual oaths as instruments of coercion and self-defence among the Adanme of Ghana'. Africa. Vol. 29, pp. 41-49.

Iwu, M. M. (1993) *Handbook of African medicinal plants*. Boca Raton, London: CRC Press, pp. 357-358.

Jeffreys, M. D. W. (1952) 'Samsonic suicide or suicide of revenge among Africans'. African Studies. Vol. 11, No. 3, pp. 118-122.

Junod, H. P. (1962) 'African penal conceptions and the emancipation of African states'. Genève-Afrique. No. 1, pp. 156-165.

Junod, H. P. (1966) 'Reform of penal systems in Africa'. East African Law Journal. Vol. 2, pp. 31-36.

Karibi-Whyte, A. G. (1977) 'Cultural pluralism and formulation of criminal policy'. Nigerian Criminal Process. pp. 9-25.

Karibi-Whyte, A. G. (1988) *Criminal policy: Traditional and modern trends*. Lagos: Nigerian Law Publications.

Karibi-Whyte, A. G. (1992) 'Sanctions in Nigerian customary criminal law'. In Bello, E. G. and Ajibola, B. A. (eds.) *Essays in honour of Judge Taslim Olawale Elias. African law and comparative public law*. Vol. 2. Dordrecht: Martinus Nijhoff.

Karibi-Whyte, A. G. (1993) *History and sources of Nigerian criminal law*. Lagos: Spectrum Law Publishing.

Katende, J. W. (1967) 'Why were punishments in pre-European East Africa mainly compensative rather than punitive?' Journal of the Denning Law Society. No. 2, pp. 122-133.

Kerr, A. J. (1956) 'Liability in delict for wrongfully causing the death of a native man married according to native law'. South African Law Journal. Vol. 73, pp. 402-408.

Killingray, D. (1986) 'The maintenance of law and order in British colonial Africa'. African Affairs. Vol. 85, No. 340, pp. 411-437.

Kirk-Greene, A. H. M. (1955) 'On swearing: An account of judicial oaths of Adamawa Province of North Nigeria'. Africa. Vol. 25, No. 1, pp. 43-53.

Kirk-Greene, A. H. M. (1980) 'The thin white line: The size of the British colonial service in Africa'. African Affairs. No. 79, pp. 25-44.

Klinghirm, A. (1971) 'The trial of a witch: A document from Ghana'. Africana Marburgensia. Vol. 4, pp. 19-26.

Krige, J. D. (1939) 'Some aspects of Lovedu judicial arrangements'. Bantu Studies Vol. 13, No. 2, pp. 113-130.

La Fontaine, J. S. (1960) 'Homicide and suicide among the Gisu'. In Bohannan, P. (ed.) *African homicide and suicide*. Princeton: University Press.

Last, M. and Chavunduka, G. L. (eds.) (1986) *The professionalisation of African medicine*. Manchester: Manchester University Press for the International African Institute.

Leaver, K. D. (1950) 'The influence of early Bantu law on modern criminal and police procedure'. Outpost. No. 27. pp. 23-25.

Levine, R. A. (1959) Gusii sex offences: A study in social control'. American Anthropologist. Vol. 61, pp. 965-990.

Lewin, J. (1940) 'Crime and punishment in Africa'. Howard Journal. Vol. 5, pp. 245-248.

Lienhardt, R. G. (1951) 'Some notions of witchcraft among the Dinka'. Africa. Vol. 21, pp. 303-318.

Lindenbaum, S. (1991) 'Anthropology rediscovers sex'. Social Science and Medicine. Vol. 33, pp. 865-866.

Lowly, M. J. (1978) 'A good name is worth more than money: Strategies of court use in urban Ghana'. In Nader, L. and Todd, H. F. (eds.) *The disputing process: Law in ten societies'*. New York: Columbia University Press, pp. 181-208.

Ludger, K. (1952) 'Control of crime in primitive society: An example from Teso'. Uganda Journal. No. 16, pp. 130-131.

Lyall, A. B. (1970) Anomy theory and deviant response with special reference to African Socialist states'. East African Law Review. Vol. 3, pp. 25-45.

Macaulay, B. (1963) 'Assessors in criminal trials in Ghana: A study from without'. Journal of African Law. Vol. 7, pp. 18-46.

MacCormack, G. (1973) 'Revenge and compensation in early law'. American Journal of Comparative Law, pp. 69-85.

MacFarlane, A. (1970) *Witchcraft in Tudor and Stuart England.* London: Routledge and Kegan Paul.

Maguire, R. A. J. (1928) 'The Masai penal code'. Journal of Royal Africa Society. Vol. 28, pp. 12-18.

Mair, L. (1969) *Witchcraft.* New York: McGraw-Hill.

Malinowski, B. (1926) *Crime and custom in savage society.* London: Routledge and Kegan Paul.

Margetts, E. L. (1967) 'Trephination of the skull by primitive cultures, with particular reference to native East African practice' In Brothwell, D. and Sandison, A. T. (eds.) *Diseases in antiquity.* Springfield, IL: Charles C Thomas.

Marshall, T. H. (1955) Gluckman on the judicial process of the Barotse'. British Journal of Sociology. Vol. 6, pp. 369-373.

Marwick, M. (ed.) (1982) *Witchcraft and sorcery.* Harmondsworth: Penquin.

McCullough, J. A. (1971) 'Defamation among the Luo of Kenya'. East African Law Journal. Vol. 7, pp. 191-230.

Medani, A. M. (1974) 'Some aspects of the Sudan law of homicide'. Journal of African Law. Vol. 18, No. 1, pp. 92-103.

Meek, C. K. (1937) *Law and authority in a Nigerian tribe: A study in indirect rule.* London: Oxford University Press.

Meek, P. M. (ed.) (1991) *African divination systems: Ways of knowing.* Bloomington: Indiana University Press.

Melland, F. H. (1935) 'Ethical and political aspects of African witchcraft'. Africa. Vol. 8, pp. 495-503.

Mensa-Bonsu, H. J. (1989) The place of 'oaths' in the constitutional set-up of Asante. Law and Anthropology. Vol. 4, pp. 259-280.

Messenger, J. C. (1959) 'The role of proverbs in a Nigerian judicial system.'. Southwestern Journal of Anthropology. Vol. 15, pp. 64-73.

Middleton, J. and Winter, E. H. (eds.) (1963) *Witchcraft and sorcery in East Africa.* London: Routledge and Kegan Paul.

Milner, A. (1965) 'The sanctions of customary criminal law: A study in social control'. Nigerian Law Journal. No. 1, pp. 173-193.

Milner, A. (1969) *African penal systems.* London: Routledge and Kegan Paul.

Monter, E. W. (1976) *Witchcraft in France and Switzerland.* Ithaca:

Morris, H. F. (1965) 'Jurisdiction of the Buganda courts and the scope of customary law in Uganda'. Journal of African Law. Vols. 9, No. 3, pp. 154-161.

Morris, H. F. (1970) 'How Nigeria got its criminal code'. Journal of African Law. Vol. 14, pp. 137-154.

Morris, H. F. (1974a) 'A history of the adoption of codes of criminal law and procedure in British Colonial Africa 1876-1935'. Journal of African Law. Vol. 18, No. 1, pp. 6-23.

Morris, H. F. (1974b) 'The award of blood money in East African manslaughter cases'. Journal of African Law. Vol. 18, No. 1, pp. 104-112.

Mutungi, O. K. (1971) *The legal aspect of witchcraft in East Africa with particular reference to Kenya.* Valparaiso University Law Review. No. 5, pp. 524-555.

Myburgh, A. C. (ed.) (1980) *Indigenous criminal law in Bophuthatswana.* Pretoria: J. L. van Schaik.

Nduka, O. (1977) 'The traditional concept of justice among the Ibo of South-Eastern Nigeria'. Odu. Vol. 15, pp. 91-103.

Noah, C. P. (1971/72) 'Xhosa and Fingo fines for seduction followed by pregnancy'. Speculum Juris. pp. 53-57.

Nsereko, D. D. N. (1989) 'Compensating the victims of crime in Botswana'. Journal of African Law. Vol. 33, No. 2, pp. 157-171.

Ojo, J. D. (1981) 'Supernatural powers and criminal law: A study with particular reference to Nigeria'. Journal of Black Studies. No. 11, pp. 327-348.

Okonkwo, C. O. and Naish, M. E. (1964) *Criminal law in Nigeria.* London: Sweet and Maxwell.

Olila, J. H. (1984) *Exaggeration and bravado: An urban anthropological view of petty crime.* Rotterdam: Bibliotheek, Erasmus Univesiteit.

Orchardson, I. Q. (1935) Kipsigis: Information collected on witchcraft'. Africa. Vol. 8, pp. 509-515.

Orde-Browne, G. St. J. (1935) Witchcraft and British colonial law'. Africa. Vol. 8, pp. 481-487.

Osinbajo, Y. (ed.) (1990) *Unification and reform of criminal laws and procedure codes of Nigeria.* Lagos: Malthouse Press.

Parker, M. (1995) 'Rethinking female circumcision'. Africa. Vol. 65, No. 4, pp. 506-523.

Parrinder, G. (1958) *Witchcraft: European and African.* London: Penquin.

Penwill, D. J. (1951) *Kamba customary law.* Nairobi: East African Literature Bureau. pp. 72-76, 78-87.

Perryman, P. W. (1937) 'Native witchcraft' Uganda Journal. Vol. 4, No. 1, pp. 7-27.

Poirier, J. (1963) La preuve judiciaire dans les droits coutumiers d'Afrique noire'. In Gilissen, J. (ed.) *Recueils de las Societé Jean Bodin pour l'histoire comparative des institutions.* La Preuve. Bruxelles. Vol. 18, pp. 37-58.

Rattray, R. S. (1929) Ashanti law and constitution. London: Oxford University Press, pp. 294-316.

Read, J. S. (1963) 'Criminal law in the Africa of today and tomorrow'. Journal of African Law. Vol. 7, No. 1, pp. 5-17.

Read, J. S. (1964) 'Crime and punishment in East Africa: The twilight of customary law'. Howard Law Journal. Vol. 10, pp. 164-186.

Read, J. S. (1965) 'Some aspects of manslaughter in East Africa'. East African Law Journal. Vol. 1, pp. 260-275.

Read, J. S. (1966) 'Some legal problems in East Africa'. East African Law Journal. Vol. 2, pp. 39-62.

Riches, D. (ed.) (1986) *The anthropology of violence.* Oxford: Basil Blackwell.

Roberts, C. C. (1933) The African native under the English system of penal law'. Journal of Comparative Legislation. Vol. 15, pp. 169-175.

Roberts, C. C. (1935) 'Witchcraft and colonial legislation'. Africa No. 8, pp. 488-497.

Rowlands, J. S. S. (1962) 'Notes on native law and customs in Kenya'. Journal of African Law. Vol. 6, No. 3, pp. 192-209.

Rugimbana, O. K. (1966) 'Various aspects of the imprisonment system in East Africa'. East African Law Journal. No. 2, pp. 18-28.

Schapera, I. (1933) 'Pre-marital pregnancy and native opinion: A note on social change. Africa. Vol. 6, pp. 59-89.

Schapera, I. (1952) 'Sorcery and witchcraft in Bechuanaland'. African Affairs. pp. 41-50.

Schapera, I. (1955) Witchcraft beyond reasonable doubt. Man. No. 55. p. 72.

Schapera, I. (1969) 'The crime of sorcery'. Proceedings of Royal Anthropological Institute. pp. 15-23.

Schapera, I. (1972) 'Some anthropological concepts of crime'. British Journal of Sociology. Vol. 23, pp. 381-394.

Seidman, R. B. (1965) 'Witch murder and mens rea: A problem of society under radical social change'. Modern Law Review. No. 28, pp. 46-61.

Seidman, R. B. (1966a) 'Mens rea and the reasonable African: The pre-scientific worldview and the mistake of fact'. International and Comparative Law Quarterly. Vol. 15, pp. 1135-1164.

Seidman, R. B. (1966b) *A sourcebook of the criminal law of Africa Cases, statutes and materials.* London: Sweet & Maxwell.

Simons, H. J. (1934) 'European civilization and African crime'. African Observer. No. 2, pp..20-27.

Spurling, A. C. (1954) Digest and guide to the criminal law of Kenya. Nairobi:

Tanner, R. E. S. (1955) 'Law enforcement by communal action in Sukumaland, Tanganyika'. Journal of African Administration. No. 7, pp. 159-165.

Tanner, R. E. S. (1965) 'Crime and punishment in East Africa'. Transition. Vol. 5, No. 2, pp. 35-38.

Tanner, R. E. S. (1966) 'Cattle theft in Musoma 1958-1959'. Tanganyika Notes and Records. pp. 31-42.

Tanner, R. E. S. (1970a) 'The selective use of legal systems in East Africa'. In Tanner, R. E. S. (ed.) *Three studies in East African criminology*. Uppsala: Scandinavian Institute of African Studies.

Tanner, R. E. S. (1970b) *Homicide in Uganda*. Uppsala: The Scandinavian Institute of African Studies.

Tanner, R. E. S. (1972) 'Penal practices in Africa: Some restrictions on the possibility of reform'. Journal of Modern African Studies. Vol. 10, Nos. 1, 2, 3 & 4, pp. 447-458.

Tennent, J. R. M. (1961) 'The administration of criminal law in some Kenya African courts'. Journal of African Law. Vol. 5, No. 3, pp. 139-144.

Turnbull, C. (1978) 'Death by decree: An anthropological approach to capital punishment'. Natural History. Vol. 87

Turnbull, C. (1984) 'The individual, community and society: Rights and responsibilities from an anthropological perspective'. Washington and Lee Law Review. Vol. 41, pp. 77-132.

Turner, V. W. (1964) 'Witchcraft and sorcery: Taxonomy versus dynamics'. Africa. Vol. 34, pp. 314-324.

Twumasi, P. K. (1985) *Criminal law*. Tema, Ghana: Ghana Publishing Corporation.

Umunna, I. (1969) 'Some aspects of indigenous African theories of crime and punishment: A case study'. African Scholar. pp. 26-30.

Vansina, J. (1969) 'The Bushong poison ordeal'. In Douglas, M. and Kaberry, P. (eds.) *Man in Africa*. London: Tavistock Publications.

Vasdev, K. (1961) 'Ghosts, evil spirits, witches and the law of homicide in the Sudan'. Sudan Law and Reports. pp. 238-244.

Warner, E. S. (1955) *Trial by sasswood'*. London: Gollancz.

Weinrich, A. K. H. (1968) 'A sociological interpretation of sorcery and witchcraft beliefs among the Karanga. NADA. pp. 47-54.

White, C. M. N. (1960) 'The role of witchcraft in Central Africa'. Horizon, pp. 26-29.

Williams, G. L. (1949) 'Homicide and the supernatural'. Law Quarterly Review. No. 65, pp. 491-503.

Winans, E. V. and Edgerton, R. B. (1964) 'Hehe magical justice'. American Anthropology. Vol. 66, pp. 745-764.

Chapter 7 — Cultural property

Most legal researchers know about the law of real property, the law of personal property, and the law of industrial and intellectual property, but are unaware of the law of cultural property. The law of cultural property covers aspects of the law of contract, commercial law, insurance law as well as capital gains tax, inheritance tax and the law of succession and inheritance. See chapter 15.

Cultural property is defined expansively by Article 1 (a-k) of the Convention on the Means of Prohibiting and Preventing the Illicit Import, Export and Transfer of Ownership of Cultural Property, 1970.

This provides that for the purposes of this Convention, the term 'cultural property' means property which, on religious or secular grounds, is specifically designated by each State as being of importance for archaeology, prehistory, history, literature, art or science and which belongs to the following categories:

(a) Rare collections and specimens of fauna, flora, minerals and anatomy, and objects of palaeontological interest;

(b) property relating to history, including the history of science and technology and military and social history, to the life of national leaders, thinkers, scientists and artists and to events of national importance;

(c) products of archaeological excavations (including regular and clandestine) or archaeological discoveries;

(d) elements of artistic or historical monuments or archaeological sites which have been dismembered;

(e) antiquities more than one hundred years old, such as inscriptions, coins and engraved seals;

(f) objects of ethnological interest;

(g) property of artistic interest, such as:

(i) pictures, paintings and drawings produced entirely by hand on any support and in any material (excluding industrial designs and manufactured articles decorated by hand);

(ii) original works of statuary art and sculpture in any material;

(iii) original engravings, prints and lithographs;

(iv) original artistic assemblages and montages in any material;

(a) rare manuscripts and *incunabula*, old books, documents and publications of special interest (historical, artistic, scientific, literary, etc.) singly or in collections;

(b) postage, revenue and similar stamps, singly or in collections;

(c) archives, including sound, photographic and cinematographic archives;

(d) articles of furniture more than one hundred years old and old musical instruments.

This chapter on cultural property covers only objects of archaeological excavations and ethnographic African antiquities, known stylistically by the name of the area within which the objects were found, such as Asante, Bakota, Benin, Dogon, Igbo-Ukwu, Mali, Nok and many more. Some of the objects are of outstanding significance for the study of African history as well as for their aesthetic value.

Contemporary African fine art has been excluded because the works are not yet fifty years old and with few exceptions, are mostly the works of living artists. Accordingly, only books and journals about archaeological and ethnographic objects of over one hundred years are included in this bibliography.

7.1 Scramble for tribal art

The question often asked by researchers is, how did so many African antiquities, bronzes, fossils, funerary pottery, gold, ivories, zoomorphic and anthropomorphic figures in terracotta, find their way to Europe from the restricted areas where they had survived for centuries? Firstly, it was mostly by imperial cultural banditry in the later half of the nineteenth century. In 1898, the bronzes and ivories looted during the 1897 Benin punitive expedition were auctioned by W. B. Webster: the auctioneer of specimens of interest to anthropologists and antiquarians. The auction sale attracted the educated public because of the "pure barbarism and exoticism" of the objects. Considerable interest in the sale was also shown by buyers from the continent, as Belgium had opened the Royal Museum for Central Africa in 1897, to exhibit the objects "collected" from their colonies, and the Musée d'Ethnographie in the Trocadero, now renamed Musée de l'Homme, had also organised an exhibition of their collection from French colonies.

Accordingly, the largest collection from Benin auction sale was bought by the Museum für Völkerkunde in Berlin, the highest bidder, because Germany was trying to codify the laws of their African territories, (see chapter 1) and Germany also had the foresight to buy up ethnographic art very cheaply. France, Belgium and Portugal augmented their collection from the auction sale. Many European states that did not benefit from the partition of Africa[8] also acquired ethnographic pieces from the sale.[9] Other objects from the punitive expedition found their way into the British Museum, the Pitt-Rivers Museum founded in 1884, the Admiral Rawson collection, and some were retained by members of the punitive expedition. There are ethnographic collections in Ambras (Tyrol), Bologna, Padua, Ireland, Zurich, America and Canada.

It was during the great exhibition of African ethnographic objects in the Trocadero that a group of sophisticated French painters, sculptors and designers "discovered" African primitive art, and borrowed amusing ideas from the unusual stylisation of the nude figures. After centuries of European naturalistic representation, African ethnographic art became a powerful stimulus in the creation of a

---

8 Signatory Powers of the Berlin Africa Conference of 1884/85. For details on the Signatory Powers of the Berlin Africa Act, see Edward Hertslet (1896:317).

9 The African ethnographic collection of some European states that have no colonies in Africa for example, Poland, Switzerland are quite modest, between five to ten thousand objects.

new European artistic movement. *Les Demoiselles d'Avignon* (1907) was the first painting by a European artist to borrow creative African stylisation and rhythm. The two *Demoiselles* on the right hand of the painting are like abstractions of African figurative masks. Clark (1956:349) noted that:

> The painting of the *Demoiselles d'Avignon* coincided with the first appreciative study of Negro sculpture, and there at last was a totally unHellenised stylisation of the body which, from its intuitive geometry, can be classified a nude.

After *Les Demoiselles d'Avignon* the scramble for 'tribal art' began. The plunder of the artistic heritage of Africa is too well known for reiteration, but what has since focused the minds of liberal minded human beings was the 1935-1936 Italian invasion of Ethiopia and the further pillage of their historical antiquities.[10] Pectoral and processional crosses made of gold, brass, iron and wood, ecclesiastical and royal crowns, several statues, obelisks, altar slabs, thousands of illuminated ecclesiastical manuscripts in Ge'ez, and the statue of the Lion of Judah were carted off to Rome on the order of Mussolini. When the statue of the Lion of Judah was remounted on a pedestal in Rome, a young man from Eritrea, Zerai Deress staged a solitary protest that the Lion of Judah should be returned to its people; he was promptly arrested by the then Fascist Police and he died in custody.

7.2 Coup d'etat and plunder of antiquities

The flow of cultural objects from Africa to well-endowed states with written history continued unabated, inspite of domestic legislation and international conventions. The preparation for independence had made some archaeologists, historians and lawyers aware that the study of their past civilisation was important. National museums, galleries and Museum Institutes of African Studies containing archaeological, ethnological and natural science collections were set up.

During the preparation for independence, the departing civil, consular officials and their many relatives and friends "collected" as many tribal antiquities as they could carry. They were abandoning Africa, but not its cultural objects. The ships loaded with African cultural objects were like floating museums of African antiquities. Some of Africa's educated elite who did not understand the significance of the cultural objects simply gave away pieces from the embryonic national collection. European royalty, UN missions, diplomatic missions and international business men who visited the newly independent states were rewarded with cultural objects as gifts.[11]

The flow of cultural objects continued because large-scale thefts from museums, galleries, depositories, more looters and scavengers' trenches occurred during a coup d'etat. In spite of intrusion alarm and case by case alarms, the antiquities on display were stripped by 'insiders' and their collaborators who saw the objects as their investment for exile. There were organised thefts from depositories and important archaeological sites were plundered and pillaged by people who were not interested in either the historical, legal or artistic message conveyed by the objects *in situ*. In Rwanda, according to Janzen (1995:63) there was also destruction of the museum's catalogue records, primary research and inventory.

---

[10] The British punitive expedition 1867-1868 against Emperor Téwodros had looted Magdala.

[11] See for example Sotheby's catalogue Monday 27 June 1983 of the auction of Prince Sadruddin Aga Khan Collection of African Art. Also the pair of ivory leopards at the Musuem of Mankind graciously given to Her Majesty the Queen.

7.3 Conventions

Some African states are parties to the Convention for the Protection of Cultural Property in the Event of Armed Conflict, 1954. This was formulated as a result of the European experience of the Second World War when most of Africa was then under colonial administration.[12] Article 35 of the 1954 Convention extended the protection to dependent territories and provides that:

> Any High Contracting Party may, at the time of ratification or accession, or at any time thereafter, declare by notification addressed to the Director-General of the United nations Educational, Scientific and Cultural Organisation, that the present Convention shall extend to all or any of the territories for whose international relations it is responsible. The said notification shall take effect three months after the date of its receipt.

Fourteen African states have ratified the Convention as at 5 July 1995 and have not made any reservations to Article 35.

Many states have also ratified the Convention on the Means of Prohibiting and Preventing the Illicit Import, Export and Transfer of Ownership of Cultural Property, 1970. Accordingly, African states are making enormous effort by legislation, as well as by the introduction of export permits or licences to prevent the illicit export of cultural property. But the Constitution of most states in Africa, as well as the African Charter on Human and Peoples' Rights, 1986 are silent on the protection of cultural property. Article 22 (1) of the African Charter only provides that:

> All peoples shall have the right to their ... cultural development with due regard to their freedom and identity and in the equal enjoyment of the common heritage of humanity.

7.4 What should be done?

Antiquities are the common heritage of humanity, but sites are being destroyed, objects are looted, dissipated, and illicitly transferred out of Africa. The OAU should either have an organ for cultural property and for indigenous laws, or it should formulate a specific Charter for the Protection of Cultural Property in the Event of a *Coup d'Etat*.

African cultural property is worth millions of pounds, millions of dollars, millions of francs, millions of marks and millions of guilders, that could pay off the international monetary debts of some African states. Therefore, should African museums accept reproductions in lieu of the states' debts while the rich countries retain the originals?

Should African states demand restitution of the enormous holdings of shelf miles of their cultural objects? The European argument is that the antiquities are the cultural heritage of humanity and that in Europe, a Benin bronze is still a Benin bronze, only its location has changed.

So what can be done? Many of the rich western states that benefit from the sale of African cultural property can make restitution by an introduction of 5% African Royalty Tax on the annual turnover of

---

[12] Except Ethiopia and Liberia.

visits to Museums, and the sale of African objects conducted by the auction houses, museums and dealers. This would be *a droit de suite* or follow-up right for African cultural objects. The European Community Parliament can make a directive on the African Royalty Tax. Other states such as Switzerland, Poland, Australia and USA could legislate for an African Royalty Tax that would be administered by their Art Dealers Association.

Since the cultural objects are the heritage of all Africa, the African Royalty Tax should be paid to the OAU for the specific education programme for rural African children, the group that needs most help.

Apart from cultural objects, issues that are becoming of increasing interest in indigenous law are hominid fossils, human remains and burials. Under many indigenous law, deceased sons that had achieved high status were buried back home in their paternal village thus putting the village on the national map. The presence in the village of such a mausoleum was to encourage the young people to admire the deceased's achievements and endeavour to be like him, if possible.

7.5 Bibliography

British Museum. (1953) *The Webster Plass Collection of African Art.* London: British Museum.

Catalogue of the rarities to be seen at Adam's at the Royal Swan in Kingsland Road. (1756) Third Edition.

'Fakes, fakers and fakery: Authenticity in African art'. African Arts. Vol. 9. No. 3, pp. 20-31 and 48-74.

'The great Nigerian Museum mystery': On the appearance on the Western art market of art from the Nigerian Museum in Lagos. Primitive Art Newsletter. November 1982. No. 5, Vol. 11, pp. 1-2.

ICOM (1995) *Illicit traffic of cultural property in Africa.* Paris: International Council of Museums.

Museums in Africa: A directory. (1970) Bonn: Deutsche Afrika Gesellschaft.

Nigeria Tribal Art (1960) The Arts Council of Great Britain.

One hundred missing objects: Looting in Africa (1994). Paris: International Council of Museums.

Raiders of the cultural ark. (1991) Paris UNESCO.

Report by the Intergovernmental Committee for Promoting the Return of Cultural Property to its Countries of Origin or its Restitution in case of Illicit Appropriation on its Activities. (1991-1993) Paris: UNESCO. Document 27C/102.

Sadruddin Aga Khan Collection of African Art. Catalogue. (1983) Monday 27 June. London: Sotheby's.

'Some home truths about repatriation'. Primitive Art Newsletter. Vol. 5, No. 10. pp. 1-3.

Treasures of ancient Nigeria legacy of 2000 years. Zagreb: Muzejski Prostor.

Abimbola, W. (1976) *Ifa: an exposition of Ifa literary corpus*. Ibadan: Oxford University Press Nigeria.

Abiodun, R. (1990) *The future of African art studies: An African perspective. African Art Studies.* The state of the discipline. Washington: Smithsonian Institution.

Abrahamsson, H. (1951) *The origin of death: Studies in African mythology*. Uppsala: Studia Ethnographica Upsaliensia 3.

Adams, M. (1989).'African visual arts from an art historical perspective'. African Studies Review. Vol. 32, No. 2, pp. 55-103.

Adepegba, C. O. (1995) 'Igbo-Ukwu and later Igbo arts'. The Nigerian Field. Vol. 60. Parts 3-4, pp. 90-103.

Afigbo, A. E. (1981) *Ropes of sand: Studies in Igbo history and culture*. Ibadan: Oxford University Press.

Agorsah, E. K. (1977) 'Restitution of cultural material to Africa'. Afrika Spectrum. Vol. 2, No. 3, pp. 305-308.

Aldrich, J. (1990) 'The nineteenth century carved wooden doors of the East African coast'. Azania. Vol. 25, pp. 1-18.

Alexander, J. C. and Seidman, S. (1990) *Culture and Society: Contemporary debates*. London: Cambridge University Press.

Alexandrow, E. (1979) *International legal protection of cultural property*. Sofia: Sofia Press.

Allen, C. (1975) 'The Afo-a-Kom: A plea to save a cultural heritage'. In Duboff, L. D. (ed.) *Art law: Domestic and international Law*. South Hackensack: Fred B Rothman.

Allison, P. et al. (1976) 'Fakes, fakers and fakery: Authenticity in African Art'. African Arts. Vol. 9, No. 3, pp. 21-31, 48-74.

Anton, F. D. J., Trowell, M. and Neuermann, H. (1979) *Primitive art: Pre Colombian, North American, Indian, African/Oceanic*. New York: Abrams.

Antubam, K. (1963) *Ghana's heritage of culture*. Leipzig: Koehler and Arneland.

Appiah, K. A. (1991) 'Is the post- in postmodernism the post- in post-colonial'. Critical Inquiry. Vol. 17, pp. 336-357.

Appiah, K. (1992) *In my father's house: Africa in the philosophy of culture*. New York: Oxford University Press.

Arundell, R. D. H. (1936) 'Rock paintings in Bukaba district'. Journal of the Royal Anthropological Institute. No. 66, pp. 113-116.

Asad, T. (ed.) (1973) *Anthropology and the colonial encounter*. London: Ithaca Press.

Asihene, E. V. (1978) *Understanding the traditional art of Ghana*. London: Associated University Presses.

Assogba, R. P. (1976) 'Revolution and the conservation of a national heritage'. Museum. Vol. 28, No. 4, pp. 212-218.

Bacon, R. H. S. (1897) *Benin the city of blood*. London: Edward Arnold.

Baker, H. (1973) 'On appraising African and Oceanic 'primitive' art'. Valuation December. Vol. 20, No. 2. pp. 1-9.

Bascom, W. (1969) *Ifa divination: Communication between Gods and men in West Africa*. Bloomington: Indiana University Press.

Bascom, W. (1973) *African art in cultural perspective: An introduction*. New York: Norton.

Bassani, E. (1994) 'Additional notes on the Afro-Portuguese ivories'. African Arts. Vol. 27, No. 3, pp. 34-45 & 100-101.

Bassani, E. and Fagg, W. B. (1988) *Africa and the Renaissance: Art in ivory*. New York: The Centre for African Art.

Bastin, M-L. (1982) *La sculpture Tshokwe*. Meudon: Alain et Françoise Chaffin.

Bator, P. M. (1982) 'An essay on the international trade in art'. Stanford Law Review. Vol. 34, pp. 275-384.

Bedaux, R. M. A. and Smits, J. (1992) 'A seventeenth century ivory figure in the Rijsmuseum voor volken kunde in Leiden'. African Arts. Vol. 25, No. 1, pp. 76-77 and 100.

Beek, W. E. A. van (1988) 'Functions of sculpture in Dogon religion'. African Arts. Vol. 21, No. 4, pp. 58-65, 91.

Bellis, J. O. (1982) *The 'place of the pots' in Akan funerary custom*. Bloomington: Indiana.

Ben-Amos, P. (1976) 'Men and animals in Benin art'. Man. Vol. 2, No. 2, pp. 243-252.

Ben-Amos, P. (1980) *The art of Benin*. London: Thames & Hudson.

Ben-Amos, P. (1986) 'Artistic creativity in Benin kingdom'. African Arts. Vol. 19, No. 3, pp. 60-63, 83.

Benthall, J. (1987) 'Ethnographic museums and the art trade'. Anthropology Today. Vol. 3, No. 3, pp. 9-13.

Berns, M. C. (1988) 'Ga'anda scarification: A model for art and identity'. In Rubin, A. (ed.) *Marks of civilization: Artistic transformation of the human body*. Los Angeles: Museum of Cultural History.

Biebuyck, D. (1969) *Tradition and creativity in tribal art*. Los Angeles: University of California.

Biebuyck, D. P. (1983) 'African art studies since 1957: Achievements and directions'. African Studies Review. Vol. 26, Nos. 3 & 4, pp. 99-118.

Blackmun, D. W. (1984) *The iconography of carved altar tusks from Benin* Ann Arbor: PhD. Thesis, University of California.

Blier, S. P. (1988-89) 'Art systems and semiotics: The question of art, craft and colonial taxonomies in Africa'. American Journal of Semiotics. Vol. 6, No. 1, pp. 7-18.

Blier, S. P. (1990) 'African art studies at the cross-roads: An American perspective'. *In African Art Studies: The state of the discipline.* Washington, DC: National Museum of African Art.

Bloch, M. (1971) *Placing the dead: Tombs, ancestral villages and kinship organisation in Madagascar.* London: Seminar Press.

Bloch, M. (1982) *Death and the regeneration of life.* Cambridge: Cambridge University Press.

Boas, F. (1975) *Primitive art.* New York: Dover Publications.

Bohannan, J. P. (ed.) (1967) *Law and warfare: Studies in the anthropology of conflict.* Garden City: Natural History Press.

Bohannan, P. (1961) 'Artist and critic in an African society'. In Smith, M. W. (ed.) *The artist in tribal society.* London: Routledge and Kegan Paul, pp. 245-273.

Boon, J. A. (1991) 'Why museums make me sad'. In Karp, I. and Lavine, S. D. (ed.) *The poetics and politics of museum display.* Washington: Smithsonian Institution Press, pp. 255-277.

Bordogna, C. (1981) 'The lure of African art: Accessible masterpieces'. Collector-Investor September Issue. pp. 35-37

Bosman, W. (1705) (1967) *A new and accurate description of the Coast of Guinea.* Reprint. London: Frank Cass.

Boylan, P. J. (1993) *Review of the Convention for the Protection of Cultural Property in the Event of Armed Conflict.* Paris: UNESCO.

Bradbury, R. E. (1973) *Benin studies: The kingdom of Benin.* London: Oxford University Press for the International African Institute.

Bravman, R. A. (1973) *Open frontiers: The mobility of art in Black Africa.* Seattle: University of Washington Press for Henry Art Gallery.

Brent, M. (1994) 'Le grand pillage du Mali'. Le Vif L'Express. No. 11, pp. 48-52.

Brothwell, D. R. (1981) *Digging up bones: The excavation, treatment and study of human skeletal remains.* London: British Museum.

Brothwell, D. R. (ed.) (1976) *Beyond aesthetics: Investigations into the nature of visual art.* London: Thomas & Hudson.

Bugner, L. (ed.) (1976) *The image of the black in western art: From the Pharaohs to the fall of the Roman empire.* Vol. 1, Cambridge, Mass: Harvard University Press.

Burnham, B. (1978) *Art theft: Its scope, its impact and its control.* New York: International Foundation for Art Research.

Chaffin, A. and Chaffin, F. (1979) *L'art Kota: Les figures de relinquaire.* Meudon: Chaffin.

Chamberlin, E. R. (1979) *Preserving the past.* London: Dent.

Chamberlin, R. (1983) *Loot!: The heritage of plunder.* London: Thames & Hudson.

Chikwendu, V. E. and Umeji, A. C. (1979) 'Local sources of raw materials for the Nigerian bronze/brass industry: With emphasis on Igbo-Ukwu'. West African Journal of Archaeology. Vol. 9, pp. 151-165.

Chikwendu, V. E., Craddock, P. T., Farquhar, R. M., Shaw, T. and Umeji, A. C. (1989) 'Nigerian sources of copper, lead and tin for the Igbo-Ukwu bronzes'. Archaeometry. Vol. 31, No. 1, pp. 27-36.

Clamens, C. (1953) Notes d'ethnologie Sénoufo'. Notes Africaines. Vol. 59, pp. 76-80.

Clark, K. (1956) *The nude.* London: John Murray.

Clarke, D. (1935) Negro art: Sculpture from West Africa'. Journal of the Royal African Society. Vol. 34, pp. 129-137.

Clifford, J. (1988) *The predicament of culture: Twentieth century ethnography, literature and art.* Cambridge, Mass: Harvard University Press.

Cole, H. M. (1969) 'Art as a verb in Igboland'. African Arts. Vol. 3, No. 1, pp. 34-41.

Cole, H. M. (1989) *Icons: Ideals and power in the art of Africa.* Washington DC: Smithsonian Institution Press.

Cole, H. M. and Ross, D. H. (1977) *The arts of Ghana.* Los Angeles: Museum of Cultural History, University of California.

Connah, G. (1972) 'Archaeology in Benin'. The Journal of African History. Vol. 13, No. 1, pp. 25-38.

Connah, G. (1981) *Three thousand years in Africa: Man and his environment in the Lake Chad region of Nigeria.* Cambridge: Cambridge University Press.

Coombes, A. E. (1994) *Reinventing Africa: Museums, material culture and popular imagination in late Victorian and Edwardian England.* New Haven: Yale University Press.

Coote, J. and Shelton, A. (eds.) (1992) *Anthropology, Art and aesthetics.* Oxford: Clarendon Press.

Cornet, J. (1975) 'African art and authenticity'. African Arts. Vol. 9. No. 1. pp. 52-55.

Cory, H. (1956) *African figurines: Their ceremonial use in puberty rites in Tanganyika*. London: Faber & Faber.

Craddock, P. T. and Picton, J. (1986) 'Medieval copper alloy production and West African bronze analysis'. Archaeometry. Vol. 38, No. 1, pp. 3-32.

Crewdson, R. (1984) 'Cultural property, a fourth estate'. The Law Society's Gazette. Wednesday 18 January, pp. 126 and 129.

Curnow, K. (1983) *The Afro-Portuguese ivories: Classification and stylistic analysis of a hybrid art form*. Ann Arbor: PhD. Thesis. Indiana University, Bloomington.

D'Azevedo, W. L. (ed.) (1973) *The traditional artist in African societies*. Bloomington: Indiana University Press.

Darish, P. (1990) *Fired brilliance: Ceramic vessels from Zaire*. Kansas City: The University of Missouri.

Dark, P. J. C. (1973) *An introduction to Benin art and technology*. Oxford: Clarendon Press.

Datta, A. (1995) 'The zoology of Africa in art'. African Research and Documentation. No. 68, pp. 36-60.

Dembélé, M. and Waals, J. D. van der (1991) 'Looting the antiquities of Mali'. Antiquity No. 65, pp. 904-905.

Diop, A. and Sokhna, G. (1972) 'Museuological activity in African countries: Its role and purpose'. Museum UNESCO Quarterly Review. Vol. 25. No. 4, pp. 250-256.

Diop, C. A. (1989) *The cultural unity of black Africa: The domains of matriarchy and of patriarchy in classical antiquity*. London: Karnack House.

Doren, J. W. van (1988) 'Death African style: The case of S. M. Otieno'. American Journal of Comparative Law. No. 36, pp. 329-350.

Doren, J. W. van (1989) 'African tradition and Western common law: A study in contradiction'. In Ojwang, J. B. and Mugambi, J. N. K. (eds.) *The SM. Otieno case: Death and burial in modern Kenya*. Nairobi: Nairobi University Press.

Drewal, H. J. (1977) 'Art and the perception of women in Yoruba culture'. Cahiers d'études Africaines. Vol. 68, No. 17, pp. 545-567.

Drewal, H. J. and Drewal, M. T. (1983) *Gelede: Art and female power among the Yoruba*. Bloomington: Indiana University Press.

Drewal, H. J., Pemberton, J. and Abiodun, R. (1989) *Yoruba: Nine centuries of African Art and thought*. New York: Harry N. Abrams.

Duboff, L. D. (ed.) (1975) *Art law: Domestic and international*. South Hackensack: Fred B Rothman.

Edwards, A. C. (1984) 'On the non-existence of an ancestor cult among the Tiv'. Anthropos. Vol. 79. Nos. 1-3, pp. 77-112.

Egharevba, J. (1934) *A short history of Benin.* Lagos: CMS Bookshop.

Eyo, E. O. (1986) *The threat to national art treasures: The illicit traffic in stolen art, the challenge to our cultural heritage.* Paris: UNESCO.

Eyo, E. (1977) *Two thousand years Nigerian art.* Lagos: Federal Department of Antiquities.

Eyo, E. (1979) 'Return and restitution of cultural property: Nigeria'. Museum. Vol. 31, pp. 18-21.

Eyo, E. and Willett, F. (1980) *Treasures of ancient Nigeria.* New York: A. A. Knopf.

Ezra, K. (1992) *Royal art of Benin: The Perls Collection in the Metropolitan Museum of Art.* New York: Metropolitan Museum of Art.

Fabian, J. (1983) *Time and the other: How anthropology makes its object.* New York: Columbia University Press.

Fagg, B. (1977) *Nok terracottas.* Lagos: Nigerian Museum.

Fagg, B. and Fleming, S. J. (1970) 'Thermoluminescent dating of a terracotta of the Nok culture'. Archaeometry. Vol. 12, No. 1, pp. 53-55.

Fagg, W. B. (1959) *Afro-Portuguese ivories.* London: Batchworth Press.

Fagg, W. B. (1963) *Nigerian images: The splendour of African sculpture.* New York: Praeger.

Fagg, W. B. (1978) *Divine kingship in Africa.* London: British Museum Publications.

Fagg, W. B. (1980) *Yoruba beadwork.* New York: Rizzoli.

Fagg, W. B. and Picton, J. (1970) *The potter's art in Africa.* London: British Museum.

Ferretti, F. (1975) *Afo-a-Kom: Sacred art of Cameroon.* New York: Joseph Okpaku.

Fitzgerald, R. T. D. (1944) 'Dakarari grave pottery'. Journal of the Royal Anthropological Institute. pp. 43-57.

Flam, J. D. (1984) 'The spell of the primitive: In Africa and Oceana artists found a new vocabulary'. Connoisseur. pp. 124-131.

Fleming, S. J. and Nicklin, K. W. (1982) 'Analysis of two bronzes from a Nigerian Asunaja shrine'. Museum of Applied Science Centre for Archaeology Journal. Vol. 2, No. 2, pp. 53-57.

Forman, W. and Dark, P. (1960) *Benin art.* London: Paul Hamlyn.

Fradier, G. (ed.) (1979) 'Return and restitution of cultural property'. Museum. Vol. 31, special issue.

Fraoua, R. (1986) *Convention concerning measures to prohibit and prevent the importation and illicit transfer of property of cultural resources.* Paris: UNESCO.

Freyer, B. (1987) *Royal Benin art in the collection of the National Museum of African Art.* Washington, D. C. Smithsonian Institution Press.

Garlake, P. S. (1977) *Excavations on the Woye Asiri family land in Ife.* West African Journal of Archaeology. Vol. 7, pp. 57-96.

Garlake, P. S. (1993) *Rock art in Zimbabwe.* PhD Thesis. London: School of Oriental and African Studies, University of London.

Garlake, P. (1978) *The making of the past: The kingdom of Africa.* Oxford: Elsevier. Phaidon.

Garrard, T. F. (1980) *Akan weights and the gold trade.* London: Longman Group Ltd.

Garrett, W. D. (1968) 'Paraphernalia of smokers and snuffers'. Antiques. No. 93, pp. 104-108.

Gauthier, J. G. and Jansen, G. (1973) *Ancient art of the Northern Cameroons, Sao and Fali.* Oosterhout, The Netherlands: Anthropological Publications.

Gillon, W. (1984) *A short history of African art.* Harmondsworth: Viking.

Glaze, A. J. (1980) 'Call and response: A Senufo female caryatid drum'. Museum Studies. Vol. 19, No. 2, pp. 118-133.

Glaze, A. J. (1981) *Art and death in a Senufo village.* Bloomington: Indiana University Press.

Glazier, J. (1984) 'Mbeere ancestors and the domestication of death'. Man. Vol. 19. No. 1, pp. 133-148.

Gluckman, M. (1937) 'Mortuary customs and the belief in survival after death among the South Eastern Bantu'. Bantu Studies. No. 11, pp. 117-136.

Goody, J. (1962) *Death, property and the ancestors: A study of the mortuary customs of the Lodagaa of West Africa.* London: Tavistock.

Greenfield, J. (1989) *The return of cultural treasures.* Cambridge: CUP.

Griaule, M. (1950) *Arts of the African native.* London: Thames and Hudson.

Griggs, A. (1974) 'Dealing in African art'. Race Relations Reporter. No. 5, pp. 17-21.

Guillaume, P. and Munro, T. (1926) *Primitive Negro sculpture.* New York: Harcourt, Brace & Co.

Gulik, W. R. van (1989) 'Holding or losing: The return of cultural property'. In Zoest van, R. (ed.) *Generators of culture: The museum as a stage.* Amsterdam: AHA Books, pp. 49-53.

Hampson, F. J. (1988) 'Belligerent reprisals and the 1977 Protocols to the Geneva Convention of 1949. International and Comparative Law Quarterly. Vol. 37, No. 4, pp. 818-843.

Harding, M. (1995) 'Soldiers of the Queen: Photographs of Africa 1867-1902 in the National Army Museum'. African Research and Documentation. No. 68, pp. 9-16.

Hart, W. A. (1993) 'A rediscovered Afro-Portuguese horn in the British Museum'. African Arts Vol. 26, No. 4, pp. 70-71 and 87.

Hart, W. A. (1995) 'African Art in the National Museum of Ireland'. African Arts. Vol. 28, No. 2, pp. 34-48.

Hertslet, E. (1896) *The map of Africa by treaty: Abyssinia to Great Britain.* Vol. 1. London: Harrison & Sons.

Holden, C. (1982) 'Curbing the antiquities trade'. Science Vol. 217, No. 4566, pp. 1230-1231.

Hollander, B. (1959) *The international law of art.* London: Bowes & Bowes.

Home, R. (1982) *City of blood revisited: A new look at the Benin expedition of 1897.* London: Rex Collins.

Houlberg, M. H. (1976) 'Collecting the anthropology of African art'. African Arts. Vol. 9, No. 3, pp. 15-19, 91.

Huntington, R. and Metcalf, P. (1979) *Celebrations of death: The anthropology of mortuary ritual.* Cambridge: Cambridge University Press.

Inskeep, R. R. and Maggs, T. M. (1975) 'Unique art objects in the iron age of the Transvaal South Africa'. South African Archaeological Bulletin. Vol. 30, pp. 114-138.

Janzen, R. K. (1995) 'The Musée National du Rwanda: Surviving the war'. African Arts. Vol. 28, No. 3, pp. 62-63.

Jones, A. (1994) 'A collection of African art in seventeenth century Germany'. Weickmann, C. Kunst-und Naturkammer. African Arts. Vol. 27, No. 2, pp. 28-43, 92.

Jones, G. I. (1984) *The art of Eastern Nigeria.* Cambridge: Cambridge University Press.

Jones, G. I. (1989) *Ibo art.* Aylesbury: Shire Publications Ltd.

Kaplan, F. S. (ed.) (1981) *Images of power: Art of the Royal Court of Benin.* New York: New York University.

Kasfir, S. L. (1984) 'One tribe, one style? Paradigms in the historiography of African art'. *History in Africa.* Vol. 11, pp. 163-193.

Kerchache, J. (1993) *Art of Africa.* New York: Abrams.

Kinahan, J. (1990) 'Four thousand years at the Spitz Koppe changes in settlement and land use on the edge of the Namib desert'. Cimbebasia. Vol. 12, pp. 1-14.

Konaré, A. O. (1995) 'Towards more efficient international collaboration. African Arts. Vol. 28, No. 4, pp. 27-31.

Kopytoff, I. (1971) 'Ancestors as elders in Africa'. Africa. Vol. 41. No. 2, pp. 129-142.

Koroma, V. H. (1939) 'The bronze statuettes of Ro-Ponka, Kafu Bolom'. Sierra Leone Studies. Vol. 22. pp. 25-28.

Kouroupas, M. P. (1995) 'U.S. efforts to protect cultural property: Implementation of the 1970 UNESCO Convention'. African Arts.. Vol. 28, No. 4, pp. 32-41.

Kuper, A. (1988) *The invention of primitive society: Transformations of an illusion*. London: Routledge.

Laude, J. (1973) *African art of the Dogon: The myth of the cliff dwellers*. New York: Brooklyn Museum in association with the Viking Press.

Lawal, B. (1974) 'Some aspects of Yoruba aesthetics'. British Journal of Aesthetics. Vol. 14, No. 3, pp. 239-249.

Lehuard, R. (1980) 'On the circulation of African art'. Arts d'Afrique Noire. No. 35, pp. 4-15.

Leiris, M. and Damase, J. (1959) *Sculpture of the Tellem and the Dogon*. London: Graphic Press Ltd.

Leyten, H. (ed.) (1995) *Illicit traffic in cultural property*. Amsterdam: Royal Tropical Institute.

Lloyd, J. B. (1971) *African animals in Renaissance literature and art*. Oxford: Clarendon Press.

M'Bow, A-M. (1979) 'A plea for the return of an irreplaceable cultural heritage to those who created it'. Museum. No. 31. pp. 58-61.

Mack, J. (1990) *Emil Torday and the art of the Congo, 1900-1909*. London: British Museum Publications.

Mandirola, R. (1984) 'Grave monuments in Ivory Coast: With special reference to the Anya and Brong'. African Arts. Vol. 17, No. 4. pp. 46-52.

Maurer, E. (1981) 'Caveat ethnos: Unmasking frauds in ethnographic art'. National Arts Guide, Vol. 3, No. 2, pp. 22-25.

McBryde, I. (ed.) (1985) *Who owns the past*? Melbourne: Oxford University Press.

McIntosh, R. J. and McIntosh, S. K. (1986) 'Dilettantism and plunder: Illicit traffic in ancient Malian art'. Museum. No. 149. pp. 49-57.

McIntosh, R. J., Togola, T. and McIntosh, S. K. (1995) 'The good collector and the premise of mutual respect among nations'. African Arts. Vol. 28, pp. 60-69.

McLeod, M. D. (1977a) 'T. E. Bowdich: An early collector in West Africa'. In Camber, R. (ed.) *Collectors and collection*. London: The British Museum Yearbook 2.

McLeod, M. D. (1977b) 'African fakes and their detection'. Antique Collector. Vol. 48, No. 6, pp. 97-99.

McLeod, M. D. (1981) *The Asante*. London: British Museum Publications Ltd.

McNaughton, P. R. (1995) 'Malian antiquities and contemporary desire'. African Arts. Vol. 28, No. 4, pp. 22-27.

Merlo, C. (1974) 'Statuettes of the abiku cult'. African Arts. Vol. 8, No. 4, pp. 30-35, 84.

Middlemas, K. (1975) *The double market: Art theft and art thieves.* Farnborough: Saxon House.

Miles, G. P. (1937) 'Ring and bronze head: A suggestion'. Ethnologica Cranmorensis. Vol. 1, p. 11.

Monari, E. (1988) 'Burial law: Reflections on the S. M. Otieno Case'. Howard Law Journal. No. 31. pp. 667-674.

Monreal, L. (1979) 'Problems and possibilities in recovering dispersed cultural heritage'. Museum. Vol. 31, No. 1, pp. 49-57.

Morton-Williams, P. (1960) 'Yoruba responses to the fear of death'. Africa. Vol. 30, pp. 34-40.

Motti, B. de (1979) A structural study of form and meaning. Ann Arbor.

Mount, M. W. (1973) *African art: the years since 1920.* Bloomington: Indiana University Press.

Mudimbe, V. Y. (1986) 'African art as a question mark'. African Studies Review. Vol. 29, No. 1, pp. 3-4.

Musanda, F. B. (1990) 'African archaeology: Looking forward'. African Archaeological Review. Vol. 8, pp. 3-22.

Nahlik, E. S. (1976) 'International law and the protection of cultural property in armed conflicts'. Hastings Law Journal. Vol. 27, pp. 1069-1087.

Nevadomsky, J. (1986) 'The Benin bronze horseman as the Ata of Idah'. African Arts. Vol. 19, No. 4. pp. 40-47.

Nicklin, K. (1975) 'The rape of Nigeria's antiquities'. African Arts. Vol. 8, No. 3, pp. 86-88.

Nicklin, K. (1981) 'Rape and Restitution: The Cross River Region considered'. Museum Vol. 33, No. 4, pp. 259-260.

Nicklin, K. (1983) 'Traditional preservation methods: Some African practices observed'. Museum. Vol. 35, No. 2, pp. 123-127.

Nooter, R. and Nooter, N. (1988) *The art of collecting African art.* New York: Centre for African Art.

Nziem, È. N. (1995) La quête des antiquitiés et l'avenir de l'Afrique. Africa. Instituto Italo-Africano. Vol. 2, pp. 249-264.

O'Keefe, P. J. (1994) *Feasibility of an international code of ethics for dealers in cultural property for the purpose of more effective control of illicit traffic in cultural property: A report for UNESCO.* Paris: UNESCO.

O'Shea, J. M. (1984) *Mortuary variability: An archaeological investigation..* Orlando: Academic Press.

Obe, A. (1981) 'Battle for Africa's stolen cultural heritage' Africa. No. 119, pp. 129-131.

Ojwang, J. B. and Mugambi, J. N. K. (eds.) (1989) *The S. M. Otieno case: Death and burial in modern Kenya.* Nairobi: Nairobi University Press.

Ottenberg, S. (1975) *Masked rituals of Afikpo.* Seattle: University of Washington Press.

Pankhurst, R. (1986) 'The case for Ethiopia'. Museum. No. 149, pp. 58-60.

Parrinder, G. (1967) *African mythology.* London: Paul Hamlyn.

Pasztory, E. (1970) 'Hieratic composition in West African art'. Art Bulletin. No. 52. pp. 299-310.

Pemberton, J. (1989) 'Art and rituals for Yoruba sacred kings'. Museum Studies. Vol. 15, No. 2, pp. 97-111.

Pennie, M. (1991) *African assortment: African art in museums in England and Scotland.* Bath: Bath College of Higher Education Press.

Phillips, T. (ed.) (1996) *Africa, the art of a continent.* Munich-New York: Prestel.

Picton, J. (1991) 'Africa and the two art worlds'. African Arts. Vol. 24. No. 3, pp. 83-86.

Pierredon-Fawcett, L. de (1991) *The droit de suite in literary and artistic property: A comparative study.* New York: Columbia University School of Law.

Pitt-Rivers, A. (1900) *Antique works of art from Benin.* Reprint with introduction by B. Fagg. New York: Dover Publications.

Plakins, A. (1983) 'A scandal that won't go away: On the thefts of Benin bronzes and other objects from the Nigerian Museum in Lagos'. Connoisseur. Vol. 213, p. 16.

Plass, M. W. (1967) *African miniatures: The goldweights of the Ashanti.* London: Percy Lund.

Portes, E. des (1995) 'The fight against illicit traffic in cultural property: A priority for museum professionals'. In Leyten, H. (ed.) *Illicit traffic in cultural property.* Amsterdam: Royal Tropical Institute.

Posnansky, M. (1975) 'The price of popularity'. African Arts. Vol. 8. No. 3. pp. 88-89.

Preston, G. N. (1977) 'More on fakery'. African Arts. Vol. 10, No. 2, pp. 89-90.

Price, S. (1989) *Primitive art in civilized places.* Chicago: University of Chicago Press.

Prott, L. V. and O'Keefe, P. J. (1983a) *National legal control of illicit traffic in cultural property.* Paris: UNESCO.

Prott, L. V. and O'Keefe, P. J. (1983b) *Legislative measures and national regulations to fight against illicit traffic of cultural resources.* Paris: UNESCO.

Prott, L. V. and O'Keefe, P. J. (1984) *Law and the cultural heritage. Volume 1 Discovery and excavation.* Abingdon, Oxon: Professional Books Ltd.

Prott, L. V. and O'Keefe, P. J. (1988) *Handbook of national regulations concerning the export of cultural property.* UNESCO.

Prott, L. V. and O'Keefe, P. J. (1989) *Law and the cultural heritage. Vol. 3, Movement.* London: Butterworths.

Prott, L. V. and O'Keefe, P. J. (1993) *National legal control of illicit traffic in cultural property.* Paris: UNESCO.

Ravenhill, P. L. (1995) 'Beyond reaction and denunciation: Appropriate action to the crisis of archaeological pillage'. African Arts Vol. 28, No. 4, pp. 56-57.

Read, C. H. and Dalton, O. M. (1899) *Antiquities from the city of Benin and from other parts of West Africa in the British Museum.* London: British Museum.

Robbins, W. M. (1966) *African art in American collections.* New York: Praeger.

Robinson, A. (1976) 'Art objects in foreign hands: The quest for restitution'. Africa. No. 59. pp. 118-123.

Rogers, A. P. V. (1996) *Law on the battlefield.* Manchester: Manchester University Press.

Rosefielde, S. (1979) 'Private collections'. African Arts. Vol. 12. No. 4, pp. 10-14.

Rosevear, D. R. (1984) 'Cross River tombstones'. African Arts. Vol. 18, No. 1, pp. 44-47.

Ross, D. H. and Garrard, T. F. (ed.) (1983) *Akan transformations problems in Ghanaian art history.* Los Angeles: University of California.

Roth, H. L. (1903) *Great Benin: Its customs, art and horror.* Halifax: F. King.

Rubin, A. (1971) 'A propos': looting of the African continent of its sculptural heritage. African Arts. Vol. 4, No. 2, p. 79.

Rubin, A. (1973) 'Bronzes of the Middle Benue'. West African Journal of Archaeology. Vol. 3, pp. 221-231.

Rubin, A. (1974) Notes on regalia in Biu Division. West African Journal of Archaeology. Vol. 4, pp. 161-175.

Rubin, A. (1982) 'New challenges to Africa's artistic heritage'. African Arts. Vol. 15. No. 2, pp. 26-27 83-85.

Rubin, W. (ed.) (1984) *'Primitivism' in 20th century art: Affinity of the tribal and the modern.* New York: Museum of Modern Art.

Ryder, A. F. C. (1964) 'A note on the Afro-Portuguese ivories'. Journal of African History. Vol. 5, No. 3, pp. 363-365.

Ryder, A. (1977) *Benin and the Europeans 1485-1897*. Ibadan: Longman.

Salim, A. I. (1990) 'Conflict between common law and customary law in Kenya: Regarding burial'. In Abun-Nasr, et al. (eds.) *Law, society and national identity*. Hamburg: Helmut Buske Verlag.

Sambo, J. S. (1995) 'Regional workshop at Arusha on the illicit trade in cultural property'. West African Museums Programme. No. 6, pp. 89-91.

Schmidt, P. R. and McIntosh, R. J. (eds.) (1996) *Plundering Africa's past*. Bloomington: Indiana University Press.

Segy, L. (1958) *African sculpture*. New York: Dover Publications.

Seidl-Hohenveldern, I. (1992) 'Artefacts as national cultural heritage and as common heritage to mankind'. In Bello, E. G. and Ajibola, B. A. (eds.) *Essays in honour of Judge Taslim Olawale Elias*. Vol. 1. Dordrecht: Martinus Nijhoff.

Shanklin, E. (1990) 'The odysssey of the Afo-a-Kom'. African Arts. Vol. 23, No. 4, pp. 62-69 & 95.

Shapiro, D. (1995) 'The ban on Malian antiquities: A matter of law'. African Arts. Vol. 28, No. 4, pp. 42-51.

Shaw, T. (1961) *Excavation at Dawu*. London: Thomas Nelson and Sons. On behalf of the University College of Ghana.

Shaw, T. (1970) *Igbo-Ukwu: An account of archaeological discoveries in Eastern Nigeria*. London: Faber for Institute of African Studies, University of Ibadan.

Shaw, T. (1975) Those Igbo-Ukwu radiocarbon dates: Facts, fiction and probabilities'. Journal of African History. Vol. 16, No. 4, pp. 503-517.

Shaw, T. (1977) *Unearthing Igbo-Ukwu*. Ibadan: Oxford University Press.

Shaw, T. (1978) *Nigeria, its archaeology and early history*. London: Thomas & Hudson.

Shaw, T. (1981) 'The Nok sculptures of Nigeria'. Scientific American. Vol. 244, No. 2, pp. 154-166.

Shaw, T. (1989) 'African archaeology: looking back and looking forward'. African Archaeological Review. Vol. 7, pp. 3-32.

Shaw, T. and MacDonald, K. C. (1995) Review article: Out of Africa and out of context. Antiquity. Vol. 69, pp. 1036-1039.

Shinnie, M. (1965) *Ancient African kingdoms*. London: Edward Arnold Ltd.

Shinnie, P. L. (1971) 'The culture of medieval Nubia and its impact on Africa'. In Hasan, Y. F. (ed.) *Sudan in Africa*. Khartoum: University of Khartoum.

Sidibé, S. (1995) 'The pillage of archaeological sites in Mali'. African Arts. Vol. 28, No. 4, pp. 52-55.

Smith, B. W. (1994) *Rock art in South Central Africa: A study based on the pictographs of Dedza district, Malawi and Kasama district, Zambia*. Cambridge: PhD Thesis. Darwin College, University of Cambridge.

Smith, E. W. (1927) *The golden stool*. London: Edinburgh House Press.

Stanley, J. L. (1983) 'The African art market: An essay and bibliography'. Africana Journal. Vol. 14. No. 2&3, pp. 157-170.

Steiner, C. B. (1994) *African art in transit*. Cambridge: Cambridge University Press.

Stevens, P. (1978) *The stone images of Esie, Nigeria*. Ibadan: Ibadan University Press.

Sutton, J. E. G. (1991) 'The international factor at Igbo-Ukwu'. The African Archaeological Review. Vol. 9, pp. 145-160.

Toman, J. (1994) *La protection des biens culturels en cas de conflit armé*. Paris: UNESCO.

Torgovnick, M. (1990) *Gone primitive: Savage intellects, modern lives*. Chicago: University of Chicago Press.

Trigger, B. (1990) 'The history of African archaeology in world perspective'. In Robertshaw, P. (ed.) *A history of African archaeology*. pp. 309-319. London: James Currey.

Trowell, M. (1970) *Classical African sculpture*. New York: Praeger.

Underwood, L. (1949) *Bronzes of West Africa*. London: Alec Tiranti.

Vansina, J. (1968) 'Kuba art in its cultural contexts'. African Forum. Vol. 3, No. 4, pp. 12-27.

Vansina, J. (1984) *Art history in Africa: An introduction to method*. London: Longman.

Verswijver, G. (1995) 'Hidden treasures of the Tervuren Museum'. African Arts Vol. 28, No. 3. pp. 22-31.

Vogel, S. M. (1983) 'Rapacious birds and severed heads:Early bronze rings from Nigeria'. Museum Studies. No. 10, pp. 331-357.

Volavka, Z. (1976) 'The fight against forgery'. African Arts. Vol. 9, No. 3, pp. 63-65.

Von Luschan, F. (1919) *Altertümer von Benin*. Berlin: Lichtdruck von W. Neumann und Co.

Von Sydow, E. (1938) 'Ancient and modern art in Benin City'. Africa. Vol. 11, pp. 55-62.

Wardell, A. (1966) 'Some notes on a substyle of the Bambara'. Museum Studies. No. 1, pp. 112-128.

Willcox, A. R. (1984) *The rock art of Africa*. London: Croom Helm.

Willett, F and Fleming, S. J. (1976b) 'A catalogue of important Nigerian copper-alloy castings dated by thermoluminescence'. Archaeometry. Vol. 18. No. 2, pp. 135-145.

Willett, F. (1966) 'On the funeral effigies of Owo and Benin and the interpretation of the life-size bronze heads from Ife, Nigeria'. Man. Vol. 1, No. 1, pp. 34-45.

Willett, F. (1967) *Ife in the history of West African sculpture*. London: Thames and Hudson Ltd.

Willett, F. (1971a) 'Nigeria' In Shinnie, P. L. *The African iron age*. Oxford: Clarendon Press. pp. 1-35.

Willett, F. (1971b) *African art: An introduction.*. New York: Praeger.

Willett, F. (1976a) 'True or false? The false dichotomy'. African Arts. Vol. 9, No. 3, pp. 8-14.

Willett, F. and Eyo, E. O. (1980) *Treasures of ancient Nigeria*. New York: Knopf in association with the Detroit Institute of Arts.

William, S. A. (1978) *The international and national protection of movable cultural property: A comparative study*. Dobbs Ferry, N Y: Oceana Publications.

Wilson, G. (1939) 'Nyakyusa convention of burial'. Bantu Studies. No. 13, pp. 1-31.

Wilson, T. H. (1996) 'The loss of cultural heritage in Mali: A perspective from Kenya'. African Arts. Vol. 29. pp. 36-41.

Yoshida, K. (1993) 'Masks and secrecy among the Chewa'. African Arts. Vol. 26. pp. 34-45.

7.6 Basic documents on the protection of cultural property

Convention for the Protection of Cultural Property in the Event of Armed Conflict, 1954. The 'Hague Convention', with Regulations for the Execution of the Convention, as well as the Protocol to the Convention and the Conference Resolutions.

Convention on the Means of Prohibiting and Preventing the Illicit Import, Export and Transfer of Ownership of Cultural Property, 1970. UNESCO.

The Vermilion Accord. 1989

The Scheme for the Protection of the Material Cultural Heritage within the Commonwealth, 1993.

Arusha Appeal 1993.

Bamako Appeal 1994.

The Return of Cultural Objects Regulations 1994 (SI 1994 No. 501)

UNIDROIT Convention on the International Return of Stolen or Illegally Exported Cultural Property, 1995.

Chapter 8 — Customary law

Africa is a large continent which has probably never had, and may never have a unitary legal system as the French, German civil law, and English common law. Following the legal historical accident of colonialism, most African states now operate two models of law. The modern official state law, which is an extension of the model imposed by the colonial powers, is co-existing with the various indigenous living laws of the citizens. Thus, the imposed civil or common law is manifestly only one form of law in Africa.

The dialectical relations of state law and indigenous laws are complex and exhilarating. For, in African states, family law is an issue of rights of choice, a lexical priority of indigenous laws, sharia law, common-law, and civil law. The official law largely serves the needs of some elite; and the indigenous laws serve the majority and nationalists who do not want to be clones of Europeans. The majority conduct their marriages, inheritance, succession, property and child law largely under the principles of the legal philosophy of indigenous law.

8.1 Minds, like parachutes, are better when open

Customary law has had a very bad press. The saying that 'minds, like parachutes are better when open' applies more readily to the early European colonisers in their misinterpretation of indigenous laws. Minds should be open to all concepts of law and their differences, and should be receptive to the purposes of law in other societies and how others organise their law for their societies. But some European colonisers and missionaries' minds were not open.

What caused the disapprobation of customary law? One answer could be the missionaries' hegemony, premised on the divine tradition of Judaeo-Christian norms of Roman law concepts and common law. Thus, Christian missionaries and colonial administrators with closed minds fragmented the communities and traumatised the natives. This briefly expressed, throws some light on the ethical, legal, economic and political turmoil all over urban Africa today.

Perhaps, I have misinterpreted the missionary ethnologists, but it is in the nature of their calling to misrepresent "heathens", then try and convert them. Critchley (1995:20) who is more subtle than I am, noted that it was "to colonise and transform other cultures according to our own world views and to conceal oppression under the cloak of a mission".

Thus, the myth that there was no law in Africa, and no moral philosophy, was generated to allow for easy domination of the Africans. This legal domination of the Africans has been used to justify further domination in the relegation of indigenous law to non-law. Africans, like other human beings in the process of centralisation of power, be it in kingdoms like Asante, Bunyoro, Buganda, Benin, or in near state level chiefdoms or in acephalous societies, have had a system of law for a very long time. Law is about power relationships. It would appear that some human beings whether black or white in different societies originally grabbed power and status either by consensus, coercion or by commerce. The radio carbon dating of some of the archaeological cultural objects described in the bibliographical references in chapter 7 were produced to enhance the authority of such men who had power and wealth.

A second answer to what caused disapprobation of indigenous law could be that before the foundation of African law schools, today, most lawyers of a certain age were trained in the London Inns of Court, or in European universities in European type of law and were usually drawn from the urban elite. Furthermore, indigenous law is not glamorous and offers very little scope to make a name or fortune at the Bar.

8.2 Customary legal problems are universal

If the meaning of law is concerned with the practical application and abstract problems of justice, reason, knowledge, existence, ethics, virtues, and not just rules and principles, then Africans, too, have had to tackle the legal problems particular to their societies. There is no ethnic or racial difference in the most basic disposition of *homo sapiens* to reason. It is in the nature of being a human being to think. There is Chinese legal thought, Japanese legal thought, Hindu legal thought, Adat legal thought, Roman legal thought, and much more. Why not African legal thought? Only the inherent injustices of colonialism and irrationality could have made one dominant group of human beings, the colonisers, ready to expound that the colonised, who did not have a written law, had no legal system. There has never been an international conference of zebras where one group of zebras could proclaim being zebras, and be thoroughly dismissive of the other group of zebras.[13]

Indigenous law need not be written to be law; what needs to be ascertained is, what kind of legal philosophy was formulated by indigenous law. See chapter 10. Indigenous law is not only about customs, tradition, usage but the encapsulated philosophical principles that make the law binding. Those are the principles that transform traditions into law which most of the people accept as binding. It is important to understand the legal reasoning of indigenous law.

Africans, like other human beings, have had moral traditions dating back for hundreds of years before the contemporary era. There is a legal reason for every principle of law based on the tradition. The indigenous law embodies the wisdom, ability and efforts of many people for hundreds of years. Some of the specific content of the principles of indigenous law has to do with what affects their lives, criminal law (see chapter 6), property law (chapter 13), marriage (chapter 11), succession (chapter 15), trade (chapter 5), even environmental conservation is very old under indigenous law.

8.3 Disapprobation of customary law

Africans have been humiliated by slavery, colonialism and technological inferiority, but the contribution of the indigenous law to their communities should not be underrated. Civil and common law are not the only protectors of human beings by the rule of law.

---

[13] Long before the trade in African antiquities, see chapter 7, exotic African animals were the first to be exploited as popular gifts for emperors and sovereigns as well as the means of entertaining the public in amphitheatres, in the circuses and *venationes*: that was, displays in killing wild animals. In one of the animal shows that Caesar gave, there were a *venatio* of 400 lions, two torch-light parades of elephants ... and the first appearance in Rome of the giraffe. See Jennison, G. (1937) citing Pliny, N. H. V111, 16(21), 55. The Zebra is indigenous to Africa, but today there are zebras all over the world where there are Zoological gardens, known affectionately as the 'zoo'.

There are many traditional practices of indigenous law disapproved of by Christendom as recorded in the references below, but what produces the disapproval? It has to do with sex in polygyny, levirate and sororate marriages, circumcision, child betrothal, bridewealth, lack of contractual paper-registered marriages and uncomplicated divorce proceedings. See chapters 11 & 15. The colonisers wanted to change the natives' property relationship to their siblings, spouses, children, matrilineal or patrilineal relatives by individuals disposing of their property as in Europe. These ancient legal activities have some utility in the societies where people are still subject to them, and where they are still practised. When they no longer serve any purpose, they will be abandoned, as happened in other civilisations. Like other ancient traditions in the world, indigenous laws are changing in the terms of the people's own priorities. Africans are not rooted in the past, as they are adapting to what they need for survival. For example, my field study shows with reference to levirate marriage that the *Himba* are not immune to socio-legal change.

When codification of indigenous law was abandoned, and when the restatement of African law project was carried out, transforming indigenous laws into written customary law, followed by recording of indigenous laws and attempted unification of written and unwritten laws (see chapter 1), it was thought that indigenous law would sooner or later fall into desuetude. But has it? It has now been accepted by some Western jurists that African customary law is law, but that Africans need to develop a theory of law comparable to western law, Woodman (1995:xv-xxvi). However, indigenous law cannot be understood in isolation from the institutions and the ethical beliefs of the people who formulated the law.

8.4 Customary law revolution

There are more citizens who are subject to customary law, and more children are being born to them and more are surviving. Indigenous laws continue to dominate the social institutions that have crucial implications for child rearing. Colonialism has been and gone unnoticed by the majority; it has proved to be a brief but traumatic episode largely in some urban areas. The rural people admit that they are technologically backward, but they cultivate one important virtue above all other virtues, 'the virtue of having an adequate sense of the tradition to which they belong', because they see urban citizens who have inherited a cocktail of many conflicting traditions and confusing moralities and can no longer live in harmony with themselves.

Those subject to customary law are not known to be in conflict or in contact with state law. There has been only a minimal impact of the respective state law, of Charters and of Conventions on the rural people. Plurality of law is not dangerous, but state law is in fact viewed as the dictatorship of the *Wa Benzi*.

There is a large scope for state law to produce a genuine, realistic ethno-jurisprudence as a source of law that will apply to all men, women and children in the communities. The indigenous law preferences of their citizens should be satisfied, because that is what they have chosen, that is what they want and that is what is meaningful to them. This in my opinion, is why customary law is important and so compelling because we need to choose indigenous institutions that are working well and modernise them, thus making statutory law relevant to the community. In most states customary law has not become a source of law for statutory law, because the urban elite argue that the state needs modern Western law if the citizens are to compete with modern Western industrialised nations. Their arguments fails at the first village out of the city, because as indigenous philosophers would say, what is legally right is not always morally right. Customary law as one of the sources of law would have validated the autonomy of indigenous law, following the principle that the laws of a democratic state should be consistent with the history and traditions of the citizens, as long as they do not violate the new Constitution which should reflect the lives led by the people.

Most rural Africans are assertively egalitarian, not in the revolutionary French style of decapitating their leaders for the people to assert their rights, but in their equality of matrilineal and patrilineal groupings. Each is given its due, in equality of power, status, cattle wealth and land. Judging by the results of my field study, it is likely that those subject to indigenous law will continue to operate outside the state law to protect their best interest as well as those of their children as there are different ways of ordering human affairs..

8.5 Bibliography

Abraham, R. C. (1933) *The Tiv people*. Lagos: Crown Agents for the Colonies.

Achimu, B. O. (1976) 'Wanted: A valid criterion for validity for customary law'. Nigerian Law Journal. Vol. 10, pp. 35-55.

Adigun, O. (1989) 'The interplay of conflicting rules: A survey of the customs of the Yoruba and the effect of modern legislation'. Law & Anthropology. Vol. 4, pp. 281-305.

Ajayi, F. A. (1960) 'The interaction of English law with customary law in Western Nigeria'. Journal of African Law. No. 4, pp. 40-50; 98-114.

Ajibola, B. (ed.) (1991) *Towards a restatement of Nigerian customary laws*. Lagos: Federal Ministry of Justice.

Ajisafe, A. K. (1924) *The laws and customs of the Yoruba people*. London: Routledge & Sons.

Allott, A. N. (1950) 'The extent of the operation of native customary law: Applicability and repugnancy'. Journal of African Administration. Vol. 2, No. 3, pp. 4-12.

Allott, A. N. (1953) 'Customary law of the Akan peoples'. African Studies. Vol. 12, No. 1, pp. 26-29.

Allott, A. N. (1957) 'The judicial ascertainment of customary law in British Africa'. Modern Law Review. Vol. 20. No. 1, pp. 244-263.

Allott, A. N. (1960) *Essays in African law, with special reference to the law of Ghana*. London: Butterworth & Co. Ltd.

Allott, A. N. (1965a) 'The future of African law' In Kuper, H and Kuper L. (eds.) *African law: Adaptation and development*. Berkeley: University of California Press.

Allott, A. N. (1965b) 'Customary law: Its place and meaning in contemporary African legal systems'. Journal of African Law. Vol. 9, No. 2, pp. 82-85.

Allott, A. N. (1968) 'Customary law'. In Rubin, N. N. and Cotran, E. (eds) Annual Survey of African Law. Vol. 2, pp. 21-23.

Allott, A. N. (1969) 'Customary law in East Africa'. Afrika Spectrum. Vol. 3, pp. 12-22.

Allott, A. N. (1970) *New essays in African law*. London: Butterworth.

Allott, A. N. (1971) '*A background paper on restatement of laws in Africa: The need, value and methods of such restatement*'. In Allott, A. N. and Cotran, E. (eds.) Integration of customary and modern legal systems in Africa. Ife.

Allott, A. N. (1984) 'What is to be done with African customary law'? Journal of African Law. Vol. 28, Nos. 1 & 2, pp. 56-71.

Ankermann, B. (1929) Ostafrika. Vol. 1, of Das Einegeborenen recht. In Schultz-Ewerth, E. and Adam, L. (eds.) Stutgart.

Anyabe, A. P. (1985) *Customary law: The war without arms*. Enugu: Fourth Dimension Publishers.

Asad, T. (ed.) (1973) *Anthropology and the colonial encounter*. London: Ithaca Press.

Asiedu-Akrofi, D. (1989) 'Judicial recognition and adoption of customary law in Nigeria'. The American Journal of Comparative Law. No. 37, pp. 571-593.

Bakari, A. H. (1989) 'Application of customary law of indigenous tribes of Tanzania Mainland'. Law & Anthropology. Vol. 4, pp. 153-166.

Beech, M. W. H. (1920) 'Sketch of Elgeyo law and custom'. Journal of the Royal African Society. Vol. 20, pp. 195-203.

Bekker, J. C. (1989) Seymour's customary law in Southern Àfrica. Kenwyn,SA: Juta.

Bekker, J. C. and Coertze, J. J. J. (1982) *Seymour's customary law in Southern Africa*. Cape Town: Juta.

Benda-Beckmann, F. von (1984) 'Law out of context: A comment on the creation of traditional laws discussion'. Journal of African Law. Vol. 28, Nos. 1 & 2, pp. 29-33.

Bennett, T. W. (1985) The *Application of customary law in Southern Africa: The conflict of personal laws* Cape Town: Juta.

Bennett, T. W. (1991) *A sourcebook of African customary law for Southern Africa*. Cape Town: Juta.

Bohannan, P. (1957) *Justice and judgment among the Tiv*. London: Oxford University Press for the International African Institute.

Brown, D. and Allen, P. A. P. J. (1968) *An introduction to the law of Uganda*. London: Sweet & Maxwell.

Bullock, C. (1913) *Mashona laws and customs*. Salisbury: Argus Publishers.

Chanock, M. (1978) 'Neo-traditionalism and customary law in Malawi'. African Studies. Vol. 16, pp. 80-91.

Chanock, M. (1982) 'Making customary law: men, women and courts in colonial Northern Rhodesia'. In Hay, M. and Wright, M. (eds.) *African women and law: historical perspectives,* pp. 53-67. Boston: Boston University, Papers on Africa, V11.

Chanock, M. (1985) *Law, custom and social order: The colonial experience in Malawi and Zambia.* Cambridge: Cambridge University Press.

Church, J. (ed.) (1993) *The future of indigenous law in Southern Africa.* Pretoria: University of South Africa.

Cohen, D. W. (1991) 'A case for the Basoga: Lloyd Fallers and the construction of an African legal system'. In Mann, K. and Roberts, R. (ed.) *Law in colonial Africa.* Portsmouth: Heinemann, pp. 239-254.

Cory, H. (1953) *Sukuma law and custom.* London: Oxford University Press for the International African Institute.

Cory, H. and Hartnoll, M. M. (1945) *Customary law of the Haya tribe, Tanganyika territory.* London: Percy Lund, Humphries, for the International African Institute.

Cotran, E. and Rubin, N. N. (1970) *Readings in African law.* New York: Africana Publishing Co.

Coxhead, J. C. C. (1914) 'The native tribes of Northern Rhodesia: Their laws and customs'. Royal Anthropological Institute. Occasional Paper, No. 5.

Critchley, S. (1995) 'Black Socrates? Questionning the philosophical tradition'. Radical Philosophy Jan/Feb 1995. pp. 17-26.

Cunnison, I. G. (1954) 'A note on the Luanda concept of custom'. Human Problems No. 14, pp. 20-29.

Dannert, E. (1905) *Zum rechte der Herero.* Dissertation (law) Erlangen. Giessen: v. Muchowsche Hof-und Universitäts-Druckerei.

Danquah, J. B. (1928) *Gold Coast: Akan laws and customs and the Akim Abuakwa constitution.* London: G. Routledge and Sons.

Deng, F. M. (1972) *The Dinka of the Sudan.* New York: Holt, Rinehart and Winston.

Douglas, M. (1963) *The Lele of the Kasai.* London: Oxford University Press for the International African Institute.

Driberg, J. H. (1928) 'Primitive law in East Africa'. Africa. Vol. 1, pp. 63-72.

Driberg, J. H. (1934) 'The African conception of law'. Journal of Comparative Legislation and International Law. Vol. 16, pp. 230-245.

Duncan, P. (1960) *Sotho laws and customs.* Cape Town: Oxford University Press.

Dundas, C. (1915) 'The organisation and laws of some Bantu tribes in East Africa'. Journal of the Royal Anthropological Institute. Vol. 45. pp. 234-306.

Dundas, C. (1921) 'Native laws of some Bantu tribes of East Africa'. Journal of the Royal Anthropological Institute. Vol. 51, pp. 217-278.

Ebo, C. (1979) Indigenous law and justice: Some major concepts and practices'. Vieteljahresberichte. No. 76, pp. 139-150.

Edel, M. M. (1969) *The Chiga of Western Uganda*. London: Dawson's of Pall Mall.

Ekow-Daniels, W. C. (1964a) 'The interaction of English law with customary law in West Africa'. International and Comparative Law Quarterly. No. 13, pp. 574-616.

Ekow-Daniels, W. C. (1964b) *The common law in West Africa*. London: Butterworths.

Elias, T. O. (1954a) *Groundwork of Nigerian law*. London: Routledge and Kegan Paul.

Elias, T. O. (1954b) 'Customary law: The limit of its validity in colonial law'. African Studies. Vol. 13, Nos. 3 & 4, pp. 97-107.

Elias, T. O. (1956) *The nature of African customary law*. Manchester: Manchester University Press.

Elias, T. O., Nwabara, S. N. and Akpamgbo, C. O. (eds.) (1975) *African indigenous law*. Enugu: Government Printer for the Institute of African Studies, University of Nigeria, Nsukka.

Evans-Pritchard, E. E. (1940) *The Nuer: A description of the modes of livelihood and political institutions of a Nilotic people*. Oxford: Clarendon Press.

Ezomo, J. U. (1967) 'Validity of customary laws in Nigeria'. The Lawyer. Vol. 2, pp. 13-15.

Falaye, F. O. A. (1988) Judicial development of customary law in Nigeria'. Journal of Legal History. No. 9, pp. 40-49.

Fallers, L. A. (1962) 'Customary law in the new African states'. Law and Contemporary Problems. Vol. 27, No. 4, pp. 605-631.

Fenton, J. S. (1948) *Outline of native law in Sierra leone*. Freetown: Government Printer.

Field, M. J. (1940) *Social organisation of the Ga people*. London: Crown Agents for the Colonies.

Fitzpatrick, P. (1984) 'Traditionalism and traditional law'. Journal of African Law. Vol. 28, Nos. 1 & 2, pp. 20-27.

Fleming, C. J. W. (1971) 'The nature of African customary law in Central Africa'. NADA. Vol. 10, No. 4, pp. 93-102.

Forde, D. (1964) *Yakö studies*. Oxford: Oxford University Press.

Gibson, G. D., Larson, T. J. and McGurk, C. R. (1981) *The Kavango peoples*. Wiesbaden: Steiner.

Gluckman, M. (1962) 'African jurisprudence'. The Advancement of Science. Vol. 18, pp. 439-454.

Gluckman, M. (1974) *African traditional law in historical perspective*. London: Oxford University Press for the British Academy.

Gluckman, M. (ed.) (1969) *Ideas and procedures in African customary law*. London: Oxford University Press for the International African Institute.

Goldin, B. and Gelfand, M. (1975) *African law and custom in Rhodesia*. Cape Town: Juta & Co Ltd.

Gonidec, P. F. (1968) *Les droits Africains*. Paris: LGDJ.

Goodman, G. R. (1987) 'Aboriginal peoples and the law of Anglophone West Africa'. (excluding Liberia) Anthropology and Law. No. 2, pp. 313-334.

Gordon, J. (1967) 'African law and the historian'. (Review article) Journal of African History. Vol. 8, No. 2, pp. 335-340.

Gordon, R. J. (1989) 'The white man's burden: Ersatz customary law and the internal pacification in South Africa'. Journal of Historical Sociology. No. 2, pp. 41-65.

Gutmann, B. (1926) *Das rechsleben der wadschagga*. Munich:

Gutmann, B. (1935) 'The African standpoint'. Africa. Vol. 8, pp. 1-17.

Hahn, C. H. L., Vedder, H. and Fourie, L. (1928) *The native tribes of South West Africa*. Cape Town: Cape Times Ltd.

Hahn, T. (1883) *Report and proceedings with appendices of the Government Commission on Native Laws and Customs*. (On Nama customary law) Cape Town: Cape Times Ltd.

Hamilton, R. W. (1910) 'East African laws and customs'. Journal of the Society of Comparative Legislation. Vol. 11, pp. 181-195.

Hamilton, R. W. (ed.) (1906) 'Some notes on native laws and customs'. East Africa Protectorate Law Reports. Vol. 1, pp. 97-111; Vol. 2, (1909) pp. 141-148; Vol. 3, (1911) pp. 117-122.

Hamnett, I. (1971) 'Some notes on the concept of custom in Lesotho'. Journal of African Law. No. 15, No. pp. 266-273.

Harries, C. L. (1929) *The laws and customs of the Bapedi and cognate tribes of the Transvaal*. Johannesburg: Hortors.

Haydon, E. S. (1960) *Law and justice in Buganda*. London: Butterworth.

Himsworth, C. M. G. (1972) 'The Botswana Customary Law Act 1969'. Journal of African Law. Vol. 16, No. 1, pp. 4-18.

Hoebel, E. A. (1954) *The law of primitive man: A study in comparative legal dynamics*. Cambridge, Mass: Harvard University Press.

Hoebel, E. A. (1961) 'Three studies in African law'. Stanford University Law Review. Vol. 13, pp. 418-442.

Hoernlé, A. W. (1925) 'The social organization of the Nama Hottentots of South West Africa'. The American Anthropologist. Vol. 27, pp. 1-24.

Hoffman, C. (1934) Sotho-texte aus dem Holzbuschgebirge in Transvaal-Aufgezeichnet von mehreren Basutho missions-gehilfen, übersetzt von Missionar C. Hoffman Rechtsgebräuchte der Basutho. Zeitschrift für eingeborenensprachen, Vol. 24, No. 1, pp. 58-76; Vol. 24, No. 2, pp. 122-150; Vol. 24, No. 3, pp. 201-230; Vol. 24, No. 4, pp. 283-303.

Holleman, J. F. (1949) 'An anthropological approach to Bantu law: With special reference to Shona law'. Rhodes-Livingstone Journal. Vol. 10, pp. 51-64.

Holleman, J. F. (1952) *Shona customary law*. London: Oxford University Press for the Rhodes-Livingstone Institute and the Beit Trust.

Holleman, J. F. (1974) *Issues in African law*. The Hague: Mouton for the Afrika-Studiecentrum, Leiden.

Howell, P. P. (1954) *A manual of Nuer law: Being an account of customary law, its evolution and development in the courts established by the Sudan Government*. Oxford: Oxford University Press.

Josselin de Jong, J. P. B. (1948) 'Customary law: A confusing fiction'. Mededelingen van de koninklijke Vereeniging Indisch Instituut 80. 3.

Khumalo, J. A. M. (1977) *Customary law of Botswana*. Cape Town: Juta.

Kohler, J. (1900) 'Rechte der deutschen Schutzgebiete. 1. Das recht der Herero'. Zeitschrift für Vergleichende Rechtswis Senschaft. Vol. 14, pp. 294-319.

Kohler, J. (1902) 'Rechte der deutschen Schutzgebiet. V1. Das Recht der Hottentotten'. Zeitschrift für Vergleichende Rechtswissenschaft. Vol. 15, pp. 337-360.

Kuper, A. (1988) *The invention of primitive society: Transformation of an illlusion*. London: Routledge.

Kuper, H. and Kuper, L. (eds.) (1965) *African Law: Adaptation and development*. Berkeley: University of California Press.

Lambert, H. E. (1956) *Kikuyu social and political insitution*. London: Oxford University Press for the International African Institute.

Le Roy, E. (1979) 'African traditional law and modernity'. Revue Monchanin. Vol. 12, No. 4, pp. 35-43.

Leakey, L. S. B. (1977) *The Southern Kikuyu before 1903*. London: Academic Press.

Leslie, R. D. (1977) 'The repugnancy rule in African law and the public policy rule in conflict of laws'. Acta Juridica. pp. 117-127.

Lewin, J. (1940) 'Native law and its background: The limits of tribal law in modern Bantu life'. Race Relations Journal. Vol. 7, pp. 42-48.

Lewin, J. (1941) 'The conflict of native law and common law in South Africa'. The South African Law Journal. No. 58, pp. 365-374.

Lewin, J. (1944) *An outline of native law*. Johannesburg: R. L. Esson.

Lewin, J. (1947) *Studies in African native law*. Cape Town: The African Bookman.

Loeb, E. M. (1950) 'The Kuanyama Ambo'. Scientific American. Vol. 183, pp. 52-55.

Makec, J. W. (1988) *The customary law of the Dinka people of Sudan: In comparison with aspects of Western and Islamic laws*. London: Afroworld.

May, J. (1983) *Zimbawean women in customary and colonial law*. Edinburgh: Holmes McDougall.

Medeiros, C. L. (1984) 'Kwandu law: The evolution of a juridical system among an Herero people of South West Angola'. Journal of African Law. Vol. 28, Nos. 1 & 2, pp. 80-89.

Mittlebeder, E. V. (1976) *African custom and western law*. New York: Africana Publishing Co.

Moore, S. F. (1986) *Social facts and fabrications 'Customary ' law on Kilimanjaro 1880-1990*. Cambridge: Cambridge University Press.

Morrison, D. L. (1967) 'Soviet work on African law: Some initial steps'. Mizan. Vol. 9. No. 6, pp. 245-251.

Morrison, D. L. (1968) 'Soviet views on African law'. Mizan. Vol. 10. No. 1. pp. 23-28.

Nadel, S. F. (1947) *The Nuba*. London: Oxford University Press.

Ncube, W. (1991) 'Dealing with inequalities in customary law: Action, reaction and social change in Zimbabwe'. International Journal of Law and the Family. Vol. 5, No. 1, pp. 58-79.

Ndulo, M. (1981) Ascertainment of customary law: Problems and perspectives with special reference to Zambia. African Social Research. No. 31. pp. 67-76.

Nekam, A. (1966) *Experiences in African customary law*. Edinburgh: Centre of African Studies.

Nekam, A. (1967) 'Aspects of African customary law'. Northwestern University Law Review. No. 62, pp. 45-56.

O'Sullivan, T. H. (1910) 'Dinka laws and customs'. Journal of the Royal Anthropological Institute. Vol. 40, pp. 171-191.

Obi, S. N. C. (1977) *The customary law manual: A manual of customary law obtaining in the Anambra and Imo States of Nigeria*. Enugu: Government Printer.

Ogwurike, C. (1966) 'The source and authority of African customary law'. University of Ghana Law Journal. Vol. 3, pp. 11-20.

Ojo, A. O. (1969) 'Judicial approach to customary law'. Journal of Islamic and Comparative Law. Vol. 3, pp. 44-53.

Ojwang, J. B. (1989) 'The meaning, content and significance of tribal law in an emergent nation: The Kenyan case'. Law & Anthropology. Vol. 4, pp. 125-140.

Okojie, C. G. (1960) *Ishan native laws and customs*. Yaba, Nigeria: John Okwesa.

Olawoye, C. O. (1970)) 'Customary law and the repugnancy provision'. The Lawyer. Vol. 4, No. 1, pp. 6-25.

Olawoye, C. O. (1971) 'Establishing customary law. *Akande* v *Akorede*'. The Nigerian Journal of Contemporary Law. Vol. 2, No. 2, pp. 260-272.

Oluyede, P. A. (1968) 'Judicial approach to customary law'. Nigeria Lawyers' Quarterly. Vol. 3, Nos. 1 & 2, pp. 11-21.

Penwill, D. J. (1951) Kamba customary law: Notes taken in the Machakos district of Kenya Colony. London: Macmillan.

Peristiany, J. G. (1949) *La vie et le droit coutimier des Kipsigis du Kenya*. Paris.

Phillips, A. (1955) 'The future of customary law in Africa'. Journal of African Administration. Vol. 7, pp. 151-159.

Pogucki, R. J. H. (1956) 'Customary law of a society in transition'. Universitas. Vol. 2, No. 4, pp. 119-121.

Poulter, S. M. (1986) *English law and ethnic minority customs*. London: Butterworth & Co. Ltd.

Poulter, S. M. (1987) 'Ethnic minority customs, English law and human rights'. International and Comparative Law Quarterly. Vol. 36, pp. 589-615.

Prinsloo, M. W. (1987) 'Restatement of indigenous law'. The Comparative and International Law Journal of Southern Africa. No. 20, pp. 411-420.

Rattray, R. S. (1929) *Ashanti law and constitution*. London: Oxford University Press.

Roberts, S. (1984) 'Some notes on African customary law'. Journal of African Law. Vol. 28, Nos. 1 & 2, pp. 1-5.

Roberts, S. (1985) 'The Tswana polity and Tswana law and custom reconsidered'. Journal of Southern African Studies. pp. 75-87.

Rohrbach, P. (1918) *Deutsche Kolonialwirtschaft: Südwest-Africa*. Berlin: Schöneberg.

Roscoe, J. (1911) *The Baganda: An account of their native customs and beliefs*. London: Frank Cass & sons.

Rowlands, J. S. S. (1962) 'Notes on native law and custom in Kenya'. Journal of African Law. Vol. 6, No. 3, pp. 192-209.

Russell, F. F. (1959) 'Eritrean customary law'. Journal of African Law. Vol. 3, pp. 99-104.

Rwezaura, B. (1995) 'From native law and custom to customary law: The changing political issue of customary law in modern Africa'. In Aleck, J. and Rannells, J. (eds.) *Custom at the crossroads*. Waigani: Faculty of Law, University of Papua New Guinea.

Sanders, A. J. G. M. (1987) 'How customary is African customary law'? Comparative and International Law Journal of Southern Africa. pp. 405-410.

Sanders, A. J. G. M. (1993) 'The Bushmen of Botswana: From desert dwellers to world citizens'. Internationales Jahrbuch für Rechtsanthropologie Vol. 4, pp. 107-122.

Sarbah, J. M. (1897) *Fanti customary laws*. London: William Clowes & Sons.

Schapera, I. (1930) *The Khoisan peoples of South Africa: Bushmen and Hottentots*. London: Routledge & Kegan Paul.

Schapera, I. (1938) *A handbook of Tswana law and customs*. London: Oxford University Press for the International African Institute.

Schiller, A. A. (1970) *African law*. South Hackensack, N. J: Rothman.

Seymour, S. M. (1953) *Native law in South Africa*. Cape Town: Juta.

Seymour, S. M. (1970) *Bantu law in South Africa*. Cape Town: Juta & Co.

Seymour, W. M. (1911) *Native law and custom: Being a compendium of the recognised native customs in force in the native territories of the colony of the Cape of Good Hope together with legislative amendments and reports of some of the more important decisions of the Native Appeal Court of Griqualand, Eas, 1901-1909*. Cape Town: Juta

Simons, H. J. (1938) 'The study of native law in South Africa'. Bantu Studies. Vol. 12, No. 3, pp. 237-242.

Snell, G. S. (1954) *Nandi customary law*. London: Macmillan.

Snyder, F. G. (1981) 'Colonialism and legal form: The creation of "customary law" in Senegal'. In Sumner, C. (ed.) *Crime, justice and underdevelopment*. London: Heinemann, pp. 90-121.

Stafford, W. G. (1935) *Native law as practised in Natal*. Johannesburg: Witwatersrand University Press.

Stopford, J. G. F. (1901) 'Glimpses of native law in West Africa'. Journal of the African Society. Vol. 1, pp. 80-97.

Sutter, R. (1984) 'The social and ideological function of African customary law in South Africa'. Social Dynamics. No. 11, pp. 49-64.

Tate, H. R. (1910) 'The native law of the Southern Gikuyu of British East Africa. Journal of the Royal African Society. Vol. 9, pp. 233-254.

Tupper, L. (1907) 'Customary and other law in the East Africa protectorate'. Journal of Comparative Legislation. Vol. 8, pp. 172-184.

Turner, V. W. (1957) *Schism and continuity in an African society: A study of Ndembu village life.* Manchester: Manchester University Press.

Twining, W. L. (1963) 'The restatement of African customary law: A comment'. The Journal of Modern African Studies. Vol. 1. pp. 221-228.

Twining, W. L. (1964) *The place of customary law in the national legal systems of East Africa.* Chicago: University of Chicago Press.

Vedder, H., Fourie, L. and Hahn, C. H. L. (1966) *The native tribes of South West Africa.* London: Frank Cass.

Verhelst, T. (1968) *Safeguarding African customary law: Judicial and legislative processes for its adaptation and integration.* Los Angeles: African Studies Centre. UCLA.

Webster, S. (1982) 'Dialogue and fiction in Ethnography'. Dialectical Anthropology. No. 7, pp. 91-114.

White, C. M. N. (1965) 'African customary law: The problem of concept and definition'. Journal of African Law. Vol. 9, No. 2, pp. 86-89.

Whitfield, G. M. B. (1948) *South African native law.* Cape Town: Juta & Co. Ltd..

Williams, D. (1986) 'The recognition of "native custom" in Tanganyika and New Zealand: Legal pluralism or monocultural imposition'. In Sack, P. and Minchin, E. (eds.) *Legal pluralism: Proceedings of the Canberra Law Workshop, V11.* Canberra Law Department, Research School of Social Sciences, Australia National University, pp. 139-154.

Wilson, G. (1937) 'Introduction to Nya Kyusa law'. Africa. Vol. 10, pp. 16-36.

Wilson, G. (1961) *Luo customary law and marriage law customs.* Nairobi: Government Printer.

Winter, C. J. (1990) 'The function of customary law in Iringa district of Tanzania: Its development until independence'. In Abun-Nasr et al. (eds) *Law, Society and national identity in Africa.* Buske Verlag.

Woodman, G. R. (1969) 'Some reaslism about customary law: The West African experience'. Wisconsin Law Review. pp. 128-152.

Woodman, G. R. (1977) 'Judicial development of customary law in Ghana and Nigeria'. University of Ghana Law Journal. Vol. 14, No. 2, pp. 115-136.

Woodman, G. R. (1987) 'Aboriginal peoples and the law of Anglophone West Africa'. (excl. Liberia) Law & Anthropology. Vol. 2, pp. 313-334.

Woodman, G. R. (1989) 'The peculiar policy of recognition of indigenous laws in British colonial Africa: A preliminary discussion'. Verfassung und Recht in Übersee. Vol. 22, pp. 273-284.

Chapter 9 — Dispute settlement and court procedure

Indigenous institutions evolved over a long period, in response to the life style, needs and choices made by the community. It is a myth that anarchy reigned in pre-colonial Africa. Many people in rural societies did not dissipate their energy and man-power in war, as they had to battle every day with their often harsh physical environment.

They have devised ways of settling disputes among themselves and between neighbouring ethnic groups. The legal institution of mediation, conciliation and child law may be the basis of indigenous law cultural conservatism. But these institutions were formulated to make peaceful co-existence and survival easy for everybody, men, women and children.

The effects of the local courts are examined without any reference to the state law, because people who only comprehend the indigenous legal system carefully avoid the formal state adjudication, mainly because of its expensive endless delay, rigorous system of imprisonment, and lack of restitution.

9.1 Thank God, I am a pagan

In order to understand the procedures in the local courts, it is essential to refer briefly to the religious beliefs and observances that serve the community which generate indigenous law. Among the *ovaHimba*, the sacred fire, *okuruuo* is a medium used by the eldest male of the patriclan for two-way communication between the ancestors and their living descendants. Their ancestors interceded for them with *Mukuru*, the Supreme Deity who created the earth. The *ovaHimba* are not sure if *Mukuru* was ever an *oruzo* man.

The leadership of the *okuruuo*, as in all the dominant religions in the world, Christianity, Confucianism, Hinduism, Islam, Judaism and Zoroastrianism, is dominated by men. Among the duolineal *Himba*, the eldest men in the *otuzo* became the keepers of the sacred fire, and the most senior wife of these men looks after the embers of the sacred flame. It was one of her duties to keep the fire smouldering every day. Any hint of rain, and it was promptly moved indoors. I did not observe any sacrifices to ancestors at the *okuruuo*, and I did not see any idols or images. The people do not use relics of dead ancestors.

The *okuruuo* is only a shrine where the ancestors advise their descendant on their existential dilemma, as well as listening to such mundane news bulletins of what to do with barren cows, sick children, or the sister who has come to live amongst them and cannot even milk a cow.

The *Himba* believe that virtuous people become venerable ancestors when they have ceased to live but also achieve immortality. Their immortal ancestors continue to live on, because the living invoke the glorified dead for good luck, in sickness, in health, marriages, birth, circumcision, deaths and succession. In short, they continuously call on their ancestors to partake in their lives vicariously. All the good things in life flow from the ancestors. Even women give birth to children who grow up strong and tall by the will of the *vicarious dei*, the ancestors. One did not need a rational faith to believe in the ancestors, as they had existed. There is no apprehension of eternal damnation in their belief, because their ancestors would not condemn their descendants to such punishment. The *Himba* theory of punishment was that ancestors, judges and jurors should themselves be able to take the punishment that they dish out if the positions were reversed.

Since the matrilineal *Himba* are pastoralists, why should the sacred fire, *okuruuo* have such an important role, rather than the cattle? Is it not the fear of the distinctive power of fire that all human beings have? Their prompt reply was that "fire gave light, warmth and energy. Fire is the spiritual face of the ancestors". *Okuruuo*, as it was explained, was the authoritative foundation of the control of fire by the *Himba*.

One cannot talk directly to the ancestors without the intercession of the head of the *oruzo*. It is like talking to a tree. It is the inner self of the individual that talked to the ancestors, and the ancestors answered the inner self. The essence is that one only solicits for something good from the ancestors, something beneficial to the supplicant and the society. The ancestors have lived on earth and they know the problems of human beings.

Malan (1973:98-100) noted that each sacred fire derives its name from the last deceased *oruzo* keeper. It becomes "the fire of Kazongovi" or "the fire of Takumua" or "the fire of Karuvapa" or "the fire of Katiti".[14] Accordingly, many sages can recite a chronology of the deceased *oruzo* keepers of their *omaruuo*. This should be of interest to oral historians.

Just as the *Himba* have a double descent system of the *eanda* and the *oruzo*, they also believe that they have a body and a spirit; a left and right half of the body, a man and a woman in each of our bodies, but it is all a question of proportion, apart from the genitalia. The good spirit is liberated when the body dies and becomes an ancestral spirit. They accept that since all human beings have to die, the *okuruuo* should be available for human beings to enable them to communicate with deceased ancestors. Consultation eases the crushing finality of death.

9.2 The local courts

As far as most of the sages can remember, matrilineal indigenous law did not have *lex talionis*: the law of retaliation, whereby the victim, or the victim's agnates gave the offender as badly as he or she gave the victim. They have always had *eanda* courts, *oruzo* courts, the deputy headman's court, the headman's and the *Omuhona* or chief's court of last resort. Most rural people have not the slightest intention of swapping their justice for the 'formal law' model with prisons.

Family complaints against a particular person, property or reputation start first in the *eanda* court consisting of the *eanda* males. Family matters of divorce and of probate are also initiated in this forum. The family court is also a children's court of hearing, for the recognition of their property rights against their maternal uncles. Furthermore, the *eanda* court is also a sort of civil and criminal injuries compensation board, if an *eanda* member has to pay a high tariff in the higher court.

As the *eanda* family court, too, needs protection against the *oruzo* court and the higher courts, like any good parent, the *eanda* family court, as court of first instance, tries to talk sense into the parties. Women are permitted to testify in the *eanda* family court; in particular, they must have their say in the dissolution of their marriage or in sororate or levirate marriage. The *eanda* court knows that the law

---

[14] Malan, J. S. (1973) 'Double descent among the Himba of South West Africa. Cimbebasia Vol. 2, No. 3, pp. 82-104.

of adultery is weighed in the husband's favour, and that divorce is easier for husbands than for their wives. After all, it was the senior men, the stronger parties in child betrothal and marriage negotiations who formulated indigenous law of divorce, adultery and polygyny to suit themselves. Thus, if the mediatory *eanda* court is unable to reach a solution, or one of the parties refuses to accept the *eanda* mediation, then the *oruzo* court attempts conciliation.

The *oruzo* court that hears appeals from the *eanda* court also has authority over its members for the sake of the good of the community. The *oruzo* acts as the ombudsmen for children in the matrilineage, because the court recognises that some children may need protection from their maternal uncles and from their parents. See chapter 4. In addition, the *oruzo* court hears complaints from children and their maternal uncles against fathers who did not provide *ozohakera* for their children. The final attempt to reconcile a husband and wife is made under the authority of the *oruzo* court. Cases of master and servant relationship, that is, when outsiders, from other ethnic groups are employed to work in the *onganda*, are also heard by the *oruzo*. The *oruzo* court has power to restrain men from inflicting gratuitous pain on women and children and to punish men who violate the moral law. If the parties are not satisfied with the mediation, they can appeal to the Headman's court or to the King or Chief's councillors and finally to the King's court for adjudication.

Everyone has access to the court, but a litigant needs cattle resources to pay the compensatory tariff, and there are restrictions on the use of family property for litigation. *Eanda* cattle and family property are the equivalent of legal aid. The plaintiff or defendant supplies the animals that will be slaughtered and cooked for meals while the court is sitting. If the accused or defendant should lose the case, the defendant or his *eanda* will pay the compensatory fine as well as the contribution made by the plaintiff.

Appealing to the impartial court of the King, Omuhona or Chief is not denied to men, women and adolescents, the accused, the innocent and the guilty: all must be given the right to have their say. They have a right to a fair trial before the community, especially if they have been accused of causing death by witchcraft or with murder. See chapter 4.

9.3 Justice of old age

In pre-colonial Omuhona's court, the job of convening the court was allocated to appointed young men who act as community justices of the peace. Jobs are allocated to men, women and children according to their abilities. The young married and unmarried men are the energetic group who roam far and wide in search of pasture, and they put the cattle capital to good use. Elderly men and women who have worked very hard all their lives are left to their own devices; some produced household materials and they are helped along by pregnant women and women with toddlers. The middle-aged men with experience of human beings who can decide 'hard cases' act as judges, jurors, peace makers as well as upholders of the institutions. The 'justice of old age' as they put it, is that the old see human nature for what it is, much more clearly than energetic young people pre-occupied with work. When these supermen are not sitting as judges and jurors, they are also the ombudsmen for children, as well as having responsibility for the welfare of their citizens. Everyone shares in the benefits produced by everybody.

When the court is summoned to sit, there could be as many as twenty to thirty men. The composition of the pre-colonial final court of appeal is mainly keepers of the sacred fire, councillors, district heads and the King, Chief or *Omuhona* and their deputies. To sublimate blatant grab for power by one faction, as most families are polygynous, they entered into a form of social contract. This agreement was that only the eldest male from a village would be eligible for office.

These supermen are the judges and jurors because they are learned in the indigenous law. They know the community, as well as being in a secure position to investigate the offence and evaluate the evidence. Since the judges and jurors have local knowledge, they also know the consequences of their verdict.

The case is conducted by the presiding judge, but all the other men act as jurors and judges in the conduct of the trial, to prevent the abuse of power. Usually the *Omuhona* or the deputy presides in court, but if one of them has an interest in the case he cannot preside. The jurors and judges with an interest in the case cannot speak, but they can hear evidence. Most people know which jurors and judges have an interest. The remaining judges and jurors are impartial and independent of the silent brothers. After hearing, the presiding judge gives his opinion, and the jurors, too, give their opinions.

9.4 Mediation without prison

The judges and jurors hear civil and criminal cases in the same court. On the appointed day, the trial judges and jurors sit in a circle under the shade of the nearest *acacia tortilis*. Some ethnic groups have what they called 'palava house' that is, a court. The presence of the public is represented by men, women and children who attend the court to see how the moral norms are reinforced. Public opinion clearly matters in the enforcement of justice in the *Omuhona's* court.

In some communities, women cannot testify. It is not because women are inferior, it is the indigenous law's basic form of holding together the foundation of *eanda* loyalty, thus they protect the institution of motherhood against the needs of the or*uzo*. Women's interests and those of children are represented by the senior male in the *oruzo*. If the woman plaintiff or defendant is married, her husband will act as surrogate, and if the child defendant has reached the age of eight or nine years, his or her *eanda* will appoint the senior maternal uncle as representative.

There is no judicial oath among the *Himba*. A man is liable for what he says before the assembled men. If what he says is *mala fide*, he would have prolonged the proceedings unnecessarily and he will be fined accordingly. As there is freedom of examination by all the jurors and judges, most people know that mendacious suitors will be caught out. The plaintiff, the defendant or the accused are their own advocate, they cannot get a relative to represent their interest, but a litigant who is mentally ill is represented by a member of her or his *eanda*. They can call as many witnesses as are willing to come forward and testify on their behalf.

There are no stands. The plaintiff sits in the centre of the circle facing the presiding judge. When one party is giving evidence, the other party is about a quarter of a mile away from the court. The plaintiff will not hear the defendant's evidence or the jeering and neither will the defendant's evidence be heard by the plaintiff. The jurors then investigate the case and the best evidence adduced to prove it. The court deals with the problems of reliability of evidence by admitting hearsay evidence as well as adducing evidence from the circumstances of each case. In open court, the jurors and judges extract the evidence by questioning the defendant and the plaintiff, then balance the testimony of their various witnesses. There is no bullying, only quiet interrogation by the judges and jurors; it is all about mercy and equilibrium in the community. All procedures in court are oral.

The judges and jurors do not retire. They deliberate in open court and the public listen to the arguments. Then they debate on the amount of compensation meted out to so and so earlier, in an identical case, and how they arrived at the conclusion. The parties and their witnesses are only brought face to face when the judges and jurors give their opinions. Among the *Himba*, after the presiding judge has explained the decision of the court, an *oruzo* counsellor or two will be appointed to help the young first-offender with rehabilitation. The offender will express his regret to the court, promise not to do further damage to his community, and will arrange the necessary reparation to the victim or his *eanda*. In other communities, it is after a fair trial that the poison ordeal is administered by the court.

Among the *Himba*, the person convicted of the wrong-doing and his *eanda* is given time to get the required number of cattle together for collection by the head of the victim's *eanda*. For, apart from the goats and sheep for domestic consumption, very few pastoralists have their herd of cattle in one place; the animals are usually bailed out to various relatives. Sometimes, the offender may pay the fine in two instalments and the victim's *eanda* is told when the cattle can be collected.

There is no incarceration, only compensatory fines are issued which will stun the offender and his *eanda*. As they explained to me, people who eat and share meat together do not hang another human being. An offender deserves to be punished, but not tortured, imprisoned or killed. No one deserves death for killing another person. As they pointed out, a just society is known by the sentences meted out against its members. The human life is more valuable than cattle. The ratio of the reasoning of the judges and jurors will be spread far and wide to the absent members, and that is how indigenous law formulated and disseminated its principles.

9.5 Case notes and adjudication

The facts were blurred because nobody was an eye witness when the incident occurred that led to the death of a child. The deceased, a girl of about ten, eleven or twelve, and a boy of about the same age, were playing outside the *onganda*, when they should have been helping with the goats and sheep inside the *onganda*.

The young girl had been visiting her paternal grandfather. It was said that the boy sometimes teased the girl mercilessly, but on that particular day he went too far. The girl went for him, and in the struggle she fell. When people heard her scream in pain, the paternal grandfather rushed to separate the two children. The girl was lying on her back, and there was no bleeding from any wound, so there was no direct evidence of the cause of death. However, some of the witnesses said that they had seen the old man holding the girl by the neck, and that it was the act of grabbing her by the neck that had killed the child. As there are no post-mortem examinations in the *ozonganda*, the cause of death could not be ascertained.

However, the girl's *eanda* wanted redress for the killing of their 'quiet' little girl who was betrothed to be married when she reached puberty. The boy's *eanda* said that the girl must have done something to their little lamb who was normally a very kind and shy boy. But circumstantial evidence was adduced that he was a teaser. The evidence of teasing the girl some while back should not be admitted, argued the boy's maternal uncles, because the girl brought the accident on herself. Some of the jurors argued that it was admissible. So, how could the boy's *eanda* explain what made the little girl have a go at the boy?

The child died, but her injury was not intentional. The old man gave evidence in his defence, and showed his hands to members of the jurors and judges. "These old hands could not have killed the girl" he said. He had no motive to kill the little girl.

"Death is very hard for human beings, we are not animals", said the presiding judge. The girl was alive on the ground and the old man had his hands around her neck. Two dissenting jurors said that based on the facts of the case, it was the boy who was the killer. The jurors and the judges did not have to prove the case 'beyond reasonable doubt'. The judges and the remaining jurors held that on the balance of probabilities it was the old man's intervention that had killed the girl. After several days sitting, the judges and the jurors found that the old man could not prove his case. The boy and the old man were jointly guilty of manslaughter and were fined forty head of cattle. The joint compensatory fine was fixed at forty head of cattle because the deceased had not reached child bearing age.

9.6 Bibliography

African Conference on Local Courts and Customary Law. *Record of the proceedings of the conference held in Dar es Salaam, Tanganyika* 8-18 September 1963. Geneva: H. Studer SA.

African Studies Branch, Colonial Office (1949) 'Developments in the administration of customary law in Kenya'. Journal of African Administration Vol. 1, No, 2, pp. 86-88.

Amsterdam Conference 1955. *The future of customary law in Africa.* Afrika Institut, Studie Centrum.

Attorney-General, Tanganyika (1941) *Handbook on native courts for the guidance of administrative officers.* Dar Es -Salaam: Government printer.

Developments in the administration of customary law in Kenya. A note by the Colonial Office African Studies Branch (1949) 'Journal of African Administration. Vol. 1, No. 2, pp. 86-88.

London Conference 1960. *The future of Law in Africa.* Allott, A. N. (ed.) London: Butterworth & Co. Ltd.

Native courts and native customary law in Africa. Record of the Judicial Advisers Conference 1953, Kampala. London: Her Majesty's Stationery Office.

Report of Native tribunal committee of Enquiry, Gold Coast, 1943. Accra: Government Printer.

Report of the Gold Coast Commission on Native Courts. Government Gazette. 31 January 1895.

Supreme Court Ordinance, 1876.

Abdul-Jalil, M. A. C. (1985) 'From native courts to people's local courts: The politics of judicial administration in Sudan'. Verfassung und Recht in Übersee. No. 18, pp. 139-153.

Abel, R. L. (1979) 'Western courts in non-western settings: Patterns of court use in colonial and neo-colonial Africa'. In Burman, S.B. and Harrell-Bond, B. E. *The imposition of law*, pp. 167-200. New York, London: Academic Press.

Abel, R. (1974) 'A comparative theory of dispute institutions in Society'. Law and Society Review. No. 8, No. 2, pp. 217-347.

Abel, R. (1980) 'Theories of litigation in society'. Jahrbuch für Recht ssoziologie und Rechtstheorie. pp. 165-191.

Abel, R. (1982) *The politics of informal justice.* New York: Academic Press.

Abrahams, R. G. (1965) 'Neighbourhood organizations: A major sub-system among the Northern Nyamwezi'. Africa. Vol. 35, pp. 168-186.

Abrahams, R. G. (1987) 'Sungusungu: Village vigilante groups in Tanzania'. African Affairs. Vol. 86, pp. 179-190.

Achike, O. (1972) 'Abolition of the customary courts in Est Central State of Nigeria: Retrograde reform'. Nigeria Lawyers' Quarterly. Vol. 6, pp. 122-135.

Adewoye, O. (1977) *The judicial system in Southern Nigeria, 1854-1954: Law and justice in a dependency.* Atlantic Highlands, New Jersey: Humanities.

Adewoye, O. (1986) 'Legal practice in Ibadan 1904-1960'. Journal of Legal Pluralism. No. 24, pp. 57-76.

Agbosu, L. K. (183-86) 'Arbitration under the customary law'. Review of Ghana Law. Vol. 15, pp. 204-215.

Aguda, A. (1973) 'Legal development in Botswana: 1885-1966'. Botswana Notes and Records Vol. 5, pp. 52-63.

Ajibola, J. O. (1982) *Administration of justice in the customary courts of Yorubaland.* Ibadan: Ibadan University Press.

Akanki, O. (1970) 'Proof of customary law in Nigerian courts'. The Nigerian Law Journal. No. 4, pp. 20-36.

Akinjide, R. O. A. (1958) 'Some aspects of justice in our native courts'. The Nigerian Bar Journal. Vol. 1, pp. 16-17.

Akpamgbo, C. O. (1978) 'Customary courts Edict No. 3, 1978. (Anambra State) The customary courts resuscitated and revisited'. The Nigerian Bar Journal. Vol. 15, No. 2, pp. 105-113.

Akyempim, O. (1955?) *The native court and its function.* Kumasi: Adom Press.

Allott, A. N. (1949) 'Native land courts'. Journal of African Administration. Vol. 1, No. 2, pp. 82-86.

Allott, A. N. (1953) '*Kwasi* v *Larbi* (1953) A. C. 164, Akan customary law of 'arbitration' in the Gold Coast'. International & Comparative Law Quarterly. Vol. 2, pp. 466-476.

Allott, A. N. (1957a) 'Arbitral proceedings in customary law'. Journal of African Administration. Vol. 9, pp. 96-100.

Allott, A. N. (1957b) 'Native tribunals in the Gold Coast 1844-1927. Prolegomena to a study of native courts in Ghana'. Journal of African Law. Vol. 1 No. 3, pp. 163-171.

Allott, A. N. (1957c) 'The authority of English decisions in colonial courts'. Journal of African Law. Vol. 1, No. 1, pp. 23-39.

Allott, A. N. (1960) *Essays in African law with special reference to the law of Ghana.* London: Butterworth.

Allott, A. N. (1963) 'Evidence in African customary law'. In Gilissen, J. (ed.) *Recueils de la Societe Jean Bodin pour l'histoire comparative des institutions. La preuve*. Brussels. Vol. 18, pp. 59-80.

Allott, A. N. (1969a) *Local and customary courts in the former British territories in Africa.* In Gilissen, J. (ed.) *Etudes sur l'Organisation judiciaire en Afrique noire.* Bruxelles: Centre d'histoires et ethnologie juridiques. Bruxelles Universite Libre.

Allott, A. N. (1969b) 'Legal personality in African law'. In Gluckman, M. (ed.) *Ideas and procedures in African law*, pp. 179-195. London: Oxford University Press. For the International African Institute.

Allott, A. N. (ed.) (1962) *Judicial and legal systems in Africa.* London: Butterworth & Co. Ltd.

Allott, A. N. (ed.) (1970) *Judicial and legal systems in Africa.* London: Butterworth & Co. Ltd.

Arnott, D. W. (1958) 'Councils and courts among the Tiv: Traditional concepts and allien institutions in a non-moslem tribe of Northern Nigeria'. Journal of African Law Vol. 2, No. 1, pp. 19-25.

Aubert, V. (1969) 'Law as a way of resolving conflict'. In Nader, L. (ed.) *Law in culture and society.* Chicago: Aldine Press.

Auerbach, J. (1983) *Justice without law? Resolving disputes without lawyers.* New York: Oxford University Press.

Barkum, M. (1968) *Law without sanctions: Order in primitive societies and the world community.* New Haven: Yale University Press.

Barnett, T. E. (1965) A report on local courts in East Africa. Port Moresby.

Beattie, J. H. M. A. (1957) 'Informal judicial activity in Bunyoro'. Journal of African Administration. Vol. 9, No. 4, pp. 188-195.

Behrman, P. (1948) 'Native appeal courts'. South African Law Journal. No. 65, pp. 413-418.

Beidelman, T. O. (1961) 'Kaguru justice and the concept of legal fictions'. Journal of African Law. Vol. 5, No. 1, pp. 5-20.

Beidelman, T. O. (1966) 'Inter-tribal tensions in some Local Government courts in colonial Tanganyika'. Journal of African Law. Vol. 10, pp. 118-130.

Benda-Beckmann, F. von (1981) 'Some comments on the problems of comparing the relationship between traditional and state systems of administration of justice in Africa and Indonesia'. Journal of Legal Pluralism. Vol. 19, pp. 165-175.

Benda-Beckmann, F. von (1985) 'Some comparative generalizations about the differential use of state and folk institutions of dispute settlement'. In Allott, A. N. and Woodman, G. R. (eds.) *People's law and state law.* The Bellagio Papers. Dordrecht: Foris Publications, pp. 187-205.

Benda-Beckmann, F. von (1985) 'Some comparative generalisations about the differential use of state and folk institutions in dispute settlement'. In Allott, A. N. and Woodman, G. R. (eds.) *People's law and state law: The Bellagio papers.* Dordrecht: Foris Publications, pp. 171-187.

Benda-Beckmann, K. von (1984) *The broken stairways to consensus: Village justice and courts in Manikabau.* Dordrecht: Foris Publications.

Bennett, T. W. (1975) 'The African court system in Rhodesia: An appraisal'. The Rhodesian Law Journal Vol. 15 Pt. 2, pp. 133-151.

Bohannan, P. (1957) *Justice and judgement among the Tiv.* Oxford: Oxford University Press for the International African Institute.

Bohannan, P. (ed.) (1967) *Law and warfare: Studies in the anthropology of conflict'.* Garden City, NY: The Natural History Press.

Bomani, M. D. (1966) 'Machinery of justice in a developing society'. East African Journal. No. 3, pp. 19-22.

Bourdillon, M. F. C. (1974) 'A note on Shona court procedures'. NADA Vol. X1, No. 1, pp. 11-14.

Bradley, K. (1942) *Native courts and authorities in Northern Rhodesia.* Ndola: African Literature Committee of Northern Rhodesia.

Brewer, I. G. (1973) 'A note on the Botswana customary courts (Amendment) Act 1972'. Comparative and International Law Journal of South Africa. No. 6, pp. 282-286.

Brooke, N. J. (1952) *Report of the Native Courts (Northern Provinces) Commission of Enquiry.* Lagos: Government Printer.

Brooke, N. J. (1954a) 'The changing character of customary courts'. Journal of African Administration No. 6, pp. 67-73.

Brooke, N. J. (1954b) 'Native courts in Sierra Leone'. Journal of African Administration. Vol. 6, pp. 185-193.

Cain, M. and Kulcsar, K. (1982) 'Thinking disputes: An essay on the origins of the dispute industry'. Law and Society Review. Vol. 16, pp. 373-402.

Cameron, D. C. (1930) *Native courts.* Dar es Salaam: Native Administration Department.

Canter, R. (1978) 'Dispute settlement and dispute processing in Zambia: Individual choice versus societal constraints'. In Nader, L and Todd, H. F. (eds.) *The disputing process: Law in ten societies.* New York: Columbia University Press.

Carson, J. B. (1958) Further notes on the African courts system in Kenya. Journal of African Administration Vol. 10, pp. 34-38.

Chamblis, W. J. and Seidman, R. B. (1982) *Law, order and power.* Reading, MA: Addison-Wesley Publishers.

Chanock, M. (1982) 'Making customary law: Men, women and courts in colonial Northern Rhodesia'. In Hay, M. and Wright, M. (eds.) *African women and the law: Historical perspectives.* Boston: Boston University Press.

Chanock, M. (1985) *Law, custom and social order: The colonial experience in Malawi and Zambia.* Cambridge: Cambridge University Press.

Coldham, S. (1990a) 'Customary law and Local Courts Act, 1990 of Zimbabwe'. Journal of African Law. Vol. 34, pp. 163-165.

Coldham, S. (1990b) 'Customary marriage and the urban local courts in Zambia'. Journal of African Law. Vol. 34, pp. 67-75.

Colson, E. (1976) 'From chief's court to local court: The evolution of local courts in Zambia'. Political Anthropology. Vol. 1, pp. 15-29.

Comaroff, J. L. and Roberts, S. (1981) *Rules and processes: The cultural logic of dispute in an African context.* Chicago: University of Chicago Press.

Comaroff, J. and Roberts, S. (1977) 'The invocation of norms in dispute settlement: The Tswana case'. In Hamnett, I. (ed.) *Social anthropology and law.* London: Academic Press, pp. 77-112.

Conley, J. M. and O'Barr, W. M. (1990) 'Rules versus relationships. The ethnography of legal thought'. Anthropology Today. Vol. 10, pp. 9-12.

Cotran, E. (1965a) 'African conference on local courts and customary law'. Journal of Local Administration, pp. 128-133.

Cotran, E. (1965b) 'Integration of courts and application of customary law in Tanganyika'. East African Law Journal. Vol. 1, pp. 108-123.

Cotran, E. (1968) 'Integration of courts and application of customary law in Kenya'. East African Law Journal. Vol. 4, pp. 14-20.

Cutshall, C. R. (1991) *Justice for the people: Community courts and legal transformation in Zimbabawe.* Harare: University of Zimbabwe Publications.

Davidson, V. G. and Barwick, D. R. (eds.) (1972) A manual concerning traditional courts in Malawi. Zomba.

Diamond, S. (1971) 'The rule of law versus the order of custom'. In Wolf, R. P. (ed.) *The rule of law.* New York: Simon and Schuster, pp. 115-144.

Doorly, A. N. (1946) 'Native tribunals'. Journal of Comparative Legislation and International Law. No. 28, pp. 25-34.

Ekineh, A. (1958) 'The customary courts'. Nigerian Bar Journal. Vol. 1, No. 3, pp. 31-34.

El nur, M. I. (1960) 'The role of the native courts in the administration of justice in the Sudan'. Sudan Notes. No. 41, pp. 78-87.

Elias, T. O. (1955) Colonial courts and the doctrine of judicial precedent. Modern Law Review. Vol. 18. pp. 356-370.

Elias, T. O. (1962) *British colonial law: A comparative study.* London: Stevens & Sons.

Elias, T. O. (1975) 'Judicial development of customary law in Nigeria'. In Elias, T. O., Nwabara, S. N. and Akpamgbo, C. O. (eds.) *African indigenous law*. Enugu: Government Printer. For the Institute of African Studies, University of Nigeria, Nsukka. pp. 145-174.

Elias, T. O. (1977) *The judicial process in Commonwealth Africa*. Legon: University of Ghana. FEP International Ltd.

Elias, T. O. (1990) *Judicial process in the newer Commonwealth*. Lagos: University of Lagos Press.

Ellickson, R. C. (1991) *Order without law: How neighbours settle disputes*. Cambridge Mass.: Harvard University Press.

Elombi, G. (1993) 'Customary arbitration: A Ghanaian trend reversed in Nigeria'. African Journal of International and Comparative Law. Vol. 5, pp. 803-824.

Epstein, A. L. (1954a) *The administration of justice and the urban African: A study of urban native courts in Northern Rhodesia*. London: Her Majesty's Stationery Office.

Epstein, A. L. (1954b) *Juridical techniques and the judicial process: A study in African customary law*. Rhodes-Livingstone Papers No. 23. Manchester: Manchester University Press.

Epstein, A. L. (ed.) (1974) 'Contention and dispute: Aspects of law and social control in Melanesia'. Canberra: Australian National University Press.

Fahey, R. P. (1971) The Poro as a system of judicial administration in Northwestern Liberia. African Law Studies. No. 4, pp. 1-25.

Fallers, L. A. (1969) *Law without precedent: Legal ideas in action in the courts of colonial Busoga*. Chicago: The University of Chicago Press.

Felstiner, W. L. F. (1974) 'Influences of social organisation on dispute processing'. Law and Society Review. Vol. 9, No. 1, pp. 63-94.

Felstiner, W. L. F., Abel, R. and Sarat, A. (1980-1981) 'The emergence and transformation of disputes: Naming, blaming and claiming'. Law and Society Review. Vol. 15, Nos. 3 & 4, pp. 631-654.

Fenton, J. S. (1948) *Outline of native law in Sierra Leone*. Freetown: Government Printers.

Findlay, M. and Zvekic, U. (eds.) (1993) *Alternative policing styles: Cross-cultural perspectives*. Deventer: Kluwer Publishers.

Forde, D. (1965) 'Justice and judgment among the Southern Ibo under colonial rule'. In Kuper, H. and Kuper, L. (eds.) *African law: Adaptation and development*. Berkeley: University of California Press.

Freeman, M. (ed.) (1995) *Alternative dispute resolution*. Aldershot: Dartmouth Publishing Co. Ltd.

Fundikira, Chief (1962) 'The reorganisation of courts in Tanganyika'. Journal of Local Administration Overseas, Vol. 1, No. 1, pp.257-258.

Gabasiane, V. (1988) 'Some common problems brought by women before the urban customary courts in Gaborone'. In Matlakala, D. (ed.) Women and the law in Botswana. The proceedings of a workshop. Gaborone: Ministry of Home Affairs.

Gallanter, M. (1981) 'Justice in many rooms: Courts, private ordering and indigenous law. Journal of Legal Pluralism Vol. 19, pp.1-47.

Geraghty, T. F. (1969) People, practice, attitudes and problems in the lower courts of Ethiopia. Journal of Ethiopian Law. No. 6. pp. 427-512.

Ghai, Y. (1991) 'The role of law in the transition of societies. The African experience'. Journal of African Law. Vol. 35, No. 1, pp. 8-20.

Gibbs, J. L. (1962) 'Poro values and courtroom procedures in a Kpelle chiefdom'. Southwestern Journal of Anthropology. Vol. 18, pp. 341-349.

Gibbs, J. L. (1963) 'The Kpelle moot: A therapeutic model for the informal settlement of disputes'. Africa. Vol. 33. pp. 1-11.

Gluckman, M. (1955) *The judicial process among the Barotse of Northern Rhodesia*. Manchester: Manchester University Press. For the Rhodes-Livingstone Institute.

Gluckman, M. (1956a) *Custom and conflict in Africa*. Oxford: Basil Blackwell.

Gluckman, M. (1956b) The reasonable man in Barotse law (5) The case of the disrespectful councillor'. Journal of African Administration. Vol. 8, pp. 151-156.

Gluckman, M. (1962) *Order and rebellion in tribal Africa: Collected essays.* London: Cohen and West.

Gluckman, M. (1965a) *The ideas in Barotse jurisprudence*. London & New Haven, Ct.: Yale University Press.

Gluckman, M. (1965b) 'Reasonableness and responsibility in the law of segmentary societies'. In Kuper, H. and Kuper, L. (eds.) *African law: Adaptation and development,* Berkeley: University of California Press, pp. 120-146.

Gluckman, M. (1972) 'Judicial process: Comparative aspects'. International Enclyclopedia of Social Science. Vols. 7-8, pp. 291-297.

Gluckman, M. (1973) 'Cross-examination and substantive law in African traditional courts'. The Juridical Review pp. 221-253.

Gluckman, M. (ed.) (1963) *Order and rebellion in tribal Africa: Collected essays*. London: Cohen and West.

Gluckman, M. (ed.) (1969) *Ideas and procedures in African customary law*. Oxford: Oxford University Press. For the Intertational African Institute.

Griffith, W. B. (1905) 'Native courts of the Gold Coast'. Journal of Comparative Legislation. Vol. 6, pp. 507-513.

Griffith, W. B. (1936) *A note on the history of the British courts in the Gold Coast colony with a brief account of the colony*. Accra: Government printers.

Griffiths, J. (1986) 'What is legal pluralism?' Journal of Legal Pluralism. Vol. 24, pp. 24-55.

Gulliver, P. H. (1973) 'Negotiations as a mode of dispute settlement: Towards a general model'. Law and Society Review. Vol. 7, pp. 667-691.

Gulliver, P. H. (1977) 'On mediators'. In Hamnett, I. (ed.) *Social anthropology and law*, pp. 15-52. London: Academic Press.

Gulliver, P. (1963) *Social control in an African society: A study of the Arusha agricultural Masai of Northern Tanganyika*. Boston: Boston University Press.

Gulliver, P. (1969) 'Dispute settlement without courts: The Ndendeuli of Southern Tanzania'. Nader, L. (ed.) *Law in culture and society*. pp. 24-68. Chicago: Aldine Press.

Gulliver, P. (1979) *Disputes and negotiations: A cross-cultural perspective*. New York: Academic Press.

Gutmann, B. (1924) 'Das rechtsleben der wadschagga im spiegel ihrer sprichwörter'. Zeitschrift für Eingeborenen Sprachen. No. 14, pp. 44-68.

Gutmann, B. (1924) 'Das rechtsleben der wadschagga im spielgel ihrer sprichwörter'. Zeitschrift fur Eingeborenen Sprachen. No. 14, pp. 44-68.

Hall, R. de Z. (1938) 'The study of native court records as a method of ethnographical enquiry'. Africa. Vol. 11. pp. 412-427.

Haydon, E. S. (1960) *Law and justice in Buganda*. London: Butterworth & Co. Ltd.

Hayford Caseley, J. E. (1903) *Gold Coast native institutions with thoughts upon a healthy imperial policy for the Gold Coast and Ashanti*. London: Sweet & Maxwell.

Heald, S. (1989) *Controlling anger: The sociology of Gisu violence*. Manchester: Manchester University Press for International African Institute.

Holleman, J. F. (1952) 'Hera court procedure: Southern Rhodesia'. Native Affairs Department Annual. Vol. 29, pp. 26-42.

Holleman, J. F. (1955) 'Indigenous administration of justice Southern Rhodesia'. Native Affairs Department Annual. Vol. 32, pp. 41-47.

Holleman, J. F. (1975) 'Some problems of evidence in Shona tribal law'. In Fortes, M and Patterson S. (eds.) *Studies in African social anthropology*. 75-94. London: Academic Press.

Holleman, J. F. (1979) 'Disparities and uncertainties in African law and judicial authority: A Rhodesian case study'. African Law Studies. Vol. 17, pp. 1-35.

Hooker, J. R. (1971),Tradition and traditional courts: Malawi's experiment with law'. American University Fieldstaff Report. Vol. 15, No. 3, pp. 1-8.

Howell, P. P. (1954) *A manual of Nuer law: Being an account of customary law its evolution and development in the courts established by the Sudan Government.* Oxford: Oxford University Press.

Jearey, J. H. (1960a) 'The structure, composition and jurisdiction of courts and authorities enforcing the criminal law in British African territories'. International and Comparative Law Quarterly. Vol. 9, pp. 396-414.

Jearey, J. H. (1960b) 'Trial by jury and trial with the aid of assessors in the superior courts of British African territories'. Journal of African Law. Vol. 4, No. 3, pp. 133-146.

Jearey, J. H. (1961) 'Trial by jury and trial with the aid of assessors in the superior courts of British African territories'. Journal of African Law. Vol. 5, No. 1, pp. 36-47.

Kayode, O. (1975) 'Judicial administration in a changing society: Customary courts in Western Nigeria'. Verfassung und Recht in Übersee. Vol. 8, pp. 435-446.

Keay, E. A. and Richardson, S. S. (1966) *The native and customary courts of Nigeia.* London: Sweet and Maxwell.

Kerr, A. J. (1957) 'The application of native law in the Supreme Court'. South African Law Journal. No. 74. pp. 313-330.

Keuning, J. (1971) Some remarks on law and courts in Africa. In integration of customary and modern legal systems in Afirca. Ile-Ife. pp. 57-71.

Khumalo, J. A. M. (1984) *The civil practice of all courts for black people in Southern Africa.* Cape Town: Juta.

Koch, K. F., Altorki, S., Arno, A. and Hickson, L. (1977) 'Ritual reconciliation and the obviation of grievances: A comparative study in the ethnography of law'. Ethnology. Vol. 16, No. 3, pp. 269-283.

Kom, E. D. (1987-88) 'Customary arbitration'. Review of Ghana Law. Vol. 16, pp. 148-170.

Korsah, K. A. (1951) Report of Commission on native courts.

Kuper, A. (1969) 'The work of the customary courts: Some facts and speculations'. African Studies. No. 28. pp. 37-48.

Lewin, J. (1944) 'Native courts and British justice inAfrica'. Africa. No. 14, pp. 448-453.

Lewis-Barned, J. F. de S. (1963) 'Integration of judicial systems: The recent reform of the local courts appeal system of Tanganyika'. Journal of African Law. Vol. 7, No. 2, pp. 84-93.

Lompo, F. and Yarga, L. (1980) *Customary courts in Upper Volta.* Ouagadougou: African Presses.

Loveridge, A. J. (1949) 'The future of native courts'. Journal of African Administration No. 1, pp. 7-18.

MacCormack, G. (1971) 'Roman and African litigation'. Revue d'histoire du droit. Vol. 39, pp. 221-255.

MacCormack, G. (1978) 'Anthropology and legal theory'. Juridical Review. pp. 216-232.

Merry, S. E. (1984) 'Athropology and the study of alternative dispute resolution'. Journal of Legal Education. Vol. 34, pp. 277-283.

Messenger, J. C. (1959) 'The role of proverbs in a Nigerian judicial system'. Southwestern Journal of Anthropology. No. 15, pp. 64-73.

Moffat, R. L. (1957) African courts and native customary law in the urban areas of Northern Rhodesia. Journal of African Administration. Vol. 9, No. 2, pp. 71-79.

Moffett, J. P. (1952) 'A history of the development of Native courts from German times'. Journal of African Administration Vol. 4, No. 1, pp. 17-28.

Moore, S. F. (1970) 'Politics, procedures and norms in changing Chagga law'. Africa Vol. 40, No. 4, pp. 321-344.

Moore, S. F. (1977) 'Individual interests and organisational structures: Dispute settlements as events of articulation'. In Hamnett, I. (ed.) *Social anthropology and law*. London: Academic Press.

Moore, S. F. (1978) *Law as process: An anthropological approach*. London: Routledge and Kegan Paul.

Moore, S. F. (1992) 'Treating law as knowledge: Telling colonial officials what to say to Africans about running their own native courts'. Law and Society Review. No. 26, pp. 11-46.

Morris, H. F. (1965) 'Uganda: Changes in the structure and jurisdiction of the courts and in the criminal law they administer'. Journal of African Law. Vol. 9, No. 1, pp. 65-73.

Nadel, S. F. (1956) 'Reason and unreason in African law'. Africa Vol. 26, No. 2, pp. 160-173.

Nader, L. (1979) 'Disputing without the force of law'. The Yale Law Journal. Vol. 88, pp. 998-1021.

Nader, L. and Todd, H. F. (eds.) (1978) *The disputing process: Law in ten societies*. New York: Columbia University Press.

Narebor, D. (1993) *Customary courts: Their relevance today*. Nigeria: Jodah Nigeria Ltd.

Nwogugu, E. I. (1976) The abolition of customary courts: The Nigerian experience. Journal of African Law. Vol. 20, No. 1, pp. 1-19.

Obilade, A. O. (1969) Reform of customary court systems in Nigeria under the military government. Journal of African Law. Vol. 13, No. 1, pp. 28-44.

Ojiako, G. G. I. (1991) 'Judicial administration of customary law in Southern Nigeria'. The Lawyers' Journal Vol. 2, No. 1, pp. 5-16.

Ojo, A. O. (1969) 'Recent reforms in the native and customary courts systems'. Nigerian Lawyer's Quarterly. No. 4, pp. 70-77.

Ojoade, O. (1988) 'Proverbial evidence of African legal customs'. Internatiional Folklore Review. No. 6, pp. 26-38.

Ollennu, N. A. (1966) 'Judicial precedent in Ghana'. University of Ghana Law Journal. Vol. 2, pp. 139-164.

Ollennu, N. A. (1970) The case for traditional courts under the constitution. University of Ghana Law Journal. No. 7, pp.82-106.

Otlhogile, B. (1994) 'Assessors and the administration of justice in Botswana'. Botswana Notes and Records Vol. 26, pp. 77-86.

Perry, J. A. G. (1977) 'Law-codes and brokerage in a Lesotho village'. In Hamnett, I. (ed.) *Social anthropology and law*. London: Academic Press.

Phillips, A. (1945) Report on native tribunals in Kenya. Nairobi: Government Printer.

Phillips, A. (1952) 'The African court system in Kenya'. Journal of African Administration Vol.4, No. 4, pp. 135-138.

Phillips, A. (1955) 'The legal factor in a changing Africa'. African Affairs. Vol. 54, pp. 280-287.

Pospisil, L. (1967) 'Legal levels and multiplicity of legal systems in human societies'. Journal of Conflict Resolution. Vol. 11, No. 1, pp. 1-26.

Poulter, S. (1976) *Family, law and litigation in Sasotho society*. Oxford: Clarendon Press.

Radcliffe-Brown, A. R. (1934) 'Sanction, social'. Encyclopaedia of the Social Sciences. Vol. 13, pp. 531-534.

Roberts, S. (1971) 'The settlement of family disputes in the Kgatla customary courts: Some new approaches'. Journal of African Law. Vol. 15, No. 1, pp. 60-76.

Roberts, S. (1976) 'Law and the study of social control in small-scale societies'. Modern Law Review. Vol. 39, pp. 663-679.

Roberts, S. (1979) *Order and dispute: An introduction to legal anthropology*. Harmondsworth: Penguin Books.

Roberts, S. (1983) 'Imposition, choice and change: Some conflicting perceptions of the relationship between state law and indigenous institutions in contemporary Africa'. Jahrbuch für Afrikanisches Recht. Vol. 2, pp. 99-106.

Roberts, S. and Comaroff, J. (1981) *Rules and processes. The cultural logic of dispute in an African context.* Chicago: University of Chicago Press.

Roberts, T. L. (1966) *Judicial organization and institutions of contemporary West Africa: A profile*. New York.

Robinson, R. E. (1949) 'The administration of African customary law'. Journal of African Administration. Vol. 1, No. 4, pp. 158-176.

Rowlands, J. S. S. (1962) 'Notes on native law and custom in Kenya'. Journal of African Law Vol. 6, No. 3, pp. 192-209.

Sa'ad, A. M. (1995) 'The politics of informal justice: A critical analysis of informal process of justice in rural Kilba, Mumuye and Jukun of Nigeria'. Afrique et Développement Vol. 20, No. 3, pp. 105-128.

Sanders, A. J. G. M. (1985) 'The internal conflict of laws in Botswana'. Botswana Notes and Records. Vol. 17, pp. 77-88.

Sarbah, J. M. (1910) 'Maclean and the Gold Coast Judicial Assesors' (1909-1910). Journal of the African Society'. Vol. 9, pp. 349-359.

Schapera, I. (1943) 'The work of tribal courts in the Bechuanaland Protectorate'. African Studies. No. 2, pp. 27-40.

Schapera, I. (1957) 'The sources of law in Tswana tribal courts: Legislation and precedent'. Journal of African Law. Vol. 1, No. 3, pp. 150-162.

Schapera, I. (1966) 'Tswana legal maxims'. Africa. Vol. 36, No. 2, pp. 121-134.

Schott, R. (1980) 'Justice versus the law: Traditional and modern jurisdiction among the Bulsa of Northern Ghana'. Law and State Vol. 21, pp. 121-133.

Seidman, R. B. (1966) 'Mens rea and the reasonable African: The pre-scientific world-view and mistake of fact'. The International and Comparative Law Quarterly. Vol. 15, No. 4, pp. 1135-1164.

Seidman, R. B. (1983) 'Rules of recognition in the primary courts of Zimbabwe: On lawyers' reasonings and customary law'. International and Comparative Law Quarterly. Vol. 32, pp. 871-903.

Sevareid, P. C. (1945) 'Evidence in Nimba'. Liberian Studies Journal Vol. 20, No. 1, pp. 15-36.

Smith, D. M. (1972) 'Man and law in urban Africa: Role of customary courts in the urbanization process'. American Journal of Comparative Law. Vol. 20, No. 2, pp. 223-246.

Smith, D. (1968) 'Native courts of Northern Nigeria: Techniques for institutional development'. Boston University Law Review. No. 48. pp. 49-82.

Smith, R. C. (1994) The struggle for control over dispute proceedings in the lower courts of Southern Rhodesia, c. 1930-c.1970. London: PhD Thesis SOAS. University of London.

Snyder, F. G. (1978) 'Legal innovation and social change in a peasant community: A Senegalese village policy'. Africa. Vol. 48, No. 3, pp. 231-247.

Snyder, F. G. (1981) 'Anthropology, dispute processes and law'. British Journal of Law and Society. No. 8, pp. 141-180.

Starr, J. and Yngvesson, B. (1975) 'Scarcity and disputing: Zeroing in on compromise decisions'. American Ethnologist. Vol. 2, pp. 553-566.

Strathern, M. (1985) 'Discovering social control'. Journal of Law and Society. Vol. 12, No. 2, pp. 111-134.

Sutherland, A. J. (1981) 'Local level dispute processes in Botswana: The Yeyi moot encapsulated'. Journal of African Law. Vol. 25, No. 1, pp. 94-114.

Tanner, R. E. S. (1955) 'Law enforcement by communal action in Sukumaland, Tanganyika territory'. Journal of African Administration. Vol. 7, pp. 159-165.

Thomas, H. B. (1944) Native tribunals in the Gold Coast colony. Journal of Comparative Legislation and International Law. No. 26, pp. 30-35.

Tobi, N. (1978) 'Recent reforms in area and customary courts in Nigeria'. Journal of African Law. Vol. 22, No. 2, pp. 133-135.

Tso, T. (1989) 'The process of decision making in tribal courts'. Arizona Law Review. Vol. 31, No. 2, pp. 225-235.

Turner, V. (1957) *Schism and continuity in an African society: A study of Ndembu village life.* Manchester: Manchester University Press.

Twining, W. (1964) *The place of customary law in the national legal systems of East Africa.* Chicago: University of Chicago Law School.

Unsworth, E. G. (1944) 'Conflict of laws in Africa: Human Problems in British Central Africa'. Rhodes-Livingstone Journal. Vol. 2, pp. 49-55.

Uwazie, E. E. (1994) 'Modes of indigenous disputing and legal interactions among the Ibos of Eastern Nigeria. Journal of Legal Pluralism and Unofficial Law. No. 34, pp.87-103.

Van Warmelo, N. J. (1971) 'Courts and court speech in Venda'. African Studies. No. 30, pp. 355-371.

Velsen, J. van (1969) 'Procedural informality, reconciliation and false comparisons'. In Gluckman, M. (ed.) *Ideas and procedures in African customary law.* London: Oxford University Press, pp. 137-152.

Verhelst, T. G. (1973) 'Legislation on the judiciaty: Fantasy law or programmed expectations'. Verfassung und Recht in Übersee. Vol. 6, pp. 137-152.

White, C. M. N. (1964) 'The changing scope of urban native courts in Northern Rhodesia'. Journal of African Law. Vol. 8, No. 1, pp. 29-33.

White, C. M. N. (1965) 'African customary law: The problem of concept and definition'. Journal of African Law. Vol. 9, No. 2, pp. 86-89.

Wood, G. S. (1966) 'Some reflections on the Bantu courts: Present and future'. Speculum Juris, pp. 17-23.

Woodman, G. R. (1981-82) 'Judicial control of the family meeting'. Review of Ghana Law. Vols. 13 & 14, pp. 222-226.

Woodman, G. R. (1987) 'How state courts create customay law in Ghana and Nigeria'. In Morse, B. W. and Woodman, G. R. (eds.) *Indigenous law and the state*. Dordrecht: Foris Publications, pp. 181-220.

Woodman, G. (1985) 'Customary law, state courts and the notion of institutionalisation of norms in Ghana and Nigeria'. In Allott, A. N. and Woodman, G. (eds.) *People's law and state law*. The Bellagio Papers. Dordrecht: Foris Publications, pp. 143-163.

Woodman, G. (1989) 'The peculiar policy of recognition of indigenous laws in British colonial Africa'. Verfassung und Recht in Übersee. Vol. 22, No. 3, pp. 273-284.

Yankah, K. (1986) 'Proverbs rhetoric and African judicial processes: The untold story'. Journal of American Folklore. No. 99, pp. 280-303.

Chapter 10 — Ethno-jurisprudence, philosophy and theology

This chapter focuses on ethno-jurisprudence and how principles of indigenous laws were distilled from the ethnography, philosophy and religious experiences of the people. Indigenous law is what the people actually do, whereas post-colonial statutory law is what the people should not get away with, and according to the American realists, law is what the courts would do.

In examining customary law, one cannot avoid the ethics of the people who formulated the law, and the morality recognised in their community, but most lawyers avoided any involvement with the ethical tradition of the people. Perhaps under the misapprehension that the people have no philosophy. Ethno-missionaries, colonial administrators, and lawyers who argued that there was no law, no religion and no philosophy had wanted to know who was the Plato of the Yoruba? The Aristotle of the Owambo? They seemed to have forgotten that there has been only one Plato. Africa could not be blamed for not producing a Plato or an Aristotle, neither did England, France, Germany or the United States.

The argument that there is no universal moral family law was not taken into account by the early jurists, although a study of any law inevitably leads to a reflection of its ethics, its moral foundation and the conditions that make the law enforceable. If philosophical questions had been asked about indigenous laws, it would have led the questioners to ponder on the nature of justice and liberty in small-scale societies. The bibliographical literature that I trawled through did not take cognisance of the thoughts of the people, even of Bantu philosophy, *négritude* or the ferocious debate in ethno-philosophy. As was reported in chapter 8, law is meaningless when studied independently of its philosophical roots.

A study of ethno-jurisprudence explains the longevity and resilience of indigenous law in the face of the arrogant modernity of post-colonial state law, apartheid, military rule, and dictators, and why indigenous law has not fallen into desuetude. Indigenous jurisprudence has a well-developed system of unwritten legal principles that are applied to men, women, children and animals. Ethno-jurisprudence still governs most people's lives, because the moral and legal authority of indigenous law lies in the general acceptance of specific virtues.

10.1 Négritude

The historical development of the legal philosophy of indigenous law is beyond the scope of these brief headnotes, but one can attempt the literature review from the origins of *négritude*, because contemporary literary critical African philosophical discourse emerged tentatively with *négritude*; at least that was the founders' point of view.

If Jeremy Bentham (1748-1832) was alive today and had to write a monograph or thesis on African customary law, he would probably have made reference to *négritude*. Even in his inimitable way, he might have described *négritude* as 'bawling upon paper', 'frippery ornament' or 'intellectuals turned into turkey-cocks'.[15] Verhelst (1968) also noted that if von Savigny had written about Africa, he would have pointed out '*négritude*' as a source of law.

In the 1930s and 1940s, some educated Africans and African Americans in Europe who were poets, artists, lawyers and philosophers, were searching for their philosophical origins, their customs and institutions, their metaphysics and their ethics. These founders of *négritude*, led by Leopold Sedar Senghor, Aimé Césaire, Cheikh Anta Diop among others had maintained that Africans could not go on philosophising in the same way as the colonial masters, as if nothing had happened to them. The philosophical crisis of these exiled black men was precipitated by the moral and legal crisis that had confronted their European counterparts after the atrocities of the Second World War and the violations of human rights that lead to the formulation of the European Convention on Human Rights in 1950.

Jean-Paul Sartre as a 'Negro philosopher' had taken the position that the Africans, too, should have their discourse. He urged his compatriots that:

> The Negro who vindicates his *négritude* in a revolutionary movement places himself, then and there, upon the terrain of reflection, whether he wishes to rediscover in himself certain objective traits growing out of African civilisation, or hopes to find the black essence in the wells of his soul.

In brief, the revival of African thought, African law, African history and black metaphysics, made visible through *négritude*, reflected the black peoples' 'existentialist integrity', according to Sartre. The principle of *négritude* has been a re-assertion of African traditional values against the imposition of christianisation and assimilation by the colonial policy of France and other countries.

Today, *négritude* has fallen out of intellectual grace and has died, because *négritude* had not advocated terrorism, violence and murder. The demise of *négritude* or its rejection by some people was because, the advocates of *négritude* had not practised what they preached. Towa's damning title to his 1971 essay was '*négritude ou servitude*'? Whereas Fanon (1965) noted that the advocates of *négritude* "are creatures of the colonial regimes who do not go out to find the mass of the people".

10.2 Ethno-philosophy

For those who read the book, *Bantu philosophy* (1945) is not about philosophy of law, but about Bantu ontology that contains some jurisprudence of indigenous law. *Bantu Philosophy* made a new liberal contribution to African thought, and it might have helped in the subsequent modifications in the literature on Africa, especially contributions by anthropologists and ethno-missionaries.

But Eboussi-Boulaga (1968) sees ethno-philosophy as a philosophy of the dominated, because of the impact of a roll call of clerics that stretched from the Reverend Father Tempels to Kagame, Mbiti and other scholarly gentlemen. This is a common phenomenon where the Churches have been very active to 'civilise' the natives and convert them to Christianity. Hountondji (1970) did not share the clerics' ethno-philosophic worldview-philosophy as community activity of people, Bantu philosophy, Dogon philosophy, rather he saw it as the thought of individuals. Hountondji's attack on Bantu ontology and Bantu philosophy generated a ferocious debate among philosophers on what is African

---

15 J. Bowring (ed.) (1843) Bentham works. Vols 11 & IV. Edinburgh: William Tait.

philosophy. In African universities, the debate sparked the schism of philosophy and theology, and as a result of the separation, academic philosophers have emerged.

The importance of *négritude* and ethno-philosophy was their influence on continental anthropologists, especially the French and German. Most British anthropologists were indifferent. Masolo (1994) remarked:

> It would be enough to compare Marcel Griaule, Germain Dieterlen or Louis V. Thomas with let us say, Meyer Fortes; E. E. Evans-Pritchard; A. R. Radcliffe-Brown, etc. While the former group is analytical and spiritualistic in the line of Cartesian reason, the latter is predominantly descriptive and bent toward a social relations aspect of culture in the empiricist tradition.

10.3 In search of a theory of law

From an examination of all the chapters in this volume, we can see that justice is the basic indigenous law principle. Indigenous law is not so jurisprudentially primitive that it does not know that lawlessness only begins when conventions are not universally followed. There are benefits in not killing or injuring people and keeping one's hands off their property, that means their cattle, land, wives, husbands, children, utensils, and benefits from social reciprocity, because of the demands they make on one another for survival.

In *Himba* culture, *oveta* can be inadequately translated as the equivalent word for justice, law, virtue, personal integrity. *Oveta* serves the purpose of rendering most small scale societies, just societies. From our theoretical understanding of pre-colonial indigenous laws, it is evident that indigenous laws have not appropriated Judaeo-Christianity, Islamic or Roman law concepts for their legal reasoning. Therefore any research into *oveta* involves detailed examination of some of the basic social contexts in which this system of justice had its origin. Many Western theorists have not taken sufficient account of cultural specifics. How is a legal theory about indigenous law possible, if the theory is silent about the family? Legal issues are involved when one theorises either about the family, moral or political philosophy. In order to describe a just society, be it the *Himba*, the English, the Owambo, the Yoruba, one must examine its justice, because that is the issue that concerns most people in their society. Indigenous societies posited a view of justice that the colonisers failed to recognise. The significance of this idea was brought out clearly to me by Derrida (1994:37) who writes that:

> justice is broader and more fundamental than human rights; nor is it to be equated with distributive justice; nor is it the same as respect for the other as a human subject, in the traditional sense of that word. It is the experience of the other as other, the fact that I permit the other to be other, which presupposes a gift without exchange, without reappropriation, without jurisdiction.

Derrida's view is interesting, because he is someone, as he puts it, 'who is making contact with actuality' or 'thinking one's time', just as people subject to indigenous law have located justice in their time.

How did they establish *oveta*? What gives *oveta* stability? Instead of asking what justice is and what it really means, I examined how justice functions in a small-scale *Himba* society. Justice does not imply formal, statutory law, because millions of people in the world live and die without setting a foot inside a court of law, yet they live in justice. Justice is clearly not the exclusive prerogative of lawyers, theorists and educated people, as justice is fundamental to all human beings.

Some Western theorists have put forward concepts on how justice originated,[16] but only Aristotle and Hume appear to be closer to the indigenous law conception of justice. I began with Aristotle and Hume's definition but reached a wider indigenous law conclusion.

Aristotle in *Nicomachean Ethics* was an early exponent of the distinction between distributive and rectificatory justice.[17] The former is concerned with the distribution of goods among people and the latter is about punishment of the individual, what he or she deserves.

Hume (1711-1776), the liberal Scottish philosopher, developed a theory of justice which maintains that certain practices are beneficial to society if the practices are universally followed, and that his convention is the origin of justice, of rights and of property. Hume explains that conventions arise very gradually and that rules of justice are conventions, but they are not mere convention. According to Hume, justice consists of a system of rules that are artificial, what he referred to as 'artifices'. Hume (1739:49) further explained that though the rules of justice are artificial, they are not arbitrary. Hume also postulates that the rules that are beneficial to society are in everybody's interest and the rules are just when they comply with a system of rules beneficial to society.

Indigenous law would appear to agree with Hume's line of thinking in that *oveta* is seen as beneficial to the community if the practices are universally followed, for example, their convention to respect others' property, to give *ohakera*, to give bridewealth. It is in everybody's interest, meaning that everybody will do well out of it, if the conventions are observed. Accordingly, under indigenous law, virtue and justice are primarily about reciprocity, just acts, or fair acts between human beings, and any infringement of this social contract is severely punished. See chapters 6 & 9.

Among the *ovaHimba* justice, then, consists of the convention that regulate their conduct to act justly to one another. Their duolineal transmission systems have produced a form of justice that serves the needs of the community. *Oveta* in their opinion is 'one of the phenomena in the legal philosophic development of human beings' of any colour. The *ovaHimba* rules of justice evolved according to the demands of their society and the environment. How did the *ovaHimba* reach such concepts of the communitarian good? Rawls (1971:136-142) has his self-interested negotiators bargaining behind 'a veil of ignorance', that is the lack of knowledge by the negotiators of their own ultimate goals in life. The *ovaHimba omaanda* and *otuzo* negotiators bargained from behind a very thin veil. They are aware of the operative principles that they can live with within their double descent system. Their moral convictions are derived from the duolineal society in which they are reared.

African indigenous laws, having survived against all the odds, almost to the twenty first century, signify that many people defy replacement of their indigenous laws. Furthermore, that meaningful indigenous ethical traditions can be adapted by contemporary ethicists. Indigenous sages think critically, they want to understand where they are going with state law which they do not see as a clean solution to their problems.

---

[16] There is the hypothetical social contract theory of Hobbes, Locke, Rousseau and Kant, whereby at some stage people got together and promised to obey the state. Then there is John Rawl's (1993) presentation of the theory of justice. He wrote on distributive justice that gave rise to justice as fairness, that is, what people in the original position, under 'a veil of ignorace' of social reality would choose.

[17] Nicomachean Ethics: 1130a6-1132a25.

Thus, ethno-jurisprudence is not a meaningless jurisprudential activity by jurists fiddling while Africa burns. Ethno-jurisprudence is about the practical application of some aspects of indigenous ethics to state law. Accordingly, ethno-jurisprudence has consequences for those who formulate policies, those who draft and enact domestic laws, as well as for the conduct of minorities, the majority, Christians and non-Christians within a state.

10.4 Bibliography

Open University (1977) *Aspects of African religion.* Milton Keynes. Open University Press.

Teaching and research in philosophy: Africa. (1984) Paris: UNESCO.

Abraham, W. E. (1962) *The mind of Africa.* London: Weidenfeld & Nicolson.

Adasu, M. O. (1985) *Understanding African traditional religion.* Sherborne: Dorset Publishing.

Allott, A. N. (1980) *The limits of law.* London: Butterworth & Co. Ltd.

Allott, A. N. (1983) 'The limits of law: A reply'. Journal of Legal Pluralism. No. 21, pp. 147-153.

An-Na'im, A. A. and Deng, F. M. (eds.) (1990) *Human rights in Africa: Cross cultural perspectives.* Washington D.C: Brookings Institute.

Anyanwu, K. C. (1981) *African philosophy.* Rome: Catholic Book Agency.

Apostel, L. (1981) *African philosophy: Myth or reality? Philosophy and anthropology.* Gent: Scientific Publishers.

Appiah, K. A. (1992) *In my father's house: Africa in the philosophy of culture.* London: Methuen.

Asante, M. K. (1990) *Kemet, Afrocentricity and knowledge.* Trenton, N.J.: Africa World Press.

Asante, M. (1987) The Afrocentric idea. Philadelphia: Temple University Press.

Awolalu, J. O. (1979) West African traditional religion. Ibadan: Onibonoje Press.

Bascom, W. (1969) *Ifa divination: Communication between gods and men in West Africa.* Bloomington: Indiana University Press.

Bediako, K. (1995) *Christianity in Africa: The renewal of a non-western religion.* New York: Orbis Books.

Beidelman, T. O. (1961) 'Kaguru justice and the concept of legal fictions'. Journal of African Law. Vol. 5, pp. 5-20.

Beidelman, T. O. (1968) 'Some Nuer notions of nakedness, nudity and sexuality'. Africa. Vol. 38, No. 2, pp. 113-132.

Beidelman, T. O. (1986) *Moral imagination in Kaguru modes of thought.* Bloomington: Indiana University Press.

Bello, E. G. (1980) *African customary humanitarian law*. Geneva: Oyez Publishing.

Bennett, T. W. (1995) *Human rights and African customary law*. Cape Town: Juta.

Berman, H. J. (1974) *The interaction of law and religion*. London: SCM Press.

Bernal, M. (1987) *'Black Athena: The Afroasiatic roots of classical civilization'. Vol. 1. Of the fabrication of ancient Greece 1785-1985*. London: Free Association Books.

Bhalla, R. S. (1990) *Concepts of jurisprudence*. Nairobi: Nairobi University Press.

Bimwenyi-Kweshi, O. (1981) *Discours théologique Négro-Africain: Problèmes de fondement*. Paris: Présence Africaine.

Binsbergen, W. van and Schoffeleers (ed.) (1985) *Theoretical explorations in African religion*. London: Routledge & Kegan Paul.

Bodurin, P. O. (ed.) (1985) *Philosophy in Africa: Trends and perspective*. Ife: University of Ife Press.

Brenner, L. (1983) *West African Sufi: The religious heritage and spiritual search of Cerno Bokar Saalif Taal*. London: C. Hurst.

Byaruhanga-Akiiki, A. B. T. (ed.) (1973) *Occasional research papers: African traditional religion and philosophy*. Kampala: Makerere University. Dept. of Religious Studies and Philosophy.

Caplan, G. M. (1964) 'The making of natural justice in British Africa: an exercise in comparative law'. Journal of Public Law Vol. 13. pp. 120-134.

Casey, J. (1990) *Pagan virtue*. Oxford: Clarendon Press.

Césaire, A. (1972) *Discourse on colonialism*. New York: Monthly Review Press.

Cottrell, R. (1989) *The politics of jurisprudence: A critical introduction to legal philosophy*. London: Butterworth & Co. Ltd.

Crahay, F. (1965) 'Conceptual take-off: Conditions for a Bantu philosophy'. Diogenes. No. 52, pp. 55-78.

Critchley, S. (1995) 'Black Socrates? Questioning the philosophical tradition'. Radical Philosophy. Jan/Feb. pp. 17-26.

Danquah, J. B. (1944) *The Akan doctrine of God: A fragment of Gold Coast ethics and religion*. London & Redhill: Lutterworth Press.

Derrida, J. (1994) 'The construction of actuality'. Radical Philosophy. Vol. 68 Autumn. pp.28-41.

Dialembonkebi, D. (1988) *Le droit de l'homme à l'existence au regard de la métaphysique négro-africaine*. Kinshasa: Lokole.

Diemer, A. (ed.) (1981) *Symposium on philosophy in the present situation of Africa*. Wiesbaden: Franz Steiner Verlag.

Dieng, A. (1983) *Contribution a l'étude des problèmes philosophiques en Afrique noire*. Paris: Nubia.

Diop, C. A. (1954) *Nations nègres et culture*. Paris: Présence Africaine.

Diop, C. A. (1989) 'Is there an African philosophy? The African Mind. Vol. 1, No. 1, pp. 2-11.

Diop, C. A. (1991) *Civilization or barbarism: An authentic anthropology*. Brooklyn: Lawrence Hill Books.

Driberg, J. H. (1934) 'The African conception of law'. Journal of Comparative Legislation. Vol. 16, pp. 230-245.

Driberg, J. H. (1935) 'The African conception of law'. Supplementary Journal of the Royal African Society. Vol. 34, pp. 230-246.

Dugard, J. (1978) *Human rights and the South African legal order*. Princeton: Princeton University Press.

Dugard, J. (1984) 'Some realism about the judicial process and positivism: A reply? South African Law Journal. Vol. 98, pp. 372-387.

Dyatlm, N. (1982) Civilisation and science juridique. Yaoundé: CIE

Ebo, C. (1979) 'Indigenous law and justice: Some major concepts and practices'. Vierteljahresberichte. Vol. 76, pp. 139-148.

Eboussi-Boulaga, F. (1968) 'Le Bantou problématique'. Présence Africaine No. 66 pp. 4-40.

Eboussi-Boulaga, F. (1977) *La crise du muntu*. Paris: Présence Africaine.

Eboussi-Boulaga, F. (1984) *Christianity without fetishes*. Maryknoll: Orbis Books.

Elias, T. O. (1956) *The nature of African customary law*. Manchester: Manchester University Press.

Elungu, P. E. A. (1987) Tradition africaine et rationalité moderne. Paris: L'Harmattan.

Evans-Pritchard, E. E. (1956) *Nuer religion*. Oxford: Clarendon Press.

Evans-Pritchard, E. E. (1980) *Theories of primitive religion*. Oxford: Oxford University Pess.

Ewing, A. C. (1951) *The fundamental question of philosophy*. London: Routledge & Kegan Paul.

Fanon, F. (1965) *The wretched of the earth*. London: MacGibbon & Kee.

Fanon, F. (1967) *Black skin, white masks*. New York: Grove Press.

Fløistad, G. (1987) *Contemporary philosophy: African philosophy*. Volume 5. Dordrecht: Martinus Nijhoff.

Forde, D. (ed.) (1967) *African worlds: Studies in the cosmological and social values of African peoples.* London: Oxford University Press.

Fortes, M. (1959) *Oedipus and Job in West African religion.* Cambridge: Cambridge University Press.

Fortes, M. (1961) 'Pietas in ancestor worship'. Journal of the Royal Anthropological Institute. Vol. 91, pp. 166-191.

Fortes, M. (1987) *Religion, morality and the person: Essays on Tallensi religion.* Cambridge: Cambridge University Press.

Fortes, M. and Dieterlen, G. (eds.) (1965) *African systems of thought.* London: Oxford University Press.

Ghai, Y. (1975) 'Notes towards a theory of law and ideology: Tanzanian perspectives'. African Law Studies, Vol. 13, pp. 31-105.

Ghai, Y. (1987 'Law, development and African scholarship'. Modern Law Review. Vol. 50, pp. 750-776.

Glover, P. E. (1968) 'The role of fire and other influences on the savanna habitat, with suggestions for further research'. East African Wildlife Journal. Vol. 6, pp. 131-137.

Gluckman, M. (1961-62) 'African jurisprudence'. Advancement of Science. Vol. 18, pp. 439-454.

Goody, J. (1977) *The domestication of the savage mind.* Cambridge: Cambridge University Press.

Griaule, M. (1965) *Conversations with Ogotommêli: An introduction to Dogon religious ideas. Oxford: Oxford University Press.* (Translated from the original French edition 1948. Paris: Edition du Chene).

Gyeke, K. (1987) *An essay on African philosophical thought: The Akan conceptual scheme.* Cambridge: Cambridge University Press.

Hallen, B. (1977) 'Robin Horton on critical philosophy and traditional thought'. Second Order Vol. 6, pp. 81-92.

Hallen, B. (1995) 'Indeterminacy, ethnophilosophy, linguistic philosophy, African philosophy. Philosophy. No. 70. pp. 377-393.

Hallen, B. and Sodipo, J. O. (1986) *Knowledge, belief and witchcraft: Analytic experiments in African philosophy.* London: Ethnographica.

Hardie, W. F. R. (1968) *Justice: Aristotle's ethical theory.* Oxford: Clarendon Press.

Hives, F. (1932) *Justice in the jungle.* London: John Lane.

Hobley, C. W. (1911) 'Further researches into Kikuyu and Kamba religious beliefs and customs'. Journal of the Royal Anthropological Institute. Vol. 41, pp. 406-457.

Horton, R. (1956) 'God, man and the land in a Northern Ibo village group'. Africa. Vol. 26, pp. 17-28.

Horton, R. (1962) 'The Kalabari world view: An outline and interpretation'. Africa. Vol. 22, pp. 197-220.

Horton, R. (1964) 'Ritual man in Africa'. Africa. Vol. 34, pp. 85-104.

Horton, R. (1967) 'African traditional thought and Western science'. Africa. Vol. 37, No. 1, pp. 50-71; 155-187.

Horton, R. (1975) 'On the rationality of conversion'. Africa. Vol. 45, No. 3, Pt. 1, pp. 220-235; Pt. 2, pp. 373-398.

Horton, R. (1976) 'Understanding traditional African religion: A reply to Professor Beattie'. Second Order. Vol. 3, pp. 3-29.

Horton, R. (1977) 'Traditional thought and the emerging African philosophy department: A comment on the current debate'. Second Order. Vol. 6, pp. 64-80.

Horton, R. (1982) 'Tradition and modernity revisited'. In Lukes, S. and Hollis, M. (eds.) *Rationality and relativism*, pp. 201-260. Oxford: Basil Blackwell.

Horton, R. (1993) *Patterns of thought in Africa and the West: Essays on magic, religion and science.* Cambridge: Cambridge University Press.

Horton, R. and Finnegan, R. (1973) *Modes of thought: Essays on thinking in Western and non-Western societies.* London: Faber and Faber.

Hountondji, P. J. (1970) 'Comments on contemporary African philosophy'. (Translated by Sally Bradshaw). Diogenes. No. 71. pp.. 109-130.

Hountondji, P. J. (1977) *Sur la 'philosophie africaine': Critique de l'ethno-philosophie.* Paris: François Maspero.

Hountondji, P. J. (1983) *African philosophy myth and reality.* London: Hutchinson University Library for Africa.

Hountondji, P. J. (1989) 'Occidentalism, elitism: Answer to two critiques'. Quest. Vol. 111, No. 2, pp. 2-29.

Hountondji, P. J. (1994) *Les savoirs endogenes: Pistes pour une recherche.* Dakar: Codesria.

Hume, D. (1739) *A treatise of human nature.* Book (iii) London: Thomas Longman.

Hund, J. (1979) 'Jurisprudence and legal anthropology: The roles of theory and method revisited'. Comparative and International Law Journal of Southern Africa. Vol. 12, pp. 188-198.

Hund, J. (1982) 'Legal and sociological approaches to indigenous law in Southern Africa'. Social Dynamics. Vol. 8, pp. 29-40.

Hund, J. (1991) 'Institutional jurisprudence'. The American Journal of Jurisprudence. Vol. 36, pp. 125-155.

Hund, J. and Kotu-Rammopu, M. (1983) 'Justice in a South African township: The sociology of Makgotla'. Comparative and International Law Journal of Southern Africa. Vol. 16, pp. 179-208.

Idowu, E. B. (1962) *Olodumare: God in Yoruba belief.* London: Longmans.

Idowu, E. B. (1973) *African traditional religion: A definition.* London: SCM Press.

James, W. (1988) *The listening ebony: Moral knowledge, religion and power among the Uduk of Sudan.* Oxford: Clarendon Press.

Jean, C. M. (1991) *Behind the Eurocentric veils: The search for African realities.* Amherst: University of Massachusetts Press.

Jules-Rosette, B. (1975) *African apostles.* Ithaca: Cornell University Press.

July, R. W. (1967) *The origins of modern African thought.* New York: Praeger.

Junod, H. A. (1912) 'Moral sense among the Bantu'. International Review of Missions. Vol. 15, pp. 85-89.

Kagame, A. (1956) *La philosophie Bantu-Rwandaise de l'être.* Bruxelles: Académie Royale des Sciences Coloniales.

Kagame, A. (1976) *La philosophie Bantu comparée.* Paris: Présence Africaine.

Kagame, A. (1989) 'The problem of 'man' in Bantu philosophy'. The African Mind. Vol. 1. No. 1, pp. 35-40.

Karp, I. and Bird, C. S. (1980) *Explorations in African systems of thought.* Bloomington: Indiana University Press.

Kidder, R. L. (1979) 'Towards an integrated theory of imposed law' In Burman S. B. and Harrell-Bond E. (eds.) *The imposition of law.* New York, London: Academic Press.

Ki-Zerbo, J. (ed.) (1989) *General history of Africa. Vol. 1. Methodology and African philosophy.* Berkeley: University of California Press.

Kopytoff, I. (1981) 'The authority of ancestors'. Man. Vol. 16, pp135-137.

Kriel, A. (1984) *Roots of African thought.* Cape Town: A. A. Balkema.

Lloyd, B. and Gay J. (ed.) (1981) *Universals of human thought: Some African evidence.* Cambridge: Cambridge University Press.

Lufuluabo, F. M. (1962) *Vers une Théodicée Bantoue.* Paris: Tournai.

M'Baye, K. (1975) 'The African conception of law'. In David, R. (ed.) *International Encyclopedia of Comparative Law,* Vol. 11, pp. 138-158. The Hague: Mouton.

MacGaffey, W. ((1981) 'African ideology and belief'. African Studies Review. No. 24. pp. 227-274.

MacIntyre, A. (1981) *After virtue: A study in moral theory*. London: Duckworth.

Makinde, M. A. (1988) *African philosophy, culture and traditional medicine*. Athens, OH: Ohio University Press.

Marasinghe, M. L. and Conklin, W. E. (eds.) (1984) *Essays on Third World perspectives in jurisprudence*. Singapore: Malayan Law Journal.

Markovitz, I. L. (1969) *Léopold Sédar Senghor and the politics of négritude*. New York: Atheneum.

Masolo, D. A. (1981) *Some aspects and perspectives of African philosophy today*. Rome: Institue Italo-African.

Masolo, D. A. (1994) *African philosophy in search of identity*. Bloomington: Indiana University Press.

Maurier, H. (1985) *Philosophie de l'Afrique noire*. St. Augustin: Anthropos Institute.

Mbembe, A. (1988) *Afriques indociles: Christianisme, pouvoir et etat en société postcoloniale*. Paris: Karthala.

Mbiti, J. S. (1969) *African religions and philosophy*. London: Heinemann.

Mbiti, J. (1972) Religions et philosophie africaines. Yaoundé: Editions Clé

Mead, M. H. (1938) 'The moral code of the Ngoni and their former military state'. Africa. Vol. 11, pp. 1-24.

Metogo, E. M. (1985) *Théologie africaine et ethnophilosophie: Problèmes de méthode en theologie africaine*. Paris: L'Harmattan.

Metuh, E. I. (1981) *God and man in African religion: A case study of the Igbo of Nigeria*. London: Chapman.

Middleton, J. (1960) *Lugbara religion: Ritual and authority among an East African people*. London: Oxford University Press for the International African Institute.

Mowoe, I. J. and Bjornson, R. (1986) *Africa and the West, the legacies of empire*. New York: Greenwood Press.

Mubengayi, C. L. (1966) *Initiation Africaine et initiation Chrétienne*. Kinshasa: CEP.

Mudimbe, V. Y. (1985) 'African gnosis: Philosophy and the order of knowledge. An introduction'. African Studies Review. Vol. 28. Nos. 2/3, pp. 149-233.

Mudimbe, V. Y. (1986) 'On the question of an African philosophy: The case of French speaking Africa'. In Mowoe, I. J. and Bjornson, R. (eds.) *Africa and the West, the legacies of Empire*. pp. 89-120. Westport., Con: Greenwood Press.

Mudimbe, V. Y. (1988) *The invention of Africa: Gnosis, philosophy and the order of knowledge.* Bloomington: Indiana University Press.

Mudimbe, V. Y. (1991) *Parables and fables: Exegesis, textuality and politics in Central Africa.* Madison: University of Wisconsin Press.

Mudimbe, V. Y. (1994) *The idea of Africa.* London: James Currey.

Mulago, V. (1969) *Vital participation: The cohesive principle of the Bantu community'.* Biblical Revelation and African beliefs. London.

Mutua, M. wa (1995) 'Conflicting conception of human rights: Rethinking the post-colonial state'. The American Society of International Law. pp. 487-490. Proceedings of the 89th Annual Meeting. New York: 5-8 April 1995.

Nadel, S. F. (1954) *Nupe religion.* London: Routledge

Nadel, S. F. (1956) 'Reason and unreason in African law'. Africa. Vol. 26. pp. 160-173.

Ndaw, A. (1983) *La pensée africaine: Recherches sur les fondements de la pensée négro-africaine.* Dakar: Les Nouvelles éditions africaines.

Nduka, O. (1977) 'The traditional concept of justice among the Ibo of South-Eastern Nigeria'. Odu. Vol. 15, pp. 91-103.

Ngùgi wa Thiong'o (1986) *Decolonising the mind: The politics of language in African literature.* London: James Currey.

Nwala, T. U. (1985) *Igbo philosophy.* Lagos: Literamed Publications.

Nyang, S. S. (1984) *Islam, Christianity and African identity.* Brattleboro (Vermon): Amana Books.

Obenga, T. (1992) *Ancient Egypt and black Africa.* London: Karnak House.

Ochieng'-Odhiambo, F. (1995) *African philosophy: An introduction.* Nairobi: Consolata Institute of Philosophy Press.

Oguah, B. E. (1977) 'African and western philosophy: A comparative study'. Journal of African Studies'. Vol. 4, No. 3, pp. 281-195.

Ogundere, J. D. (1992) 'The philosophy of justice, the parameter and ends of justice, jus naturale: Natural justice and unjust laws'. In Bello, E. G. and Ajibola, B. A. (eds.) Essays in honour of Judge Taslim Olawale Elias. Vol. 11. *African law and comparative public law.* Dordrecht: Martinuis Nijhoff.

Ogunmokun, D. (1982) 'Equity and Yoruba traditional legal system'. Lawyer University of Lagos. Vol. 12, pp. 37-44.

Ogwurike, C. (1966) 'The source and authority of African customary law'. University of Ghana Law Journal. Vol. 3, pp. 11-20.

Ogwurike, C. (1979) *Concept of law in English speaking Africa.* New York: Nok Publishers.

Ojwang, J. B. (1989) 'The meaning, content and significance of tribal law in an emergent nation: The Kenyan case'. Law and Anthropology. Vol. 4, pp. 125-140.

Ojwang, J. B. (1992) 'Laying a basis for rights: Towards a jurisprudence of development'. Nairobi University Press. pp. 1-47.

Ojwang, J. B. and Kuria, G. K. (1977) 'The rule of law in general and Kenya perspectives'. Zambia Law Journal. Vol. 7-9, pp. 109-127.

Okafor, F. U. (1992) *Igbo philosophy of law*. Enugu: Fourth Dimension Publishing & Co.

Okafor, F. U. (1993) 'Issues in African philosophy re-examined'. International Philosophical Quarterly. Vol.33, No. 1 pp. 91-99.

Okere, T. (1983) *African philosophy: A historico-hermeneutical investigation of the conditions of its possibility*. London: University Press of America.

Okolo, C. B. (1984) 'Négritude: A philosophy of social action'. International Philosophical Quarterly. Vol. 24, pp. 427-438.

Okolo, C. B. (1987) *What is African philosophy? A short introduction*. Enugu: Freemans Press.

Olupona, J. K. (ed.) (1991) *African traditional religions in contemporary society*. New York: Paragon House.

Oruka, H. O. (1981) 'Four trends in current African philosophy'. In Diemeer, A. (ed.) *Symposium on philosophy in the present situation of Africa*. Wiesbaden: Franz Steiner Verlag GMBH.

Oruka, H. O. (1984) *Philosophy of Eastern Africa and the future of philosophical research in Africa*. Paris: UNESCO.

Oruka, H. O. (ed.) (1990) *Sage philosophy: Indigenous thinkers and modern debate on African philosophy*. Leiden: E. J. Brill.

Outlaw, L. (1990) 'African philosophy: Deconstructive and reconstructive challenges'. In Oruka, H. O. (ed.) *Sage Philosophy: Indigenous thinkers and modern debate on African philosophy*. Leiden: E. J. Brill.

Panikkar, R. (1982) 'Is the notion of human rights a western concept?' Diogenes. Vol. 120, pp. 75-102.

Paris, P. J. (1995) *The sprituality of African peoples*. Minneapolis: Fortress Press.

Park, A. E. W. (1963) *The sources of Nigerian law*. Lagos: African Universities Press.

Parrinder, E. G. (1954) *African traditional religion*. London: Hutchinson.

Parrinder, E. G. (1961) *West African religion*. London: Epworth Press.

Parrinder, E. G. (1962) *African traditional religion*. London: Sheldon Press.

Peel, J. D. Y. (1977) 'Conversion and tradition in two African societies: Ijebu and Buganda'. Past and Present. Vol. 77, pp. 108-141.

Post, A. H. (1887) *Afrikanische jurisprudenz: Ethnologisch-juristiche Beiträge zur Kenntnis der einheimischen rechte Afrikas.* Oldenburg und Leipzig: Schulze.

Radin, P. (1927) *Primitive man as philosopher.* New York: D. Appleton

Read, K. E. (1955) 'Morality and the concept of the person among the Gahuku-Gama'. Oceania. Vol. 25, pp. 233-282.

Read, M. (1938) 'The moral code of the Ngoni and their former military state'. Africa. Vol. 11, pp. 1-24.

Reyntjens, F. and Wolf-Phillips, L. (1984) 'Revolution in the legal systems of third world states'. In Marasinghe, M. L. and Conklin, W. E. (eds.) *Essays on Third World perspectives in jurisprudence.* Singapore: Malayan Law Journal. pp. 105-136.

Richards, A. I. (1967) 'African systems of thought: An anglo-French dialogue'. Man. Vol. 2, pp. 286-298.

Roberts, C. C. (1937) *Tangled justice: Some reasons for a change of policy in Africa.* London: Macmillan.

Rokumoto, K. (ed.) (1994) *Sociological theories of law.* Aldershot: Dartmouth Publishing Co. Ltd.

Ross, W. D. (tr.) (1984) *Aristotle. The Nicomachean ethics.* Oxford. Oxford University Press.

Ruch, E. A. (1989) 'African philosophy: Regressive or progressive?' The African Mind. Vol. 1, No. 1, pp. 41-54.

Ruch, E. A. and Anyanwu, K. C. (1981) *African philosophy: An introduction to the main philosophical trends in contemporary Africa.* Rome: Catholic Book Agency.

Sanders, A. J. G. M. (1979) *International jurisprudence in African context.* Durban: Butterworth & Co. Ltd.

Sartre, J. P. (1948) 'Orphée noir' In *Les Temps Modernes*, pp. 577-606.

Scheffler, H. W. (1966) 'Ancestor worship in anthropology: Or observations on descent and descent groups'. Current Anthropology Vol. 7, pp. 541-551.

Senghor, L. S. (1964) *Liberté 1: Négritude et humanisme.* Paris: Editions des Seuil.

Senghor, L. S. (1977) *Liberté 111: Négritude et civilisation de l'universel.* Paris: Editons des Seuil.

Senghor, L. S. (1988) *Ce que je crois: Négritude, francité et civilisation de l'universel.* Paris: Bernard Grasset.

Serequeberhan, T. (1991) *African philosophy: The essential readings.* New York: Paragon House.

Serequeberhan, T. (1993) 'African philosophy: An exposition'. Quest. Vol. 7, No. 2, pp. 92-106.

Serequeberhan, T. (1994) *The hermeneutics of African philosophy: Horizon and discourse*. London: Routledge.

Shivji, I. (1989) *The concept of human rights in Africa*. Dakar: Codesria.

Shweder, R. A. and Levine, R. A. (eds.) (1984) *Culture theory: Essays on mind, self and emotion*. Cambridge: Cambridge University Press.

Silberbauer, G. (1991) 'Ethics in small-scale societies. In Silberbauer, G and Singer, P. (eds.) *A companion to ethics*, pp. 14-18. Oxford: Blackwell.

Smet, A. J. (1980) *Histoire de la philosophie africaine contemparaine*. Kinshasa: Faculté de theologie Catholique.

Smet, A. J. (ed.) (1975) *Philosophie Africaine*. Kinshasa: Presses Universitaires du Zaïre.

Storm, W. (1993) 'Bantoe-filosofie v Bantu philosophy'. Quest. Vol. 7, No. 2, pp. 67-75.

Sumner, C. (1986) *The source of African philosophy: The Ethiopian philosophy of man*. Stuttgart: Steiner-Verlag-Weisbaden-GmbH.

Sylla, A. (1978) La philosophie morale des Wolof. Dakar: Sankoré.

Tangwa, G. (1992a) 'African philosophy: appraisal of a recurrent problematic. The sources of traditional African philosophy'. Cogito. Vol. 6, No. 2, pp. 78-84.

Tangwa, G. (1992b) 'African philosophy, Part 2'. Cogito. Vol. 6, No. 3, pp. 138-143.

Tempels, P. (1945) *La philosophie Bantoue*. Elisabethville: Lovania.

Tempels, P. (1962)*Notre rencontre 1.*. Léopoldville: Centre d'Etudes Pastorales.

Towa, M. (1971) *Leopold Sedar Senghor: Négritude or servitude?* Yaounde: Clé.

Towa, M. (1979a) L'idée d'une philosophie négro-africaine. Yaoundé: Editions Clé.

Towa, M. (1979b) Essai sur la problématique philosophieque dans l'afrique actuelle. Yaoundé: Editions Clé.

Tsenay, S. (1993) 'African philosophy: An exposition'. Quest. Vol. 7, No. 2, pp. 92-105.

Twesigye, E. K. (1987) *Common ground: Christianity, African religion and philosophy*. New York: Peter Lang.

Van Hook, J. (1993) 'African philosophy: Its quest for identity'. Quest. Vol. 7, No. 1, pp. 29-43.

Vanderlinden, J. (1983) *Les systèmes juridiques Africains*. Paris: Presses universitaires de France.

Vansina, J. (1985) *Oral tradition as history*. Madison: University of Wisconsin Press.

Varga, C. (ed.) (1992) *Comparative legal cultures*. Aldershot: Dartmouth Publishing Co. International Library of Essays in Law and Legal Theory.

Wacks, R. (1984) 'Judges and injustice'. South African Law Journal. No. 101, pp. 266-285.

Wamba-dia-Wamba, E. (1979) 'La philosophie en Afrique ou les défis de l'Africain philosophe'. Revue Canadienne des etudes Africaines. Vol. 13, No. 1-2, pp. 223-244.

Wamba-dia-Wamba, E. (1991) 'Philosophy in Africa: Challenges of the African philosopher'. In Serequeberhan, T. (ed.) *The essential readings*. New York: Paragon House.

Wilson, G. (1936) 'An African morality'. Africa. Vol. 9, pp. 25-98.

Wiredu, K. (1980) *Philosophy and an African culture*. Cambridge: Cambridge University Press.

Woodman, G. R. (1983) 'The limits of the limits of law'. Journal of Legal Pluralism. No. 21, pp. 129-146.

Woodman, G. R. (1995) 'Introduction' In. Woodman, G. R. and Obilade, A. O. *African law and legal theory*. Aldershot: Darmouth Publishing Co. Ltd.

Woodman, G. R. (1996) 'Legal pluralism and the search for justice'. Journal of African Law. Vol. 40, No. 2, pp. 152-167.

Woodman, G. R. and Obilade, A. O. (eds.) (1995) *African law and legal theory*. Aldershot: Darmouth.

Wright, R. A. (ed.) (1984) *African philosophy: An introduction*. Lanham: University Press of America.

Yai, O. (1977) 'Theory and practice in African philosophy: The poverty of speculative philosophy'. Second Order Vol. 6, No. 2, pp. 3-20.

Zahan, D. (1970) *The religion, spirituality and thought of traditional Africa*. Chicago: University of Chicago Press.

Zahan, D. (1979) *The religion, spirituality and thought of traditional Africa*. Chicago: University of Chicago Press.

Zuesse, E. M. (1979) *Ritual cosmos: The sanctification of life in African religion*. Athens (Ohio): Ohio University Press.

Chapter 11 — Formalities of marriage

In this chapter, the focus will be on the formalities of indigenous marriage, marriage settlement now popularly known as bridewealth, as well as an examination of *ondjova* wife, that is, a man's first betrothed wife, and finally divorce.

Marriage of a man and a woman is a universal institution as old as humankind. What differs from society to society is the variation in the formalities or the rituals of procreation that proclaim a couple husband and wife. Indigenous law marriage is a contractual relationship between the man's *oruzo* and the girl's *oruzo*, their *omaanda*, as well as the union of the bridegroom and bride or subsequent brides. Since it is both families who officiate at indigenous marriage, it is impossible for an indigene to marry in defiance of the families or have a clandestine or fictitious indigenous marriage.

Among the *Himba*, one ceremony of marriage is held at the bride's sacred fire, and the other at the bridegroom's sacred fire. Marriage is a happier version of a funeral ceremony, because both are public spectacles. The publicity is what gives everyone notice that the couple are going to become husband and wife; technically therefore, everyone is a witness at the ceremony, and this is the public registration of the marriage.

Indigenous law allows two forms of marriages, monogamy (one) and polygamy (many).

The residence in monogamy or polygamy could be virilocal or uxorilocal, where the husband moved and set up home in his wife's *onganda*. The matrilineal *Himba* would prefer to have nothing to do with uxorilocal marriage, because as they said, "the wife's *eanda* would get their grubby hands on the man's cattle".

There are also two forms of polygamy. First polyandry, this is where the community permits a woman to have two or three husbands simultaneously, usually brothers, (adelphogamy). Secondly, polygyny where a man can marry many wives simultaneously. Accordingly, rich and powerful polygynists are related by marriage to several men.

In some societies monogamy is not absolute, as there are grounds for divorce, furthermore a widow or widower can remarry. There was no bibliographical reference in which a widow was buried alive with her deceased husband.

Marriage under indigenous law is a very serious business not to be left in the hands of the couple. The girls do not usually make their own decision on whom to marry or when to marry, and neither do the boys decide whom to marry. The *Himba oruzo* argued that a young man cannot be trusted to make a sensible choice, as he is still a child himself, the choice has to be made for boys and girls to protect them from their own folly. But adult men and women usually make their own decisions to marry the second and subsequent spouses, their 'love' spouse. They are then considered able to sort out the social and economic consequences of polygyny. However, for the first marriage, the *ondjova*, boys and girls who have reached puberty do not have such a right to decide with whom to start having children. They marry whosoever they have been betrothed to and fall in love later, and hopefully live happily ever after with the selected spouse. If they are unhappy, they can petition their *eanda* to renegotiate the return of a percentage of the bridewealth for divorce settlement. Marriage under indigenous law is not a private prison created for men and women in a polygamous society.

11.1 Child betrothal and the *ondjova* wife

Indigenous child betrothal is much maligned. The myth that betrothed girls marry very early was sustained by 'informants' of missionaries, ethnographers and administrators. They failed to distinguish between betrothal and marriage.

If poor *eanda* and *oruzo* married off their daughters and nieces without the formalities of *ovivareke* and *ovitunya*, they of course got poorer. Neither do poor men abduct the daughters and nieces of cattle barons because husbands do not inherit their wife's property. See chapter 16.

Among the *ovaHimba*, there is still much child betrothal, but I did not come across child marriages. Child betrothal amongst pastoralists, as elsewhere in Africa, is nothing more sinister than 'cattle alliances', major cattle transactions in which the *oruzo* and *eanda* males move their cattle about in different ceremonies for the benefit of the next generation. First, for the *ovivareke*, the child betrothal cattle, then for the bridewealth cattle, *ovitunya*, then for *eanda* succession, bailment, and finally *oruzo* succession cattle.

There were no reported cases of forced marriages of children among the *ovaHimba*, and marriage by proxy is prohibited by the indigenous law, because the couple must be physically present before the presiding heads of the *otuzo* and *okuruuo*, to be smeared with herbs and fat to hasten reproduction.

Under indigenous law, child betrothal is not consummated because the child bride cannot procreate. The institution of marriage is for the procreation of the next generation, and children themselves who are still 'technically disabled' because of their minority, need a good start to their own life, before they start having children. Furthermore, polygynists and paedophiles do not make comfortable bed partners in such small-scale indigenous societies.

If a girl is not old enough to bear children she should remain with her *eanda*. During my fieldwork paedophilia was not the *Himba* preoccupation. The *ovaHimba* believe rightly or wrongly that pre-pubertal sexual activity causes infertility and that childless women are childless because they married too young. Accordingly, betrothed girls are not propelled into marriage immediately after puberty. Fathers and maternal uncles decide when girls should leave the matrilineage for a virilocal marriage. Puberty was not only the decisive factor, but her physical maturity was a prerequisite. "She should have a pair of well-formed breasts on her. In the absence of breasts how will she feed her child?" The *ovaHimba* believe implicitly in the merits of breast feeding.

Indigenous law argument for child betrothal is that it instils obedience and the ethics of the society into the young couple and that it is easier to find putative husbands for girls at an early age. Accordingly, the matriclan and the patriclan have a duty to find suitable, marriageable spouse. Child betrothal as we would see in chapters 14 and 15 in my opinion, is a social device that conditions girls as progenitors to accept the institution of polygyny. Child betrothed girls are more likely to become wives who will be subservient to in-laws, and who will not challenge their material deprivations, not having had much as young wives.

When a suitable potential spouse has been found and if their *omaanda* and *otuzo* and the couple agree, then they become engaged to marry, a few years after the girl's puberty rites and menstruation. In some patrilineal polygynous societies, girls undergo clitoridectomy, to prevent nymphomania, an extreme degree of sexual promiscuity in some women who are married polygynously. Because, polygynists should have wives who are sexually docile and who wait passively to be serviced, instead of going on a frolic of their own. This was the justification for clitoridectomy and infibulation in which the labia are stitched together.

When the contractual betrothal gifts, *otjivareke* provided by the young man or his *eanda* are accepted, the oral contract to marry is sealed. After sometime, the betrothed girl is taken to visit her putative in-laws for approval. The young girl sleeps in the same hut as her future mother-in-law. A week or two later, the child is taken back to her *eanda* relatives or her own parents.

However, when the girl reaches puberty, her prospective in-laws would propose again on behalf of their son. Even after both sets of *omaanda* and *otuzo* agree that the young lady is physically mature for marriage, she can still reject the putative husband on the grounds of repugnancy. There is no pressure exerted on the girl to marry for cattle, if after negotiations between the contracting *otuzo*, and mediation by the *omaanda*, she resolutely refuses to budge, the *otjivareke*, the betrothal settlement is refunded plus agreed damages. The man's family may have entertained her, probably several times, and some families might have given gifts to the girl and her family for several years. The correct measure of damages for the breach is exacted, because they have relied on her to marry their son.

Marriage is also not obligatory for the man. The young man or his *oruzo*, can refuse to go through with the marriage to the betrothed girl. One cannot enforce on him the obligation to marry the girl now that she has come of age. In spite of every precaution, she may have grown up into an undesirable young woman, unfit to be their son's *ondjova* wife. His *eanda* would then forfeit only the *otjivareke*, the betrothal cattle. No contractual damages are recoverable on the loss of marital expectations. The girl's *eanda* has not been unjustly enriched, because they will have to restart the search for a suitable spouse.

The girl whose mother has many children is the favoured woman to become the *ondjova* wife because the fertile genes will have been transmitted to her. It is preferable in matrilineal societies if the woman is also a cross-cousin, for a man could marry a daughter of his mother's brother, or a daughter of his father's sister. It is not a rule, but it has the added advantage that the man and woman already know and perhaps like each other, as well as keeping the cattle property, cocoa plantation or real estate within the matriclan.

A bride who had undergone the *ondjova* ritual would always remain X's *ondjova* wife. Even as an ex-wife, the *ondjova* wife takes precedence at burials, homages, and family gatherings over X's subsequent wife or wives, because she is the child betrothed wife who had undergone the *ondjova* ritual.

Since child betrothal is not consummated and some girls live with their prospective mothers-in-law, my argument is that child betrothal is a way of providing young girl skivvies for old women. In most societies under the provenance of indigenous law, marriage arrangements are now made much later, especially for girls who go to school because schooling has raised the marriageable age of girls.

11.2 Marriage settlement

The marriage settlement has been variously described in the ethnographic literature below as bridewealth, brideprice, brideservice, childprice, dowry, marriage consideration, marriage payment and wife purchase. Many communities in Africa have their own name for it such as, *aseda, bohali, bogadi, emabeka, hunda, idana, lobola, long, ngurario, tirinsa and many more*. However, my preference is for *ovitunya*, an *otjiHerero* word used in North West Namibia where I did my fieldwork. There are many interesting papers on indigenous law marriage settlement.

What is *ovitunya*? It depends on the status of the man, and whether descent is matrilineal or patrilineal. If descent is matrilineal *ovitunya* tends to be small, whereas in patrilineal societies, the marriage settlement is large. In some societies *ovitunya* consists of either a herd of pedigree cattle, gold, jewellery, agricultural produce or fine clothes. In some societies, poor young men offered their services to the bride's family, in lieu of bridewealth and worked for love for an agreed number of lunar months. *Ovitunya* is not purchase, because a husband cannot sell his wife to another man. His limited right in his wife does not include the right to dispose of her by sale.

When both *omaanda* and *otuzo* of the parties agree to become affines, and the couple consent to marry, then the contract of *ovitunya*, the marriage settlement cattle is negotiated. The marriage contract of *ovitunya* creates an affinal bond between the *otuzo* of the spouses. The successful *otuzo* marriages constructed *ozonganda* cohesion and loyalties to members of the various *omaanda*, *otuzo* and *oviwondo*. In short, the successful *ovitunya* marriage of a man and woman maximises the happiness of many people.

Today *ovitunya* is keeping pace with inflation. The standard going rate at the time of my fieldwork had become a very fat ox with excellent picturesque horns and fine long bushy tail. Such a fine ox is known as *ongombe yotjitunya*. Any old 'scrub' ox would be returned with the utmost alacrity. In addition, a pedigree heifer calf, known as the *ongombe yorutombe*, two sheep rams known as *ondu yondjova* and one sheep with a lamb are also given. They make up the matrilineal *ovitunya*, but some people gave over and above this amount. As a result of contact with Liberation Movements, *ovitunya* could now be part payment in cattle and cash or designer blankets or cases of liquor. These new style *ovitunya* status goods were not acceptable to some old uncles and fathers who prefer animals. Cattle *ovitunya* means circulating cattle wealth, whereas monetary bridewealth is akin to purchase.

Indigenous law did not allow a man to enter marriage without the obligation of paying *ovitunya*, because it was not easy to extract cattle payment from husbands who had kicked out their wives. On the other hand, it was effortlessly simple to enforce the *ovitunya* before marriage. No *ovitunya*, no wife. No cattle, no sex, thus no children. *Ovitunya* underpins marriage and the rights of the *oruzo* over the children of the *eanda*. Indigenous law, therefore, refuses to acknowledge a marriage without *ovitunya*; the man or his family must put the *ovitunya* "up front" as they say. It is not a purchase price, it is seen as a financial provision should he discard, divorce or desert her. Without *ovitunya*, indigenous marriage would have been a temporary arrangement for men, because women are burdened with children who depend on them for several years and need meat and milk to rear them.

In patrilineal societies *ovitunya* has an important law 'job' of *pater est quem nuptiae demonstrant*, that is, the legal father is one who can show marriage to the mother. For ex-husbands can claim paternity rights in children born to their ex-wives if the women did not observe at least a nine months period of ritual purity before remarriage. People in the rural areas do not have indigenous law blood tests and DNA finger-printing to verify the child's paternity. The indigenous law period of purity takes priority.

Christendom, relies on the power of the Matrimonial Courts to make orders for financial provison and support for discarded wives, and the state also provides supplementary benefits. In England, for example, to make support for ex-wives and children more effective, the Child Support Act, 1991, the Child Support Collecting and Enforcement Agency, and the Department of Social Security are working together to pursue liable ex-husbands for the maintenance of their child or children. Indigenous law solved this dilemma with *ovitunya*, as Roman law did with *donatio ante nuptias*.[18]

11.3 Divorce

Since the union of a man and woman is marriage and not sale, dissolution of the marriage is found in indigenous law. Like all marriages, whether they are child betrothal, marriage at nineteen or thirty, marriage in the Registry Office, in the cathedral, or before the sacred fire, divorce may follow when the parties are unhappy. Indissolubility of polygynous marriage is an alien concept to some communities; husbands and wives are free to divorce each other. *Himba* women could not see any merit in indissolubility of marriage, perhaps because, as a result of the duolineal transmission system they are financially independent of their husbands.

Couples who married under indigenous law, like other married couples, hope that the marriage they have entered into with the blessings of their ancestors and both families would last forever, but matrilineal societies have no double standards for men and women. A man can neither beat his wife to death for adultery, nor can the *oruzo* inflict death sentence for adultery, when the husband has access to two or three wives, and 'carries on' with his best friend's wife. Matrilineal indigenous law regards it as only fair that between a husband and wife, the wife could have sexual intercourse with a man designated by her husband, but she should not go out on a frolic of her own. Usually, the designated man is the husband's closest friend.

Divorce in matrilineal societies is a strong balancing institution between the *eanda* and the *oruzo*. Although husbands and wives are equal in initiating divorce proceedings, divorce seems to be easier for a man than for a woman, particularly if she is still of child bearing age.

There are two main grounds for the dissolution of an indigenous marriage. The wife's adultery is one reason for her to leave her husband. Adultery under indigenous law means voluntary sexual intercourse between a married woman and another man, without her husband's consent.

Adulterous sexual intercourse should involve penetration, and the parties must be seen together in the act; corroboration by at least three or four people is necessary to prove adultery. The corroboration by eye witnesses was essential, because that was the evidence admissible before the *oruzo* court. Sexual play behind the mopane trees is not sufficient to deprive a man of ten head of cattle, and confession by the wife is inadmissible, as it could be an act of revenge to extort cattle from a rich man. But if the couple spend a night in the same hut, without her husband's permission that will raise a presumption of adultery.

Adultery is an offence committed only by married women as a man is permitted to be polygynous. In consequence of her adultery, a wife can leave her husband and cohabit happily with the other man while she seeks dissolution of the marriage. In spite of her adulterous relationship with the co-respondent, the happy wife can be unhappily re-united again with her husband. For she can be ordered by her matrilineage to return to her husband for mediation, to establish her grievances.

---

[18] In Roman law, the bridegroom's family gave the *donatio ante nuptias* to the bride, usually an estate. For details see Institutes of Iustinian 2. 3. 7.

However, if the run-away wife refuses to join her enraged husband for mediation, and the *otuzo* admit that the marriage has ended, the co-respondent will pay damages to her husband as well as *ovitunya* to her *eanda*. Most husbands do not usually rush off and dissolve their marriage for adultery. It was succinctly put that one does not throw away a perfectly good chair just because someone else sat on it. Forde (1941:72) also noted that "but of itself adultery appears rarely to result in divorce".

Adultery in duolineal transmission is a matter between the wife, the outraged husband and the other man, the co-respondent. So that adultery is not used to extract cattle from rich men, sexual intercourse had to be proved before a husband could claim damages for "robbery". What is adultery worth? The tariff is six to ten head of cattle as exemplary damages and loss of future profits payable to the aggrieved husband. The punitive damages compensate for the husband's wounded virility.

Some oral historians have argued that a woman caught in adultery was put to death. But they have failed to tell us how the woman died. Who executed her? Did her agnates agree to the execution? Was her bridewealth refunded? What of the woman's children?

The second major ground for divorce was taking a second wife without just cause, and without the consent of the *ondjova* wife. Matrilineal and patrilineal descent recognise polygyny, but in order for a man to take a second 'love' wife, he must provide *ovitunya* for the subsequent wife as well as be in a position to support two wives. See chapter 14. There are many more grounds for divorce, but today the most common ground has become drunkenness and the neglect of minor children.

11.4 Social reality of indigenous divorce

Matrilineal societies have managed to minimise the effects of divorce on their children's lives. Divorce is less acrimonious, because the parties have nothing to lose or gain. The ex-wife expects no maintenance and gets none, as the *eanda* is liable for the uterine children and not the divorcing parents. Divorce involves a clean break, hence the provision of *otjivareke*, *ovitunya* and *ohakera*. These conventions create obligations that are some of the ways in which indigenous laws produce a community of responsible fathers. The conventions are men's legal obligations for the support of their children in their *eanda*, and are important principles of justice in indigenous law. See chapter 4. Custody of the children is the pride of the matrilineage, because no woman should be burdened with the duty of bringing up the next generation of children for the community, she should be free to remarry and move on alone to the new husband's *onganda*. As a divorced father may also take a subsequent wife or wives, children of the matrilineage are not brought up by indulgent or wicked step-parents.

11.5 Bibliography

Colloquium on African Law. School of oriental and African Studies, London (1961) 'The legal status of women in Africa, practice, procedure and evidence in the native African local or customary courts'. Journal of African Law. Vol. 2, pp. 125-138.

Kalema Report (1965) Report of the Commission on Marriage, Divorce and the Status of Women. Entebbe, Uganda: Government Printer.

Native Custom and the Colonial Courts: Lobola. (1891) Cape Law Journal. Vol. 8, pp. 37-41.

Native marriage law: Ukulobola (1891) Cape Law Journal. Vol. 8, pp. 218-222.

Report of the Kenya Commission on the Law of Marriage and Divorce. (1968) Nairobi: Government Printer.

Achike, O. (1976a) Problems of creation and dissolution of customary marriages in Nigeria. In Roberts, S. (ed.) *Law and the family in Africa*. The Hague: Mouton.

Achike, O. (1976b) 'The myth of Registrar's Certificate in Act marriages examined'. Nigerian Juridical Review. Vol. 1, pp. 57-66.

Achike, O. (1977) 'Problems of creation and dissolution of customary marriage in Nigeria. In Roberts, S. (ed.) (1977) *Law and the family in Africa*. The Hague: Mouton.

Adams, B. and Mburugu, E. (1994) 'Kikuyu bridewealth and polygyny today'. Journal of Comparative Family Studies. Vol. 25. No. 2, pp. 159-166.

Adesanya, S. A. (1976) 'Divorce law in Ghana and Nigeria: A comparative study in law reform'. The Review of Ghana Law. Vol. 8, pp. 91-115.

Adigun, O. (1989) 'The interplay of conflicting rules: A survey of the customs of the Yoruba and the effect of modern legislation'. Law and Anthropology. Vol. 4, pp. 281-305.

Adinkrah, K. O. (1980) 'The essentials of a customary marriage: A new approach'. Review of Ghana Law. Vol. 12, pp. 40-52.

Agbede, I. O. (1968) 'Recognition of double marriage in Nigerian law.' International and Comparative Law Quarterly. Vol. 17, pp. 735-743.

Agbede, I. O. (1971) 'Inter-racial marriage under Nigerian customary law'. The Nigerian Bar Journal. Vol. 9, pp. 35-47.

Agbosu, L. K. (1981-82) 'Individualisation of interests under the customary law of Ghana'. Review of Ghana Law. Vols. 13&14, pp. 35-50.

Agbosu, L. K. (1983-86) 'The legal composition of the Akan family'. Review of Ghana Law. Vol. 15, pp. 96-111.

Agbosu, L. K. (1987-88) 'Seduction actions in Ghana: *Benya* v *Lawani*'. Review of Ghana Law. vol. 16, pp. 171-190.

Ahmed, A. (1968) 'The general philosophy behind grounds for divorce, a comparative study of both statutory and customary systems'. The Lawyer. Vol. 3, No. 1. pp. 25-30.

Akande, J. O. (1979) *Laws and customs affecting women's status in Nigeria*. Lagos: International Federation of Women Lawyers. (Nigeria).

Akers, S. (1994) 'Female genital mutilation: Cultural or criminal.' Journal of Child Law. Vol. 6, No. 1, pp. 27-31.

Akpaloo, G. A. (1994) 'The impact of legislation on the customary practices of the Ga-Dangme peoples of South Eastern Ghana. Law and Anthropology. Vol. 7, pp. 203-238.

Akpamgbo, C. (1977) 'A woman to woman marriage and the repugnancy clause: A case of putting new wine into old bottles'. African Law Studies. Vol. 14, pp. 87-95.

Allen, J. V. (1972) 'Sitting on a man: Colonialism and the lost political institutions of Igbo women. Canadian Journal of African Studies. Vol 6, No. 2, pp. 165-181.

Allott, A. N. (1958) 'Marriage and internal conflict of laws in Ghana'. Journal of African Law. Vol. 2, No. 3, pp. 164-184.

Allott, A. N. (1968) 'Family law'. In Rubin, N. N. and Cotran, E. (eds.) Annual Survey of African Law. Vol. 2, pp. 23-27.

Amadiume, I. (1987) *Male daughters, female husbands: Gender and sex in an African society.* London: Zed Books.

Amarteifio, E. (1958) Customary marriage in Ghana. African Women Vol. 3, pp. 4-5.

Anderson, J. N. D. (ed.) (1968) *Family law in Asia and Africa.* London: Allen & Unwin.

Aniagolu, A. N. (1977) 'Aspects of customary marriage and divorce and their incidents upon family life'. In Elias, T. O., Nwabara, S. N. and Akpamgbo, C. O. (eds.) *African Indigenous laws.* Enugu: Government Printer. pp. 91-121.

Arens, W. and Arens Antos, D. (1978) 'Kinship and marriage in a polyethnic community'. Africa. Vol. 48, pp. 149-160.

Arhin, K. (1987) 'The political and military roles of Akan women'. In Oppong, C. (ed.) *Female and male in West Africa.* London: Allen & Unwin.

Armstrong, A. et. al (1993) 'Uncovering reality: Excavating women's rights in African family law'. International Journal of Law and the Family. Vol. 7, No. 3, pp. 314-369.

Arnold, J. (1963) 'Lobola: Marriage customs of the Xhosa'. Bantu. Vol. 10, pp. 123-126.

Atiyah, P. S. (1958) 'Some problems of family law in the Sudan Republic'. Sudan Notes and Records. No. 39, pp. 88-100.

Ault, J. M. (1983) 'State power and the regulation of marriage in colonial Zambia. Theory, Culture and Society No. 1, pp. 181-210.

Babalola, K. (1969) 'The use of proverbs in settling and developing customalry law with particular reference to the family'. The Advocate. Vol. 2, No. 1, pp. 41-48.

Balls-Headley, W. (1894) *The evolution of the diseases of women.* London: Smith Elder & Co.

Barker-Benfield, G. J. (1976) *The horrors of the half-known life: Male attitudes towards women and sexuality in the nineteenth century America.* NewYork: Harper & Row.

Barnard, A. (1992) *Hunters and herders of Southern Africa: A comparative ethnography of the Khoisan peoples.* Cambridge: Cambridge University Press.

Barnes, J. A. (1949) 'Measures of divorce frequency in simple societies. Journal of the Royal Anthropological Institute. Vol. 79. pp.37-62.

Barnes, J. A. (1951) *Marriage in a changing society: A study in structural change among the Fort Jameson Ngoui.* Cape Town: Rhodes-Livingstone Paper.

Barnes, R. (1880) Lectures on the diseases of women. Lancet. pp. 1, 4-6, 155-157, 121-123, 923-925.

Barnes, R. (1884) *On the relations between medicine, surgery and obstetrics in London.* New York: W. Wood.

Bassir, O. (1954) Marriage rites among the Aku (Yoruba) of Freetown'. Africa. Vol. 24, pp. 251-256.

Beattie, J. H. M. (1958) Nyoro marriage and affinity (Uganda). Africa. Vol. 27. pp. 1-22.

Beckett, W. E. (1932) 'The recognition of polygamous marriages under English Law'. Law Quarterly Review. No. 48, pp. 341-373.

Bledsoe, C. H. (1980) *Women and marriage in Kpelle society.* Stanford, Calif.: Stanford University Press.

Bloomhill, G. (1961) 'Africa en famille: Women and children in a primitive (Matabele) Society'. African World. pp. 12-14.

Bohannan, P. and Middleton, J. (eds.) (1968) *Marriage, family and residence.* Garden City, NY: Natural History Press.

Borgerhoff Mulder, M. (1989) 'Polygyny and the extent of women's contribution to subsistence: A reply to White'. American Anthropologist. Vol. 91, No. 1, pp. 178-180.

Borgerhoff, M. (1992) 'Women strategies in polygynous marriage: Kipsigis, Datoga and other East African Cases'. Human Nature. Vol. 3, No. 1, pp. 45-70.

Borneman, J. (1996) 'Until death do us part: Marriage, death in anthropological discourse'. American Ethnologist. Vol. 23, No. 2, pp. 215-234 & 237-238.

Brabin, L. (1984) 'Polygyny: An indicator of nutritional stress in African agricultural societies'. Africa. Vol. 54, No. 1, pp. 31-45.

Brain, R. (1972) *Bangwa kinship and marriage.* Cambridge: Cambridge University Press.

Bretschneider, P. (1992) 'Sociological models of polygyny: A critical review'. Anthropos. Vol. 87, pp. 183-191.

Bretschneider, P. (1995) *Polygyny: A cross-cultural study.* Uppsala. Uppsala University.

Broderick, G. E. P. (1945) 'Betrothal ceremony among the Wazeruru of the Salisbury district'. NADA Vol. 22, pp. 49-50.

Brown, E. F. (1935) 'Hehe grandmother'. Journal of the Royal Anthropological Institute. Vol. 65, pp. 83-96.

Brown, S. D. (1994) 'The divorce of Zanjiili's daughter: Poly-ethnic litigation in Northern Ghana. Droit et Cultures. No. 27, pp. 225-249.

Brown, W. (1960) 'Status of Uganda women in relation to marriage laws'. African Women. Vol. 4, No. 1, pp. 1-4.

Bukh, J. (1979) *The village woman in Ghana.* Uppsala: Scandinavian Institute of African Studies.

Buxton, J. (1958) 'The significance of bridewealth and the levirate among the Nilotic and Nilo-Hamitic tribes of the Southern Sudan'. Anti-Slavery Reporter. Vol. 11, pp. 66-75.

Cairncross, J. (1974) *After polygamy was made a sin. The social history of christian polygamy.* London: Routledge and Kegan Paul.

Chalifoux, J. J. (1980) 'Secondary marriage and levels of seniority among the Abisi (Piti) of Nigeria'. In Levine, N. E. (ed.) *Women with many husbands: Polyandrous alliance and marital flexibility in Africa and Asia.* Journal of Comparative Family Studies. (special issue) Vol. 11, No. 3, pp. 325-334.

Chanock, M. (1989) 'Neither customary nor legal: African customary law in an era of family law reform'. International Journal of Law and the Family. Vol. 3, No. 1, pp. 72-88.

Chesoni, Z. R. (1966) 'Divorce and succession in Luyia customary law'. East African Law Journal. Vol. 2, pp. 165-178.

Chigwedere, A. (1988) *Lobolo: The pros and cons in relation to the emancipation of women in Zimbabwe.* Harare: Books for Africa.

Chigwedere, A. (1988) *Lobolo: The pros and cons in relation to the emancipation of women in Zimbabwe.* Harare: Books for Africa.

Child, H. F. (1932) 'Amandebele custom: Impotency as a ground of divorce and payment of second dowries'. NADA. No. 10, pp. 36-39.

Christensen, J. B. (1954) Double descent among the Fanti. New Haven: Human Relations Area Files.

Clerc, A. (1938) 'The marriage laws of the Ronga tribe'. Bantu Studies. Vol. 12, pp. 75-104.

Clive, E. (1980) 'Marriage: An unnecessary legal concept?' In Eekelaar, J. and Katz, S. (eds.) *Marriage and cohabitation in contemporary societies.* Toronto: Butterworths & Co. Ltd.

Coldham, S. (1990) 'Customary marriage and the urban local courts in Zambia'. Journal of African Law. Vol. 34, No. 1, pp. 67-75.

Colson, E. (1958) *Marriage and the family among the Plateau Tonga of Northern Rhodesia.* Manchester: Manchester University Press for the Rhodes-Livingstone Institute.

Comaroff, J. L. (ed.) (1980) *The meaning of marriage payments.* London & New York: Academic Press.

Comaroff, J. and Roberts, S. (1977) 'Marriage and extra-marital sexuality: The dialectics of legal change among the Kgatla'. Journal of African Law. Vol.. 21, No. 1, pp. 97-123.

Conte, E. (1982) Marriage patterns, political change and the perpetuation of social inequality in South Kanem (Chad) London: PhD Thesis. University College, University of London.

Cotran, E. (1968) The law of marriage and divorce: Kenya. London: Sweet and Maxwell.

Cotran, E. (1979) 'The rejection of the Marriage Bill in Kenya'. Journal of African Law. Vol. 23, No. 2, pp. 109-116.

Cotran, E. (1996) 'Marriage, divorce and succession laws in Kenya: Is integration or unification possible?' Journal of African Law. Vol. 40, No.2, pp. 194-204.

Cotran, E. and Rubin, N. N. (1970) *Readings in African Law*. Vol 11, London: Frank Cass.

Cotton, J. C. (1905) 'The Calabar marriage law and custom'. Journal of the African Society. Vol. 4, No. 16, pp. 427-432.

Crandall, D. P. (1991) 'The strength of the ovaHimba patrilineage'. Cimbebasia. Vol. 13, pp. 45-51.

Cretney, S. (1967) 'Some problems in the marriage laws of Kenya'. East African Law Journal. Vol. 3, pp. 1-26.

Cripps, H. (1947) Should lobolo be restricted by legislation? NADA No. 24, pp. 41-47.

Culwick, A. T. and Culwick, G. M. (1934) 'The functions of bridewealth in Ubena of the rivers'. Africa. Vol. 7, No. 1, pp. 140-159.

Dalton, G. (1966) 'Bridewealth v Brideprice'. American Anthropologist. pp. 732-738.

Date-Bah, S. K. and Fiadjoe, A. K. (1971) 'Seduction actions: The Ghanaian experience'. The Review of Ghana Law. Vol. 3, pp. 29-38.

De Haas, M. (1987) 'Is there anything more to say about lobolo'? African Studies. Vol. 46, pp. 33-55.

Dickemann, M. (1979) 'The ecology of mating systems in hypergynous dowry societies'. Social Science Information. Vol. 18, pp. 163-195.

Divale, W. T. (1974) 'Migration, external warfare and matrilocal residence'. Behaviour Science Research. Vol. 9, pp. 75-133.

Dlamini, C. R. N. (1994) *The juridical analysis and critical evaluation of ilobolo in a changing Zulu society*. Pretoria: Co-operative Research Programme on Marriage and Family Life.

Donzelot, J. (1979) *The policing of families*. New York: Pantheon.

Dupire, M. (1974) 'Residence, land tenure and marriage in a double descent society: The Serer from the Sine and Boal regions of Senegal'. Cahiers d'etudes Africaines. Vol. 14, pp. 417-452.

Edwards, W. (1929) 'From birth to death: Notes on the natives of the Mrewa district, Southern Rhodesia'. NADA Vol. 7, pp. 16-42.

Ekow-Daniels, W. C. (1965) 'Towards the integration of the laws relating to husband and wife in Ghana'. University of Ghana Law Journal. Vol. 11, pp. 20-58.

Ekow-Daniels, W. C. (1971) 'Notes and comments: Ghana Matrimonial Causes Act, 1971'. Review of Ghana Law. Vol. 3, No. 3, pp. 231-238.

Ekow-Daniels, W. C. (1972) 'The legal position of women under our marriage laws'. University of Ghana Law Journal. Vol. 9, pp. 39-63.

Ekow-Daniels, W. C. (1973) 'Damages for adultery now?' Review of Ghana Law. Vol. 5, No. 2, pp. 148-150.

Ekow-Daniels, W. C. (1977) 'Dissolution of customary law marriages by the court' Review of Ghana Law. Vol. 9, pp. 71-82.

Ekow-Daniels, W. C. and Woodman, G. R. (eds.) (1976) *Essays in Ghanaian law Supreme Court centenary publication 1876-1976.* Legon: University of Ghana Faculty of Law.

Ekundare, R. O. (1969) *Marriage and divorce under Yoruba customary law*. Ile-Ife: University of Ife Press.

Elias, T. O. (1956) *The nature of African customary law*. Manchester: Manchester University Press.

Elias, T. O. (1957) 'Hausa marriage'. Nigeria. No. 53. pp. 135-149.

Elias, T. O., Nwabara, S. N. and Akpamgbo, C. (eds.) (1975) *African indigenous laws*. Enugu: Nigerian Government Printer.

Ember, M. and Ember, C. R. (1971) 'The conditions favouring matrilocal versus patriloval residence'. American Anthropologist. Vol. 73, pp. 571-594.

Engelbrecht, J. A. (1931) 'Swazi customs relating to marriage'. Annals of the University of Stellenbosch. Vol. 8, No. 6, Sect. B.

Epstein, A. L. (1954) 'Divorce law and the stability of marriage among the Lunda of Kazembe'. Human Problems in British Central Africa. Rhodes-Livingstone Journal. Vol. 14. pp. 1-19.

Esenwa, S. E. (1948) 'Marriage customs in Asaba Division. Nigerian Fields. Vol. 13, pp. 71-81.

Evans-Pritchard, E. E. (1931) 'An alternative term for brideprice'. Man. Vol. 30, pp. 36-39.

Evans-Pritchard, E. E. (1934) 'Social character of bride-wealth with special reference to the Azande'. Man. Vol. 34. pp. 172-175.

Evans-Pritchard, E. E. (1946) 'Nuer bridewealth'. Africa. Vol. 16, pp. 247-257.

Evans-Pritchard, E. E. (1947) 'Bridewealth among the Nuer'. African Studies. Vol. 6, pp. 181-188.

Evans-Pritchard, E. E. (1948) 'Nuer marriage ceremonies'. Africa. Vol. 18, pp. 29-40.

Evans-Pritchard, E. E. (1949) *Nuer rules of exogamy and incest: Essay in social structure.* Oxford: Oxford University Press.

Evans-Pritchard, E. E. (1950) 'Marriage custom of the Luo of Kenya'. Africa. Vol. 20, pp. 132-142.

Evans-Pritchard, E. E. (1951) *Kinship and marriage among the Nuer.* Oxford: Clarendon Press.

Fako, T. (1983) The family and national development in Botswana'. Botswana Notes and Records. Vol. 15, pp. 452-464.

Fallers, L. A. (1957) 'Some determinants of marriage stabillity in Busoga: A reformulation of Gluckman's hypothesis. Africa. Vol. 27, pp. 106-121.

Famodu, A. O. (1968) 'The rights of women under Yoruba customary law'. The Advocate. Spring. pp. 76-78.

Fardon, R. (1984) Sisters, wives, wards and daughters: A transformational analysis of the political organization of the Tiv and their neighbours'. Africa. Vol. 54, No. 4, pp. 2-21.

Farran, C. O. (1963) *Matrimonial laws of the Sudan: Being a study of the divergent religious and civil laws in African society.* London: Butterworth & Co. Ltd..

Faubion, J. D. (1996) 'Kinship is dead: Long live kinship'. Comparative Studies in Society and History. Vol. 38, No. 1, pp. 67-91.

Feraro, G. P. (1991) 'Marriage and conjugal roles in Swaziland: Persistence and change'. International Journal of Sociology of the Family. Vol. 21. No. 2. pp. 89-128.

Field, J. O. (1936) 'Bride wealth as a bar to marriage'. Man. Vol. 36, pp. 38-39.

Field, M. J. (1940) *Social organization of the Gã people.* Accra: Government Printer for the Crown Agents for the Colonies.

Filer, C. (1985) 'What is this thing called brideprice'? Mankind. Vol. 15, pp. 163-183.

Fisher, H. (1973) 'Conversion reconsidered: Some historical aspects of religious conversion in Black Africa'. Africa. Vol. 43, No. 1, pp. 27-40.

Fleming, C. J. W. (1973) 'The constitution of the indigenous family'. NADA Vol. 10. No. 5, pp.56-65.

Forde, D. C. (1946) Marriage and family among the Yoruba. London.

Forde, D. (1941) Marriage and the family among the Yakö in South Eastern Nigeria. London: Percy Lund Humphries.

Fortes, M. (1937) Marriage law among the Tallensi. Accra: Government Printer.

Fortes, M. (1945) *The dynamics of clanship among the Tallensi.* Oxford: Oxford University Press.

Fortes, M. (1949) The web of kinship among the Tallensi. London: Oxford University Press.

Fortes, M. (1953) 'The structure of unilineal descent groups'. American Anthropologist. No. 55, pp. 17-41.

Fox, R. (1967) *Kinship and marriage: An anthropological perspective*. Harmondsworth: Penguin Books.

Fox, R. (1980) *The red lamp of incest*. New York: Dutton.

Fox, R. (1985) 'Paternity irrelevance and matrilineal descent'. The Behavioral and Brain Sciences. Vol. 8, No. 4, pp. 674-675.

Fox, R. (1993) *Reproduction and succession: Studies in anthropological law and society*. New Brunswick: Transaction Publishers.

Gelfand, M. (1975) 'Upombwe: Adultery in Shona law. NADA Vol. 11, No. 2, pp. 192-199.

Gelfand, M. (1976) 'Seduction and elopment in Shona law. NADA Vol. 11. No. 3, pp. 321-327.

Gluckman, M. (1950) 'Marriage payments and social structure among the Lozi and Zulu'. In Goody, J. (ed.) *Kinship: Selected readings*. Baltimore: Penguin Books.

Gluckman, M. (1954) Bridewealth and the stability of marriage. Man. Vol. 54. p. 67.

Gluckman, M. (1955) 'The reasonable man in Barotse law: The case of the eloping wife'. Journal of African Administration. Vol. 7, No. 1, pp. 127-131.

Gluckman, M. (1959) 'Kinship and marriage among the Lozi of Northern Rhodesia and the Zulu of Natal'. In Radcliffe-Brown, A. R. and Dorde, D. (eds.) *African systems of kinship and marriage*. Oxford: Oxford University Press.

Goody, J. (1973) 'Bridewealth and dowry in Africa and Eurasia'. In Goody, J. and Tambiah, S. J. (eds.) *Bridewealth and dowry*. pp. 1-58. Cambridge: Cambridge University Press.

Goody, J. (1983) *The development of the family and marriage in Europe*. Cambridge: Cambridge University Press.

Gray, R. F. (1960) 'Sonjo bride price and the question of African 'wife purchase'. American Anthropologist. Vol. 62, pp. 34-57.

Griew, E. (1960) 'Ohochuku v Ohochuku divorce, polygamous marriage'. International and Comparative Law Quarterly. Vol. 9, pp. 503-508.

Griffiths, A. (1984) 'Support for owmen with dependent children under the customary system of the Bakwena and the Roman-Dutch common and statuttory law of Botswana'. Journal of Legal Pluralism. Vol. 22, pp. 1-15.

Griffiths, A. (1989) 'The legal heritage of colonialism: Family law in a former British protectorate'. Law and Anthropology. Vol. 4, pp. 75-105.

Håkansson, T. (1989) 'Family structure, bridewealth and environment in Eastern Africa: A comparative study of house-property systems'. Ethnology. Vol. 28, No. 2, pp. 1117-134.

Halleran, T. H. (1951) Krobo marriage customs Anthropos Vol. 46, pp. 996-997.

Harrell-Bond, B. E. and Rijnsdorp, U. (1977) 'The emergence of the 'stranger-permit marriage' and other new forms of conjugal union in rural Sierra leone'. In Roberts, S. (ed.) *Law and the family in Africa*. The Hague: Mouton.

Harries-Jones, P. (1964) 'Marital disputes and the process of conciliation in a copperbelt town: Human Problems in British Central Africa'. Rhodes-Livingstone Journal. Vol. 35, pp. 29-72.

Hartland, E. S. (1909-10) *Primitive paternity*. London: David Nutt.

Herskovitz, M. J. (1937) 'A note on "woman marriage" in Dahomey'. Africa. Vol. 10, pp. 335-341

Himonga, C. N. (1987) 'Property disputes in law and practice: Dissolution of marriage in Zambia'. In Armstrong, A. and Ncube, W. (eds.) *Women and law in Southern Africa*. Harare: Zimbabwe Publishing House.

Himonga, C. N. (1991) 'Family law reform and the integration of the laws of succession in Zambia'. Verfassung und Recht in Übersee. Vol. 24, pp. 340-361.

Himonga, C. (1994) 'The dual family law system in Zambia: Co-existence and operation'. Law and Anthropology. Vol. 7, pp. 239-260.

Holleman, J. F. (1951) 'The dissolution of native marriages'. National Affairs. Vol. 2, No. 7, pp. 3-4.

Holleman, J. F. (1952) *Shona customary law: With reference to kinship, marriage, the family and the estate*. London: Oxford University Press for the Rhodes-Livingstone Institute.

Holleman, J. F. (1960) 'Bantu marriage at the cross-roads'. Race Relations Journal. Vol. 27, No. 2, pp. 153-157.

Holleman, J. (1974) *Issues in African law*. The Hague: Mouton.

Howell, P. P. (1953) 'Some observations on divorce among the Nuer'. Journal of Royal Anthropological Institute. Vol. 83, pp. 136-146.

Huber, H. (1973) *Marriage and the family in rural Bukwaya*. Fribourg, Switzerland: University Press.

Hunter, M. (1933) 'The effects of contact with Europeans on the status of Pondo women'. Africa. Vol. 5, pp. 259-276.

Ibik, J. O. (1970) *Restatement of African law: The law of mariage and divorce. Malawi*. London: Sweet and Maxwell.

Imoagene, S. (1969) 'Kinship and marital stability among the Weppa-Wano'. (Mid Western Nigeria) Journal of Business and Social Studies. Vol. 2, No. 1, pp. 42-52.

Jeffreys, M. D. W. (1951) 'Lobolo's child-price'. African Studies. Vol. 10, pp. 145-184.

Jennings, A. E. (1933) *Bogadi: A study of the marriage laws and customs of the Bechuana tribes of South Africa.* Vryburg: London Missionary Society.

Kane, M. (1972) 'The status of married women under customary law in Senegal'. American Journal of Comparative Law. Vol. 20. No. 4. pp. 716-723.

Kassam, F. M. (1969) *Report of the Kenya Commission on Marriage and Divorce: A critique'.* Eastern Africa Law Review. Vol. 2, pp. 179-219.

Kasunmu, A. B. (1966) *Nigerian Family Law.* London: Butterworth & Co. Ltd.

Kasunmu, A. B. (1969) 'Proof of a polygamous marriage in Nigerian High Courts. *Lawal v Younan* re examined'. Journal of Islamic and Comparative Law. Vol. 3, pp.27-43.

Kenning, J. (1963) *Customary laws and customary courts in Yorubaland.* Ibadan: Institute of Social and Economic Research.

Kilbride, P. (1994) Plural marriage for our times: A reinvented option? Westport, Conn.: Greenwood Press.

Knowles, O. S. (1956) 'Some modern adaptations of customary law in the settlement of matrimonial disputes in the Luo, Kisii and Kuria tribes of South Nyanza'. Journal of African Administration. Vol. 8, pp. 11-15.

Kohler, J. (1895) *On the pre-history of marriage, totemism, group marriage, mother-right.* Chicago: University of Chicago Press.

Kouassigan, G. A. (1974) *Quelle est ma loi? Tradition et modernisme dans le droit privé de la famille en Afique noire francophone.* Paris: Pedone.

Krige, E. J. (1974) 'Woman-marriage, with special reference to the Lovedu: Its significance for the definition of marriage'. Africa. Vol. 44, pp. 11-37.

Krige, E. J. and Comaroff, J. L. (eds.) (1981) *Essays on African marriage in Southern Africa.* Cape Town: Juta.

Kuenyehia, A. (1986-89) 'Women and family law in Ghana: An appraisal of property rights of married women'. University of Ghana Law Journal. Vol. 17, pp. 72-99.

Kuenyehia, A. (1990-92) 'Distribution of matrimonial property on dissolution of marriage: A reappraisal'. University of Ghana Law Journal. Vol. 18, pp. 94-108.

Kuper, A. (1982) *Wives for cattle: Bridewealth and marriage in Southern Africa.* London: Routledge & Kegan Paul.

Kurian, G. (1979) *Cross-cultural perspectives of mate-selection and marriage.* Westport, Conn.: Greenwood Press.

Kurland, J. (1979) 'Paternity, mother's brother and human sociality'. In Chagnon, N. and Irons, W. (eds.) *Evolutionary biology and human social behaviour.* North Scituate, MA: Duxbury.

Lamb, C. (1992) 'Female excision: the feminist conundrum'. Ufahamu. Vol. 20, No. 3, pp. 13-31.

Lamber, J. C. (1973) 'A married woman's surname: Is custom law?' Washington University Law Quarterly. pp. 779-819.

Lancaster, C. S. (1974) 'Brideservice, residence and authority among the Goba (N. Shona) of the Zambesi Valley'. Africa. Vol. 44, pp. 46-64.

Langenbahn, H. J. (1989) 'Bridewealth and brideservice among the Ingessana'. Sociologus. Vol. 39, pp. 177-189.

Leach, E. R. (1953) 'Bridewealth and the stability of marriage'. Man. Vol. 53. pp. 179-180.

Lee, G. R. (1979) 'Marital structure and economic systems'. Journal of Marriage and the Family. Vol. 41, pp. 701-707.

Lestrade, G. P. (1926) 'Some notes on the bogadi system of the Bahurutshe'. South African Journal of Science. Vol. 23, pp. 937-942.

Lévi-Strauss, C. (1967) *Les structures élémentaires de la parente*. Paris: Mouton.

Lewin, J. (1939) 'Some legal consequences of marriage by native Christians in British Africa'. Modern Law Review. Vol. 3, pp. 48-52.

Lewin, J. (1944) 'Some lobolo cases in native law'. African Studies. Vol. 3, pp. 129-139.

Lloyd, P. C. (1955) 'The Yoruba lineage'. Africa. Vol. 25, pp. 235-251.

Lloyd, P. C. (1968) 'Divorce among the Yoruba'. American Anthropologist. Vol. 70, No. 1, pp. 67-81.

Lowy, M. J. (1977) 'Establishing paternity and demanding child support in a Ghanaian town. In Roberts, S. (ed.) Law and the family in Africa. pp. 15-37. The Hague: Mouton.

Lystad, R. (1959) 'Marriage among the Ashanti and Agni' In Bascom, W. R. and Herskovits, M. J. (eds.) *Continuity and change in African cultures*, pp. 187-204. Chicago: University of Chicago Press.

M'Baye, K. (1968) *Le droit de la famille en Afrique noire et à Madagascar*. Paris: G. P. Maisonneuve et Larose

MacGaffey, W. (1983) 'Lineage structure, marriage and the family amongst the Central Bantu'. Journal of African History. Vol. 24, No. 2, pp. 173-187.

Magutu, W. (1983) 'Lesotho's African marriage is not a 'customary union'. Comparative and International Law Journal of Southern Africa. No. 16, pp. 374-382.

Mair, L. (1971) *Marriage*. Harmondsworth: Penguin Books.

Mair, L. (ed.) (1969) *African marriage and social change*. London: Cass.

Mamashela, M. (1991) *Family law through cases in Lesotho*. Roma: National University of Lesotho.

Mamashela, M. P. (1989) 'Legal dualism in Lesotho (with particular reference to marriage and succession'. Law and Anthropology. Vol. 7, 4, pp. 59-73.

Mann, K. (1985) *Marrying well: Marriage, status and social change among the educated elite in colonial Lagos.* Cambridge: Cambridge University Press.

Marks, S. and Rathbone, R. (1983) 'The history of the family in Africa: Introduction'. Journal of African History. Vol. 24, No. 2, pp. 145-161.

Marshall, L. (1976) *The !Kung of Nyae Nyae.* Cambridge, Mass: Harvard University Press.

May, J. (1983) *Zimbabwean women in customary and colonial law.* Gweru: Mambu Press.

Mayer, P. (1950) *Gusii bridewealth law and custom.* Cape Town: Geoffrey Cumberledge

Mbilinyi, M. (1988) 'Runaway wives in colonial Tanganyika: Forced labour and forced marriage in Rungwe District 1919-1961'. International Journal of the Sociology of Law. Vol. 16, pp. 1-29.

Meek, C. K. (1936) 'Marriage by exchange in Nigeria: A disappearing institution'. Africa. Vol. 9, No. 1, pp. 64-74.

Meek, D. (1992) 'The process of marriage in African societies: A multiple indicator approach'. Population and Development Review. Vol. 18, No. 1, pp. 61-78.

Mell, A. H. (1951) 'Notes on family and marriage in primitive societies'. Nyasaland Journal. Vol. 4, No. 1, pp. 7-23.

Mercer, C. L. (1971) 'Engagement, breach of promise and seduction in African law'. Rhodesia Law Journal. pp. 156-158.

Meyer, F. (ed.) (1962) *Marriage in tribal societies.* Cambridge: Cambridge University Press.

Moller, V. and Welch, G. J. (1990) Polygamy, economic security and well-being of retired Zulu migrant workers'. Journal of Cross-Cultural Gerontology. Vol. 5, No. 3, pp. 205-216.

Molokomme, A. L. (1990-91) Disseminating family law reforms: Some lessons from Botswana. Journal of Legal Pluralism. Nos. 30 & 31, pp. 303-329.

Molokomme, A. (1994) 'Caught between indigenous law and state law: The strategies of mothers in maintenance cases in a Bangwaketse village'. Law and Anthropology. Vol. 7, pp. 287-310.

Morris, H. F. (1966) 'Uganda: Report of the Commission on Marriage, Divorce and the Status of Women. Journal of African Law. Vol. 10. No. 1, pp. 3-7.

Morris, H. F. (1968) *Marriage law in Uganda: Sixty years of attempted reform in Family law in Asia and Africa.* London: Allen and Unwin.

Morris, H. F. (1971) 'Review of developments in African marriage law since 1950'. In Phillips, A. and Morris, F. (eds.) *Marriage laws in Africa.* London: Oxford University Press for International African Institute.

Morris, H. F. (1979) 'The development of statutory marriage law in 20th century British colonial Africa'. Journal of African Law. Vol. 23, No. pp. 37-64.

Mulago, V. (1965) 'Mariage africain et mariage chrétien: Perspectives liturgico pastorales'. Revue du Clergé Africain. Vol. 20, No. 6, pp. 547-564.

Mulago, V. (1971) 'Le mariage traditionnel bantu'. Revue du Clergé Africain Vol. 26, Nos. 3-4, pp. 5-61.

Mulder, M. B. (1995) 'Bridewealth and its correlates: Quantifying changes over time'. Current Anthropology. Vol. 36, No. 3, pp. 573-589

Muller, J. C. (1978) 'On bridewealth and meaning among the Rukuba, Plateau State, Nigeria'. Africa. Vol. 48, No. 2, pp. 161-175.

Muller, J. C. (1984) 'Marriage rules on the Plateau: An exchange (between Muller and B. Sharpe)' Africa. Vol. 54, No. 4, pp. 22-24.

Muller, J. C. and Sangree, W. H. (1973) 'Irigwe and Rukuba marriage: A comparison'. The Canadian Journal of African Studies. Vol. 7, pp. 27-57.

Murray, C. (1977) 'High bridewealth, migrant labour and the position of women in Lesotho'. Journal of African Law. Vol. 21, pp. 79-95.

Ncube, W. (1990) 'Re-allocation of matrimonial property at the dissolution of marriage in Zimbabwe'. Journal of African Law. Vol. 34, No. 1, pp. 1-8.

Needham, R. (ed.) (1971) *Rethinking kinship and marriage*. London: Tavistock Publications.

Nhlapo, R. T. (1989) 'International protection of human rights and the family: African variations on a common theme'. International Journal of Law and the Family. Vol. 3, No. 1, pp. 1-20.

Nhlapo, R. T. (1991) 'The African family and women's rights: Friends or foes'. Acta Juridica. pp. 135-146.

Nhlapo, R. T. (1995) Cultural diversity, human rights and the family in contemporary Africa: Lessons from the South African Constitution debate. International Journal of Law and the Family. Vol. 9, No. 2, pp. 208-225.

Nhlapo, T. (1992) *Marriage and divorce in Swazi law and custom*. Mbabane: Websters

Nii-Aponsah, D. A. (1978) 'Law and social reality: The effect of marriage and paternity of membership of family among Ga Mashie people'. Review of Ghana Law. Vol. 10, No. 1, pp. 32-46.

Nsereko, D. D. (1975) 'The nature and function of marriage gifts in customary African marriages'. American Journal of Comparative Law. Vol. 23, pp.682-704.

Nukunya, G. K. (1969) *Kinship and marriage among the Anlo Ewe*. London: The Athlone Press.

Nwogugu, E. I. (1974) *Family law in Nigeria*. Ibadan: Heinemann.

Nylander, A. V. J. and Kasunmu, A. B. (1968) In Rubin, N. N. and Cotran, E. (eds.) Annual Survey of African Law. Vol.2, pp. 44-52.

O'Brien, D. (1977) 'Female husbands in Southern Bantu societies'. In Schlegel, A. (ed.) *Sexual stratification: A cross-cultural view*. New York: Columbia University Press.

Obi, S. N. C. (1966) *Modern family law in Southern Nigeria*. London: Sweet & Maxwell.

Obilade, A. O. (1966) 'Customary law marriages rights fall into abeyance'. The Lawyer. Vol. 2, No. 1, pp. 1-2.

Oboler, R. S. (1980) 'Is the female husband a man? Woman/woman marriage among the Nandi of Kenya'. Ethnology. Vol. 19, pp. 69-88.

Ogbu, J. (1978) 'African bridewealth and women's status'. American Ethnologist. Vol. 5, No. 2, pp. 241-262.

Okagbue, R. O. (1975) 'The marriage dilemma'. In Elias, T. O. et al. (eds.) *African indigenous laws*. Enugu: Government Printer.

Ollennu, N. A. (1968) 'The family law in Ghana'. In *Le droit de la famille en Afrique noire et à Madagascar*. Etudes preparées a la requête de l'UNESCO. Paris.

Olufon, K. (1970) 'A critique of the law relating to conversion of marriages in Nigeria'. The Lawyer. Vol.4, No. 1, pp. 26-33.

Opoku, K. (1972) 'Divorce in Ghana'. Verfassung und Recht in Übersee. Vol. 5, pp. 507-414.

Oppong, C. (1972) 'A note on matriliny and marriage in Accra'. Journal Asian and African Studies. Vol. 7, pp. 211-218.

Oppong, C. and Adaba, G. (1978) *Marriage, fertility and parenthood in West Africa*. Canberra. Australian National University.

Osmond, M. W. (1965) 'Toward monogamy: A cross-cultural study of correlates of type of marriage'. Social Forces. Vol. 44, pp. 6-16.

Ottenberg, S. (1968) *Double descent in an African society: The Afikpo village-group*. Seattle: University of Washington Press.

Paliwala, A. (1993) 'Family transformation and family law: Some African developments in financial support on relationship breakdown'. In Adelman, S. and Paliwala, A. (eds.) *Law and crisis in the third world*. London: Hans Zell.

Parkin, D. and Nyamwaya (eds.) (1987) *Transformation of African marriage*. Manchester: Manchester University Press.

Perlman, M. L. (1969) 'Law and the status of women in Uganda: A systematic comparison between the Ganda and the Toro'. Tropical magazine. Vol. 2, pp. 60-106.

Perlman, M. L. (1985) 'Family law and social change among the Toro of Uganda'. Journal of African Law. Vol. 29, No. 1, pp. 82-93.

Phillips, A. (1949) 'The African marriage survey. Journal of African Administration. Vol. 1, No. 1, pp.39-40.

Phillips, A. (1950) 'African marriage in the Belgian Congo'. Journal of African Administration. Vol. 2, No. 2, pp. 15-19.

Phillips, A. (1959) Marriage and divorce laws in East Africa. Journal of African Law. Vol. 3, pp. 93-98.

Phillips, A. (1963) Marriage laws in Africa. In Phillips, A. (ed.) *Survey of African marriage and family life.* London: Oxford University Press for the International African Institute.

Phillips, A. (ed.) (1953) *Survey of African marriage and family life*. London: Oxford University Press for the International Africn Institute.

Pigault, G. and Rwegera, D. (1975) 'Marriages in Sub-Saharan Africa'. Africa. International bibliography 1945-1975. RIC Supplement. pp. 23-26.

Posselt, F. (1928) 'Native marriage'. NADA No. 6, pp. 67-73.

Poulter, S. (1976) *Family law and litigation in Basotho Society.* Oxford: Clarendon Press.

Poulter, S. (1977) 'Marriage, divorce and legitimacy in Lesotho'. Journal of African Law. Vol. 21, No. 1, pp. 66-78.

Poulter, S. (1981) *Legal dualism in Lesotho: A study of the choice of law question in family law matters.* Morija Lesotho: Morija Sesuto Books.

Pradelles de Latour, C. H. (1994) 'Marriage payments, debt and fatherhood among the Bangoua: A Lacanian analysis of a kinship sytem'. Africa. Vol. 64. No. 1, pp. 21-33.

Preston-Whyte, E. (1974) Kinship and marriage'. In Hammond-Tooke, W. D. (ed.) *The Bantu-speaking peoples of Southern Africa.* pp. 177-210. London: Routledge and Kegan Paul.

Quansah, E. K. (1994) 'Proposals for the reform of the law of marriage in Botswana: Some observations'. Pula. Vol. 8, No. 2, pp. 37-45.

Radcliffe-Brown, A. R. (1924) 'The mother's brother in South Africa'. South African Journal of Science. Vol. 21, pp. 542-555.

Radcliffe-Brown, A. R. and Forde, D. (eds.) (1950) *African systems of kinship and marriage.* London: Oxford University Press for International African Institute.

Rattray, R. S. (1929) *The family: The wife in Ashanti law and constitution.* Oxford: Clarendon Press.

Read, J. S. (1963) Women's status and law reform'. In Anderson, J. N. D. (ed.) *Changing law in developing countries.* pp. 210-239. London: Allen & Unwin.

Read, J. S. (1964) 'When is a wife not a wife?' Journal of the Denning Law Society. Vol. 2, pp. 47-75.

Read, J. S. (1969) 'Marriage and divorce: A new look for the law in kenya?' East African Law Journal. Vol. 5, pp. 107-140.

Read, J. S. (1972) 'A milestone in the integration of personal laws: The new law of marriage and divorce in Tanzania'. Journal of African Law. Vol. 16, No. 1, pp. 19-39.

Reynolds, W. S. (1979-80) 'Wives and co-wives in Marachi, Kenya. Folk. Vol. 21-22, pp. 133-146.

Richards, A. I. (1933) 'Mother-right in Central Africa'. In Evans-Pritchard, E. E., Firth, R., Malinowski, B. and Schapera I. (eds.) *Essays presented to C. G. Seligman*. London: Kegan Paul, Trench and Trubner.

Richards, A. I. (1940) *Bemba marriage and present economic conditions*. Rhodes-Livingstone papers. No. 4, Livinstone, Northern Rhodesia: Rhodes-Livingstone Institute.

Richards, E. H. (ed.) *Ordinances, Orders and Rules in force in the Colony of Lagos, 1893*. London: Stevens & Sons.

Roberts, S. (1964) 'Matrilineal family law and custom in Malawi: A comparison of two systems'. Journal of African Law. Vol. 8, No. 2, pp. 77-90.

Roberts, S. (1972) *Tswana family law. Restatement of African Law*, No. 5, Botswana 1. London: Sweet & Maxwell.

Roberts, S. (1977b) 'The Kgatla marriage: Concepts of validity'. In Roberts, S. (ed.) *Law and the family in Africa*. The Hague: Mouton.

Roberts, S. (ed.) (1977a) *Law and the family in Africa*. The Hague: Mouton.

Rubin, N. N. (1970) 'Matrimonial law among the Bali of West Cameroon: A restatement'. Journal of African Law. Vol. 14, No. 2, pp. 69-97.

Rwezaura, B. A. (1986) 'Tanzania: The Law Reform Commission's Paper on proposed changes in family law'. Journal of Family Law. Vol. 10, pp. 213-220.

Rwezaura, B. A. (1988b) 'The changing role of the extended family in providing economic support for an indicidual in Africa'. Bayreuth African Studies Series. pp. 57-89.

Rwezaura, B. A. (1989) 'The changing community obligations to the elderly in contemporary Africa'. Journal of Social Development in Africa. Vol. 4, pp. 5-24.

Rwezaura, B. A. (1990) 'The integration of marriage laws in Africa with special reference to Tanzania' In Abun-Nasr, et al (eds.) *Law, society, and national identity in Africa, pp. 139-161*. Hamburg: Helmut Buske Verlag.

Rwezaura, B. A. (1994-95) 'Tanzania: Building a new family law out of a plural legal system'. Journal of Family Law. Vol. 33, pp. 523-540.

Rwezaura, B. (1984) 'Some aspects of mediation and conciliation in the settlement of matrimonial disputes in Tanzania'. In Eekelaar, J. M. and Katz, S. N. (eds.) *The resolution of family conflict: Comparative legal perspectives.*Toronto: Butterworth & Co. Ltd. pp. 52-69.

Rwezaura, B. (1985) *Traditional family law and change in Tanzania: A study of the Kuria social system*. Baden Baden: Nomos Verlagesellschaft.

Rwezaura, B. 91974) 'The legal status of woman-to-woman marriages in Tanzania'. Eastern Africa Law Review. Vol. 7, No. 3, pp. 319-325.

Rwezaura, B. and Wanitzer, U. (1988a) 'Family law reform in Tanzania: A social legal report'. International Journal of Law and the Family. Vol. 2, No. 1, pp. 1-26.

Rwezaura, B. et al. (1995b) 'Parting the long grass: Revealling and reconceptualising the African family'. Journal of Legal Pluralism. No. 35, pp. 25-73.

Sabean, D. W. (1983) 'The history of the family in Africa and Europe: Some comparative perspectives'. Journal of African History. Vol. 24, No. 2, pp. 163-171.

Sangree, W. H. (1969) 'Going home to mother: Traditional marriage among the Irigwe of Benue-Plateau State'. American Anthropologist. Vol. 71. pp. 1046-1057.

Sawyerr, A. (1977) 'Judicial manipulation of customary family law in Tanzania'. In Roberts, S. (ed.) *Law and the family in Africa*. The Hague: Mouton, pp. 115-128.

Schapera, I. (1929) 'Matrilocal marriage in Southern Rhodesia'. Man. No. 29, pp. 113-117.

Schapera, I. (1933) 'Pre-marital pregnancy and native opinion. A note on social change'. Africa. Vol. 6, pp. 59-91.

Schapera, I. (1940) *Married life in an African tribe*. London: Faber and Faber.

Schapera, I. (1946) *Married life in an African tribe*. London: Faber & Faber.

Schapera, I. (1949) 'The Tswana conception of incest' In Fortes, M. (ed.) *Social structure: Essays presented to A. R. Radcliffe-Brown*. Oxford: Clarendon Press.

Schapera, I. (1950) 'Kinship and marriage among the Tswana'. In. Radcliffe-Brown, A. and Forde, D. (eds.) *African systems of kinship and marriage*. London: Oxford University Press, pp. 140-165.

Schapera, I. (1957) 'Marriage of near kin among the Tswana'. Africa. Vol. 27, pp. 139-159.

Schapera, I. (1978) 'Some notes on Tswana bogadi'. Journal of African Law. Vol. 22, No. 2, pp. 112-124.

Schlegel, A. (1972) *Male dominance and female autonomy: Domestic authority in matrilineal societies*. New Haven: Human Relations Area Files.

Schneider, D. M. (1953) 'A note on bridewealth and the stability of marriage'. Man. Vol. 53. pp. 55-57.

Schneider, D. and Gough, K. (1961) *Matrilineal kinship*. Berkeley: University of California Press.

Schultz, T. W. (1974) *Economics of the family: Marriage, children and human capital.* A Conference Report of the National Bureau of Economic Research. Chicago: The University of Chicago Press.

Seymour, S. M. (1960) *Native law in South Africa.* Cape Town: Juta

Sharp, B. (1984) 'Marriage rules on the Plateau: An exchange (between Sharp and J. C. Muller)'. Africa. Vol. 54, No. 4, pp. 23-30.

Shaw, K. C. (1932) 'Some preliminary notes on Luo marriage customs'. Journal of East Africa and Uganda Natural History Society. Vol. 45, pp. 39-50.

Shostak, M. (1981) *Nisa: The life and words of a !Kung woman.* Cambridge, Mass.: Harvard University Press.

Shropshire, D. W. T. (1941) *The Bantu women under the Natal Code of Native Law.* Lovedale: Lovedale Press.

Shropshire, D. (1927) 'Marriage rites and their meaning'. NADA No. 5 pp. 85-95.

Silberbauer, G. B. (1963) 'Marriage and the girl's puberty ceremony of the G/wi Bushmen'. Africa. Vol. 33, pp. 12-23.

Simmons, D. C. (1960) 'Sexual life, marriage and childhood among the Efik'. Africa. Vol. 30, No. 2, pp. 153-165.

Skinner, E. P. (ed.) (1973) *Peoples and cultures of Africa.* Garden City. N. Y.: Doubleday.

Smart, H. M. J. (1983) *Sierra Leone customary family law.* Free town: Atlantic Printers.

Smith, E. W. (1953) 'A survey of African marriage and family life'. Journal of African Administration. Vol. 5, No. 3, pp. 102-112.

Smith, M. G. (1953) 'Secondary marriage in Northern Nigeria'. Africa. Vol. 23, No. 3, pp. 298-323.

Snell, G. S. (1954) *Nandi customary law.* London: Macmillan.

Solivetti, L. M. (1994) 'Family, marriage and divorce in a Hausa community: A sociological model'. Africa. Vol. 64, No. 2, pp. 252-271.

Southall, A. W. (1960) 'On chastity in Africa'. Uganda Journal. Vol. 24, No. 2, pp. 207-216.

Storrs-Fox, D. (1931) 'Notes on marriage customs among the Masai'. Journal of East Africa and Uganda Natural History Society. Vol. 42-43, pp. 183-192.

Takirambudde, P. N. (ed.) (1982) *The individual under African law.* (Proceedings of the All-Africa Law Conference) Kwaluseni: University of Swaziland.

Tambiah, S. J. (1989) 'Bridewealth and dowry revisited'. Current Anthropology. Vol. 30, pp. 413-435.

Taylor, O. P. (1975) The position of women under Sierra Leone customary family law. In Elias, T. O. (ed.) *African indigenous laws*. Enugu: Government Printer.

Thomas, N. W. (1910) 'Marriage and legal customs of Edo-speaking peoples of Nigeria'. Journal of Comparative Legislation. pp. 94-101.

Thompson, B. (1989) 'Internal conflicts in marriage and inheritance laws in Sierra Leone: Some anachronisms'. African Journal of International and Comparative Law. Vol. 1, pp. 392-406.

Thompson, C. F. (1967) 'African customary law'. Law Library Journal. Vol. 60, No. 1, pp. 21-30.

Tillett, G. A. (1965) 'A family law and the women of Africa: UN Seminar on the status of women in Family law'. U. S. Department of State Bulletin. 15 February 1965. Vol. 52, pp. 229-233.

Topouzis, D. (1985) 'The men with many wives'. New Society. Vol. 74, No. 1188. pp. 13-15.

Torday, E. (1929) 'The principles of Bantu marriage'. Africa. Vol. 2, pp. 255-290.

Tuupainen, M. (1968) *Marriage in a matrilineal African tribe: A social anthropological study of marriage in the Ondonga tribe in Ovamboland.* Helsinki:Academic Bookstore.

Ukaegbu, A. O. (1976) 'Traditional marriage habits and population growth'. Africa. Vol. 46, pp. 390-398.

Usman, H. B. (1987) 'Brideprice and the law' Annals of Borno. vol.4, pp. 95-111.

Uzoma, A. C. (1971) 'The changing position of married women of one Ibo community (Nkwerre) in township village'. Friedrich Ebert Stiftung Viertel-Jahresberichte. No. 44, pp. 113-150.

Verdier, R. (1983) 'Customary family law'. International Encyclopedia of Comparative Law. Vol. 4, pp. 98-128.

Wanda, B. P. (1988) Customary family law in Malawi: Adherence to tradition and adaptability to change. Journal of Legal Pluralism. No. 27, pp. 117-134.

Ward, E. (1938) The Yoruba husband-wife code. PhD. Thesis Catholic University of America.

Warmelo, N. J. van (1948) *Venda law: Betrothal, thakha wedding*. Pretoria: Government Printer.

Watson, W. (1954) Bridewealth and the stability of marriage'. Man. Vol. 54, pp. 67-68.

Weinrich, A. (1982) *African marriage in Zimbabwe and the impact of christianity*. Gweru: Mambo Press.

Welch, G. and Sachs, A. (1987) 'The bride price, revolution, and the liberation of women'. International Journal of the Sociology of Law. No. 15 pp. 369-392.

Westermarck, E. (1891) *The history of human marriage*. London: MacMillan.

Wieschhoff, H. A. (1941) 'Divorce laws and practices in modern Ibo culture'. Journal of Negro History. Vol. 26, pp. 299-324.

Wilson, G. (1961) *Luo customary law and marriage laws and custom*. Nairobi: Government Printer.

Woodman, G. R. (1974) 'The family as a corporation in Ghanaian and Nigerian law'. African Law Studies. No. 11, pp. 1-35.

Woodman, G. R. (1981-82) 'Adaptation of customary law to the Matrimonial Causes Act, 1971'. Review of Ghana Law. Vols. 13 &14, pp. 218.

Woodman, G. R. (1988) 'Unification or continuing pluralism in family law in Anglophone Africa: Past experience, present realities and future possibilities'. Lesotho Law Journal. Vol. 4, No. 2, pp. 33-79.

Woodman, G. R. (1993) 'Essentials of an Akan customary law marriage'. Journal of African Law. Vol. 37, No. 2, pp. 199-205.

Woodman, G. (1977) 'Judicial development of customary law: The case of marriage law in Ghana and Nigeria. University of Ghana Law Journal. Vol. 14, No. 2, pp. 115-136.

Worsley, P. M. (1956) 'The kinship system of the Tallensi: A revaluation'. Journal of the Royal Anthropological Institute. No. 86, pp. 37-75.

Zabel, S. C. (1970) 'Hyde v Hyde in Africa: A comparative study of the law of marriage in the Sudan and Nigeria'. Utah Law Review. September. pp. 526-554.

Chapter 12 — Legal anthropology

This chapter could have had a different title as legal anthropology is undergoing a revolution in its name. It started first as anthropology and colonialism, law and anthropology, then anthropological jurisprudence, anthropology of law, legal pluralism, law and development, and now comparative law and social change.

At its inception, legal anthropology, was an amalgam of native laws and customs, law in stateless societies, how order was maintained in uncivilized society. Legal anthropology, the study of those exotic primitive people doing piquant things to three or four wives, was for them. Whereas, the sociology of law, because it had society and social appended to it, was for 'us', civilized, monogamous, Austinian positivists. There has been a legal revolution in the status of legal anthropology, and the subject has now found a temporary new home, in 'law and development studies' and 'law and society' that are guaranteed to induce social engineering in the developing world.

But as Bohannan (1969:401) rightly noted, legal anthropology is "a small field in which the general quality of the work is extraordinarily high". It should also be noted that even if the titles of the works in the international bibliography appear to be legal, Gluckman (1955:xix), for example cautioned that "this is ... primarily a social anthropologist book for social anthropology".

Accordingly, the literature of legal anthropology examined and selected for this chapter did not encapsulate the philosophical foundation of the indigenous law, hence a separate chapter on philosophy, ethno-jurisprudence and religion is included. See chapter 10.

12. 1 Crises in law and anthropology

Legal anthropologists have analysed and interpreted African indigenous laws but with very little reference to the philosophical input of the people who formulated the principles of the customary law. For example, the indigenous child law and succession law that govern the matrilineal *Himba* and the patrilineal Tiv may be similar but the underlying jurisprudence may vary enormously. What has emerged when one trawled through the literature on legal anthropology was that most writers did not take cognisance of *négritude*, Bantu philosophy or the ferocious debate in ethno-philosophy. Hardly any jurisprudential or anthropological notice was taken of the philosophy of the indigenous law.

Matriliny is a common-sense approach that has taken millennia to evolve. Legal anthropology is not the kind of law where there is a right answer waiting to be subpoenaed, accordingly, legal anthropology is languishing because it cannot be studied independently of indigenous philosophy, in spite of its new names. Whose law and legal institutions are required for development?

Anthropologists are by definition participant observers, and their fieldwork experience or expertise is usually with one tribe, accordingly, they have tended to specialise in a particular group. Adam Kuper (1983:111) noted that Schapera worked for many years in close alliance with the government of Bechuanaland (Botswana). Schapera (1938) recorded Tswana law and customs, for the chiefs and the courts, and wrote an account of the various systems of contract law and land tenure in the country.

The historical development of legal anthropology, law and anthropology is beyond the scope of this brief headnote. However, the first survey of law and anthropology was recorded by Sarbah (1897) and was followed by Seymour (1911) and Danquah (1928) Malinowski had attempted to rehabilitate the natives from the scorn of Ankermann (1905), and Lévy-Brühl (1910). Malinowski (1922:10) recorded that:

> Their social institutions have a very definite organisation ... they are governed by authority, law and order in their public and personal relations, while the latter are under the control of extremely complex ties of kinship and clanship ... a picture of the natives subjected to a strict code of behaviour and good manners to which in comparison the life at the Court of Versailles or Escurial was free and easy.

Furthermore, Malinowski (1926:14) also argued that primitive societies had law and that law should not only be construed as "central authority, codes, courts and constable".

Accordingly, some ethnographers started to examine the functions of law in primitive societies. This was the period of tribal law school, when the imperial government ethnographers described the function of law in a particular 'tribe'. The leading exponents of this genre were Rattray (1929) on the Ashanti, Schapera (1935) among the Tswana, Evans-Pritchard (1940) on the Nuer, Forde (1941) on the Yakö and Cory (1945) on the Haya, and many others.

After the Second World War, the colonial powers realised the importance of the study of Asian and African civilisations and languages, and they established Centres for African Studies in Europe. But the demise of the functional tribal law school under Radcliffe-Brown (1952), Max Gluckman (1955) and Paul Bohannan (1957) on the Tiv, was hastened when several law schools were also opened in Africa, and Kwame Nkrumah (1962) called for the Africanisation of the law of Ghana, for colonialism was not yet over and done with until the collapse of colonial law.

12. 2 Plurality of laws

The functional tribal law school of legal anthropology was replaced by jurists such as Elias (1956), Allott (1960) and others who maintained that African law ought to transcend the anthropological connection into which it had got bogged down, and there emerged out of this school, another group of lawyers who concentrated more specifically on an aspect of indigenous law, such as land law and family property, succession, contract, family law, and criminal law.

Today, indigenous law is evolving according to the needs and requirements of the majority of the population under its jurisdiction, and it is receiving recognition as law, the way some human beings order their affairs.

12.3 Bibliography

Ahmed, A. (1973) 'Some remarks from the Third World on anthropology and colonialism: The Sudan'. In Asad, T. (ed.) *Anthropology and the colonial encounter*. London: Ithaca Press, pp. 259-270.

Akbar, N. (1984) 'Africentric social sciences for human liberation'. Journal of Black Studies. Vol. 14, No. 4, pp. 385-414.

Alliot, M. (1968) 'L'acculturation juridique'. In Poiriér, J. (ed.) *Ethnologie générale*, Paris: Gallimard, pp. 1180-1236.

Allott, A. N. (1956) 'Review of Gluckman's the judicial process among the Barotse of Northern Rhodesia'. Law Quarterly Review. Vol. 72, pp. 144-147.

Allott, A. N. (1960) *Essays in African law*. London: Butterworths.

Allott, A. N. (1961) 'The changing law in a changing Africa'. Sociologus. Vol. 11, pp. 115-131.

Allott, A. N. (1967) 'Law and social anthropology with special reference to African law'. Sociologus. Vol. 17, pp.1-19.

Allott, A. N. (1969) 'Legal personality in African law: A comparative study with special reference to Ghana'. In Gluckman, M. (ed.) *Ideas and procedures in African customary law*. London: Oxford University Press for the International African Institute.

Asad, T. (ed.) (1973) *Anthropology and the colonial encounter*. London: Ithaca Press.

Beattie, J. (1956) 'Ethnographic and sociological research in East Africa: A review'. Africa. Vol. 26, pp. 265-276.

Beattie, J. (1957) 'Informal judicial activity in Bunyoro'. Journal of African Administration. Vol. 9, No. 4, pp. 188-195.

Benda-Beckmann, K. von and Strijbosch, F. (1986) *Anthropology of law in the Netherlands: Essays on legal pluralism*. Dordrecht: Foris Publication

Bentley, G. C. and Westermark, G. D. (1983) *'Law, anthropology and mediation in Windsor Yearbook of access to justice*. Ontario, Canada: Windsor University Press.

Black, D. (1981) 'The relevance of legal anthropology'. Contemporary Sociology. Vol. 10, No. 1, pp. 43-46.

Bloch, M. (1983) *Marxism and anthropology: The history of a relationship*. Oxford: Clarendon Press.

Bohannan, P. (1957) *Justice and judgment among the Tiv*. London: Oxford University Press.

Bohannan, P. (1964) 'Anthropology and the law'. In Bohannan, P. (ed.) *Horizons of anthropology*, pp. 191-199. Chicago: Aldine Publishing

Bohannan, P. (1965) 'The differing realms of law: The ethnography of law'. Supplement to The American Anthropologist. Vol. 67, pt. 2, pp. 33-42.

Bohannan, P. (1968) 'Law and legal institutions'. In Sills, D. L. (ed.) *International encyclopedia of the social science*. Vol. 9. New York: Macmillan and the Free Press.

Bohannan, P. (1969) 'Ethnography and comparison in legal anthropology'. In Nader, L. (ed.) *Law in culture and society,* Chicago Aldine Publishing, pp. 401-418.

Bohannan, P. (ed.) (1967) '*Law and warfare: Studies in the anthropology of conflict*. Austin, TX: University of Texas Press.

Brown, R. (1973) 'Anthropology and colonial rule: The case of Godfrey Wilson and the Rhodes-Livingstone Institute'. In Asad, T. (ed.) *Anthropology and the colonial encounter*. London: Ithaca Press, pp. 174-197.

Brown, R. (1979) 'Passages in the life of a white anthropologist: Max Gluckman'. Journal of African History. No. 20, pp. 525-541.

Bryde, B-O. (1976) *The politics and sociology of African legal development*. Frankfurt am Main: Alfred Metzner Verlag.

Burman, S. B. and Harrell-Bond, B. E. (eds.) (1979) *The imposition of law*. London: Academic Press.

Burton, J. W. (1985) 'Christians, colonists and conversion: A view from the Nilotic Sudan'. Journal of Modern African Studies. Vol. 23, pp. 349-369.

Burton, J. W. (1992) 'Representing Africa: Colonial anthropology revisited'. Journal of Asian and African Studies. Vol. 27. Nos. 3-4. pp. 181-201.

Cairns, H. (1931) 'Law and anthropology'. Columbia Law Review. Vol. 31, pp. 32-55.

Chamblis, W. J. and Seidman, R. B. (1982) *Law, order and power*. Reading, MA: Addison-Wesley Publishing Co.

Chanock, M. (1983) 'Signposts or tombstones? Some reflections on recent works in the anthropology of law'. Law in Context 1.

Chanock, M. (1985) *Law, anthropology and history*. Cambridge: Cambridge University Press.

Chiba, M. (1984) 'Cultural universality and particularity of jurisprudence'. In Marasinghe, M. L. and Conklin, W. E. (eds.) *Essays on third world perspectives in jurispprudence*. Singapore: Malayan Law Journal Pte Ltd.

Comaroff, J. L. and Roberts, S. (1977) 'The invocation of norms in dispute settlement: The Tswana case'. In Hamnett, I. (ed.) *Social anthropology and law*. London: Academic Press, pp. 77-112.

Cory, H. and Hartnoll, M. M. (1945) *Customary law of the Haya*. London: Frank Cass & Co. Ltd.

Cotran, E. and Rubin, N. N. (ed.) (1970) *Readings in African law*. London: Frank Cass.

Cox, B. (1971) 'Some recent trends in ethnographic studies of law'. Law and Society Review. Vol. 5, pp. 407-415.

Danquah, J. B. (1928) *Gold Coast: Akan laws and customs and the Akim Abuakwa constitution*. London: G. Routledge & Sons.

David, R. (1974) *Les grands système de droit contemporains*. Paris: Dalloz.

De Sousa Santos, B. (1987) 'Law: A map of misreading. Toward a postmodern conception of law'. Journal of Law and Society. Vol. 14, No. 3, pp. 279-302.

Diamond, A. S. (1951) *The evolution of law and order*. London: Watts.

Diamond, A. S. (1971a) 'The rule of law versus the order of custom'. Social Research. Vol. 38, pp. 42-72.

Diamond, A. S. (1971b) *Primitive law, past and present*. London: Methuen.

Diamond, A. S. (1981) 'The rule of law versus the order of custom'. In Wolff, R. P. (ed.) *The rule of law*. New York: Simon & Schuster.

Donnelly, J. (1985) 'In search of the unicorn: The jurisprudence and politics of the right to development'. California Western International Law Journal. Vol. 15, pp. 475-509.

Doucet, M. and Vanderlinden, J. (eds.) (1994) *La réception des systèmes juridiques: Implantation et destin*. Bruxelles: Bruylant.

Driberg, J. H. (1934) 'The African conception of law'. Journal of Comparative Legislation and International Law. Vol. 16, pp. 230-246.

Dundas, C. (1915) The organisation and laws of some Bantu tribes in East Africa'. Journal of the Royal Anthropological Institute. Vol. 45, pp. 234-306.

Dwyer, D. H. (1979) 'Substance and process: Reappraising the premises of the anthropology of law'. Dialectical Anthropology. Vol. 4, pp. 309-320.

Elias, T. O. (1956) *The nature of African customary law*. Manchester: Manchester University Press.

Epstein, A. L. (1954) 'Juridicial techniques and the judicial process'. Rhodes-Livingstone Papers, No. 23.

Epstein, A. L. (1973) 'Reasonable man revisited: Some problems in the anthropology of law'. Law and Society Review. Vol. 7, No. 4, pp. 643-666.

Evans-Pritchard, E. E. (1946) 'Applied anthropology'. Africa. No. 16, pp. 92-98.

Evans-Pritchard, E. E. (1949) 'Anthropology and colonial affairs'. Man. No. 49, pp. 137-138.

Fallers, L. A. (1977) 'Administration and the supremacy of the law in colonial Busoga'. In Hamnett, I. (ed.) *Social anthropology and law*, pp. 53-76. London: Academic Press.

Firth, R. (1977) 'Whose frame of reference? One anthropologist's experience'. Anthropological Forum. No. 4, pp. 145-167.

Fitzpatrick, P. (1985) 'Is it simple to be a Marxist in legal anthropology? Modern Law Review. Vol. 48, No. 4, pp. 472-485.

Forde, D. (1953) 'Applied anthropology in Government: British Africa'. In Kroeber, A. (ed.) *Anthropology Today*. Chicago: University of Chicago Press, pp. 841-865.

Forde, D. (1965) 'Tropical African studies'. Africa. Vol. 35, pp. 30-97.

Foster, P. (1973) 'Empiricism and imperialism: A review of the new left critique of social anthropology'. In Asad, T. (ed.) *Anthropology and the colonial encounter*. London: Ithaca Press.

Fox, R. (1975) *Biosocial anthropology*. London: Ithaca Press.

Fox, R. (1993) *Reproduction and succession: Studies in anthropology, law and society*. New Brunswick: Transaction Publishers.

Franck, T. M. (1972) 'The new development: Can American law and legal institutions help developing countries'? Wisconsin Law Review. Vol. 12, pp. 767-801.

Gadacz, R. (1987) 'Folk law and legal pluralism: Issues and directions in the anthropology of law in modernizing societies. Legal Studies Journal. Vol. 11, No. 2, pp.125-144.

Geertz, C. (1983a) *Local knowledge: Further essays in interpretive anthropology*. New York: Basic Books Inc.

Geertz, C. (1983b) 'Slide show: Evans-Pritchard's African transparencies'. Raritan. No. 3, pp. 62-80.

Ghai, Y. P. (1975) 'Notes towards a theory of law and ideology: Tanzanian perspectives'. African Law Studies. Vol. 13, pp. 31-105.

Ghai, Y., Luckham, R. and Snyder, F. (1987) *The political economy of law*. Delhi: Oxford University Press.

Gluckman, M. (1955a) *Judicial process among the Barotse of Northern Rhodesia*. Manchester: Manchester University Press for the Rhodes-Livingstone Institute.

Gluckman, M. (1955b) 'The reasonable man in Barotse law'. Journal of African Administration. Vol. 7, No. 1, pp. 51-55, 127-131.

Gluckman, M. (1956) 'The reasonable man in Barotse Law (111) The case of the dog-in-the manger headman'. Journal of African Administration. Vol. 8, No. 4, pp. 101-105.

Gluckman, M. (1959) 'The technical vocabulary of Barotse jurisprudence'. American Anthropologist. Vol. 61, No. 5, pp. 743-759.

Gluckman, M. (1962) 'African jurisprudence'. The Advancement of Science. Vol. 18, pp. 439-454.

Gluckman, M. (1964) 'Natural justice in Africa'. Natural Law Forum. Vol. 9, pp. 25-44.

Gluckman, M. (1965) *The ideas in Barotse jurisprudence*. New Haven: Yale University Press.

Gluckman, M. (1967) *The judicial process among the Barotse of Northern Rhodesia*. Manchester: Manchester University Press.

Gluckman, M. (1969) 'Concepts in the comparative study of tribal law'. In Nader, L. (ed.) *Law in culture and society*. Chicago: Aldine Press.

Gluckman, M. (1971) *Politics, law and ritual in tribal Society*. Oxford: Blackwell.

Gluckman, M. (1974) 'African traditional law in historical perspective'. London: Oxford University Press.

Gluckman, M. (ed.) (1972) *The allocation of responsibility*. Manchester: Manchester University Press.

Gordon, J. (1967) 'African law and the historian'. Review article. Journal of African History. Vol. 8, pp. 335-340.

Gough, K. (1968) 'Anthropology and imperialism'. Monthly Review. No. 19, pp. 12-27.

Greenberg, D. F. (1980) 'Law and development in light of dependency theory'. Research in Law and Sociology. Vol. 3, pp. 129-159.

Griffiths, J. (1986) 'What is legal pluralism?' Journal of Legal Pluralism. Vol. 24, pp. 24-55.

Hamnett, I. (1975) *Chieftainship and legitimacy: An anthropological study of executive law in Lesotho*. London: Routledge & Kegan Paul.

Hamnett, I. (ed.) (1977) *Social anthropology and law*. London: Academic Press.

Hoebel, E. A. (1946) 'Law and anthropology'. Virginia Law Review. Vol. 30, pp. 834-854.

Hoebel, E. A. (1954) *The law of primitive man*. Cambridge Mass: Harvard University Press.

Holleman, J. F. (1949) 'An anthropological approach to Bantu law: With special reference to Shona law'. Rhodes-Livingstone Journal. Vol. 10, pp. 51-64.

Holleman, J. F. (1973) 'Trouble-cases and trouble-less cases in the study of customary law and legal reform'. Law and Society Review. Vol. 7, pp. 585-609.

Holleman, J. F. (1974) *Issues in African law*. The Hague: Mouton.

Holleman, J. F. (1975) 'Some problems of evidence in Shona tribal law'. In Fortes, M. and Patterson, S. (eds.) *Studies in African social anthropology*. London: Academic Press, pp. 75-94.

Holleman, J. F. (1979) 'Law and anthropology: A necessary partnership for the study of legal change in plural systems. Journal of African Law Vol. 23, pp. 117-130.

Hooker, M. B. (1975) *Legal pluralism: An introduction to colonial and neo-colonial laws*. Oxford: Clarendon Press.

Hund, J. G. (1979) 'Jurisprudence and legal anthropology: The roles of theory and method revisited'. Comparative and International Law Journal of Southern Africa. Vol. 12, pp. 188-198.

Hund, J. (1982) 'Legal and sociological approaches to indigenous law in Southern Africa'. Social Dynamics. Vol. 8, pp. 29-40.

Hund, J. (1984) 'The new legal anthropology: A critical review of rules and processes'. Comparative and International Law Journal of Southern Africa Vol. 27, No. 2, pp. 211-223.

James, W. (1973) 'The anthropologist as reluctant imperialist'. In Asad, T. (ed.) *Anthropology and the colonial encounter*. London: Ithaca Press, pp. 41-70.

Jones, G. I. (1974) 'Social anthropology in Nigeria during the colonial period'. Africa. Vol. 44, pp. 280-289.

Kidder, R. L. (1979) 'Toward an integrated theory of imposed law'. In Burman, S. B. and Harrell-Bond, B. E. (eds.) *The imposition of law*. London: Academic Press, pp. 289-306.

Koch, K. F. (ed.) (1979) 'The anthropological perspective, patterns of management: Essays in the ethnology of law'. *Access to Justice. Vol. 4*, Milan: Giuffrè.

Kucklick, J. (1978) 'The sins of the fathers: British anthropology and African colonial administration'. Research in Sociology of Knowledge, Science and Art. Vol. 1, pp. 93-119.

Kulcsár, K. (1970) Historical development of the law applying functions. In Péteri, Z. (ed.) *Hungarian law-comparative law*. Budapest: Akadémiai Kiadó.

Kuper, A. (1983) *Anthropology and anthropologists*. London: Routledge and Kegan Paul.

Kuper, H. and Kuper, L. (eds.) (1966) *Introduction to African law: Adaptation and development*. Los Angeles: University of California Press.

Lafond, M. (1985) *Recueil de thèses africanistes (droit et science politique) 1967-1984)* Pairs: Centre d'Etudes juridiques comparatives, Université de Paris.

Lampe, E. J. (1970) *Rechtsanthropologie: Eine strukturanalyse des menschen im recht*. Berlin: Duncker & Humbolt.

Le Roy, E. (1984) 'Legal paradigm and legal discourse: The case of the law of French-speaking black Africa'. International Journal of Sociology of Law. Vol. 12, pp. 1-22.

Lévy-Brühl, L. (1910) *Les fonctions mentales dans les sociétés inferieurs*. Paris: Alcan.

Lewis, D. (1973) 'Anthropology and colonialism'. Current Anthropology. No. 14. pp. 5381-5391.

Loizos, P. (1977) 'Personal evidence: Comments on an acrimonious debate'. Anthropological Forum. Vol. 4, pp. 137-144.

MacCormack, G. (1978) 'Anthropology and legal theory'. Juridical Review. pp. 216-238.

Malinowski, B. (1922) *Argonauts of the Western Paficic*. New York: E. P. Dutton & Co. Inc.

Malinowski, B. (1926) *Crime and custom in savage society*. London: Kegan Paul, Trench and Trubner.

Malinowski, B. (1936) 'Native education and culture contact'. International Review of Missions. Vol. 25, pp. 480-517

Medeiros, C. L. (1984) 'Kwandu law: The evolution of a juridical system among an Herero people of South West Angola'. Journal of African Law. Vol. 28, No. 1, pp. 80-89.

Meek, C. K. (1937) *Law and authority in a Nigerian tribe*. London: Oxford University Press.

Merry, S. E. (1988) 'Legal pluralism'. Law and Society Review. Vol. 22, No. 5, pp. 869-896.

Merry, S. E. (1992) 'Anthropology, law and the transnational process'. Annual Review in Anthropology. Vol. 21, pp. 357-379.

Moore, S. F. (1969) 'Law and anthropology'. In Siegel, B. J. (ed.) *Biennial Review of Anthropology*. pp. 259-293. Stanford: Stanford University Press.

Moore, S. F. (1973) 'Law and social change: The semi-autonomous social field as an appropriate subject of study. Law and Society Review. Vol. 7, pp. 719-746.

Moore, S. F. (1978) *Law as process: An anthropological approach*. London: Routledge and Kegan Paul.

Moore, S. F. (1986) 'Legal systems of the world: An introductory guide to classification, typological interpretations and bibliographical resources'. In Lipson, L. and Wheeler, S. (eds.) *Law and the social sciences*, pp. 11-62. New York: Russel Sage Foundation.

Nadel, S. F. (1956) *Reason and unreason in African law: Africa in ten societies*. New York: Columbia University Press.

Nader, L. (1965) 'The anthropological study of law'. American Anthropologist. Vol. 67, No. 6, pp. 3-32.

Nader, L. (1965) 'The anthropological study of law'. American Anthropologist. Vol. 67, No. 6, pp. 3-32.

Nader, L. (1967) 'The anthropological study of law'. American Anthropologist. Vol. 6, No. 2, pp. 26-32.

Nader, L. (1969c) *Law in culture and society*. Chicago: Aldine Press.

Nader, L. (ed.) (1969a) *The anthropology of law*. Berkeley: University of California.

Nader, L. (ed.) (1969b) *Ethnography and comparison: Legal anthropology*. Chicago: Aldine Publishing.

Nader, L. and Todd, H. F. (eds.) (1978) *The disputing process: Law in ten societies*. New York: Columbia University Press.

Nader, L. and Yngvesson, B. (1973) 'On studying the ethnography of law and its consequences'. In Honigmann, J. J. (ed.) *Handbook of social and cultural anthropology*. Chicago: Rand McNally, pp. 883-921.

Nader, L., Koch, K. F. and Cox, B. (1966) 'The ethnography of law: A bibliographical survey'. Current Anthropology. Vol. 7, No. 3, pp. 276-294.

Newman, K. S. (1983) *Law and economic organisation: A comparative study of pre-industrial societies.* Cambridge: Cambridge University Press.

Nkrumah, K. (1962) 'Law in Africa'. (Address at the Opening of the Ghana Law School, 4 January 1962) Journal of African Law. Vol. 6, pp. 103-112.

Ojwang, J. B. (1989) 'The meaning, content and significance of tribal law in an emergent nation: The Kenya case'. Law and Anthropology. Vol. 4, pp. 125-140.

Ortner, S. B. (1984) 'Theory in anthropoogy since the sixties'. Comparative Studies in Society and History. Vol. 26, pp. 126-166.

Owusu, M. (1978) 'Ethnography of Africa: The usefulness of the useless'. American Anthropologist. No. 80 pp. 310-334.

Park, A. E. W. (1963) *The sources of Nigerian law.* London: Sweet & Maxwell.

Paul, J. C. N. and Dias, C. F. (1982) 'State-managed development: A legal critique and alternative development: A legal prospectus'. Third World Legal Studies. pp. 35-58.

Poirier, J. (1970) 'The current state of legal ethnology and its future tasks'. International Social Science Journal. Vol. 22, No. 3, pp. 476-494.

Pospisil, L. J. (1956) 'The nature of law'. Transactions of the New York Academy of Sciences. Vol. 18, No. 8, pp. 746-755.

Pospisil, L. J. (1971) *Anthropology of law: A comparative theory.* New York: Harper & Row.

Pospisil, L. J. (1985) *The ethnology of law.* New Haven, CT. Human Relations Area Files.

Post, A. H. (1887) *Afrikanische jurisprudenz*: Ethnologisch-juristische Beitrage zur Kenntnis der einheimischen rechte Afrikas. Oldenburg: Schulze.

Post, A. H. (1894-95) *Grundriss der ethnologischen jurisprudenz.* 2 vols. Oldernburg and Leipzig: Schulzesche Hof-Buchhand-lung und Hof Buchdruckerei.

Rattray, R. S. (1928) 'Anthropology and christian missions: Their mutual bearing on the problems of colonial administration'. Africa. Vol. 1, pp. 98-106.

Redfield, R. (1967) 'Primitive law'. In Bohannan, P. (ed.) *Law and warfare: Studies in the anthropology of conflict.* Austin, TX: University of Texas Press.

Rijnsdorp, U. (1975) 'Different views about paternal rights in Bo (Sierra Leone)'. Kroniek van Afrika Vol. 1, pp. 23-37.

Roberts, C. C. (1937) *Tangled justice.* London: MacMillan.

Roberts, S. (1981) 'Where two worlds meet: A time for reassessment in the anthropology of law'. Michigan Law Review. Vol. 79, March, pp. 737-747.

Robertson, A. F. (1975) 'Anthropology and government in Ghana'. African Affairs. Vol. 74, pp. 51-64.

Rokumoto, K. (ed.) (1994) *Sociological theories of law*. Aldershot: Dartmouth Publishing Co Ltd. The International Library of Essays in Law and Legal Theory.

Rouland, N. (1994) *Legal anthropology*. Stanford: Stanford University

Sack, P. and Aleck, J. (eds.) (1992) *Law and anthropology*. Aldershot: Dartmouth Publishing Co Ltd.. The International Library of Essays in Law and Legal Theory.

Saltman, M. (1985) 'The law is an ass: An anthropological appraisal'. In Overing, J. (ed.) *Reason and morality*. London: Tavistock Publication, pp. 226-239.

Sanders, A. J. G. M. (1994) 'Legal anthropology in a changing South Africa'. Comparative and International Law Journal of Southern Africa. Vol. 27, No. 1, pp. 70-76.

Sarbah, J. M. (1897) *Fanti customary laws*. London: William Clowes & Sons.

Schapera, I. (1935) 'The social structure of the Tswana ward'. Bantu Studies. Vol. 9, pp. 203-224.

Schapera, I. (1938) *A Handbook of Tswana law and custom*. London: Oxford University Press for The International African Institute.

Schapera, I. (1943) *Tribal legislation among the Tswana of Bechuanaland Protectorate: A study in the mechanism of social change*. London: Percy Lund, Humphries & Co.

Schapera, I. (1951) 'Anthropology and the administrator'. Journal of African Administration. Vol. 3, pp. 128-135.

Schapera, I. (1957) 'The sources of law in Tswana tribal courts: Legislation and precedent'. Journal of African Law. Vol. 1, No. pp. 150-162.

Schiller, A. A. (1965) 'Law'. In Lystad, R. A. (ed.) *The African world: A survey of social research*. New York: Praeger for African Institute Columbia University.

Schott, R. (1980) 'Justice versus the law: Traditional and modern jurisdiction among the Bulsa of Northern Ghana'. Law and State. No. 21. pp. 121-133.

Schott, R. (1982) 'Main trends in German ethnological jurisprudence and legal ethnology.' Journal of Legal Pluralism. No. 20. pp. 37-68.

Seidman, R. B. (1966) 'Mens rea and the reasonable African: The pre-scientific world-view and mistake of fact'. The International & Comparative Law Quarterly. Vol. 15. Pt. 4, pp. 1135-1164.

Seymour, W. M. (1911) *Native law in South Africa*. Cape Town: Juta.

Snyder, F. G. (1981) 'Anthropology, dispute processes and law: A critical introduction'. British Journal of Law and Society. Vo. 8, No. 2, pp. 141-180.

Starr, J. and Collier, J. F. (1987) 'Historical studies of legal change'. Current Anthropology. Vol. 28, No. 3, pp. 367-372.

Starr, J. and Collier, J. F. (eds.) (1989) *History and power in the study of law: New directions in legal anthropology*. Ithaca & London: Cornell University Press.

Street, B. (1975) *The savage in literature*. London: Routledge and Kegan Paul.

Thornton, R. (1983) 'Narrative ethnography in Africa 1850-1920: The creation and capture of an appropriate domain for anthropology'. Man. Vol. 18, pp. 502-220.

Trubek, D. M. (1972) 'Toward a social theory of law: An essay on the study of law and development'. Yale Law Journal. Vol. 82, pp. 1-50.

Turnbull, C. M. (1984) 'The individual, community and society: Rights and responsibilities from an anthropological perspective'. Washington and Lee Law Review. Vol. 41, pp. 77-132.

Twining, W. L. (1973) 'Law and anthropology: A case study in inter disciplinary collaboration'. Law and Society Review. Vol. 7, pp. 561-584.

Vansina, J. (1965) 'A traditional legal system'. In Kuper H. and Kuper L. (eds.) *African law: Adaptation and development*. Los Angeles: University of California Press.

Varga, C. (1984) 'Is law a system of enactments? In Peczenik, A Alexander et al. (eds.) *Theory of legal science*. Dordrecht: Reidel.

Varga, C. (1992) *Comparative legal culture*. Aldershot: Dartmouth Publishing Co. Ltd. The International Library of Essays in Law and Legal Theory.

Wilson, G. (1940) 'Anthropology as a public service'. Africa. Vol. 12, pp. 43-61.

Zagaris, B. (1988) 'Law and development or comparative law and social change: The application of old concepts in the Commonwealth Caribbean'. University of Miami Inter-American Law Review. Vol. 19, pp. 549-593.

Chapter 13 — Land and family property

There have been far more unprecedented changes in customary land law than in the customary law of marriage, customary child law, law of succession and inheritance. The changes were brought about, firstly, because urban land has become capital money that could be exchanged for valuable consideration. Secondly, because of the introduction of land law reforms, such as the registration of individual title, nationalisation of the land and some states introduced co-operate village farm lands.

The focus of this chapter is only on indigenous land law.

Originally, under the indigenous law of some communities, land and water were owned jointly by men, women and children and animals. Everyone, according to the Herero has a right to be alive, and to survive. Accordingly, in order to survive, a person should have a place to graze the cattle, a place to farm, a home, and a piece of ground in which to be buried. Thus, the living that is men, women, children and animals have possession of the land, but they do not own it, as the land is the joint property of the living, the dead ancestors, as well as the generations yet to be born.

By clearing a definite piece of land and building their homes on it, the Herero make that area the family *onganda*, because it is the labour of every member of the family that created the *onganda*. This was their recognisable way of taking possession of the land. By labouring on the land, the matriclan, or the patriclan, acquired possession of that particular piece of land and the adjoining areas for farming.

The families who have worked on the land to make it habitable are entitled to possession but they do not own it, but the huts, the chattels, the farms and the animal enclosures that they built with their own labour are their properties. They have possesory rights in the products of their labour.

Among pastoralist with a large herd of cattle, it is necessary to obtain the consent of the most senior men and women for permission to live or graze near an existing village. A council meeting of the *otuzo* is summoned to take a decision regarding the new herders. More often than not, the new nomadic family is given permission to remain, but their cattle must go further afield for grazing. The new-comers are not tenants under the senior men, as there is no system of tenure. Land is not conveyed or alienated by the ovaHerero. If permission to settle in the village is refused, probably because of drought, the new-comers and their cattle, goats, sheep and donkeys will simply move on.

During the 1992 Namibia National Land Conference, the ovaHerero representative explained the ownership of land.

> Before the Europeans settled among them, or even at the time of the arrival of the first Rhenish missionaries, no member of the tribe would have thought of selling the land, for such a transaction did not exist in their minds.

According to the Herero, it would appear that pre-colonial indigenous law did not create or transfer estates or interests in land, as there was inexhaustible supply of virgin land.

The 'strangers' or white settlers simply allocated to themselves highlands to build their homes, their farms, their churches and cemeteries and declared the rest Crown land. They recognised the titles of the natives, but not to the fertile land. Germany and England had entered into Protection Treaties with the local chiefs and their councillors. See chapter 1. According to the account of oral historians, the purpose of the treaties was to take possession of the land. Rohrbach (1918:18) who was head of the Settlement Commission unusually agreed with the later oral historians that the decision to colonise means nothing else than:

> that the native tribes must withdraw from the lands on which they have pastured their cattle and so let the white man pasture his cattle on these self same lands. If the moral right of this standpoint is questioned, the answer is that for people of the culture standard of the natives, the loss of their free national barbarism and the development of a class of workers in the service of and dependent on the Whites is primarily a law of existence in the highest degree.

This was the thinking at the time of colonialism when land was being appropriated. Agitators and firebrands who revolted had their lands confiscated because thinking natives were seen as dangerous, and land titles were given to loyal natives who declared openly for the administration. In white settlers territories, native reserves were created. The administrator could move hundreds of people from one part of the territory to another and he was also vested with the power to appoint any person as a chief or headman or depose or remove such a person. Head tax and hut tax were introduced and were collected for the Crown by the traditional functionaries.

13.1 Trust property, family property

In the bibliography cited below, the various writers propounded several concepts of land ownership, land tenure and equitable interests. Some communities also have a law of stool property and a law of family property. The concept of family property fits well into the structure of a society in which polygynous marriage is recognised, thereby benefiting all the man's children from all his wives. Matrilineal pastoralists also have the *eanda* family cattle.

Their use of the trust concept illustrates the distinction between family property and personal property. Among the matrilineal pastoralists, only the senior married men of the *eanda* have the capacity to be trustees of the family trust cattle. If one member dies, the surviving hierarchy of trustees is re-arranged. If a trustee moves out of the *onganda* for various reasons, he still remains a trustee of the family property, because trusteeship is for life. On the death of a trustee, however, his trusteeship of the trust herd terminates. His *eanda* heir will succeed him as one of the trustees of the family cattle property under the principle of survivorship.

The trust cattle or matrilineal land cannot be alienated, except in case of dire necessity, such as the payment of compensatory cattle fines and helping with bridewealth which brings in more women and children. But the meat and milk from the trust herd can be drunk and eaten by members of the *eanda*, who are the ultimate beneficiaries. The calves from the trust cattle also become family property. Accordingly, some trustees have a large herd of trust cattle, as well as individual herd.

Today, statutory land law is moving very fast, and in some states indigenous law is being superseded by several land legislations. However, the modern changes in land law have not as yet affected the majority of the people in the rural hinterland. Accordingly, in some instances one can safely write about rural land law and urban land law.

13.2 Bibliography

Bibliography of published sources relating to African land tenure, 1950. London: HMSO.

Bibliography on land tenure in Africa, 1970). Rome: Food and Agricultural Organisation of the UN.

British House of Commons. *Papers relating to Her Majesty's possessions in West Africa*. Parliamentary Papers session 1875. Vol. 52, pp. 843-907.

Chief Commissioner, Sierra Leone Protectorate (1949) *Land tenure in Sierra Leone Protectorate: Mende land tenure, Kono land tenure, Temne land tenure*. Journal of African Administration. pp. 119-123.

Native land tenure in Kikuyu Province. Colony and protectorate of Kenya. Report of a Committee. November 1929. Nairobi: Government Printer.

Tanganyika Government African land tenure. (1954) Dar es Salaam.

Acquaye, E. (1970) 'The administration and development of Stool land in Ghana'. The Review of Ghana Law. Vol. 2, pp. 22-29.

Adeetuk, A. T. (1991) *Land tenure and food production in Northern Ghana, 1900-1985*. Madison: PhD Thesis, University of Wisconsin.

Adegboye, R. O. (1966) 'An analysis of land tenure structures in some selected areas in Nigeria'. Bulletin of Rural Economics and Sociology. Vol. 2, No. 1, pp. 38-51.

Afonja, S. (1986) 'Land control: A critical factor in Yoruba gender stratification'. In Robertson, C. and Berger, I. (eds.) *Women and class in Africa*. New York: African Publishing.

Agbosu, L. K. (1980) 'Land administration in Northern Ghana'. Review of Ghana Law. Vol. 12, pp. 104-133.

Agbosu, L. K. (1980a) *Land administration and land titles registration in Ghana*. London: PhD Thesis. School of African and Oriental Studies, University of London.

Agbosu, L. K. (1980b) 'Land administration in Northern Ghana'. Review of Ghana Law. Vol. 12, pp. 104-133.

Agbosu, L. K. (1981 & 1982) 'Individualisation of interests under the customary land law of Ghana'. Review of Ghana Today. Vols. 13 & 14, pp. 35-50.

Agbosu, L. K. (1981-82) 'Individualisation of interests under the customary land law of Ghana'. Review of Ghana Today. Vols. 13 & 14, pp. 35-50.

Aidoo, E. S. (1980) 'The conveyancer's confusion'. Review of Ghana Law. Vol. 12, pp. 53-66.

Akinkugbe, O. O. (1975) 'Damages for trespass: Ouster of a claim for possession'. The Nigerian Journal of Contemporary Law. Vol. 6, No. 1 & 2. pp. 66-90.

Allan, W., Gluckman, M., Peters, D. U. and Trapnell, C. G. (1948) *Land holding and law usage among the Plateau Tonga of Mazabuka District. A reconnaissance survey.* The Rhodes Livingstone papers, No. 14. Oxford: Oxford University Press.

Allott, A. N. (1949) 'Native land courts'. Journal of African Administration. Vol. 1, No. 1, pp. 82-86.

Allott, A. N. (1954) *Akan law of property.* PhD Thesis, London: School of Oriental and African Studies, University of London.

Allott, A. N. (1956) 'The effect of marriage on property in the Gold Coast'. International and Comparative Law Quarterly. Vol. 5, pt. 4, pp. 519-533.

Allott, A. N. (1961) 'Towards a definition of absolute ownership'. Journal of African Law. Vol. 5, No. 2, pp. 99-102.

Allott, A. N. (1968) 'Family property in West Africa: Its juristic basis, control and enjoyment'. In Anderson, J. N. D. (ed.) *Family law in Asia and Africa.* London: Butterworths, pp. 121-142.

Allott, A. N. (1970a) 'Modern changes in African land tenure'. In Cotran, E. and Rubin, N. (eds.) *Readings in African law.* London: Frank Cass, pp. 236-249.

Allott, A. N. (1970b) 'Language and property: A universal vocabulary for the analysis and description of proprietary relationships'. African Language Studies. Vol. 11, pp. 12-20.

Allott, A.N. (1966) *The Ashanti law of property.* Stuttgart: Ferdinand Enke Verlag.

Almagor, U. (1982) 'Pastoral identity and reluctance to change: The Mbanderu of Ngamiland'. In Werbner, R. (ed.) *Land reform in the making: Tradition, public policy and ideology in Botswana.* London: Rex Collings.

Asante, S. K. B. (1965b) 'Interests in land in the customary law of Ghana: A new appraisal'. Yale Law Journal. Vol. 74, pp. 848-885.

Asante, S. K. B. (1975) *Property law and social goals in Ghana 1844-1966.* Accra: Ghana University Press.

Asante, S. K. (1965a) 'Fiduciary principles in Anglo-American law and the customary law of Ghana: A comparative study'. International and Comparative Law Quarterly. Vol. 14, pp. 1144-

Asante-Ansong, S. (1981-1982) Title registration in Ghana: What is registrable, land, estate in land or facts?' The Review of Ghana Law. Vols. 13 & 14, pp. 51-72

Ault, D. E. and Rutman, G. L. (1979-80) 'The development of individual rights to property in tribal Africa'. Journal of Law and Economics. Vol. 22, pp. 163-182.

Barrows, R. (1974) 'African land reform policies: The case of Sierra Leone'. Land Economics. Vol. 50, pp. 402-410.

Barzel, Y. (1989) *Economic analysis of property rights.* Cambridge: Cambridge University Press.

Bassett, T. J. and Crummey, D. E. (eds.) (1993) *Land in African agrarian systems.* Wisconsin: The University of Wisconsin Press.

Bassett, T. (1986) 'Fulani herd movements'. Geographical Review. Vol. 76, No. 3, pp. 233-248.

Bates, R. (1987) 'The agrarian origins of Mau Mau'. Agricultural History. Vol. 61, pp. 1-28.

Beattie, J. H. M. (1954) 'The Kibanja system of land tenure in Bunyoro, Uganda'. Journal of African Administration. Vol. 6, No. 1, pp. 18-28.

Beech, M. H. (1917) 'Kikuyu system of land tenure'. Journal of the African Society. Vol 17, No. 65, pp. 46-59.

Beinart, W., Delius, P. and Trapido, S. (eds.) (1986) *Putting a plough to the ground: Accumulation and dispossession in Rural South Africa 1850-1930.* Johannesburg: Ravan Press.

Bennett, T. W. (1985) 'Terminology and land tenure in customary law: An exercise in linguistic theory'. Acta Juridica. pp. 173-187.

Bennett, T. W. (1993) 'Redistribution of land and the doctrine of aboriginal title in South Africa'. South African Journal of Human Rights. Vol. 9, pp. 443-476.

Bennett, T. W. and Roos, J. W. (1992) 'The 1991 Land Reform Acts and the future of African customary law'. South African Law Journal. Vol. 109, pp. 447-471.

Bentsi-Enchill, K. (1964) *Ghana land law.* London: Sweet & Maxwell.

Bentsi-Enchill, K. (1965) 'Do African systems of land tenure require a special terminology? Journal of African Law. Vol. 9. No. 2, pp. 114-139.

Bentsi-Enchill, K. (1975) 'The traditional legal systems of Africa'. International Encyclopaedia of Comparative Law. Vol. 6, pp. 68-102.

Berry, S. (1988a) 'Property rights and rural resource management: The case of tree crops in West Africa'. Cahiers d'ORSTOM Sciences Humains. Vol. 24, No. 1, pp. 3-16.

Berry, S. (1988b) 'Concentration without privatization? Some consequences of changing patterns of land control in Africa'. In Reyna, S. P. and Downs, R. E. (eds.) *Land and society in contemporary Africa.* pp. 53-75. Hanover, N. H.: University Press of New England for the University of New Hampshire.

Besteman, C. (1994) 'Individualisation and the assault on customary tenure in Africa: Title registration programmes and the case of Somalia'. Afrika. Vol. 64. No. 4, pp. 484-515.

Biebuyck, D. (1964) 'Land holding and social organization'. In Herskovitz, M. J and Harwitz, M. (eds.) *Economic transition in Africa.* London: Routledge and Kegan Paul, pp. 99-112.

Biebuyck, D. (ed.) (1963) *African agrarian systems.* London: Oxford University Press for the International African Institute.

Bohannan, P. (1954) *Tiv farm and settlement.* London. Her Majesty's Stationery Office.

Bohannan, P. (1963) '"Land" "tenure" and "land-tenure"' In Biebuyck, D. (ed.) *African agrarian systems.* London: Oxford University Press, pp. 101-115.

Bohannan, P. (1964) 'Land use, land tenure and land reform'. In Herskovits, M. and Harwitz, M. (eds.) *Economic transition in Africa.* Evanston: Northwestern University Press, pp. 133-149.

Brink, R. van den, Bromley, D. W. and Chavas, J. P. (1994) 'The economics of Cain and Abel: Agro-pastoral property rights in the Sahel'. The Journal of Development Studies. Vol. 31, No. 3, pp. 373-399.

Brock, B. (1969) 'Customary land tenure, 'individualism' and agricultural development in Uganda'. East African Journal of Rural Development. Vol. 2, No. 2, pp. 21-22.

Brokensha, D. and Glazier, J. (1976) 'Land law and the transformation of customary tenure: The Mbeere case'. Journal of African Law. Vol. 20, No. pp. 39-50.

Brooke, N. J. (1946) 'Some legal aspects of land tenure in Nigeria'. African Studies. Vol. 5, pp. 111-120.

Bruce, J. W. (1988) 'A perspective on indigenous land tenure systems and land concentration'. In Downs, R. E. and Reyna, S. P. (eds.) *Land and society in contemporary Africa.* Hanover, NH.: University Press of New England for the University of New Hampshire.

Bruce, J. (1986) *Land tenure issues in project design and strategies for agricultural development in Sub-Saharan Africa.* Land Tenure Centre Paper 128. Madison.

Burton, R. F. (1873) *The lands of Cazembe.* London: John Murray.

Cameron, D. (1933) *Note on land tenure in the Yoruba Province.* Lagos: Government Printer.

Carey Jones, N. S. (1965) 'The decolonisation of the White Highlands of Kenya'. Geographical Journal. Vol. 131, No. 2, pp. 186-201.

Casely Hayford, J. E. (1913) The truth about the African land question. London: Phillips.

Chanock, M. L. (1991a) 'A peculiar sharpness: An essay on property in the history of customary law in colonial Africa'. Journal of African History, Vol. 32, No. 1. pp. 65-88.

Chanock, M. (1977) 'Agricultural change and continuity in Malawi'. In Palmer, R. and Parsons, N. (eds.) *The roots of rural poverty in Southern Africa.* London: Heinemann, pp. 369-409.

Chanock, M. (1991b) 'Paradigms policies and property: A review of the customary law of land tenure'. In Mann, K. and Roberts, R. (eds.) *Law in colonial Africa.* London: Heinemann.

Cheater, A. P. (1990) 'The ideology of 'communal land tenure' in Zimbabwe: Mythogenesis enacted?' Africa. Vol. 60. pp. 188-206.

Chubb, L. T. (1948) *Ibo land tenure.* Nigeria: Gaskiya Corporation.

Cohen, J. M. and Koehn, P. D. (1977) 'Rural and urban land reform in Ethiopia'. African Law Studies. Vol. 14, pp. 3-26.

Cohen, J. (1980) 'Land tenure and rural development in Africa'. In Bates, A. F. and Lofchie, M. F. (eds.) *Agricultural development in Africa: Issues of public policy*, pp. 349-389. New York: Praeger.

Coker, G. B. A. (1962) *Family property among the Yoruba*. London: Sweet and Maxwell.

Coldham, S. F. R. (1978) 'The effect of registration of title upon customary land rights in Kenya'. Journal of African Law. Vol. 22, No. 2, pp. 91-111.

Coldham, S. (1982a) 'Land reform in Kenya: Some problems and perspectives'. In *Law in alternative strategies of rural development*. Third World Legal Studies. New York: Intworlsa.

Coldham, S. (1982b) 'The registration of group ranches among the Masai of Kenya: Some legal problems'. Journal of Legal Pluralism. no. 20, pp. 1-16.

Coldham, S. (1985) 'A comparative study of land tenure legislation in Africa'. Acta Juridica. pp. 189-212.

Coldham, S. (1995) 'Land tenure reform in Tanzania: Legal problems and perspectives'. The Journal of Modern African Studies. Vol. 33, No. 2. pp. 227-242.

Colson, E. (1960) *The social organisation of the Gwembe Tonga*. Manchester: Manchester University Press.

Colson, E. (1971) 'The impact of the colonial period on the definition of land rights'. In Duignan, P. and Gann, L. H. (eds.) *Profiles of change: African society and colonial rule*, 193-215. Vol. 3 of *Colonialism in Africa: 1870-1969*. Cambridge: Cambridge University Press.

Comaroff, J. (1982) 'Class and culture in a peasant economy: The transformation of land tenure in Barolong'. In Werbner, (ed.) *Land reform in the making: Tradition, public policy and ideology in Botswana*. London: Rex Collings.

Cotran, E. and Rubin, N. (eds.) (1970) *Readings in African law*. London: Frank Cass.

Cowen, D. V. (1967) 'Land tenure and economic development in Lesotho'. South African Journal of Economics. Vol. 35, No. 1, pp. 57-74.

Cross, C. (1992) 'An alternative legality: The property rights question in relation to South African land reform'. South African Journal of Human Rights. Vol. 8, pp. 305-343.

Cummins, S. K., Lofchie, M. and Payne, R. (1986) *African agrarian crisis: The roots of famine*. Boulder, Colo.: Westview Press.

Davison, J. (1987) 'Without land we are nothing: The effect of land tenure policies and practices upon rural women in Kenya'. Rural Africana. Vol. 27, pp. 19-33.

Davison, J. (ed.) (1988) *Agriculture, women and land: The African experience*. Boulder, Colo.: Westview Press.

Dewees, P. A. (1995) 'Trees and farm boundaries: Farm forestry, land tenure and reform in Kenya'. Africa. Vol. 65, No. 2, pp. 217-235.

Dobson, E. B. (1940) 'Land tenure of the Wasambaa'. Tanganyika Notes and Records. Vol. 10. pp-27.

Dorjahn, V. R. and Fyfe, C. (1962) 'Landlord and stranger: Changes in tenancy relations in Sierra Leone'. Journal of African History. Vol. 3, No. 3, pp. 391-397.

Dosekun, A. O. (1978) 'Socio-economic aspects of customary tenancy'. The Lawyer. Vol. 7, No. 1, pp. 55-64.

Downs, R. E. and Reyna, S. P. (eds.) (1988) *Land and society in contemporary Africa*. Hanover: N. H.: University Press of New England for the University of New Hampshire.

Drinkwater, M. (1989) 'Technical development and peasant impoverishment: Land -use policy in Zimbabwe's Midlands Province'. Journal of Southern African Studies. Vol. 15, No. 2, pp. 287-305.

Ekow-Daniels, W. C. (1978) 'The ascertainment of property rights between husband and wife'. Review of Ghana Law. Vol. 10, Nos. 2 & 3, pp. 137-151.

Elias, T. O. (1953) *Nigerian land law and custom*. London: Routledge and Kegan Paul.

Elias, T. O. (1956) 'Some current problems in African land tenure'. Tropical Agriculture. Vol. 33, pp. 287-296.

Elias, T. O. (1962) *Nigerian land law*. London: Routledge & Kegan Paul.

Elias, T. O. (1971) 'Ilorin land and the land tenure law'. Nigerian Law Journal. Vol. 5, pp. 159-161.

Emiko, G. I. (1976) 'Nigeria, customary land law of the Itsekiris: A look at *Idundun* v *Okumagba*'. Journal of African Law. Vol. 20, No. 2, pp. 107-126.

Ezejiofor, G. O. (1975) 'Alienation of family property in Nigeria'. African Law Studies. Vol. 12. pp. 4-20

Famoriyo, S. (1974) 'Land transactions and agricultural development in Nigeria'. East African Journal of Rural Development. Vol. 7, pp. 177-188.

Feldman, R. (1974) 'Custom and capitalism: Changes in the basis of land tenure in Ismani, Tanzania'. Journal of Development Studies. Vol. 10, Nos. 3 & 4, pp. 305-320.

Field, J. O. (1945) 'Sale of land in an Ibo community'. Man. Vol. 45. No. 47. p. 70.

Fimbo, G. M. (1992) *Essays in land law, Tanzania: A source book*. Dar es Salaam: Faculty of Law.

Fitzgerald, J. F. et al. (ed.) (1995) *African greenhouse gas emission inventories and mitigation options forestry, land-use change and agriculture*. Dordrecht: Kluwer Academic.

Fleming, C. J. W. (1974) 'Systems of land tenure'. NADA. Vol. 11, No. 1. pp. 53-83.

Fosbrooke, H. A. (1952) 'Public opinion and changes in land tenure'. Journal of African Administration. Special Supplement. pp. 28-36.

Friedman, H. (1986) 'Patriarchy and property'. Sociologica Ruralis, Vol. 26, No. 2, pp. 186-193.

Gayer, C. (1957) *Report on Land Tenure in Bugisu. Land Tenure in Uganda.* Entebbe: Government Printer.

Gershenberg, I. (1971) 'Land tenure as a constraint to rural development: A re-evaluation'. East African Journal of Rural Development Vol. 4, pp. 51-62.

Gildea, R. Y. (1964) 'Culture and land tenure in Ghana'. Land Economics. Vol. 40, No. 1, pp. 102-104.

Glazier, J. (1985) *Land and the uses of tradition among the Mbeere of Kenya.* Lanham, Md.: University Press of America.

Gluckman, M. (1943) *Essays on Lozi land law and royal property.* Rhodes-Livingstone Papers, 10. Livingstone: Rhodes-Livingstone Institute.

Gluckman, M. (1945) 'African land tenure'. Human Problems in British Central Africa. Rhodes-Livingstone Institute. Paper No. 3, pp. 1-12.

Gluckman, M. (1969) 'Property rights and status in African traditional law'. In Gluckman, M. (ed.) *Ideas and procedures in African customary law.* Oxford: Oxford University Press for the International African Institute, pp. 252-265.

Gondwe, Z. S. (1986) 'Agricultural policy in Tanzania at the cross-roads'. Land Use Policy. Vol. 3, No. 1, pp. 31-36.

Gray, R. F. and Gulliver, P. H. (1964) *The family estate in Africa: Studies in the role of property in family structure and lineage continuity.* London: Routledge and Kegan Paul.

Green, J. (1986) *Evaluating the impact of consolidation of holdings, individualization of tenure, and registration of title: Lessons from Kenya.* Madison: Land Tenure Center, University of Wisconsin.

Grove, A. T. and Klein, F. M. G. (1979) *Rural Africa.* Cambridge: Cambridge University Press.

Gulliver, P. H. (1958) *Land tenure and social change among the Nyakyusa: A study of the Ngoni and Ndendeuli of Southern Tangayika. East African Studies. No. 11,* Kampala: East African Institute of Social Research.

Gulliver, P. (1955) *The family herds: A study of two pastoral tribes in East Africa, the Jie and Tarkana.* London: Routledge & Kegan Paul.

Guttmann, E. (1956) 'Land tenure among the Azande people of Equatoria Province in the Sudan'. Sudan Notes and Records. Vol. 37, pp. 48-55.

Gyasi, E. A. (1994) 'The adaptability of African communal land tenure to economic opportunity: The example of land acquisition for oil palm farming in Ghana'. Africa. Vol. 64, No. 3, pp. 391-405.

Hailey, P. C. (1952) 'The land tenure problem in Africa'. Journal of African Administration. Special Supplement. pp. 3-7.

Håkansson, T. (1986) *Landless Gusii women: A result of customary land law and modern marriage patterns.* Uppsala: African Studies Programme. Dept of Cultural Anthropology.

Håkansson, T. (1988) *Bridewealth, women and land.* Uppsala: Uppsala University Press.

Hamilton, P. O. (1974) 'Termination of customary tenancy by forfeiture'. The Lawyer. Vol. 6, No. 11, pp. 14-18.

Hannigan, A. St. J. (1967) 'Equity and the law in Ghana'. University of Ghana Law Journal. Vol. 4, No. 1, pp. 28-39.

Haugerud, A. (1983) 'The consequences of land tenure reform among small holders in the Kenya Highlands'. Rural Africana Vols. 15 & 16, pp. 65-89.

Haugerud, A. (1989) 'Land tenure and agrarian change in Kenya'. Africa, Vol. 59, No. 1, pp. 62-90.

Hennings, R. O. (1952) 'Some trends and problems of African land tenure in Kenya'. Journal of African Administration. Vol. 4, pp. 122-134.

Heyer, J. (1975) 'The origins of regional inequalities in small-holder agriculture in Kenya, 1920-1973'. East African Journal of Rural Development Vol. 8, pp. 1-2.

Hitchcock, R. (1980) 'Tradition, social justice and land reform in Central Botswana'. Journal of African Law. Vol. 24, No. 1, pp. 1-34.

Homan, F. D. (1958) 'Inheritance in the Kenya native land units'. Journal of African Administration. Vol. 10, pp. 131-135.

Homan, F. D. (1962) 'Consolidation, enclosure and registration of title in Kenya'. Journal of Local Administration Overseas. Vol. 1, No. 1, pp. 4-14.

Homewood, K. (1994) *Methods in the study of African land use.* Boston, Mass.: African Studies Centre, Boston University Press.

Hopkins, A. G. (1980) *Property rights and empire building: Britains annexation of Lagos, 1861.* The Journal of Economic History. Vol. 40, pp. 777-798.

Hughes, A. J. B. (1964) 'Reflections on traditional and individual land tenure in Swaziland'. Journal of Local Administration Overseas. Vol. 3, No. 1, pp. 3-13.

Hyden, G. (1980) *Beyond Ujamaa in Tanzania: Underdevelopment and an uncaptuared peasantry.* London: Heinemann.

Ibik, J. O. (1971) *The law of land, succession, movable property argreements and civil wrongs. Restatement of African Law. 4: Malawi, Vol. 2.* London: Sweet and Maxwell.

Jacoby, E. H. (1971a) *Man and land: The fundamental issue in development.* London: Deutsch.

James, R. W. (1965) 'The changing role of land in Southern Nigeria'. Odu. Vol. 1, No. 2, pp. 3-23.

James, R. W. (1971) *Land tenure and policy in Tanzania.* Toronto: University of Toronto Press.

James, R. W. (1976) 'Land tenure reform in developing countries: From westernization to indigenization'. East African Law Review. Vol. 9, pp. 1-46.

James, R. W. (1982) *Modern land law of Nigeria*. Ile-Ife, Nigeria: University of Ife Press.

James, R. W. and Fimbo, G. M. (1973) *Customary land law of Tanzania: A source book*. Dar es Salaam: East African Literature Bureau.

James, R. W. and Kasunmu, A. B. (1966) *Alienation of family property in Southern Nigeria*. Ibadan: Ibadan University Press.

Jegede, M. I. (1970) 'Nature and extent of a family member's rights and interests in family land: A re-appraisal'. Eastern Africa Law Review. Vol. 3, pp. 229-255.

Jegede, M. I. (1971) 'The changing features of family ownership of land in Nigeria'. Nigerian Law Journal. Vol. 5, pp. 19-40.

Jones, C. (1996) 'Plus ça change, plus ça reste le même? The new Zanzibar land law project'. Journal of African Law. Vol. 40, No. 1, pp. 19-42.

Jones, G. I. (1949) *Ibo land tenure*. Africa. Vol. 19, pp. 309-323.

Josiah-Aryeh, N. A. (1995) *Family property and the state in Ghana: Changing customary law in an urban setting*. London: PhD Thesis. School of Oriental and African Studies, University of London.

Keith, A. B. (1902) 'Tribal ownership of land'. Journal of the African Society. Vol. 1, No. 4, pp. 455-461.

Kerr, A. J. (1990) *The customary law of immovable property and of succession*. Grahamstown: Rhodes University.

Kimani, S. M. (1972) 'The structure of land ownership in nairobi'. Canadian Journal of African Studies, Vol. 6, pp. 379-402.

Kishindo, P. (1995) 'Differential security of tenure on Malawi's customary land: Implications for investment'. Development Southern Africa. Vol. 12, No. 2, pp. 167-174.

Kludze, A. K. P. (1973) *Restatement of African Law. Ghana: Ewe law of property*. London: Sweet & Maxwell.

Klug, H. (1995) 'Defining the property rights of others: Political power, indigenous tenure and the construction of customary land law'. Journal of Legal Pluralism. No. 35, pp. 119-148.

Köbben, A. J. F. (1963) 'Land as an object of gain in a non-literate society: Land tenure among the Bete and Dida (Ivory Coast, West Africa)'. In Biebuyck, D. (ed.) *African agrarian systems*, London: Oxford University Press, 245-266.

Kom, E. D. (1966) 'The nature of a member's interest in family land in Nigeria and Ghana'. University of Ghana Law Journal. Vol. 3, pp. 122-138.

Kom, E. D. (1967) 'Unlawful disposition of family land: Void or voidable'. University of Ghana Law Journal. Vol. 4, No. 2, pp. 11-121.

Kom, E. D. (1983-1986) 'Defences to an action for declaration of title to land'. Review of Ghana Law. Vol. 15, pp. 152-169.

Lambert, H. E. (1947) 'Land tenure among the Akamba'. African Studies. Vol. 6, No. 4, pp. 159-162.

Lawrence, J. C. D. (1957) *The Iteso*. Oxford: Oxford University Press.

Le Roy, E. (1982) 'Caractères des droits fonciers coutumiers'. Encyclopédie juridique de l'Afrique. Vol. 5, pp. 39-47.

Lennihan, L. (1982) 'Rights in men and rights in land'. Slavery and Abolition. Vol. 3, pp. 111-139.

Lewis, C. (1985) 'The modern concept of ownership of land'. Acta Juridica. pp. 241-266.

Lipton, M. (1977) *Why poor people stay poor: Urban bias in world development*. Cambridge, Mass: Harvard University Press.

Little, P. (1985) 'Absentee herdowners and part-time pastoralists: The political economy of resource use in Northern Kenya'. Human Ecology. Vol. 13, No. 2, pp. 131-151.

Lloyd, P. C. (1959) 'Family property among the Yoruba'. Journal of African Law. Vol. 3, pp. 105-115.

Lloyd, P. C. (1960) 'Some modern developments in Yoruba customary land law'. Journal of African Administration. Vol. 12, pp. 11-20.

Lloyd, P. C. (1962) *Yoruba land law*. London: Oxford University Press for the Nigerian Institute of Social and Economic Research.

Lofchie, M. (1978) 'Agrarian crisis and economic liberalisation in Tanzania'. Journal of Modern African Studies. Vol. 16, No. 3, pp.451-475.

MacCormack, G. (1983) 'Problems in the description of African systems of landholding'. Journal of Legal Pluralism. Vol. 21, pp. 1-14.

Mackenzie, F. (1996) 'Conflicting claims to custom: Land and law in Central Province, Kenya 1912-1952'. Journal of African Law. Vol. 40, No. 1, pp. 62-77.

Main, K. M. (1967) *Land law in East Africa*. Nairobi: Oxford University Press.

Mair, L. P. (1931) 'Native land tenure in East Africa'. Africa. Vol. 4, pp. 314-329.

Manners, R. A. (1964) 'Colonialism and native land tenure: A case study in ordained accommodation'. In Manners, R. A. (ed.) *Process and patterns in culture*. Chicago: Aldine Press.

Martin, J. (1946) 'Married women's property'. The Nigeria Law Quarterly Review. Vol. 1, No. 3, pp. 9-13.

Mbagwu, T. (1978) 'Land concentration around a few individuals in Igbo-land of Eastern Nigeria: Its processes, scope and future'. Africa. Vol. 48, No. 2, pp. 101-115.

McAuslan, J. P. W. B. (1967) 'Control of land and agricultural development in Kenya and Tanzania'. In Sawyer, G. F. A. (ed.) *East African law and social change*. Nairobi: East African Institute of Social and Cultural Affairs, pp. 172-257.

McDowell, C. M. (1965) An introduction to the problems of ownership of land in Northern Nigeria. Nigerian Law Journal Vol. 1, pp. 202-226.

McDowell, C. M. (1969) 'The breakdown of traditional land tenure in Northern Nigeria'. In Gluckman, M. (ed.) *Ideas and procedures in African customary law*. Oxford: Oxford University Press for the International African Institute, pp. 252-265.

Meek, C. K. (1946) *Land law and custom in the colonies*. London: Oxford University Press.

Meek, C. K. (1948) *Colonial law: A bibliography with special reference to native African systems of law and land tenure*. London: Oxford University Press.

Meek, C. K. (1951) 'A note on primitive systems of land-holding and on methods of investigation'. Journal of African Administration Vol. 3, No. 1, pp. 9-13.

Meek, C. K. (1957) *Land tenure and land administration in Nigeria and the Cameroons*. London: Her Majesty's Stationery Office.

Mifsud, F. M. (1967) *Customary land law in Africa with reference to legislation aimed at adjusting customary tenures to the needs of development*. Rome: FAO Legislative Series No. 7.

Morton-Williams, P. (1961) 'Review of family property among the Yoruba by G. B. A. Coker'. Africa. Vol. 31. No. 3, pp. 291-292.

Mugerwa, N. (1966) 'Land tenure in East Africa: Some contrasts'. East African Law Today. for British Institute of International and Comparative law. pp. 101-105.

Mukwaya, A. B. (1953) *Land tenure in Buganda: Present day tendencies*. Kampala: East Africa Institute of Social Research.

Mulumbwa, A. C. (1993) 'Rural land tenure in Zambia and agricultural development: Recent perspectives'. Lesotho Law Journal. Vol. 8, No. 2, pp. 113-141.

Munro, A. P. (1966) 'Land law in Kenya'. In Hutchison, T. (ed.) *Africa and law: Developing legal systems in African Commonwealth nation*. Madison: University of Wisconsin Press, pp. 75-103.

Mvungar, M. P. (1982) *Land law and policy in Zambia*. Lusaka: Mambo Press for the University of Zambia, Institute for African Studies.

Mvungi, S. (1994) 'Populism and invented traditions: The new Land Tenure Act of 1992 and its implications on customary land rights in Tanzania'. Afrika Spectrum. Jg. 29, H.3, pp. 327-338.

Nasser, S. F. (1966) 'Statutory and customary land tenure'. In Smith, H. E. (ed.) *Agricultural development in Tanzania*. London: Oxford University Press, pp. 56-59.

Ng'ong'ola, C. (1985) 'Colonial law and the inception of a dual land system in Nyasaland'. Verfassung und Recht in Übersee. Vol. 18, pp. 283-302.

Niamir, M. (1995) 'Indigenous systems of natural resource management among pastoralists of arid and semi-arid Africa'. In Warren, D. M., Slikkerveer, L., Jan and Brokensha, D. (eds.) *The cultural dimension of development: Indigenous knowledge systems*. London: Intermediate Technology Publications.

Njonjo, A. I. (1978) 'The Africanization of the 'white highlands': A study in agrarian class struggles in Kenya, 1950-1974. PhD. Thesis. Princeton University.

Northcote, R. C. (1945) *A memorandum on native land tenure*. Dar es Salaam:

Nothale, D. W. (1986) 'Land tenure systems and agricultural production in Malawi. In Arntzen, J. W., Ngcongoco, L. D. and Turner, S. D. (eds.) *Land policy and agriculture in Eastern and Southern Africa*. Selected papers presented at a workshop held in Gaborone, Botswana, 14-19 February 1982. Tokyo, Japan: United Nations University, pp. 127-132.

Obi, S. N. C. (1963) *Ibo law of property*. London: Butterworth & Co. Ltd.

Obi, S. N. C. (1969) 'Women's property and succession thereto in modern Ibo law'. (Eastern Nigeria) Journal of African Law. Vol. 6, No. 1, pp. 6-18.

Obilade, A. O. (1965) 'Customary law and the Registered Land Act, 1965'. The Lawyer. Vol. 2, No. 1, pp. 16-20.

Ogbobine, R. A. I. (1974) *Materials and cases on Benin land law*. Benin City, Nigeria: Midwest Newspapers Corp.

Ohonbamu, O. (1964) 'Current trends in the Nigerian customary law of mortgage'. Nigerian Law Journal. Vol. 1, No. 1, pp. 1-9.

Okanu, M. C. (1986) *Nigerian law of property*. Enugu, Nigeria: Fourth Dimension Publishers.

Okoth-Ogendo, H. W. O. (1974) 'Property theory and land-use analysis: An essay in the political economy of ideas'. Journal of Eastern African Research and Development. Vol. 5, No. 1, pp. 37-53.

Okoth-Ogendo, H. W. O. (1976) 'African land tenure reform'. In Heyer, J. Maitha, J, and Senga, W. (eds.) *Agricultural development in Kenya*. Nairobi: Oxford University Press.

Okoth-Ogendo, H. W. O. (1978) *The political economy of land law: An essay in the legal organisation of underdevelopment in Kenya, 1895-1974*. DSL Thesis. Law School, Yale University.

Okoth-Ogendo, H. W. O. (1981) 'Land ownership and land distribution in Kenya's large-farm areas'. In Killick, T. (ed.) *Papers on the Kenyan economy*. Nairobi: Heinemann.

Okoth-Ogendo, H. W. O. (1986) 'The perils of land tenure reform: The case of Kenya'. In Arntzen, J., Ngcongco, L. and Turner, S. (eds.) *Land policy and agriculture in Eastern and Southern Africa.* Tokyo: United Nations University, pp. 79-92.

Okoth-Ogendo, H. W. O. (1989) 'Some issues of theory in the study of tenure relations in African agriculture'. Africa. Vol. 59, No. 1, pp. 6-17.

Olaitan, M. O. (1982) *Cases on Nigerian land law*: Index 1971-1975. Lagos, Nigeria: Libriservice Publications.

Olawoye, C. O. (1970a) Disposition of family land: Burden of proving consent'. Nigerian Journal of Contemporary Law. Vol. 1, No. 1, pp. 157-168.

Olawoye, C. O. (1970b) 'The meaning of family property, comments on *Abeje* v *Ogundairo'*. Nigerian Journal of Contemporary Law. Vol. 1, No. 2, pp. 300-316.

Oldaker, A. A. (1957) 'Tribal customary land tenure in Tanganyika'. Tanganyika Notes and Records. pp. 117-144.

Ollennu, N. A. (1962) *Principles of Customary land law in Ghana.* London: Sweet & Maxwell.

Omotola, J. A. (1974) 'Adverse possession of land and the intention of the true owner'. The Conveyancer and Property Lawyer. Vol. 38, pp. 172-175.

Omotola, J. A. (1976) 'The customary tenant and transfer of land in Nigeria'. The Nigerian Journal of Contemporary Law. Vol. 6, Nos. 1 &2, pp. 44-65.

Onala, P. L. (1986) *Land law and conveyancing in Kenya.* Nairobi: Heinemann.

Onwuamaegbu, O. (1975) 'Nigerian indigenous land law. In Elias, T. O., Nwabara, S. N. and Akpamgbo, C. O. (eds.) *African indigenous law.* Enugu, Nigeria: Government printer. For the Institute of African Studies, University of Nigeria, Nsukka. pp. 340-362.

Oshio, P. E. (1990) 'The Land Use Act and the institution of family property in Nigeria'. Journal of African Law. Vol. 34, No. 2, pp. 79-92.

Pachai, B. (1973) 'Land policies in Malawi: An examination of the colonial legacy'. Journal of African History. Vol. 14, No. 4, pp. 681-698.

Palmer, R. and Parsons, N. (eds.) (1977) *The roots of rural poverty in Central and Southern Africa.* London:

Park, E. A. W. (1965) 'A dual system of land tenure: The experience of Southern Nigeria'. Journal of African Law. Vol. 9, No. 1, pp. 1-19.

Parsons, K. H. (1971) *Customary land tenure and the development of African agriculture.* Madison: Land tenure Centre, University of Wisconsin.

Picard, L. A. (1980) 'Bureaucrats, cattle, and public policy: Land tenure changes in Botswana'. Comparative Political Studies Vol. 13, pp. 313-356.

Pogucki, R. J. H. (1955) 'Gold Coast land tenure: Land tenure in Ghana: A survey of land tenure in customary law of the Protectorate of the Northern territories'. Vols. 1-5, titled: *Gold Coast land tenure*. Vol. 2, *Report on land tenure in Adangme customary law*. Vol. 6, *General principles of land tenure in Ghana*. Accra: Government Printer.

Price, W. (1933) Land tenure in the Yoruba Provinces. Lagos: Government Printer.

Quansah, E. K. (1988) 'Ownership of matrimonial property under African customary law: A search for criteria'. Calabar Law Journal. Vol. 2, pp. 109-121.

Rogers, M. (1973) 'The Kenya land reform programme: A model for modern Africa?' Verfassung und Recht in Übersee. Vol. 6, pp. 49-63.

Rohde, R. F. (1993) *Afternoons in Damaraland: Common land and common sense in one of Namibia's former 'homelands'*. Edinburgh: University of Edinburgh Centre of African Studies.

Rowling, C. W. (1948) *Study of land tenure in the Cameroons provinces*. Lagos: Government Printer.

Rowling, C. W. (1951) 'African land tenures: A plea'. Journal of African Administration. Vol. 3. No. 1, pp. 4-8.

Rowling, C. W. (1952) 'An analysis of factors effecting changes in land tenure in Africa'. Journal of African Administration. Special Supplement. pp. 21-28.

Rowling, C. W. (1956) *Land tenure in Ijebu Province*. Lagos: Government printer.

Schapera, I. (1943) *Native land tenure in the Bechuanaland Protectorate*. Alice: The Lovedale Press.

Schapera, I. (1983) 'The system of land tenure on the Barolong Farms' (Bechuanaland Protectorate) Botswana Notes and Records Vol. 15, pp. 15-37.

Schmidt, W. (1935) 'The position of women with regard to property in primitive society'. American Anthropologist. Vol. 37, No. 2, pp. 224-256.

Sender, J. and Smith, S. (1990) *Poverty, class and gender in rural Africa: A Tanzanian case study*. London: Routledge & Kegan Paul.

Sheddick, V. (1954) *Land tenure in Basutoland*. London: Her majesty's Stationery Office.

Shelford, F. (1911) 'Land tenure on the Gold Coast'. Journal of the Royal African Society. Vol. 10, pp. 473-476.

Simmance, A. J. F. (1961) 'Land redemption among the Fort Hall Kikuyu'. Journal of African Law. Vol. 5, No. 2, pp. 75-81.

Simpson, S. R. (1970) 'Towards a definition of absolute ownership'. Journal of African Law. Vol. 5, No. 3, pp. 145-150.

Smith, I. O. (1995) *The law of real property in Nigeria*. Lagos: Lagos State University.

Snyder, F. G. (1977) 'Land law and economic change in rural Senegal: Diola pledge transactions and disputes'. In Hamnett, I. (ed.) *Social anthropology and law*. London: Academic Press, pp. 113-157.

Sonius, H. W. J. (1963) *Introduction to aspects of customary land law in Africa as compared with some Indonesian aspects.* Leiden: Universitaire.

Sorrenson, M. P. K. (1967) *Land reform in the Kikuyu country: A study in Government policy.* London: Oxford University Press for East African Institute of Social Research.

Ssempebwa, E. F. (1978) 'The law and problems of urban housing finance in Uganda'. In Kanyeihamba, G. W. and McAuslan, J. P. W. B. (eds.) *Urban legal problems in Eastern Africa.* Uppsala, Sweden: Scandinavian Institute of African Studies, 163-183.

Thomas, M. F. and Whittington, G. W. (eds.) (1969) Environment and land use in Africa. London: Methuen.

Tipple, A. G. (1986) 'Revolution in property rights'. West Africa. No. 27, pp. 79-80.

Toulmin, C. (1983) 'Herders and farmers or farmer-herders and herder-farmers?' Pastoral Network Paper. Vol. 15d. pp. 1-22.

Uchendu, V. (1970) 'The impact of changing agricultural technology on African land tenure'. Journal of Developing Areas. Vol. 4, pp. 477-486.

Utuama, A. A. (1989) *Nigerian law of real property*. Ibadan: Shaneson, C. I. Ltd.

Vail, L. (ed.) (1989) *The creation of tribalism in Southern Africa.* London James Currey.

Verhelst, T. (1968) *Materials on land law and economic development in Africa.* Los Angeles: African Studies Centre, UCLA.

Verhelst, T. (1969-70) 'Customary land tenure as a constraint on agricultural development: A re-evaluation'. Cultures et Développement Vol. 2, pp. 627-656.

Wagner, G. (1949) *The Bantu of Western Kenya: With reference to the Vugusu and Logoli.* London: Oxford University Press for the International African Institute..

Wanjala, S. C. (1990) *Land law and disputes in Kenya.* Nairobi: Oxford University Press.

Watson, D. J. (1962) 'The cattle-owner settlement scheme in Sierra Leone'. Empire Journal of Experimental Agriculture. Vol. 30, No. 117, pp. 42-48.

Watts, M. (1983) '"Good try, Mr. Paul": Populism and the Politics of African land use'. African Studies Review. Vol. 26, No. 2, pp. 73-83.

Werbner, R. (1982) 'The quasi-judicial and the experience of the absurd: Remaking land law in North-Eastern Botswana'. In Werbner, R. (ed.) *Land reform in the making: Tradition, public policy and ideology in Botswana.* pp. 131-150. London: Rex Collings.

Werbner, R. (ed.) (1982) *Land reform in the making: Tradition, public policy and ideology in Botswana*. London: Rex Collings.

White, C. M. N. (1958) 'Terminological confusion in African land tenure'. Journal of African Administration. Vol. 10, pp. 124-130.

White, C. M. N. (1959) 'A survey of land tenure in Northern Rhodesia. Journal of African Administration. Vol. 11, No. 4. pp. 171-178.

White, C. (1963) 'Factors determining the content of African land tenure systems in Northern Rhodesia'. In Biebuyck, D. (ed.) *African agrarian systems: Studies presented and discussed at the Second International African seminar*. Lovanium University, Leopoldville. January 1960. London: Oxford University Press for the International African Institute.

Williams, D. V. (1981) 'State coercion against peasant farmers: The Tanzanian case'. Journal of Legal Pluralism. Vol. 20, pp. 95-127.

Willoughby, P. G. (1965) 'Land registration in Nigeria: Past, present and future'. Nigerian Law Journal. Vol. 1, No. 2, pp. 260-283.

Wilson, G. (1938) The land rights of individual among the Nyakyusa. Livingstone: Rhodes-Livingstone Institute. Paper No. 1.

Woodman, G. R. (1964) 'The alienation of family land in Ghana'. University of Ghana Law Journal. Vol. 1, pp. 23-41.

Woodman, G. R. (1967a) 'A note on voidable grants in customary law'. Law in Society. Vol. 3, pp. 59-64.

Woodman, G. R. (1967b) 'The formalities and incidents of conveyances in Ghana'. University of Ghana Law Journal. Vol. 4, pp. 1-.

Woodman, G. R. (1968) 'The allodial title to land'. University of Ghana Law Journal. Vol. 5, pp. 79-114.

Woodman, G. R. (1969) 'Some realism about customary law'. Wisconsin Law Review. Vol. 1, pp. 128-152.

Woodman, G. R. (1970) 'Rights to fixtures in customary law'. University of Ghana Law Journal. Vol. 7, pp. 70-76.

Woodman, G. R. (1971) 'Acquiescence in English law and the customary land law of Ghana and Nigeria'. Journal of African Law. Vol. 15, No. 1, pp. 41-59.

Woodman, G. R. (1971) 'Land law controversies: Does the fee simple exist? What is tribute?' University of Ghana Law Journal. Vol. 8, pp. 148-152.

Woodman, G. R. (1975) *Customary land law in the Ghanaian Courts*. Accra: Ghana University Press.

Woodman, G. R. (1981-82a) 'Land use policy and the extent of the usufruct'. Review of Ghana Law. Vols. 13 & 14. pp. 200-204.

Woodman, G. R. (1981-82b) 'Family lands as stool lands'. Review of Ghana Law. Vols. 13 & 14, pp. 187-190.

Woodman, G. R. (1989-90) 'The head of family immunity principle: The Supreme Court proposes, the PNDC disposes'. Review of Ghana Law. Vol. 17, pp. 359-369.

Yakubu, M. G. (1985) *Land law in Nigeria*. London: Macmillan.

Young, P. C. (1963) *Yoruba land law*. London: Oxford University Press for the Nigerian Institute of Social and Economic Research.

Young, R. and Fosbrooke, H. (1960) *Land and politics among the Liguru of Tanganyika*. London: Routledge and Kegan Paul.

Chapter 14 — Right to a husband

Polygyny is one of the last indigenous law institutions that revolve around real life and has not fallen into desuetude. See chapter 11. Not because it is practised only by black men doing exciting things to two or more women, but it suffices to note that most men everywhere have a vested interest in polygyny, albeit monogamy with mistresses.

In matrilineal societies, because women are the progenitors and transmitters of the *eanda*, women are considered to have a right to a husband. The right to a husband presupposes that a man has the privilege of polygyny. The woman's right of sharing a half, or a quarter of a rich, virtuous husband is preferable to having no husband at all.

What was most undesirable was for a beautiful woman of child bearing age to be left at home unmarried. This was seen as an indictment by the community of the woman's *eanda*, *oruzo* and parents, because men did not wish to marry into such a family. Marriage, be it monogamous, polygamous, levirate or sororate was specially difficult for the intellectually disabled and the poor. As an old *Himba* sage said: "A poor man may be an excellent husband, but you wouldn't want your niece to marry one".

An unmarried woman is not in a position to bring in bridewealth, marriage settlement property and children. A community that does not reproduce itself will sooner or later die out completely. Accordingly, children are very important in the scheme of polygyny, because after all, blood is a more natural tie than land and cattle wealth.

Children are considered to be the only vital gift that a woman could give. If death should take the woman in child birth as a substitute for the child's life, then children become more valuable because their lives were bought at a very high price. Patrilineal societies discouraged philandering, having children outside marriage, because it is considered unjust enrichment by the mother's matriclan who have full custody of the children, owing to lack of marriage settlement. Children, they argued ought to increase the population of the patriclan, not that of the matriclan.

As descent and inheritance of property are usually recognised through the female line, the *eanda* takes a great deal of interest in the selection of a man and a woman's first spouse, the *ondjova* wife, the couple who would have mating rights with each other and whose sons and daughters would one day become *oruzo* heir or *eanda* heir. See chapter 11. Matrilineal pastoralists know a great deal about how to cross-breed their cattle and they apply this knowledge to the selection of a husband or wife. It is a way of selecting one's heirs and giving the children a reasonable chance in the starting line of life. But the husband's second and subsequent 'love' marriages, if he can afford them, are his own affair.

14.1 Sororate marriage

If his *ondjova* is sterile, he would discuss his intention of marrying a second wife with her. Just as other couples would discuss their intention of having an artificial insemination by donor, *in vitro* fertilisation, embryo transfer and replantation, surrogacy or adoption. If the *ondjova* wife consents, then he will take a second wife. However, his *ondjova* wife, his sisters and nephews and friends must accompany him to the marriage ceremony of the 'love' wife to show their approval. If the *ondjova* wife declines and thus shows her disapproval, he will still get married to his 'love' wife in any case, and will install her in another *onganda* with his *oruzo* relatives.

When an *ondjova* wife with children died, it was considered appropriate for the widower to marry his deceased wife's unmarried sister, if she had one. This is the sororate marriage. The rationale of sororate marriage is that an aunt would take better care of her nephews and nieces than any other woman.

Indigenous law formalities for a sororate marriage required the widower to make another separate bridewealth settlement. There is no pressure exerted on the sister to marry her brother-in-law. Her paternal uncles will participate in this determination and will not permit the maternal uncles to sacrifice her for another bridewealth cattle. She might not want to marry into a family where her sister had died. On the other hand, the deceased wife's *eanda* might not like the widower well enough to accept his offer of marriage to a second niece.

14.2 Levirate marriage

Indigenous moral law also permits a man to marry his deceased brother's young widow, and a young widow could also marry her deceased husband's brother who is nearer to her own age group. This is the levirate marriage or widow inheritance.[19] A uterine brother has a moral obligation to look after his brother's young widows and minor children, but leviratic marriage is not compulsory.

Furthermore, the individual couple has a say in the matter, they do not have to marry. There is no coercion. Like other people under civil law or common law, some people under customary law, because they are rational human beings, do not obey all their legal rules like ants. If a leviratic marriage is in their best interest as well as in the best interest of their children, *eanda* and *oruzo,* then they entered into it. At the same time, a couple without the inclination to submit to a leviratic yoke is not condemned, but it requires the virtue of courage for a widow to fly in the face of the generally accepted moral law. Nevertheless, in some cases nieces of powerful men and cattle barons returned home as widows, but if they decide to remarry outside the deceased's agnate group, the *ovitunya* was refundable.

In a matrilineal leviratic marriage, the uterine brother of the deceased becomes the genitor without any marriage formalities, because the widow is already a member of his *oruzo*. The childless widow and her cattle simply move into the surviving brother's *onganda*. The widow's first child born out of the new leviratic marriage, is begotten on behalf of the deceased brother, and named after him, but the subsequent children "belong" to the living husband. The children of the leviratic marriage call the man who fathers them *inyangu*, (in Herero, a father's younger brother) not *tate* meaning father. It was explained that some modern widow-inheritors have a tendency to forget the deceased brother and claimed all the children as their own offspring. Whereas, in widow inheritance, there is a new marriage ceremony to change the *oruzo* of the widow to that of the new genitor.

My interviewees explained that widows who willingly entered leviratic polygyny were usually young childless women who probably had married infertile old men. Old battle axes are not inherited. The

[19] For more details on ancient levirate see Deuteronomy 25:5 and Leviticus 18:16. The leading ethnographic study is P. P. Howell (1954:78-80). See also Arthur Phillips and Henry Morris (1971:103 & Note 5)

older women who have passed child bearing age, explained that they would not submit to the yoke of levirate polygyny if death should dissolve their current marriage.

The bibliographical study in this chapter covers polygyny and the demographic argument; widows, wife inheritance and the levirate, but not much research has been conducted on harem polygyny or polyandry among the Lele, Kadara, Kagoro and many small scale societies.

Today, the incidences of sororate marriage and leviratic polygyny are gradually dying out as in Christendom. This is not as a result of Christianity, international treaties, charters and statutes, because legislation alone does not change human beings. The changes are brought about by education of girls and the growing perception that women are autonomous beings, furthermore, that marriage is not only about procreation.

14.2 Bibliography

Abrahams, R. G. (1973) 'Some aspects of levirate'. In Goody, J. (ed.) *The character of kinship.* Cambridge: Cambridge University Press.

Adams, B. and Mburugu, E. (1994) 'Kikuyu bridewealth and polygyny today'. Journal of Comparative Family Studies. Vol. 25, No. 2, pp. 159-166.

Adjetey, P. A. (1961) 'Some legal consequences of polygamous marriages in Ghana'. Universitas. No. 4, pp. 168-171.

Ames, D. W. (1955) 'The economic basis of Wolof polygyny'. South Western Journal of Anthropology. Vol. 11, No. 4, pp. 391-403.

Ardener, E. W. (1962) *Divorce and fertility: An African study.* London: Oxford University Press.

Barnes, J. A. (1971) *Three styles in the study of kinship.* Berkeley: University of California Press.

Bauman, H. (1928) 'The division of work according to sex in African hoe culture'. Africa. Vol. 1, pp. 289-319.

Bazeley, W. S. (1929) 'Manyika law and custom regarding inheritance of wives and property and the guardianship of children'. NADA No. 7, pp. 110-112.

Beckett, W. E. (1932) 'The recognition of polygamous marriages under English law'. Law Quarterly Review. No. 48, pp. 341-373.

Begler, E. (1978) 'Sex, status and authority in egalitarian society'. American Anthropologist. Vol. 80, pp. 571-588.

Béjin, A. (1985) 'The extra-marital union today'. In Ariès, P. and Béjin A. (eds.) *Western sexuality: Practice and precept in past and present times.* Oxford: Basil Blackwell.

Betzig, L. L. (1986) *Despotism and differential reproduction: A Darwinian view of history.* New York: Aldine Press.

Borgerhoff Mulder, M. (1988) 'Is the polygyny threshold model relevant to humans'? In Mascie-Taylor, C. G. N. and Boyce, A. J. (eds.) *Mating patterns*, pp. 209-230. Cambridge: Cambridge University Press.

Borgerhoff Mulder, M. (1989a) 'Polygyny and the extent of women's contribution to subsistence: A reply to White'. American Anthropologist. Vol. 91, No. 1, pp. 178-180.

Borgerhoff Mulder, M. (1989b) 'Marital status and reproductive performance in Kipsigis women: Re-evaluating the polygyny-fertility hypothesis'. Population Studies. Vol. 43, No. 2, pp. 285-304.

Borgerhoff Mulder, M. (1992) 'Women strategies in polygynous marriage: Kipsigis, Datoga and other East African cases'. Human Nature. Vol. 3, No. 1, pp. 45-70.

Brabin, L. (1984) 'Polygyny: An indicator of nutritional stress in African agricultural societies'. Africa. Vol. 54, No. 1, pp. 31-45.

Bretschneider, P. (1992) 'Sociological models of polygyny: A critical review'. Anthropos. Vol. 87, pp. 183-191.

Bretschneider, P. (1995) *Polygyny: A cross-cultural study*. Uppsala: Academia Ubsaliensis. Uppsala Studies in cultural anthropology.

Burton, M. L. and Reitz, K. (1981) 'The plow, female contribution to agricultural subsistence and polygyny: A long-linear analysis'. Behaviour Science Research. Vol. 16, No. 4, pp. 275-305.

Buxton, J. (1958) 'The significance of bridewealth and the levirate among the Nilotic and Nilo-Hamitic tribes of the Southern Sudan'. Anti-Slavery Reporter. Vol. 11, pp. 66-75.

Cairncross, J. (1974) *After polygamy was made a sin: The social history of christian polygamy.* London: Routledge and Kegan Paul.

Caldwell, J. C. and Caldwell, P. (1987) 'The cultural context of high fertility in Sub-saharan Africa'. Population and Development Review. Vol. 13, pp. 409-437.

Chalifoux, J. J. (1980) 'Secondary marriage and levels of seniority among the Abisi (Piti) of Nigeria'. In women with many husbands: Polyandrous alliance and marital flexibility in Africa and Asia. Journal of Comparative Family Studies. (Special issue) Vol. 11, No. 3, pp. 325-334.

Christensen, J. B. (1954) *Double descent among the Fanti*. New Haven: Human Relations Area Files.

Clarke, E. (1957) *My mother who fathered me*. London: Allen & Unwin.

Clignet, R. (1970) *Many wives, many powers: Authority and power in polygynous families.* Evanston: Northwestern University Press.

Clignet, R. (1987) 'On dit que la polygamie est morte: Vive la polygamie!' In Parkin, D. and Nyamwaya, D. (eds.) *Transformations of African marriage*, Manchester: Manchester University Press, pp. 199-209.

Colson, E. (1958) *Marriage and family among the Plateau Tonga of Northern Rhodesia.* Manchester: Manchester University Press.

Crandall, D. P. (1991) 'The strength of the ovaHimba patrilineage'. Cimbebasia. Vol. 13, pp. 45-51.

Cronk, L. (1991) 'Wealth, status and reproductive success among the Mukogodo of Kenya'. American Anthropologist. Vol. 93, pp. 345-360.

Crosby, K. H. (1937) 'Polygamy in Mende country'. Africa. Vol. 10, No. 2, pp. 249-264.

D'Hondt, W. and Vandewiele, M. (1980) 'Attitudes of Senegalese Secondary School students towards traditional African way of life and western way of life'. Psychological Reports. Vol. 47, No. 1, pp. 235-242.

Dee Vellenga, D. (1986) 'The widow among the matrilineal Akan of Southern Ghana'. In Potash, B. (ed.) *Widows in African societies: Choices and constraints*. Stanford: Stanford University Press, pp. 220-240.

Dickemann, M. (1979) 'The ecology of mating systems in hypergynous dowry societies'. Social Science Information. Vol. 18, pp. 163-195.

Dorjahn, V. R. (1959) 'The factor of polygyny in African demography'. In Bascom, W. R. and Herskovits, M. J. (eds.) *Continuity and change in African cultures*. Chicago: University of Chicago Press, pp. 87-113.

Dorjahn, V. R. (1988) 'Changes in Temne polygyny'. Ethnology. No. 27, pp. 367-390.

Douglas, M. (1964) 'Matriliny and pawnship in Central Africa'. Africa. Vol. 34, pp. 301-313.

Douglas, M. (1969) 'Is matriliny doomed in Africa?' In Douglas, M. and Kaberry P. M. (eds.) *Man in Africa*. London: Tavistock, pp. 121-135.

Eades, J. S. (1980) *The Yoruba today*. Cambridge: Cambridge University Press.

Ember, M. (1974) 'Warfare, sex ratio and polygyny'. Ethnology. Vol. 13, pp. 197-206.

Ember, M. (1984) 'Alternative predictors of polygyny'. Behaviour Science Research. Vol. 19, pp. 1-23.

Essock-Vitale, S. M. (1984) 'The reproductive success of wealthy Americans'. Ethology and Sociobiology. Vol. 5, pp. 45-49.

Evans-Pritchard, E. E. (1965) *The position of women in primitive societies and other essays in social anthropology*. New York: Free Press.

Fadipe, N. A. (1970) *The sociology of the Yoruba*. Ibadan: Ibadan University Press.

Fallers, L. (1957) 'Some determinants of marriage stability in Busoga'. Africa. Vol. 27, No. 2, pp. 106-123.

Folarin, A. (1939) *The laws and customs of Egbaland*. Abeokuta, Nigeria: ENA Press.

Forde, D. (1950) 'Double descent among the Yakö'. In Radcliffe-Brown, A. R. and Forde, D. (eds.) *African systems of kinship and marriage*. Oxford: Oxford University Press. pp. 285-332.

Garenne, M. and Walle, E. van de (1989) 'Polygyny and fertility among the Sereer of Senegal'. Population Studies. Vol. 43, pp. 267-283.

Gbadegesin, S. (1993) 'The ethics of polygyny'. Quest. Vol. 7, No. 2, pp. 2-29.

Gibson, G. (1956) 'Double descent and its correlates among the Herero of Ngamiland'. American Anthropologist. Vol. 58, pp. 109-139.

Goode, W. (1963) World revolution and family patterns. New York: Free Press.

Goody, J. (1973) 'Polygyny, economy and the role of women'. In Goody, J. (ed.) *The character of kinship*. Cambridge: Cambridge University Press, pp. 175-190.

Hartung, J. (1982) 'Polygyny and the inheritance of wealth'. Current Anthropology. Vol. 23, pp. 1-12.

Heald, S. (1982) 'The making of men'. Africa. Vol. 52, pp. 15-36.

Heusch, L. de (1981) *Why marry her?* Cambridge: Cambridge University Press.

Howell, P. P. (1954) *A manual of Nuer law: Being an account of customary law its evolution and development in the courts established by the Sudan Government*. Oxford: Oxford University Press.

Karanja, W. (1987) 'Outside wives' and 'inside wives' in Nigeria: A study of changing perceptions of marriage. In Parkin, D. and Nyamwaya, D. (eds.) *Transformations of African marriage*. Manchester: Manchester University Press for the International African Institute, pp. 247-261.

Karanja, W. (1994) 'The phenomenon of 'outside wives': Some reflections on its possible influence on fertility'. In Bledsoe and Pison, G. (eds.) Nuptiality in sub-saharan Africa: Contemporary anthropological and demographic perspectives. Oxford: Clarendon Press, pp. 194-214.

Kilbride, P. (1994) Plural marriage for out times: A reinvented option? Westport:

Kirwen, M. C. (1979) *African widows: An empirical study of the problems of adapting western christian teachings on marriage to the leviratic custom for the case of widows in four rural African societies*. New York: Orbis Press.

Kuper, A. (1975) 'Preferential marriage and polygyny among the Tswana'. In Fortes, M. and Patterson, S. (eds.) *Studies in African social anthropology*. London: Academic Press.

Leslie, R. D. (1972) 'Polygamous marriages and bigamy'. The Juridical Review. pp. 113-123.

Little, K. and Price, A. (1973) 'Some trends in modern marriage among West Africans'. In Trunbull, C. (ed.) *Africa and change*. New York: Knopf. pp. 185-207.

Lopata, H. Z. (1979) *Women as widows: Support systems*. New York: Elsevier-North Holland.

Low, B. S. (1988) 'Pathogen stress and polygyny in humans'. In Betzig, L., Borgerhoff Mulder, M. and Turke, P. (eds.) *Human reproductive behaviour: A Darwinian perspective*Cambridge: Cambridge University Press, pp. 115-127.

Marasinghe, M. L. (1968) 'Monogamy, polygamy and bigamy'. Journal of Islamic and Comparative Law. Vol. 2, pp. 54-78.

Marris, P. (1958) *Widows and their families*. London: Routledge & Kegan Paul.

Meekers, D. and Franklin, N. (1995) 'Women's perception of polygyny among the Kaguru of Tanzania'. Ethnology. Vol. 34, No. 4, pp. 315-329.

Moller, V. and Welch, G. J. (1990) 'Polygamy, economic security and well being of retired Zulu migrant workers'. Journal of Cross-Cultural Gerontology. Vol. 5, No. 3, pp. 205-216.

Morris, I. H. C. (1953) 'The recognition of polygamous marriages in English law'. Harvard Law Review. No. 66, pp. 961-1012.

Muhsam, H. V. (1958) 'The fertility of polygamous marriages'. Population Studies. Vol. 10, pp. 3-16.

Muller, J. C. (1980) 'On the relevance of having two husbands: Contribution to the polygynous/polyandrous marital forms of the Jos Plateau'. *In women with many husbands: Polygandous alliance and marital flexibility in Africa and Asia.* Journal of Comparative Family Studies. Vol. 11, No. 3, pp. 359-369.

Naden, D. and Naden T. (1991) 'Polygyny: Further factors from Mamprusi'. American Anthropologist. Vol. 93 & 94, pp. 948-950.

Obbo, C. (1976) 'Dominant male ideology and female options: Three East African case studies'. Africa. Vol. 46, pp. 371-389.

Okonjo, K. (1992) Aspects of continuity and change in mate selection among the Igbo West of the Niger River. Journal of Comparative Family Studies. Vol. 23, No. 3, pp. 339-360.

Okonkwo, C. O. (1976) 'Bigamy in a polygamous society (Nigeria)'. The Nigerian Juridical Review. Vol. 1, pp. 76-87.

Osmond, M. W. (1965) 'Toward monogamy: A cross cultural study of correlates of type of marriage'. Social Forces. Vol. 44, pp. 6-16.

Owuamanam, D. O. (1984) 'Adolescents' perception of polygamous family and its relationship to self-concept'. International Journal of Psychology. Vol. 19, No. 6, pp. 593-598.

Phillips, A. and Morris, H. F. (1971) *Marriage laws in Africa.* Oxford: Oxford University Press.

Potash, B. (ed.) (1986) *Widows in African societies: Choices and constraints.* Stanford: Stanford University Press.

Reynolds, W. S. (1979-80) 'Wives and co-wives in Marachi, Kenya'. Folk. Vol. 21, No. 22, pp. 133-146.

Sacks, K. (1982) *Sisters and wives: The past and future of sexual inequality.* Urbana: University of Illinois Press.

Sagay, I. E. (1974a) 'Multiple marriages in Nigeria a conflict of law and culture'. The Nigerian Bar Journal. Vol. 12, pp. 82-87.

Sagay, I. (1974b) 'Widow inheritance versus monogamous marriage: The Oba's dilemma'. Journal of African Law. Vol. 18, No. 2, pp. 168-172.

Samuels, A. (1984) 'The polygamous wife: How far is she treated as a wife in English law?' Journal of Social Welfare Law, pp. 271-276.

Sichona, F. J. (1992) *The polygyny-fertility hypothesis revisited: The situation in Ghana.* Carolina Population Centre Papers. Chapel Hill.

Simmons, D. C. (1960) 'Sexual life, marriage and childhood among the Efik'. Africa. Vol. 30. pp. 153-165.

Smith, M. G. (1953) 'Secondary marriage in Northern Nigeria'. Africa. Vol. 23, pp. 298-323.

Smith, R. S. (1988) *Kingdoms of the Yoruba.* Madison, Wis: University of Wisconsin Press.

Solway, J. S. (1990) 'Affines and spouses, friends and lovers: The passing of polygyny in Botswana'. Journal of Anthropological Research. Vol. 46, pp. 41-66.

Spencer, P. (1980) 'Polygyny as a measure of social differentiation in Africa'. In Mitchell, C. (ed.) *Numerical techniques in social anthropology.* Philadelphia: Institute for the Study of Human Issues, pp. 117-160.

Topouzis, D. (1985) 'The men with many wives'. New Society. Vol. 74, No. 1188, pp. 13-15.

Ukaegbu, A. (1977) 'Fertility of women in polygynous unions in rural Eastern Nigeria'. Journal of Marriage and the Family. Vol. 39, No. 4, pp. 397-404.

Ware, H. (1979) 'Polygyny: Women's views in a transitional society, Nigeria 1975'. Journal of Marriage and the Family. Vol. 41, No. 1, pp. 185-195.

White, D. R. (1988a) 'Rethinking polygyny: Co-wives, codes and cultural systems'. Current Anthropology. Vol. 29, No. 4, pp. 529-558.

White, D. R. (1989) 'Questioning the correlational evidence for Kipsigis wealth as a cause of reproductive success rather than polygyny as a cause of both extra children and extra wealth. American Anthropologist. Vol. 91, No. 1, pp. 175-178.

White, D. R. and Burton, M. L. (1988b) 'Causes of polygyny: Ecology, economy, kinship and warfare'. American Anthropologist. Vol. 90, No. 4, pp. 871-887.

Wittrup, I. (1990) 'Me and my husband's wife: An analysis of polygyny among Mandinka in the Gambia'. Folk. Vol. 33, pp. 117-142.

Chapter 15 — Succession and inheritance

The indigenous law of succession is a minefield for researchers as well as for practising lawyers. The transmission of status and the inheritance of chattels become effective only after death, but the validity of some indigenous succession laws depends on whether the deceased belonged to a matrilineal, patrilineal, or duolineal group, and whether the deceased's marriage was virilocal, uxorilocal, or polygynous. See chapter 11. There are fixed indigenous provisions among some groups for matrilineal, and patrilineal succession, as well as for inheritance in polygynous families. Furthermore, in some states it has to be ascertained if indigenous law, <u>The Marriage Ordinance</u> or the <u>Intestate Succession Law</u> applies to the estate of the intestate.

In succession and inheritance, the welfare of the deceased's children under the age of puberty is also paramount and the intestate's young widows too deserve attention. Accordingly, young children and widows of child bearing age tend to be assimilated into the deceased's estate. Not because the young widows and children are property to be devised, but because a magnanimous husband makes provision for his widows continued maintenance and sexuality.

The levirate succession and widow inheritance are usually for the protection of young and beautiful widows in a locality where they have contracted virilocal marriage, far away from home. See chapter 14. The beautiful young widows already know their deceased husband's agnates, accordingly, the union is not considered repugnant. See chapter 8. However, no widow is under obligation to enter into a leviratic polygynous marriage, as there are no rules of enforcement in a community where couples already have rules of separate matrimonial property.

15.1 Oral will

In matrilineal societies men and women can make oral will, but it has no effect whatsoever until it is made as a dying disposition. Among the *Herero,* a dying adult who has capacity can make an oral will, *okurumatisa.* The matrilineal *Akan* also made oral will, *samansiw.* This should settle the legal argument between Kludze (1975: 22-25), Dankwa (1978-81: 97-98) and Kludze (1988:149-156) on the origin of the oral will characteristic of the matrilineal Akan. Forde (1941) did not discuss Yakö matriliny oral will and neither did Beidelman (1971) on the Kaguru.

Okurumatisa, oral will was made before witnesses. More often than not, the oral will was a reiteration of what the witnesses already knew from years of conversations. However, only *okurumatisa,* the dying disposition made before agnatic men who are not beneficiaries was valid; this followed from the *ovaHimba* practice that a person who was terminally ill should never be left alone. There was nothing mystical about dying, as the *ovaHimba* say, but the owner of life knew when he or she was dying and required contact with loved ones. The wail, *omuvere wa zu po* (the sick person is dying) is relayed from *onganda* to *onganda.* The dying person was then held up to give him or her love and courage, although death was a very simple affair, one did not die lying prone on one's back. The dying person's last words were listened to attentively.

A dying man may express the wish that his brothers should look after his wife, or wives and young children. The wife or wives who bore him children should not be left as destitute widows and that his young children should neither starve nor become orphans. He can ask any of his immediate agnates to marry his widows and he can appoint *oruzo* guardians for the young children. As a result of matriliny, *okurumatisa*, gives the dying an opportunity to make small bequests, *donatio mortis causa*, gifts conditional on death of his favourite insignificant objects to specially deserving patrilineal relatives. In some matrilineal societies, most people know that the freedom of the oral will should not interfere with the beneficial rights of the *eanda* heirs, the blood relatives. Among the *ovaHimba*, it is unthinkable to bequeath *eanda* property or a significant self-acquired property by *okurumatisa* to non *eanda* beneficiaries for example, a wife's brother. The bequests would be revoked by the indigenous court.

The dying could also indicate where he would like to be buried, as the living and the dead co-existed until the colonial law forbade the burying of the dead within the village. The *Himba* bury their dead under the earth, whereas some riverine communities, where there are many potters, buried their dead in large funerary urns, vessels. See the archaeological collections in the Lagos Museum.

The dying is permitted to identify the cattle with picturesque well constructed horns that would be slaughtered after the interment. The horns make splendid tomb decorations. Having been provided with all the necessaries for the land of the ancestors, the *Himba* dead did not return to torment the living.

15.2 Administration of the estate

As the deceased would never be present to arrange his or her funeral, it is the function of the *eanda heirs* and the *oruzo* to give the dead a befitting funeral. The *eanda* heirs are assisted by the personal representative, the *omujanua*, the oldest surviving agnate of the deceased. Since a widow or widows are not related to their husband, they cannot bury him. They have no property in his corpse.

The *omujanua* administers the estate, arranges the funeral and the 'paying of homage'. He also helps with the payment of the deceased's debts and the distribution of the chattels to the rightful *eanda* beneficiaries. The deceased's cattle are separated from those of the survivors' cattle. First, the widow or widows' livestock are isolated from those of the deceased, then the children's cattle are also identified. Dead cattle that had belonged to the widow or widows and their children are replaced. If the joint ownership of cattle accumulated during the marriage had not been severed in the man's lifetime, then the cattle will devolve to the deceased's *eanda* estate. Cattle to be used as payment for the deceased's debts are set aside and cattle for the funeral feast are also deducted. Funerals and marriages are public affairs, accordingly, at the funeral of a rich man or woman many poor people expect to feed themselves on meat twice a day for three weeks. After all, the animals were the self-acquired property of the deceased and no expense was spared for the funeral feast.

Cattle capitalism make certain pastoralists a few of the richest people in Africa. A man or woman could own two to four hundred head of cattle and hundreds of sheep and goats. Thus, the personal chattels of a deceased *omuHimba* may include his or her herd of cattle, a horse or donkey, sheep, goats, blankets, sandals, slippers, leather bags, fine ethnographic snuff containers, headrest, wooden spoons, drinking vessels, jewellery, musical instruments, kieries, a knife, transistor radio, a four wheel drive, some coins and bank notes.

15.3 Cattle dung is thicker than water

In matrilineal societies, a deceased man's sister's sons, his nephews, usually inherit his personal chattels. His nephews are the recognisable, fixed *eanda* heirs who have the same blood relationship as the deceased. In the absence of surviving nephews and nieces, the chattels will vest in the deceased's maternal aunt's eldest son, following whom, the deceased's younger uterine brothers will take. However, if the deceased was an old man who had outlived everybody in his immediate *eanda*, a matrilineal descendant from his maternal grandmother or great grandmother will inherit the chattels.

The deceased's son is disqualified from succeeding to the chattels, because he is not of the same *eanda*, uterine blood as his father. In succession and inheritance, the *ovaHimba* say that "cattle dung is thicker than water" or more precisely, uterine blood that inherits the cattle is thicker than water. In pastoral matriliny, property had already devolved on the deceased's sons and daughters long before the death of their father, for they had received the *ohakera* cattle, and more cattle when they reached puberty. Furthermore, they are the beneficiaries of the estate of their maternal uncles. A deceased woman is succeeded by her children and uterine siblings.

Duolineal succession has to do with the religious, political and cultural relationship of mostly the adult men. The status of the keeper of the cultural property is based exclusively on male seniority in the patrilineage. The position vacated by the dead must be filled so the cultural property vested in the deceased's nearest and oldest surviving male, first the immediate uterine brother. If the deceased has no more surviving uterine brothers, or uncles, then the next person entitled to the cultural property is the deceased's eldest son by the *ondjova* wife. See chapter 11. If the deceased had only daughters, then the oldest surviving brother of the half-blood takes the title of the keeper of the cultural property.

In patrilineal societies, the birth of the first born son is exhilarating, because he is destined to carry on the indigenous duty, whereas the other children born after number one are simply love children. On the other hand, in matrilineal societies daughters are *okurangerera*, they bring good luck and wealth, because daughters bring in bridewealth, men and sons.

However, in some patrilineal societies where descent was by primogeniture, the men had no need for an oral will as the immovable property devolved on the preferred first son. He was the sole trustee of the family property and he was liable to maintain his siblings and make provisions for the intestate's elderly relatives.

There is another form of patrilineal distribution of the intestate's estate, that is, when all the sons hold the real property as joint tenants, but the chattels are shared equally with their sisters. If a son had predeceased the intestate and left surviving children, his share did not lapse. It devolved on the issue.

Another variation of patrilineal distribution was when sons and daughters shared equally in the real property and in the chattels, followed by the deceased's brothers and sisters of the full blood, then father and mother in equal shares, uncles and aunts of the whole blood, then brothers and sisters of the half-blood.

Yet another form of patrilineality is where the real property devolved on only the deceased's siblings, with maintenance of widows and children as optional extras.

Some patrilineal groups did not recognise widowhood as the death of the husband did not dissolve the marriage. Since the wife or wives did not bring any dower to the husband at the start of the marriage, they have no entitlement to his estate on his intestacy. Wives of child bearing age were not propelled into a leviratic marriage, they could divorce their deceased husband by returning a percentage of the bridewealth to the heirs, thus they are free to remarry.

15.4 Intestacy of a patrilineal polygynist

Generally, the poor are not polygynous, polygyny is the privilege of rich men, or powerful men, and marriage is virilocal. See chapters 11 & 14. There are fixed rules for the distribution of the estate of a rich patrilineal polygynous intestate. If as an example, the deceased is survived by four widows and nine children, the question is, should the estate be divided into four *stirpes,* W, X, Y, Z representing the four 'roots' and branches of each household or into nine equal parts *per capita*?

The widows have a right to reside in their matrimonial homes and the right to be maintained by their children, but as non-relatives of the deceased they have no intestate succession rights.

Accordingly, some Yoruba communities have formulated two methods of distributing the estate of an intestate polygynist.

Idi-igi, is a stirpital construction whereby each household W, X, Y, Z irrespective of the number of children in the root takes one quarter of the estate. A childless widow or widow with a single child benefited. In *ori-ojori*, the distribution is *per capita* among the nine children. If a child has predeceased the intestate and leaves no issue, that child gets nothing. See chapter 4 on children and *abiku*. But the child *in utero* is a person and thus has a claim right to the deceased's estate to take in the *ori-ojori*.

Some fathers spend a great deal of money in the education of the eldest son, and the wedding feast of the eldest daughter in each root, but the eldest children do not bring these gifts into the *hotchpot*. Education of the eldest son is evaluated as a right. However, each mother and a whole spider web of sisters help to educate the other children as best they can. These sons educated expensively by their women folks are expected to give something back in gratitude for the women's sacrifice.

The colonial argument was that indigenous succession law deprived the surviving widow and children of the deceased's estate in favour of his siblings, accordingly, The Marriage Ordinance for monogamous marriage was introduced. Only the deceased's surviving legal wife and her children were the recognised beneficiaries. However, the Intestate Succession Law in some states, has made marriage by customary law, Church rites or statutory law irrelevant to the devolution of the intestate's estate.

Rich men are being urged to make written wills, but some of the published wills so far, have not contravened the deceased's indigenous laws, only it simply made it easier to disinherit wayward daughters. The rich testators had a tendency to appoint the same indigenous law personal representative as the executor of the will. Provisions are made for the 'inside' statutory wife and children as well as pecuniary legacies and general annuities for the 'outside' wives and children.

15.5 Bibliography

N. C. W. S. B. (1929) 'Manyika law and custom regarding inheritance of wives and property and the guardianship of children'. NADA No. 7, pp. 110-112.

Reform of the Law of Succession in Ghana. (1959) Journal of African Law. Vol. 3, No. 2, pp. 90-92.

'Succession according to native custom upset owing to marriage by Christian rites: Restitutio in integrum' (1906) South African Law Journal. No. 23, pp. 106-107.

WLEA (1994) *The law of succession in Uganda: Women, inheritance laws and practices*. Kampala, Uganda: WLEA Publications.

WLEA: Women and Law in East Africa

WLSA (1994) *Inheritance in Botswana*. Gaborone: WLSA Publications

WLSA (1994) *Inheritance in Lesotho*. Maseru: WLSA Publications.

WLSA (1994) *Inheritance in Zambia: Law and practice*. Lusaka: WLSA Publications.

WLSA (1994) *Inheritance in Zimbabawe: Law, customs and practice*. Harare: WLSA Publications.

WLSA (1995) *Inheritance laws and practice in Swaziland*. Mbabane: WLSA Publications.

WLSA: Women and the Law in Southern Africa: Research Project.

Abrahams, R. G. (1973) 'Some aspects of levirate'. In Goody, J. (ed.) *The character of kinship*. Cambridge: Cambridge University Press.

Adesanya, M. O. (1974) 'Devolution and distribution of intestate estates among the Yoruba'. Zeitschrift für Vergleichende Rechtswissenschaft. Vol. 74, pp. 1-38.

Adigun, O. (1987) *Cases and texts on equity, trusts and administration of estates*. Abeaokuta: Ayo Sodimu.

Allott, A. N. (1953) 'A note on the Ga law of succession'. Bulletin of School of Oriental and African Studies. pp. 164-169.

Allott, A. N. (1970) 'The law of inheritance, family structure and modern economic order in Africa'. Zeitschrift für Vergleichende Rechtswissenschaft. pp. 105-118

Arhim, K. (1994) 'The economic implications of transformations in Akan funeral rites: With special reference to the Asante'. Africa. Vol. 64, No. 3, pp. 307-322.

Asemota, S. A. (1969) 'Intestate succession in Nigeria'. The Lawyer. Vol. 3, No.2, pp. 18-24.

Bailey, S. R. (1988-89) *The dramatization of mourning: Essays on Asante funeral rites in reference to Kumasi*. Legon: University of California Education programme at the University of Ghana.

Barnes, B. H. (1922) 'Survival after death among the Ba-Bemba of North-Eastern Rhodesia'. Man. Vol. 22, No. 22, pp. 41-41.

Beidelman, T. O. (1971) *The Kaguru, a matrilineal people of East Africa*. Case studies in cultural anthropology. Prospect Heights, IL.

Beinart, B. (1958) 'Liability of a deceased estate for maintenance'. Acta Juridica Vol. 1, pp. 92-111.

Beinart, B. (1965-66) 'The forgotten widow'. Acta Juridica. Vol. 8, pp. 285-325.

Bentsi-Enchill, K. (1964) *Ghana land law: An exposition, analysis and critique*. London: Sweet & Maxwell.

Bentsi-Enchill, K. (1972) 'Intestate succession revisited'. University of Ghana Law Journal. No. 9, pp. 123-134.

Bimpong-Buta, S. Y. (1983-86) Benefits conferred on customary marriage spouses by the Intestate Succession Law, 1985. (PNDCL iii) Review of Ghana Law. Vol. 15, pp. 239-247.

Binet, J. (1965) 'Le droit successorial chez les Ewe'. In Poirie, J. (ed.) *Etudes du droit africain et malgache*. pp. 307-315. Paris: Cujas.

Bullock, C. (1929) 'Can a native make a will'? NADA No. 7, pp. 104-109.

Bullock, C. (1950) 'Succession of Bemba chiefs'. NADA. No. 27, pp. 85-96.

Carstens, P. (1983) 'The inheritance of private property among the Nama of Southern Africa reconsidered'. Africa. Vol. 53, No. 2, pp. 58-70.

Cheater, A. P. (1987) 'Fighting over property: The articulation of dominant and subordinate legal systems governing the inheritance of immovable property among blacks in Zimbabawe'. Africa. Vol. 57, No. 2, pp. 173-196.

Chesoni, Z. R. (1966) 'Divorce and succession in Luyia customary law'. East African Law Journal. Vol. 2, pp. 165-178.

Christensen, J. B. (1954) *Double descent among the Fanti*. New Haven: Human Relations Area Files.

Cockcroft, I. G. (1934) 'Is the right of disinheritance recognised in native law'? NADA. No. 12, p. 36.

Coissoró, Narana (1966) *The customary laws of succession in Central Africa*. Lisboa:Technical University of Lisbon.

Coldham, S. F. R. (1983) The law of succession in Zambia: Recent proposals for reform'. Journal of African Law. Vol. 27, No. 2, pp. 162-168.

Colson, E. (1950) 'Possible repercussions of the right to make wills upon the Plateau Tonga of Northern Rhodesia'. Journal of African Administration. Vol. 2, No. 1, pp.24-34.

Cotran, E. (1969) *The law of succession: Kenya*. London: Sweet & Maxwell.

Cotran, E. (1987) *Casebook on Kenya customary law*. Abingdon, Oxon: Professional Books.

Crandall, D. P. (1991) 'The strength of the ovaHimba patrilineage'. Cimbebasia. Vol. 13, pp. 45-51.

Dankwa, E. V. O. (1985) 'Progress and regress in samansiw 1978-1981'. University of Ghana Law Journal. Vol. 15, pp. 97-112.

Dankwa, E. V. O. (1985) 'Property rights of widows in their deceased husband's estate'. University of Ghana Law Journal. Vol. 16, pp. 1-24.

Danquah, J. B. (1928) *Akan laws and customs and the Akim Abuakwa constitution*. London: Routledge.

Dengu-Zvgbo, K. et al. (eds.) (1994) *Inheritance in Zimbabwe: Law, customs and practice*. Harare: Women & Law in Southern Africa Research Trust.

Derret, J. D. N. (1965) *Studies in the laws of succession in Nigeria*. London: Oxford University Press.

Douglas, M. (1964) 'Matriliny and pawnship in Central Africa'. Africa. Vol. 34, pp. 301-313.

Douglas, M. (1969) 'Is matriliny doomed in Africa?' In Douglas, M. and Kaberry, P. (eds.) *Man in Africa*. London: Tavistock, pp. 121-135.

Driberg, J. H. (1929) 'Inheritance fees'. Man. No. 29. pp. 87-90.

Edwards, W. (1929) 'From birth to death'. NADA pp. 16-42.

Elias, T. O. (1957) 'Fulani inheritance'. Nigeria. No. 54. pp. 198-207.

Forde, D. (1941) *Marriage and the family among the Yakö in South Eastern Nigeria*. London: Percy Lund, Humphries & Co. Ltd.

Fox, R. (1993) *Reproduction and succession: Studies in anthropological law and society*. New Brunswick: Transaction Publishers.

Garbett, G. K. (1966) 'Religious aspects of political succession among the valley Korekore'. In Stokes, E. and Brown, R. (eds.) *The Zambesian past: Studies in Central African history*. Manchester: Manchester University Press, pp. 137-170.

Gibson, G. (1956) 'Double descent and its correlates among the Herero of Ngamiland'. American Anthropologist. Vol. 58, pp. 109-139.

Gilbert, M. (1988) 'The sudden death of a millionaire: Conversion and consensus in a Ghanaian kingdom'. Africa. Vol. 58, No. 3, pp. 291-314.

Gluckman, M. (1954) 'Succession and civil war among the Bemba: An exercise in anthropological theory'. Human problems. Vol. 16, pp. 6-25.

Goldfarb, A. (1990) 'A Kenyan wife's right to bury her husband: Applying the Conventions of the Elimination of all Forms of Discrimination Against Women'. ILSA. Journal of International Law. No. 14, pp. 1-24.

Goody, J. (1959) 'The mother's brother and the sister's son in West Africa'. Journal of the Royal Anthropological Institute. Vol. 89, pp. 59-88.

Goody, J. (1961) 'The classification of double descent systems'. Current Anthropology. Vol. 2, No. 11, pp. 3-25.

Goody, J. (1962) *Death, property and the ancestors: A study of the mortuary customs of the LoDagaa of West Africa*. London: Tavistock.

Goody, J. and Buckley, J. (1973) 'Inheritance and women's labour in Africa'. Africa. No. 43. pp. 108-121.

Gough, K. (1961) 'The modern disintegration of matrilineal descent groups'. In Schneider, D. M. and Gough, K. (eds.) *Matrilineal kinship*. Berkeley: University of California Press. pp, 631-652.

Gray, R. F. and Gulliver, P. (eds.) (1964) *The family estate in Africa*. Boston, Mass: Boston University Press.

Gulliver, P. H. (1955) *The family herds: A study of two pastoral tribes in East Africa, the Jie and the Turkama*. London: Routledge.

Guyer, J. I. (1987) *Women and the state in Africa: Marriage law, inheritance and resettlement*. Boston, Mass: Boston University, African Studies Centre.

Hannigan, A. St. J. J. (1954) 'The present system of succession amongst the Akan people of the Gold Coast'. Journal of African Administration. No. 6, pp. 166-171.

Hartung, J. (1976) 'On natural selection and the inheritance of wealth'. Current Anthropology. Vol. 17, pp. 607-622.

Hartung, J. (1982) 'Polygyny and the inheritance of wealth'. Current Anthropology. Vol. 23, pp. 1-12.

Hartung, J. (1985) 'Matrilineal inheritance: New theory and analysis'. The Behavioral and Brain Sciences. Vol. 8, No. 4, pp. 661-688.

Hay, M. and Wright, M. (eds.) (1982) *African women and the law: Historical perspectives*. Boston: Boston University Press.

Himonga, C. H. (1991) 'Family law reform and the integration of the laws of succession in Zambia'. Verfassung und Recht in Übersee. Vol. 24, pp. 340-361.

Himonga, C. N. (1989) 'The law of succession and inheritance in Zambia and the proposed reform'. International Journal of Law and the Family. Vol. 3, No. 2, pp. 160-176.

Himonga, C. N. (1993) 'Protection of widows and administration of customary estates in Zambian courts'. In Ludwar-Ene, G. and Reh, M. (eds.) *Focus on women in Africa*. Bayreuth: Breitinger.

Himonga, C. N. (1995) *Family and succession laws in Zambia: Developments since independence*. Münster: Lit Beiträge zur Afrikaforschung.

Holleman, J. F. (1952) *Shona customary law with reference to marriage, kinship, the family and the state*, pp. 318-368. London: Oxford University Press for the Rhodes-Livingstone Institute.

Holy, L. (1986) *Strategies and norms in a changing matrilineal society: Descent, succession and inheritance among the Toka of Zambia*. Cambridge: Cambridge University Press.

Homan, F. D. (1958) 'Inheritance in the Kenya native land units'. Journal of African Administration. Vol. 10, No. 3, pp. 131-135.

Howell, P. P. (1954) 'Some observations on divorce among the Nuer'. Journal of Royal Anthropological Institute. Vol. 83, pp. 136-146.

Howman, E. G. (1923) 'Some replies to questions in the native customs examination of 1923'. NADA. Vol. 1, pp. 84-86.

Ibik, J. O. (1971) *Restatement of African law. 4. The law of land, succession, movable property, agreements and civil wrongs.* London: Sweet & Maxwell.

Kaggwa, D. (1989) 'A Christian interpretation of the customs of the Baganda relating to death and inheritance'. The African Mind. Vol. 1, No. 1, pp. 108-135.

Kasunmu, A. B. (1964) 'Intestate succession in Nigeria'. Nigerian Law Journal. Vol. 1, pp. 50-58.

Kerr, A. J. (1961) *The native law of succession in South Africa.* London: Butterworths.

Kerr, A. J. (1969) 'A fidei commissum incorporating conditions based on Bantu law'. South Afircan Law Journal. No. 86, pp. 25-26.

Kintu, M. (1967) 'The Basonga customary law of succession'. Journal of Denning Law Society. No. 2, pp. 71-81.

Kludze, A. K. P. (1972) 'Problems of intestate succession in Ghana'. Universitas. Vol. 2, No. 1, pp. 3-37.

Kludze, A. K. P. (1975) 'The formalities of the customary law will'. University of Ghana Law Journal. Vol. 12. pp. 21-47.

Kludze, A. K. P. (1976) 'A century of changes in the law of succession'. In Ekow-Daniel, W. C. and Woodman, G. R. (eds.) *Essays in Ghanaian law.* Legon: The Faculty of Law, University of Ghana.

Kludze, A. K. P. (1988) *Modern law of succession in Ghana.* Dordrecht: Foris Publications

Lawuyi, O. B. (1991) 'The social marketing of elites: The advertised self in obituaries and congratulations in some Nigerian Dailies'. Africa. Vol. 61, No. 2, pp. 247-263.

Lehmann, F. R. (1951) 'Order of the hereditary succession of chiefs among the Herero'. Zeitschrift für Ethnologie. Vol. 76, pp. 94-102.

Levtzion, N. (1972) Was royal succession in ancient Ghana matrilineal? International Journal of African History Studies. pp. 91-93.

Lewin, J. (1945) 'Some cases of inheritance in native law'. African Studies. Vol. 4, No. 2, pp. 71-87.

Lloyd, P. C. (1955) 'The Yoruba lineage'. Africa. Vol. 25, pp. 235-251.

Lloyd, P. C. (1959) 'Some notes on the Yoruba rules of succession and on family property'. Journal of African Law. Vol. 3, pp. 7-32.

Loveridge, A. J. (1950) 'Wills and the customary law in the Gold Coast'. Journal of African Administration. Vol. 2, No. 4, pp. 24-28.

Lyall, A. (1988) 'Gwao bin kilimo: The Administor's reaction'. Journal of African Law. Vol. 32, No. 1, pp. 64-71.

Lyall, A. (1988) 'Gwao bin Kilimo: The administrator's reaction'. Journal of African Law. Vol. 32, No. 1, pp. 64-71.

Madhuku, L. (1993) 'Is custom customary law? The case of *Murisa* v *Murisa* S. 41-92, and a reply to Mrs. Julie Stewart'. Legal Forum. Vol. 5, No. 1, pp. 32-34.

Marris, P. (1958) *Widows and their families*. London: Routledge & Kegan Paul.

Matson, J. N. (1953) 'Testate succession in Ashanti'. Africa. Vol. 23, No. 3, pp. 224-232.

McCaskie, T. C. (1989) 'Death and the Asantehene: A historical meditation'. Journal of African History. Vol. 30, No. 2, pp. 417-444.

Moore, T. R. (1968) 'Dower, homestead and testamentary freedom in Liberia'. Liberia Law Journal. Vol. 4, pp. 101-125.

Morris, H. F. (1970) 'Attitudes towards succession law in Nigeria during the colonial period'. Journal of African Law. Vol. 14, No. 1, pp. 5-16.

Mtengeti-Migiro, R. (1991) 'Legal developments on women's rights to inherit under customary law in Tanzania'. Verfassung und Recht in Übersee. Vol. 24, pp. 362-371.

Mvunga, M. P. (1979) 'Law and social change: A case study in the customary law of inheritance in Zambia'. African Social Research. No. 28, pp. 643-654.

Ndou, R. S., Letsoala, Essy M. (eds.) (1994) *The future of the institution of hereditary rule and customary law in South Africa.* Papers from the customary law conference held at the Alpha Training Centre in Broederstroom from 16-18 July 1993. Maarshalltown, SA: Contralesa.

Nii-Aponsah, D. A. (1974) 'Ga-Mashie succession'. The Review of Ghana Law. Vol. 6, pp. 116-121.

Obi, S. N. C. (1962) 'Women's property and succession thereto in modern Ibo law '(Eastern Nigeria) Journal of African Law. Vol. 6, No. 1, pp. 6-18.

Okoro, N. (1966) *The customary laws of succession in Eastern Nigeria and the statutory and judicial rules governing their application.* London: Sweet & Maxwell.

Okoro, N. (1966) *The customary laws of succession in Eastern Nigeria and the statutory and judicial rules governing their application.* London: Sweet & Maxwell.

Ollennu, N. A. (1960) *The law of succession in Ghana*. London: Sweet & Maxwell.

Ollennu, N. A. (1962) *Principles of customary land law in Ghana*. London: Sweet & Maxwell.

Ollennu, N. A. (1966) *The law of testate and intestate succession in Ghana*. London: Sweet & Maxwell.

Owiredu, P. A. (1959) 'The Akan system of inheritance today and tomorrow'. African Affairs. No, 48, pp. 161-165.

Phibri, K. M. (1983) 'Some changes in the matrilineal family system among the Cherwa of Malawi since the nineteenth century'. Journal of African Law. Vol. 3, pp. 93-98.

Poewe, K. O. (1978) 'Matriliny in the throes of change: Kinship, descent and marriage in Luapula, Zambia'. Africa. Vol. 48, No. 3, pp. 205-219.

Potash, B. (1986) *Widows in African societies: Choices and constraints*. Stanford: Standord University press.

Powell, R. J. (1953) 'Notes on the Kutaya, Kukumba and Kugare. NADA No. 30, pp. 14-22.

Quartey-Papafio, A. B. (1910) 'Law of succession among the Akras of Ga tribes proper of the Gold Coast'. Journal of African Society. No. 10, pp. 64-72.

Radcliffe-Brown, A. R. (1935) 'Patrilineal and matrilineal succession. Iowa Law Journal. Vol. 20, reprinted as *Structure and function in primitive society*. London: Cohen and West.

Ramolefe, A. M. R. (1965-66) 'Customary law inheritance and succession: In particular the status of customary heir'. Lesotho. no 5, pp. 18-21.

Rehfisch, F. C. (1960) 'The dynamics of multilineality on the Mambila Plateau'. Africa. Vol. 30, pp. 246-261.

Roberts, S. A. and Comaroff, J. L. (1979) 'A chief's decision and the devolution of property in a Tswana chiefdom'. In Shack, W. and Cohen, P. (eds.) *Power in leadership*. Oxford: Clarendon Press.

Roberts, S. (1966) 'A revolution in the law of succession of Malawi'. Journal of African Law. Vol. 10, No. 1, pp. 21-32.

Roberts, S. (1968) 'The Malawi law of succession: Another attempted reform'. Journal of African Law. Vol. 12, No. 2, pp. 81-88.

Roberts, S. and Schapera, I. (1980) 'Ngwaketse inheritance: The devolution of cattle on women in a Tswana chiefdom'. African Law Studies. Vol. 28, pp. 63-81.

Rubin, N. (1965) 'Swazi law of succession: A restatement'. Journal of African Law. Vol. 9, No. 2, pp. 90-113.

Sagay, I. E. (1995) Customary law and freedom of testamentary power'. Journal of African Law. Vol. 39, No. 2, pp. 173-182.

Salim, A. I. (1990) 'Conflict between common law and customary law in Kenya: Regarding burial rights'. In Abun-Nasr, et al. (eds.) *Law, society and national identity*. Hamburg: Helmut Buske Verlag.

Sarbah, J. M. (1897) *Fanti customary laws*. London: William Clowes & Sons.

Selwyn-Bazeley, W. (1929) 'Manyika law and custom regarding inheritance of wives and property and the guardianship of children'. NADA. pp. 110-112.

Smart, H. M. J. (1969) 'Inheritance to property in Sierra Leone: An analysis of the law and problems involved. Sierra Leone Studies. No. 24, pp. 2-25.

Stamp, P. (1991) 'Burying Otieno: The politics of gender and ethnicity in Kenya'. Signs. No. 16, pp. 808-845.

Stewart, J. (1989-90) 'Who gets the money?: Some aspects of testate and intestate succession in Zimbabwe'. Zimbabawe Law Review. Vols. 7 & 8, pp. 85-103.

Warmelo, N. J. van (1949) *Venda law: Inheritance*. Pretoria: Government Printers.

Whitehead, G. O. (1950) 'Property and inheritance among the Bari'. Sudan Notes. No. 31. pp. 143-147.

Wild, N. C. (1977) 'A question of succession'. NADA Vol. 11. No. 4, pp. 415-427.

Woodman, G. R. (1969) 'Two problems in matrilineal succession'. Review of Ghana Law. Vols. 1 & 2, pp. 6-30.

Woodman, G. R. (1985) 'Ghana reforms the law of intestate succession'. Journal of African Law. Vol. 29, No. pp. 118-128.

Woodman, G. (1974) 'The rights of wives, sons and daughters in the estates of their deceased husbands and fathers'. In Oppong, C. (ed.) *Domestic rights and duties in Southern Ghana.* Legon: Institute of African Studies.

Chapter 16 — Bibliography

Many authors have taken on the Herculean task of compiling a bibliography of African studies. But the early attempts of African law bibliography were an amalgam of all the provinces of English, French, and Portuguese law, Roman Dutch law, international law, domestic law, and African customary law appended when it was found.

However, editors and compilers began to produce a legal bibliography of their states, but with identical format of dealing with all the provinces of the law. A researcher in only customary law had to trawl through international law and statutory law to find customary law.

The bibliography in this chapter can be used in conjunction with the material in chapter 3 on case books, Law Reports and legal research methodology. Included in this bibliographical section, however, are some bibliographies of other disciplines, because sometimes the compilers include some notes on African customary or indigenous law. The bibliographic references may help researchers to find more material on indigenous laws.

Africa, bibliographic survey of literature, 1973. Washington, DC: Headquarters Department of the Army.

African books in print: An index by author, title and subject. Fourth edition, 1993. London: Hans Zell.

Annual Survey of African Law from School of Oriental and African Studies. London: University of London.

Bibliography of African Law (1957) Journal of African Law. Vol. 1, No. 2, p.144.

Bibliography of African Law (1961) Part 2: *West Africa. Restatement of African Law Project.* London: SOAS. University of London.

Bibliography of African Law (1967) Journal of African Law. Vol. 11, No. 1, pp. 67-69.

'Bibliography of African Law' (1967) Journal of African Law. Vol. 11, No. 3, pp. 194-198.

'Bibliography of African Law' (1968) Journal of African Law. Vol. 12, No. 3, pp. 194-198.

'Bibliography on chiefs and African states' (1987) Journal of Legal Pluralism. Nos. 25 & 26, pp. 30-46.

Bibliography on land tenure in Africa. (1970) Food and Agricultural Organisation. Rome.

'Bibliography of the works of Antony Allott 1948-1988'. Journal of African Law. (1987) Vol. 31, Nos. 1 & 2, pp. 226-231.

Current bibliography on African affairs, 1995-1996. Vol. 27, No. 1. Farmingdale, N.Y: Baywood Publishing Company, Inc.

The future of customary law in Africa. (1956) Leiden: Afrika Instituut-Studie Centrum-Leiden.

International African Bibliography. Vol. 1, 1971-1975. London: William Dawson for International African Institute. Vol. 1-5.

International library of essays in law and legal theory. Aldershot: Dartmouth Publishing Co. Ltd.

Joint acquisition list of Africana. Evanston, Il: Northwestern University Library

Publications on Africa in USSR 1961-1985: List of books, pamphlets and articles on Africa published in the USSR. Moscow: Institute of Africa USSR Academy of Science.

Restatement of African Law Project. Bibliography for East Africa (Kenya, Somali Republic, Sudan, Tanganyika, Uganda, Zanzibar) London: SOAS.

Standing Conference on Library materials on Africa 1965-1970. Parts 1-10. London: SOAS, University of London.

United Kingdom publications and theses on Africa 1920-1966. Standing Conference on Library materials on Africa. Cambridge. W. Heffer.

Abel, R. L. (1970) 'A bibliography of the customary laws of Kenya: With special reference to the laws of wrongs'. East African Law Journal. Vol. 6, No. 2, pp. 100-151.

Allen, C. H. (1995) Africa bibliography. Edinburgh: Edinburgh University Press.

Allott, A. N. (1959) 'The law of Buganda: Some recent publications'. Journal of African Law. Vol. 3, No. 1, pp. 1-6.

Alman, M. (1973) United Kingdom publications and theses on Africa 1967 and 1968. Standing Conference on Library materials on Africa. London: Frank Cass.

Baker, P. (1994) International Directory of African Studies Research. London: Hans Zell for International African Institute.

Bennett, T. W. (1973) *A select index of NADA relating to African law and custom.* Salisbury: Dept. of Law, University of Rhodesia.

Bennett, T. W. and Phillips, S. (1975) A bibliography of African law, with special reference to Rhodesia. Salisbury: University of Rhodesia.

Bertie, O. B. (comp.) (1961) African documentation. Bibliography of African law. Part 1: East Africa. Restatement of Africn Law Project. The Royal Institute of International Affairs. London: SOAS. University of London.

Besterman, T. (1975) *A world bibliography of African bibliographies.* Totowa, N.J: Rowman and Littlefield.

Blackhurst, H. (ed.) (1985) *Africa bibliography 1984.* Manchester: Manchester University Press.

Blake, D. and Travisi, C. (1984) Periodicals from Africa. A bibliography and union list of periodicals published in Africa. First supplement. Boston, Mass: G. K. Hall.

Blaustein, A. P. (1966) 'African legal periodicals: A bibliography'. Law Library Journal. Vol. 59, pp. 93-96.

Blaustein, A. P. (1970) 'Selected bibliography on law and development in East Africa'. East African Law Journal. Vol. 6, No. 3, pp. 229-238.

Blaustein, A. P. and Beede, B. R. (1974) 'African legal periodicals: A bibliography'. African Law Studies. No. 11, pp. 71-79.

Breem, W. and Phillips, S. (1991) Bibliography of Commonwealth Law Reports. London: Mansell.

Bruce, J. W. (1979) *A bibliographical guide to the customary law of the Sudan*. Khartoum: Customary Law Project. Faculty of Law. University of Khartoum.

Burt, E. C. (1983) Bibliography of the visual arts in East Africa, Supplement. Africana Journal. Vol. 14. Nos. 2 &3, pp. 205-252.

Cardinall, A. W. (1932) *A bibliography of the Gold Coast*. Accra: Government Printer.

Cottrell, G. (1973) 'A bibliography of materials on Nigerian law published in Nigeria'. Africa Law Studies. Vol. 9, pp. 1-37.

Duignan, P. et al. (comps.) (1971) Africa South of the Sahara: A bibliography for undergraduate libraries. Willimasport, Penn.: Bro-Dart.

E Britto de Sousa de Marais Pina Elisa Maria (1972) Sociology of Law: A selected bibliography. Lisboa: Junta de investigoções do Ultramar.

East, J. W. (1987) The German Administration in East Africa. A select annotated bibliography of the German colonial administration in Tanganyika, Rwanda and Burundi 1884-1918. Thesis submitted for the Fellowship of the Library Association, London.

Falode, J. B. (1970) *Bibliography of legal materials concerning Africa in the University Library*. Dar es Salaam: University Library.

Gaskin, L. J. P. (1965) A bibliography of African arts. London: International African Institute.

Gorman, G. E. and Mills, J. J. (1987) Guide to current national bibliographies in the Third World. London: Hans Zell.

Hall, D. (comp.) (1995) International African bibliography. Current books, articles and papers in African Studies. London: Hans Zell.

Hall, D. (ed.) (1982) International African bibliography: Current books, articles and papers in African Studies. 1982-1983. Vols. 12-13. No. 1. London: Mansell.

Hall, D. (ed.) (1984) International African bibliography: Current books, articles and papers in African Studies. Vol. 14, No. 1. London: Mansell.

Hall, D. (ed.) (1985) International African bibliography: Current books, articles and papers in African Studies. 1985-1986. Vols. 15-16. London: Mansell.

Hall, D. (ed.) (1987) International African bibliography: Current books, articles and papers in African Studies. 1987-1988. Vols. 17-18. London: Mansell.

Hall, D. (ed.) (1989) International African bibliography: Current books, articles and papers in African Studies. 1989-1990. Vols. 19-20. London: Mansell.

Hall, D. (ed.) (1991) International African bibliography: Current books, articles and papers in African Studies. Vol. 21, No. 1. London: Mansell.

Hall, D. (ed.) (1993) International African bibliography: Current books, articles and papers in African Studies. Vol. 23, No. 1. London: Hans Zell.

Holdsworth, M. (1961) *Soviet African Studies* (1918-1959) An annoted bibliography. Oxford University Press for the royal Insitute of International Affair.

Howell, J. B. (1978) Kenya: Subject guide to official publications. Washington: Library of Congress.

Jegede, O. (1975) Nigerian legal bibliography. New York: Oceana Publications.

Jegede, O. (1983) Nigerian legal bibliography: A classified list of materials related to Nigeria. Dobbs Ferry, N.Y.: Oceana Publications for the Nigerian Institute of Advanced Legal Studies.

Kerr, A. J. (1956) 'Some recent studies of native law'. Africa Studies. Vol. 15. pp. 139-144.

Kratochvil, L. and Shaw, S. (comps.) (1974) *African women: A select bibliography*. Cambridge: African Studies Centre.

Kuper, B. (1962) *A bibliography of native law in South Africa 1941-1961*. Johannesburg: Witwatersrand.

Lafond, M. (1990) 'Bibliographie sur la justice en Afrique: Recension des ouvrages anglais et français parus de 1982 à 1990 Afrique Contemporaine No. 156. pp. 293-309.

Lansky, R. (1981) Handbook of bibliographies on law in the developing countries. Frankfurt/M: Vittorio Klostermann.

Leon, M. and Shier, J. (eds.) (1979) International African Bibliography: Current books, articles and papers in African Studies. 1979-1981. Vols, 9-11. London: Mansell.

Lewin, J. (1941) Short survey of native law in South Africa. Bantu Studies, Vol. 15. pp. 65-90.

Mahoney, M. and Pearson, J. D. (eds.) (1976) International African Bibliography: Current books, articles and papers in African Studies. Vols. 6-8. 1976-1978. London: Mansell.

Maxwell, L. F. (1964) A legal bibliography of the British Commonwealth of Nations. London: Sweet and Maxwell.

McIlwaine, J. H. St. J. (1978) Theses on Africa 1963-1975 accepted by universities in the United Kingdom and Ireland. London: Mansell.

Meek, C. K. (1948) Colonial law: A bibliography with special reference to native African system of law and land tenure. London: Oxford University Press.

Musiker, R. (1970) South African bibliography: A survey of bibliographies and bibliographical work. London: Crosby Lockwood.

Musiker, R. (1975) South African bibliography: A survey of bibliographies and bibliographical work. Supplement 1970-1974. Johannesburg: University of Witwatersrand.

Mwalimu, C. (1988) A bibliographic essay of selected secondary sources on the common law and customary law of English-speaking sub-Saharan Africa. Law Library Journal. Vol. 80, No. 2, pp.241-289.

Nader, L., Koch, K. F. and Cox, B. (1966) The ethnography of law: A bibliographical survey. Current Anthropology. Vol. 7. pp. 267-294.

Ochai, A. (comp.) (1974) Catalogue of Africana, Kashim Ibrahim Library. Ahmadu Bello University. Zaria: Ahmadu Bello University Press.

Olaitan, M. O. and Jegede, O. (1983) *Basic resources on Nigerian Law*. Lagos: Libriservice.

Oluwakuyide, A. (1975) 'Nigerian legal studies: A bibliographical discussion of the sources and resources. Current Bibliography on Affrican Affairs Vol. 8, No. 2, pp. 127-133.

Oni, W. K. and Gbinigie, O. O. (1975) Sources of African law. A preliminary bibliography of African legal materials. Lagos: University of Lagos.

Panofsky, H. E. (1975) A bibliography of Africana. Westport, Conn: Greenwood Press.

Pearson, J. D. (ed.) (1982) *International African bibliography 1973-1978*: Books, articles and papers in African studies. London: Mansell.

Pearson, J. D. and Jones, R. (eds.) (1970) The bibliography of Africa. Collected papers of the International Conference on African Bibliography, 1967. Nairobi: University College, Nairobi.

Pechota, V. (1994) *Szladits' Bibliography on foreign and comparative law. Books and articles in English. (1989-1990.* Vols. 1, 2, & 3.

Rabie, A. (1987) *A bibliography of South African criminal law*. Cape Town: Juta & Co Ltd.

Raistrick, D. and Rees, J. (1977) *Lawyers' law books: A practical index to legal literature*. Abingdon,Oxon: Professional Books Ltd.

Read, J. S. (1968) Bibliographical introduction to legal history and ethnology, Kenya, Tanzania, Uganda. Bruxelles: Université Libré de Bruxelles.

Redden, K. R. (ed.) (1985) *Modern legal systems cyclopedia*. Vol. 6, Africa. New York: William S. Hein & Co.

Risch, A. (1969) Selected bibliography of recent publications on East African law. Afrika Spectrum. Vol. 3. pp. 43-46.

Roberts, A. A. (1942) A South African legal bibliography. Pretoria: University of South Africa, Hiddingh-Currie Publication.

Salaam, M. O. (comp.) (1980) An index to conference proceedings, symposia and seminar papers held by the Africana Unit. Research and Bibliographic services Division. Africana Unit. Ahmadu Bello University.

Saulniers, S. S. and Rakowski, C. A. (1977) Women in the development process: A select bibliography on women in sub-Saharan Africa and Latin America. Austin, Texas: University of Texas Press.

Scheven, Y. (1988) *Bibliographies for African Studies* 1970-1976. London: Hans Zell.

Scheven, Y. (ed.) (1994) Bibliographies for African studies, 1987-1993. London: Hans Zell.

Schiller, A. A. (1969) 'Customary land tenure among the Highland people of Northern Ethiopia: A bibliography'. African Law Studies. Vol. 1 pp. 1-22.

Schiller, A. A. (1971) 'African law books in 1969 and 1970: Survey'. African Law Studies. Vol. 4, pp. 65-89.

Sevareid, P. (1983) The future of customary law. Appendix: A basic bibliography of customary law for Anglophonic Africa'. Africana Journal. Vol. 14, No. 1, p. 47.

Simpson, A. W. B. (ed.) (1984) *Biographical dictionary of the common law*. London: Butterworth & Co Ltd.

Stanley, J. L. (1985) *African art: A bibliographical guide*. New York and London: Africana Publishing Co.

Stanley, J. L. (1990) *The arts of Africa: An annotated bibliography, 1986 and 1987*. Atlanta.

Szladits, C. (1955) *A bibliography on foreign and comparative law: Books and articles*. Dobbs Ferry N.Y: Oceana

Travis, C. and Alman, M. (comps.) (1977) Periodicals from Africa: A bibliography and union list of periodicals published in Africa. Standing Conference on Library Materials on Africa. Boston, Mass.: G. K. Hall.

Twining, W. L., Twining, P. and Nasri, A. B. (comps) (1960) Bibliography of Sudan law. Sudan Law Journal. pp. 313-334.

Vanderlinden, J. (1966) Outline of a bibliography on Ethiopian law. Journal of Comparative law. Vol. 3, p. 257.

Vanderlinden, J. (1967) 'A supplement to the bibliography of Ethiopian law'. Journal of Ethiopian Law. Vol. 4, No. 2, pp. 433-437.

Vanderlinden, J. (1972) African law bibliography, 1947-1966. Centre for African Legal Development. Bruxelles: Presses universitaires de Bruxelles.

Vanderlinden, J. (1975) An introduction to the sources on contemporary African laws. Independent sub-Saharan Africa. Belgrade: Institute of Comparative Law.

Vanderlinden, J. (1976) African law bibliography 1967-1976. Vol. 2, A-G. Bruxelles: Presses Universitaires de Bruxelles.

Vanderlinden, J. (1982) *African law bibliography. Third Supplement.* Geneva: Nordic Law Consultants.

Vanderlinden, J. (1986) African law bibliography 1977-1986. Bruxelles: Presses Universitaires de Bruxelles.

Vanderlinden, J. (1992) Bibliographies internationales de la doctrine juridique africaine. Moncton: Editions du Centre international de la common law en français. Université de Moncton. Vol. 5, Cameroon. Vol. 6, Central African Republic. Vol. 7, Congo. Vol. 11, Gabon, Vol. 16, Niger. Vol. 17. Rwanda. Vol. 18, Senegal. Vol. 19, Chad.

Verhelst, T. G. (ed.) (1972) Legal process and the individual: African source materials including background papers, a bibliography and selected legislation. Addis Ababa: Faculty of Law, Haile Selassie 1 University. The Centre for African Legal Development.

Vogel, J. (1977) 'Bibliography of unpublished dissertations and papers on African law, 1965-1976'. African Law Studies. Vol. 15, pp. 62-74.

Wilkinson, P. J. (1980) *Bibliography in socio-legal studies.* No. 1. Oxford: Centre for Socio-Legal Studies, Wolfson College.

Witherell, J. W. (1973) Africana acquisitions. General reference and bibliography division. Washington: Library of Congress.

Conclusion

The conclusion is necessarily brief because the purpose is simply to remind the Ankermanns and the Lévy-Brühls of this world that Africa was the cradle of modern humanity. If the early Africans had not had the technology to survive the first million years of human evolution on this planet, where would the Europeans be today with their much vaunted technology? The European achievements were preceded by millions of years of Africa's invention of food production, specialised animal husbandry, fishery, metallurgy, herbal medicine and indigenous law, which today is taught in universities.

One is not arguing that all aspects of the indigenous laws should be retained at all cost in a pre-colonial mindset, because the laws were beneficial to our foreparents. Human beings move with their times, and laws fall into desuetude when they no longer have meaningful roles to uphold in the society's justice system. Increasingly, when people become aware that the adoption of new laws would make their life better, the old laws quickly fall into abeyance. The argument is that indigenous law jurisprudence having survived almost into its second millennium, signify that some of its ethical traditions can be adapted by contemporary ethicists.

Monogamous marriage could be taken as an example of a step towards modernisation by the people. There is freedom of choice as to how a couple become husband and wife. There are now triple forms of marriages for believers and non-believers alike. First, there is religious marriage before a priest, in the eyes of God or in the eyes of Allah. Secondly, there is marriage in the eyes of the state, before the registrar. Both forms of marriages guarantee that on divorce or on intestacy, the assets of the couple can be divided and distributed according to the prevailing statutory law.

However, in spite of the bridal outfit, organ music and certificate of marriage, some couples do not feel truly married without the formalities of the indigenous marriage, marriage in the eyes of the 'tribe' with both families officiating. Even if parents no longer have a role in the selection of marriage partners made by a Yoruba and a Luo couple in London, Paris, or New York, sometimes both will eventually undergo a Luo indigenous marriage ceremony or a Yoruba marriage ceremony.

A great deal of research needs to be carried out on various aspects of African indigenous law, and its harmonisation with Western jurisprudence, because in the great scramble to adopt Western law in order to be modern, we should be careful not to throw out the baby with the bath water.

Indices

Author index

A

B

C

D

H

I

J

K

L

M

N

O

S

T

U

Subject index

A

B

C

I

J

K

L

M

N

O

P

Q

R

S